COUPLES IN THE BIBLE

Examples to Live By

by

Sylvia Charles

HENSLEY
PUBLISHING

DEDICATION

I dedicate this study to my husband, Don, the one who makes "us" a "couple." I'm grateful not only for the counsel and support he has given me in the preparation of this study, but for the love we have shared in our forty-five years of marriage. Most of all, I give praise to God for His grace and mercy, which has kept us related to Him and to each other through it all.

ACKNOWLEDGMENTS

I have been blessed, as I have sought out modern examples to be used at the conclusion of each lesson. Some of these are stories of couples of previous centuries, who have had an impact upon our world because of what God did in their lives. Some stories were taken from present-day books and periodicals, which are ever-available to build faith and give encouragement to those of us who are are seeking to follow the Lord. Other stories were graciously given me to use by personal friends and acquaintenances, whose lives so aptly illustrate the lessons I wanted to get across. Finally, some of the modern examples have come from my own life. I do want to give God the glory for making me aware of these stories so that you, as couples desiring to follow God's Word, can benefit from His work in the lives of other couples, both around us now and throughout the ages.

BIBLE VERSIONS

Unless otherwise noted, all Scripture quotation are taken from *The Holy Bible, New International Version (NIV)*. Copyright © 1973, 1978, 1984, International Bible Society. Used by permission of Zondervan.

Scripture quotations marked KJV are taken from the *King James Version* of the Bible.

Scripture quotations marked TLB are taken from *The Living Bible*, copyright © 1971 by Tyndale House Publishers, Wheaton, IL. Used by permission.

COUPLES IN THE BIBLE
 EXAMPLES TO LIVE BY
ISBN 1-56322-062-8
EAN 9781563220623

FOREWORD

God's finale to the creation of the heavens and earth was to make a man to have dominion over the earth — a man with whom He could have fellowship. But almost as soon as He had made this man, God saw that the man needed someone to share his earthly life. So, God took a rib from the man and made a woman…male and female created He them. God communicated with this couple, even as He told them to be fruitful, to multiply, to replenish the earth, and to subdue it. God had provided all their physical needs. He also imparted His authority, as He gave them dominion over the fish of the sea, the fowl of the air, and every living thing that moved upon the earth. Through this first couple, Adam and Eve, the Lord God Almighty ordained His divine plan for the marriage relationship as He made them not only one with each other, but also in perfect fellowship with Him.

Adam and Eve, however, became separated from God through sin. Thus, their unique oneness with Him, and with each other, was broken. So, God provided a way to reconcile man back into fellowship with Himself. The Bible is the story of how God accomplished this — first, through a system of animal sacrifices, and ultimately, through the sacrifice of His only-begotten Son, Jesus Christ. Now, by accepting the sacrifice of God's unblemished Lamb in atonement for sin, we can receive His forgiveness and gain fellowship with Him. As we are, thus, transferred from the kingdom of darkness into this new kingdom, we become part of the Church, the Body of Jesus Christ!

Following Jesus' death and resurrection, He ascended into heaven, where He is now seated at the right hand of the Father, interceding for us. On the day of Pentecost, following Jesus' ascension, God sent His Holy Spirit to lift up Jesus, to call people to Him, and to equip the Church, as well as to prepare the Bride for the consummation of her relationship with the Bridegroom. The Word tells us that when she is joined with Him at the Marriage Supper of the Lamb, she will be found righteous, without spot and blemish…conformed to His nature.

The Bible begins with the story of a couple, Adam and Eve, and the institution of the marriage relationship. Likewise, the Bible ends with the story of a couple, Jesus Christ and His Bride — He, as King of Kings and Lord of Lords, and she, as the glorious Church for whom He gave His life.

Between the stories of these two couples we find glimpses of many other couples in the Bible from whom we, as the Bride-in-preparation, can benefit as we allow the Holy Spirit to teach and conform us to the nature of our Bridegroom-to-be.

We will consider twenty-eight couples in the Bible who experienced many of the same situations and problems that husbands and wives face today. Each lesson will primarily look at one teaching per couple to see how they succeeded or failed in that area…and, thus, how they can be examples to us in our marriage relationship.

The study is written with the prayer that couples found in God's written Word will minister truth and life to each couple today who seek to abide in His Word and obey it. What glory it will be when all couples in His Word — past and present — are united at the Marriage Supper of the Lamb with Jesus, our Lord, Savior, and soon-coming Bridegroom!

ABOUT PHOTOCOPYING THIS BOOK

Some people who would never walk into a store and shoplift a book may think nothing of photocopying the same book. The results are the same. Both acts are wrong. Many people have the mistaken understanding that making copies of copyrighted material is legal if it is for their own personal use and not for resale. Making unauthorized copies of any copyrighted material is against the law.

First Timothy 5:17-18 instructs us to give the laborer his wages, specifically those who labor in the Word and doctrine. As a publisher, we have a moral as well as a legal responsibility to see that our authors receive fair compensation for their efforts. Many of them depend on the income from the sale of these books as their sole livelihood. So, for that matter, do the artists, printers, and the numerous other people who work to make these books available to you.

Please help us abide by the laws of both man and God by discouraging those who would copy this material in lieu of purchase.

Table of Contents

Lesson 1

Adam and Eve

Maintaining Oneness in Marriage

But at the beginning of creation, God made them male and female. For this reason, a man will leave his father and mother and be united to his wife, and the two will become one flesh. So they are no longer two, but one. Therefore, what God has joined together, let not man separate.

Mark 10:6-9

SETTING THE STAGE

Adam and Eve, the first "couple" on earth, were created in the image of God. They were the only couple to begin their life together without sin. They were privileged to experience a unique oneness as husband and wife — neither had previously had any kind of relationship with another person; and they were "married" from the time they met! They were God's ideal of what a perfect marriage should be — until sin came into their lives and destroyed the "oneness" God had intended them to have with both Him and each other.

Now, every couple on earth has to deal with sin in order to obtain and maintain a oneness, an intimate relationship with God and with each other in body, soul and spirit. As I Corinthians 15:45-50 reminds us, Adam was the "natural man." Only when Jesus, the "second man" or "last Adam," is united with His Bride, the Church, will there be the complete spiritual relationship God desires between husband and wife. Meanwhile, we can learn how to restore brokenness so we can enjoy oneness in our marriage relationship while here on earth.

INTRODUCING ADAM AND EVE

(Based on Genesis 1:26-28; 2:7-3:24)

On the last day of creation, God formed Adam from the dust of the ground. He breathed the breath of life into Adam's nostrils, and Adam became a living soul. God gave Adam dominion over all the plants and trees, and over everything that had the breath of life in it. It would seem that Adam had all he needed — a beautiful garden in which to live, an abundance of good food, a fulfilling vocation, perfect health, and a relationship with a God who loved him enough to communicate and have fellowship with him. But one thing was missing. He had no earthly companion with whom to share his life!

God recognized that it wasn't good for Adam to be alone. So, God took a rib from Adam and made a helpmeet, a companion with whom Adam could be intimate — body, soul, and spirit. When Adam awoke from this divine surgery, he saw a beautiful creature and called her "woman." They were as "one" as two persons could ever be. Eve was literally part of Adam; and both had been created in the image of God.

This first couple had a relationship of perfect innocence and purity. They saw themselves so wholly belonging to one another that they had no need to cover their bodies. They were completely transparent before God as well. God's glory covered them. Theirs was the ideal marriage — perfect oneness with each other and with God.

LESSONS FROM ADAM AND EVE

Sin and Its Consequences

At the end of the sixth day of creation, God declared that everything He had made was very good! He had made man for His pleasure and His fellowship, as well as to be part of the plan in restoring and ruling the earth. In the process, He had given man free will, hoping that he would desire to obey Him and trust in His Word.

What was the *one* thing God forbade man to do? (Genesis 2:15-17)

_____

What were the consequences of such action?

_____

Who tempted Eve to sin? (Genesis 3:1-6; II Corinthians 11:3)

_____

What temptation did she yield to?

_____

What were the consequences for her? (Genesis 3:16, 22-24)

_____

_____

How did Adam sin? (Genesis 3:6)

_____

What was the consequence for him? (Genesis 3:17-19, 22-24)

_____

_____

How did sin affect their fellowship with God? (Genesis 3:7-10)

_____

_____

How did God provide atonement (a covering) for their sin? (Genesis 3:21)

_____

What Does God Say About Sin?

Deuteronomy 25:16 _____

Psalm 5:4-6 _____

_____

Proverbs 6:16-19 _____

_____

Ezekiel 18:20-21 _____

_____

Romans 3:23 _____

Romans 6:23 _____

Because God is Holy, He had to provide a covering for sin. So, He brought into being a system of atonement whereby shed blood would cover sin. (See Hebrews 9:22.) From Genesis (where God provided Adam and Eve with skins from an animal which had been slain to pay the penalty for their sin), to Malachi, we read of altars, tabernacles and temples — all places where innocent animals were slain in payment for man's sins. The Hebrew people were burdened with this impossible system. Eventually, God sent His only-begotten Son, Jesus, into the world as the ultimate sacrifice for sin. Because this Lamb of God shed His blood upon the cross, we can now repent of sin and be forgiven as we accept what He has done for us.

> *God made him who had no sin to be sin for us, so that in him we might become the righteousness of God.* II Corinthians 5:21

> *He did not enter by means of the blood of goats and calves; but he entered the Most Holy Place once for all by his own blood, having obtained eternal redemption.* Hebrews 9:12

> *So Christ was sacrificed once to take away the sins of many people; and he will appear a second time, not to bear sin, but to bring salvation to those who are waiting for him.* Hebrews 9:28

Oneness in the Marriage Relationship

Since we are made in God's image and are triune in nature, coming into a oneness in the marriage relationship involves being intimate not only in body, but also in soul and spirit. Couples in the world never truly experience this oneness, for it takes obedience to God's Word, and a relationship with Him, to have the true intimacy of body, soul, and *spirit*.

Becoming "one" as husband and wife does not mean we become clones of one another. It means we come into a unity of love in which each person can become all that he or she was meant to be. Even opposite personalities can complement one another as God brings about a "oneness."

As soon as God had created Adam and Eve as male and female, He declared, in Genesis 2:24, that the husband is to _____

_____

_____

If a person is physically or emotionally tied to past relationships, that person is not free to become "one" in a new relationship. One cannot "cleave" until he "leaves," for "to cleave" means to stick together like glue, to be so joined that the two cannot be separated without damage to both.

At the "Fall," God placed Eve under the rule and protection of her husband's authority. We are reminded in I Timothy 2:11-15 that the wife is to _____

_____

because _____

_____

Ephesians 5:22-23 confirms this _____

_____

_____

Though the husband must take a definite step to assume responsibility of his wife by leaving his father and mother, the wife is transferred from the covering of her parents to that of her husband as she obeys God's will in submitting to her husband in the marriage relationship. Thus, they are both free to become "one."

Oneness of Body, Soul, and Spirit

Body   As a temple of the Holy Spirit, we are to keep our bodies disciplined. We must respect the body of our mate.

Soul   Because the soul includes the mind, will, and emotions, we must deal with the "flesh" (anger, pride, self-pity, etc.) and forgive offenses.

Spirit   By being "born-again" and filled with the Holy Spirit, we can have a oneness of spirit never experienced by those in the world.

How Oneness Can Be Restored

Through Repentance

True repentance brings about change in the mind, heart, and will. The prodigal son, in Luke 15:11-24, is the perfect example of one who saw his sin, had a change of heart, and did what he knew his father would want him to do. Whenever even one marriage partner truly repents, the way is opened for reconciliation.

Through Confession of Sin

First John 1:9 says *"If we confess our sins, he is faithful and just and will forgive us our sins and purify us from all unrighteousness."* Confessing sin, to both God and those we have offended, continues the process towards forgiveness.

Through Forgiveness

According to Matthew 6:14-15, God will forgive (or not forgive) as we forgive (or don't forgive). When we either ask for or receive forgiveness, we experience God's grace, which makes it possible to find oneness with our mate restored.

SUMMARY

Adam and Eve, the first couple in a marriage relationship, broke their perfect oneness by sinning. Because of their disobedience and rebellion, every couple since, has had to deal with sin and its resulting separation from one another and from God. And, as in the beginning, Satan continues to do all that he can to destroy the oneness in marriage.

The only way to restore oneness, with each other and with God, is to recognize sin for what it is, repent, confess it to God and to one another, and allow God to cleanse it with the blood of Jesus Christ. True repentance and the exchange of forgiveness restores the oneness God ordained in the marriage relationship between husband and wife.

CONSIDER THIS

Have you, as a husband, left your father and mother so that you can truly cleave to your wife? Explain.

_____

_____

Do you love her as Jesus loves the Church? Explain.

_____

_____

Do you, as a wife, submit to your husband's authority *as unto the Lord?* Explain.

_____

_____

How do you now experience oneness of body, soul, and spirit?

_____

_____

How do you restore your oneness when it is broken for any reason?

_____

_____

MODERN EXAMPLE

In our forty-five years of marriage, sin has broken our oneness a number of times. Though we haven't experienced long periods of physical separation, we both definitely recall nights when we each slept on our own edge of the bed because of a grievance for which pride would not allow neither of us to quickly repent!

It took a while for us to come into a oneness of the soul — particularly our emotions —partly, because Don was an only child. His mother was simply unable to let him go, even though we were both college graduates when we married. So, he found it emotionally difficult to leave her and cleave to me. When we lived many miles from his parents, his mother would write or call only him...and that made me resentful. It would have been even more difficult if we hadn't realized that it wasn't "me," but would have been anyone he married. (She and I did begin to have a much better relationship after I became the mother of their first grandchild!)

A real lack of spiritual oneness occurred about sixteen years into our marriage. Don had attended a very liberal seminary and was pastoring a church in Arizona. He had become acquainted with other like-minded pastors, one of whom was dabbling in the occult. He soon began seeing a medium, who introduced him to all kinds of supernatural "signs and wonders," something he was hungry for in his own relationship with God. Though I did not know all that I now know concerning the ways of Satan, I knew enough to not like what He was doing. Spiritually, we were becoming far apart until, by God's grace, we were introduced to some truly born-again, Spirit-filled Christians who prayed for and ministered to us. When Don repented of his involvement with the occult and we both experienced the reality of the Holy Spirit in our lives, we came into a spiritual oneness that has continued to this day. We praise God for the oneness He has brought us...body, soul, and spirit.

Abraham and Sarah

Living by Faith in God

> *He (Abraham) did not waver through unbelief regarding the promise of God, but was strengthened in his faith and gave glory to God, being fully persuaded that God had power to do what he had promised.*
>
> Romans 4:20-21

SETTING THE STAGE

Several generations after Adam and Eve, man had become so wicked that God sent a flood upon the earth and destroyed every human being, except Noah and his family. Even with this new beginning, man soon fell into disobedience again, and God was grieved. He longed for a people who would love and trust Him as a father. He determined to bring this about by establishing a covenant between a chosen nation and Himself.

So God appeared to a man named Abram who was living in the Mesopotamian region. He asked Abram to leave his country, and his people, and go into a land that He would show him. God would begin anew with Abram by making a covenant with him, allowing him to become the father of a new nation, a chosen people who would be God's family and heirs of all His provision. God would extend His love, His mercy, and His blessing as these people would, in faith, trust and obey Him. His desire for those people, as part of the "old" covenant, was the same as His desire for those of us of the "new" covenant — a daily walk of faith in Him. How do we do this? We'll look at the life of Abraham and Sarah and see how they lived by faith in God.

INTRODUCING ABRAHAM AND SARAH

(Based on Genesis 11:27-12:20; 16:1-16; 17:15-22; 18:10-15; 21:1-7)

Abram, his wife (and half-sister), Sarai, his father, Terah, and his nephew, Lot, left their homeland, Ur of the Chaldees, to go to Canaan. But when they came to Haran, they settled there instead. After Terah died, Abram heard the call of God — to move to a land God would show him. So Abram and Sarai (later called Abraham and Sarah) and Lot set out for Canaan. They encountered a number of obstacles, including famine. Yet, God told Abram He would give him the land, and He made a covenant to raise Abram up to be the father of a great nation. In time, Abraham and Lot separated because they had accumulated too many flocks and possessions to move about together.

When Abraham was ninety-nine years old, and Sarah ninety, God finally gave them Isaac, the heir He had promised. This was several years after Abraham and Sarah had tried to fulfill God's promise by their own means — allowing Abraham to father a child by Sarah's handmaid, Hagar. That child, Ishmael, became the father of twelve rulers of nations, most of which we know to be Arab nations today. Thus, the age-old conflict between Jews and Arabs began with the competition between the child of promise and the child of the flesh.

When Isaac was a young man, God asked Abraham to sacrifice him upon an altar. Just as Abraham was about to put a knife to Isaac's throat, God provided a ram instead, and Isaac was spared. Sarah died at age 127. Abraham married again, had other children, and lived to be 175 years old.

LESSONS FROM ABRAHAM AND SARAH

Living by Faith in God

How did Abram (Abraham) know that it was the voice of God Almighty speaking to him, a "nobody" in a pagan land? What gave him the courage to pick up stakes and leave his own country, not knowing where he was going? Why was his wife, Sarai (Sarah) willing to follow her husband in this strange venture?

We have no way of knowing the answers to these questions except that, somehow, Abraham was given the faith to believe God's Word. James 2:23 does say that "*Abraham believed God, and it was credited to him as righteousness, and he was called God's friend.*" When God spoke, Abraham believed His Word and acted upon it. Evidently Sarah had been given a submissive spirit, for she was willing to trust her husband so that she, too, could follow in faith.

Hebrews 11:8-12 reminds us of some of the ways Abraham and Sarah lived by faith. One would think that, through their long walk of faith they would have realized the fulfillment of every promise God had made them. In reality, they died in faith, able only to see and welcome many promises from a distance. Thus, it was not their accomplishments that pleased God, but their *faith* in Him.

Let's now look at some of the ways they acted in faith:

- After leaving Mesopotamia, they had to trust God to lead them into the land He had promised and to supply all their needs in the process.
- After they arrived in the land of promise, a great famine drove them to Egypt. Here, Sarah was given to Pharaoh. She had to have faith that God would set her free. He did.
- In the division of the land, Lot chose the fertile plains and left Abraham with the barren desert. As God renewed the covenant, Abraham had to trust that the land would provide an inheritance for offspring as great in number as the dust of the earth!
- A big test of faith came when God told Abraham that he and Sarah (at ages ninety-nine and ninety) would have a son by natural means!
- Abraham had faith to intercede for the people of Sodom (where Lot lived) when all looked hopeless because of their great sin. He was willing to pray if only ten were saved.
- Probably the greatest test of faith came when God asked Abraham to take Isaac, the long-awaited child of the covenant, up to a mountain and lay him on an altar as a sacrifice. When God saw Abraham's obedience, He rescued Isaac at the last minute.

What is Faith?

The simplest definition of *faith* is "absolute dependence upon God's Word." It involves taking God seriously, totally trusting in His Word regardless of what circumstances are saying. Faith does not deny the reality of difficulties; it declares God's power in the midst of them.

According to the following scriptures, what is faith?

Ephesians 2:8 _____

Galatians 5:22 _____

Hebrews 11:1 _____

It is important to understand that faith has more to do with our attitude than with the end result. Abraham and Sarah had many struggles believing God for what He had promised them. We do also. It is doubt, or unbelief, that cancels out faith.

According to Hebrews 4:1-6, we can only enter God's rest (provision) by believing in His Word — and that only comes by mixing faith with what we have heard preached. Romans 10:17 tells us *"faith comes from hearing the message, and the message is heard through the word of Christ."*

Faith is a gift of God, a fruit of the Spirit, the title deed of things hoped for. It becomes reality in us as we hear and believe in God's Word.

Living Our Faith

Other scriptures, which will help us to live by faith, include:

Hebrews 11:6: We please God by _____

Romans 14:23: Everything we do that is not done in faith is _____

Romans 10:17: Faith comes to us by _____

II Corinthians 5:7: Faith is not just a one-time experience. We are to _____

Hebrews 4:2 KJV: To profit from God's Word, we need to combine what we read (hear) with _____

James 2:17, 26: Our faith will be dead, or useless, unless _____

_____

Luke 18:8: One thing Jesus will look for when He returns to earth is _____

_____

In the 11th chapter of Hebrews, we find many people listed who had real faith in God. Abraham and Sarah are the only couple named. List some of the individuals and what they did by faith.

Name	What They Did
_____	_____
_____	_____
_____	_____
_____	_____
_____	_____
_____	_____
_____	_____

Beginning halfway through verse 35 and continuing through the end of verse 39, what does the Bible tell us happened to others who were commended for their faith, yet didn't receive what they had been promised?

_____

_____

_____

_____

_____

_____

These men of faith, though they trusted God and won his approval, none of them received all that God had promised them; for God wanted them to wait and share the even better rewards that were prepared for us.

Hebrews 11:39-40 TLB

SUMMARY

It took faith, a gift of God, for Abraham to hear God's voice in a pagan land and go into an unknown land God had promised to give him. But that was only the beginning. By faith, Abraham and Sarah settled there, overcame many obstacles as they acquired wealth, and had a son. It took a real gift of faith to be willing to then give this son as a sacrifice to God at His command.

God honored this couple's faith and, indeed, made Abraham the father of His chosen people when He gave Abraham an heir with whom He would renew His covenant. No step of faith is easy; but Abraham and Sarah were able to obey God as they trusted in His goodness — even though they did not have the "advantage" of those of us who live today, after God, in the flesh, gave His life on the cross so we can have eternal life by faith in Him! Nor did they have the Bible and the testimony of believers who have been willing to be martyred for their faith. To live by faith in God is still not easy, but it is what God desires. In fact, without faith, we cannot please Him.

CONSIDER THIS

How do we get faith in God?

_____

_____

Can you recount an example in your life of living by faith?

_____

_____

In what ways can you improve your walk in faith?

_____

_____

What do you do when you don't see immediate results after taking a step of faith?

_____

_____

MODERN EXAMPLE

In January 1956, five young couples from various parts of the United States, and from differing walks of life, found themselves living together in the jungles of Ecuador. By faith in God, each couple had left families and the comforts of home to take the Gospel to a stone-age tribe with whom they first had to learn to communicate.

The families of the Youderians, the Saints, the McCullys, the Flemings, and the Elliotts included several small children who were left fatherless when the five men were killed by the Auca Indians. Elisabeth Elliott wrote a book entitled *Through Gates of Splendor,* about their story. Reading it, one marvels at the faith of the five young widows, some in their 20's when they had to face the future without their husbands. Would they leave Ecuador where they sincerely believed God had led them? Would they become angry because it seemed that God had not honored their steps of faith?

On the 25th anniversary of the massacre, a new edition of Elliott's book was released.

In it she told how God continued to use the women as they again, by faith in His mysterious ways, sought His will for the rest of their lives. Marj Saint married Abe Van Der Puy, president of the World Radio Missionary Fellowship, and has lived many years in Quito, Ecuador. Barbara Youderian also lived in Quito, where she ran a missionary guest house of the Gospel Missionary Union. Olive Fleming married Walter Liefeld, head of the New Testament Department at Trinity Evangelical Divinity School in Deerfield, Illinois. Marilou McCully worked as accounting supervisor in a hospital in the Seattle area. And Elizabeth Elliott Gren became the author of many inspirational books. Until 1976, Nate Saints' sister Rachel lived with the Auca Indians, many of whom became Christians! Waorani villagers now welcome pilots distributing the life-giving Word of God.

Only God knows why He allowed five young couples to go, by faith, into the jungles of Ecuador just to have the husbands die at the hands of those with whom they had believed God wanted them to share the Gospel. With many questions to be answered only in heaven, the widows and families have continued to walk by faith in God who will, in the end, receive all the glory for what *He* has done!

Lesson 3

Lot and His Wife

Separating From the World

You adulteress people, don't you know that friendship with the world is hatred towards God? Anyone who chooses to be a friend of the world becomes an enemy of God.

James 4:4

SETTING THE STAGE

In the story of Abraham and Sarah, we find the parallel story of Lot and his wife.

As Abraham and Sarah are examples of the walk of faith that God desires in His people, so Lot and his wife are examples of what happens when God's people are double-minded. Being double-minded means being unable to walk in faith, because we're yielding to the lust and enticement of the world. It's like serving two gods, as we'll see in the story of Lot and his wife. We fail to live by faith in God because we fail to let go of our friendship with the world.

INTRODUCING LOT AND HIS WIFE

(Based on Genesis 11:31; 19:1-38)

Lot and Abraham were members of the same family. They left Ur of Chaldees together. They entered the Promised Land and shared some of the same blessings. Then, the 13th chapter of Genesis tells us, they separated. Their herds and households had become too large to travel together any longer. So, Abraham gave Lot the choice of where he would like to settle down. Lot immediately chose the fertile Jordan plain.

The first we read about Lot's wife and family is after he is living in Sodom. One evening, two angels approached Lot at the city gate to tell him that God was going to destroy the city because of its grievous sin. Lot invited these angels (who appeared to be men) into his home for the night. Then, a crowd of men from the city surrounded Lot's house, begging Lot to give them the "men" guests so that they could have sex with them. Lot not only refused, he also offered his virgin daughters to them instead! The angels struck the lusting men with blindness before taking Lot and his family from the city. They escaped Sodom just before fire fell from heaven and consumed Sodom, Gomorrah, and the surrounding plains. Lot's wife looked back to watch and was turned into a pillar of salt. Lot and his two daughters found safety in the little town of Zoar before moving on to the nearby mountains.

LESSONS FROM LOT AND HIS WIFE

Double-Mindedness

At the separation of Abraham and Lot, we begin to see what was in Lot's heart and mind. He appeared to be following God, yet he, apparently, also still loved the world. When given a choice, he pitched his tent in the fertile plains *near* Sodom, a thriving, but wicked, city.

A double-minded man tries to both please God and be friends with the world. Even Peter (in II Peter 2:7-8) described Lot as a righteous man living in a wicked city, yet tormented by the things he saw. Lot knew God, but he also gave in, at times, to surrounding circumstances.

For instance, when the angels came to rescue Lot before God sent fire to consume the city, Lot insisted they spend the night in his home instead of the public square. Then, when the homosexuals of the city wanted the angels, Lot offered his own daughters to them instead! He was caught between his desire to appease the men and his desire to please the angels sent by God! It took a supernatural act of God, smiting the men with blindness, to free Lot. Genesis 19:16 tells us that when the angels told him to hurry up and take his daughters out of the city while there was yet time, Lot "lingered" (KJV) or "hesitated" (NIV) and they had to literally pull him and his family out!

Next, the angels told him to escape to the mountain so that he wouldn't be consumed; but Lot chose, instead, to go to Zoar, a little city nearby. Lot's story doesn't have a happy ending. He barely escaped destruction in the burning city, and he lost his wife on the way out. He ended up living in a cave with his two daughters who caused him to become drunk and then committed incest with him.

We don't know how much Lot's wife influenced him, but we can gather from the story that she, too, was double-minded. She looked back at Sodom while trying to go toward the mountains, and she was turned into a pillar of salt! Many years later, Jesus singled her out as one we are to remember — one who looked back as God was delivering her from destruction.

Double-mindedness keeps us from walking by faith in God. A double-minded person is always confused and indecisive. He tries to please both God and man's system. He's unable to hold on to a fixed belief.

Summarize James 1:5-8. _____

_____

_____

To "cure" double-mindedness, we are instructed to (See James 4:8-10.): _____

_____

_____

_____

Separation From the World

God says specific things about separating from the world (letting go any friendship with it). When Lot chose to pitch his tent near Sodom (Genesis 13:12), he put himself in jeopardy. Second Peter 2:4-19 tells how God rescued Lot; it also describes men of the world who surrounded him.

What are these men like (beginning in v. 10)?

_____

_____

_____

_____

_____

In Jesus' prayer for His disciples in John 17:6-19, what relationship does He want His followers to have with the world?

_____

_____

_____

James 4:4 tells us that friendship with the world is

_____

First John 2:15-17 reminds us that _____

_____

James 4:1-10 tells us that to separate from the world, we should do the following:

_____

_____

In Matthew 6:24, Jesus says no one can serve two masters because he will

_____

In II Timothy 2:3-4, Paul tells Timothy that a good soldier of Jesus Christ will not get involved (NIV) or entangled with (KJV) _____

In II Peter 2:20, the warning given to Christians is to _____

_____

because _____

In II Corinthians 6:14-17, Paul warns Christians not to be yoked together with unbelievers (those in the world) because _____

_____

How does Ephesians 2:1-3 describe the world, of which Christians used to be part?

_____

_____

In II Peter 3:14-18, Peter tells Christians how to live until Jesus Christ returns. What is his specific advice in verse 17? _____

_____

_____

Single-Mindedness

The man without the Spirit does not accept the things that come from the Spirit of God, for they are foolishness to him, and he cannot understand them, because they are spiritually discerned. The spiritual man makes judgments about all things, but he himself is not subject to any man's judgment: 'For who has known the mind of the Lord that he may instruct him?' But we have the mind of Christ.

II Corinthians 2:14-16

Our desire and our goal is to be single-minded — to have the mind of Christ, untainted by the ways men think. To have this, we must know and speak God's Word. Make notes on the following scriptures, then write a summary of what the Bible says you should do to be single-minded — to have the mind of Christ.

Romans 12:1-2 _____

Luke 9:62 _____

James 4:7-10 _____

Philippians 2:1-11 _____

_____

II Peter 3:14-18 _____

_____

II Corinthians 4:18 _____

_____

Summary of the above: _____

_____

_____

SUMMARY

In Luke 17:32, Jesus gives the simple command to remember Lot's wife. He is telling the Pharisees some of the things that would take place just prior to His return. Though they probably didn't understand what He was saying, we, who are living in the end times, should especially take to heart the message Jesus was trying to convey. We need to remember Lot's wife and not look back longingly to the things and people we have left behind. Nor, should we be double-minded — part "in the world" and part "with the Lord." God's desire is for us to keep our eyes on Jesus and be submissive to His Holy Spirit as we become a holy people, separated unto Him — doing what He wants us to do now and in the future.

He does not want us to look *back*, or *around*...only *up*, for His redemption is drawing near! (Luke 21:28)

CONSIDER THIS

Do you tend to look back to either the good things of your past or to the failures you have experienced?

_____

_____

What is your relationship with the world?

_____

_____

Are you teaching your children to have the right attitude toward the world? How?

_____

_____

Are you double-minded or single-minded in your relationship with God?

_____

_____

MODERN EXAMPLE

Sam and Paula home school their three children, because they want to instill Christian principles in their education instead of leaving the secular public schools to have their humanistic influence upon them.

The two younger children have always been home-schooled and aren't really aware of what they are "missing." The oldest child, a son, was in public school until sixth grade and now resents being taught at home. His old friends taunt him, and he misses some of the things he used to do with them...not realizing that it was because of some of these "things" his parents decided to home-educate their children!

One of the questions most frequently asked of Sam and Paula is, "What about the socialization your children are missing because they aren't in school?" Their reply is, "Secular socialization is exactly what we fear most for our children. We want them to associate with children whose parents are also concerned about Christian values. We also want them to be grounded in God's Word so they can better withstand the influence of the world." But it's not easy. Even within their home, regular TV programming and other worldly influences can undo what they try to teach.

Sam and Paula are finding that it's one thing for them, as parents, to have a commitment to God's principles and it's quite another thing to pass those principles on to sometimes-rebellious children. They are finding that being good role models and praying for each child is just as important as preparing academic lessons each day. As they try to become a family pleasing to God, separated from the world they're discovering that an education is "caught" as much as it is "taught."

Lesson 4

Isaac and Rebekah

Parenting God's Way

---

*Children, obey your parents in everything, for this pleases the Lord. Fathers,
do not embitter your children, or they will become discouraged.*

Colossians 3:20-21

SETTING THE STAGE

All parents have problems, to some extent, in raising their children. Even Christian
parents who do all they can to train, discipline, and love their children in the fear of the
Lord, face difficult situations when raising children in our society. So, the issue is not that
we have problems; the issue is: how do we go about dealing with the problems so that God's
best is realized for all concerned?

Isaac and Rebekah had some problems raising their twin sons, Jacob and Esau, partly
because they had not dealt with some of the sins or "flesh" in their own personalities. In this
lesson, we'll consider some of the things God expects us to do to avoid some of the pitfalls
in parenting. We'll use Isaac and Rebekah as examples to see if, perhaps, we are making
some of the same mistakes — which may have a long-range effect on our children.

INTRODUCING ISAAC AND REBEKAH

(Based on Genesis 25:19-34; 26:34-28:9)

Isaac sat down under the scrubby desert bush, grateful for some shade and a cool breeze.
He just wanted to rest and listen to the bleating of the sheep grazing nearby. Even with a
staff, he was finding it increasingly difficult to walk on the rocky ground because of his
failing eyesight.

Though he closed his eyes and tuned his ears to the familiar sounds of the flocks, it
wasn't long before he was thinking, again, of a subject much on his mind of late — his
advancing years and the need to pass on his blessing to Esau, his firstborn. He wished he
could make it the happy occasion it ought to be. But he knew that Rebekah had always
favored Jacob, even though he was the younger of the twins. There always seemed to be
such rivalry between the boys!

Suddenly, he heard the sound of footsteps, and he said, "Esau, is that you?"

"Yes, father, I've just come in from the field."

"I wish I could go out with you, but I think those days are gone. Esau, would you go find
some wild game and fix me a meal? I want to bless you before I die," Isaac replied.

Rebekah overheard the conversation and knew she had to act quickly. She called Jacob
and told him to run to the flocks and get a couple of goats. She would make Isaac a meal

and use the goatskins to cover Jacob's arms so that they would feel hairy like Esau's. She would then get Jacob to take her meal to Isaac before Esau returned. That way, Isaac would mistake Jacob for Esau and Jacob would receive their father's blessing instead of Esau.

Jacob did as instructed by his mother and ended up with the blessing of his father, as well as the hatred of his brother. Rebekah, no doubt, secretly delighted in the success of her scheme. Isaac was both surprised and disappointed in what had happened, and, the Bible says, Esau lifted up his voice and wept.

LESSONS FROM ISAAC AND REBEKAH
Parenting

Isaac had lived his whole life as a receiver instead of a giver. Born to elderly parents, he had inherited all his father's vast wealth. We can see an example of his passive submission to his father as he was being prepared as a sacrifice. Even his wife was found for him. Since Rebekah seems to have been the more dominant, Isaac was probably a rather passive father to his children, though he was more partial to the more "outdoorsy" life style of Esau.

Rebekah, a more assertive person, seems to have assumed the leadership role, even when it meant deceiving or controlling others to fit into her plans. It is significant to note that *she* sought the Lord concerning the conflict she felt in her womb before the twins were born. Perhaps she did not even tell Isaac that the Lord had told her she would have twins and that the elder would serve the younger. It may have been that she felt she had to help God bring this to pass. It's possible that, because of suffering the reproach of barrenness for many years prior to the birth of the twins, she had allowed bitterness to take root in her life.

Esau had a problem with bitterness. We read of this in Hebrews 12:16-17. After selling his birthright for a simple meal, he was remorseful, which allows for bitterness instead of repentance.

Jacob was much like his mother in that he manipulated people and situations. Like her, he was adept at schemes, bribery, and deception. Because of this, God later dealt with him severely.

The Lord had promised Isaac and Rebekah a child of the covenant, a seed from whom all the nations of the earth would be blessed. But inadequacies in the personalities of the parents, showing favoritism, indulgence, confused roles as a mother and father, sins of the children, bitterness and lack of discipline all had varying effects on each member of the family. It's easy to understand why Isaac and Rebekah would have problems parenting their children.

According to scripture, parents' responsibilities toward their children include:

> Protecting them
> Teaching/Training them
> Disciplining them
> Providing for them
> Loving them

Let's look at each of these areas.

Protecting Children

Hebrews 11:23 reminds us how Amram and Jochebed protected their baby, Moses, during a time when all male babies were being killed by order of the Pharaoh. Parents have the responsibility to protect their children from evil, temptation, enemies, dangers, and calamities. When we claim the protection provided in Psalm 91, what does verse 11 say the reward will be? (KJV uses the term *dwelling*; NIV uses *tent*.)

_____

_____

Teaching/Training Children

To teach or to train children is to give them knowledge of the truth. Teaching deals with the mind; training deals with the will.

Proverbs 22:6 clearly tells us that we are to do this, for it says: *"Train up a child in the way he should go, and when he is old, he will not turn from it."*

Deuteronomy 4:9 confirms it: *"Only be careful, and watch yourselves closely so that you do not forget the things your eyes have seen or let them slip from your heart as long as you live."*

Ephesians 6:4 gives fathers a clue as to what their attitude should be when teaching/training their children: *"Fathers, do not exasperate your children; instead, bring them up in the training and instruction of the Lord."*

Someone once said that every child comes into this world with sealed orders. It's up to parents to unseal them and discover what God intends for each child. That is why Proverbs 22:6 says *"in the way he* (the child*) should go,"* not "according to the parent's desires and ambitions."

So, how do we go about teaching/training our children?

1. Be an example. Children learn as much by what they see as by what they hear.
2. Instruct them. Give specific directions and knowledge that they need. Don't assume they already know everything, and don't leave the teaching to society and friends.
3. Set some rules. Children need directions and limitations to function well, not only in the home, but also in society.
4. Discipline them. This is the way teaching is reinforced.

Teaching is a continuous, ongoing process. Read Deuteronomy 6:4-9 and summarize what it says about teaching/training our children.

_____

_____

_____

_____

Disciplining Children

Webster's dictionary defines discipline as training that corrects, molds or perfects. For the Christian parent, this will be according to what scripture teaches. We have seen in Isaac and Rebekah how problems in their own personalities affected the way they disciplined their children. So, perhaps parents need to be disciplining themselves in the process as well!

Some of the guidelines given in the book of Proverbs will help parents know how to discipline their children. Write down the following:

Proverbs 3:11-12

_____

_____

_____

Proverb 13:24

_____

_____

Proverb 19:18

_____

_____

Proverb 22:15

_____

_____

Proverbs 23:13-14

_____

_____

_____

Proverb 29:15

_____

_____

Proverb 29:17

_____

_____

If you check your dictionary you'll find punishment is defined as a system of rules governing conduct. We find an example of this in Deuteronomy 21:18-21.

If a man has a stubborn and rebellious son who does not obey his father and mother and will not listen to them when they discipline him, his father and mother shall take hold of him and bring him to the elders at the gate of his town. They shall say to the elders, 'This son of ours is stubborn and rebellious. He will not obey us. He is a profligate and a drunkard. Then all the men of his town shall stone him to death. You must purge the evil from among you. All Israel will hear of it and be afraid.

For discipline to work, parents must be in agreement as to the goals they want to accomplish in bringing their children to maturity. They will also need to be in agreement as to the type of punishment or consequences appropriate for each age level. These won't be as harsh as taking the child to the elders at the city gate and having them stone him to death, but they should include suffering logical consequences, spanking, separation from the situation, deprivation of something they want, lack of expected reward, etc.

What are some of the methods you have found that work?

For pre-schoolers _____

_____

For elementary age children _____

_____

For teenagers _____

_____

Providing for Our Children

Second Corinthians 12:14b says *"children should not have to save up for their parents, but parents for their children."* As parents, we provide the material needs of our children. At the same time, we need to be guard against oversaturating them with materialism. In his book *The New Dare to Discipline*, Dr. James Dobson discusses this problem, which is peculiar to our modern American society.

> Many American children are inundated with excesses that work toward their detriment. It has been said that prosperity offers a greater test of character than does adversity, and I'm inclined to agree. There are few conditions that inhibit a sense of appreciation more than for a child to feel he is entitled to whatever he wants, whenever he wants it.

He continues on pages 44 and 45,

> Although it sounds paradoxical, you actually cheat him of pleasure when you give him too much. Pleasure occurs when an intense need is satisfied. If there is no need, there is no pleasure.

And, so, in providing for our children, sometimes the best thing we can do is *not* give them things — and say "no" to their pleas for more.

Loving Our Children

Parents should try to make the home the center of the child's security, happiness, and pleasant memories — a place where he knows he is loved. Giving love takes time and attention, two things parents often have little of today. Even discipline is a sign of love. God says so in Hebrews 12:6: *"because the Lord disciplines those he loves, and he punishes everyone he accepts as a son."*

List ways you show your children that you love them.

_____

_____

_____

_____

_____

_____

_____

Do they *know* that you love them?

_____

SUMMARY

God *"knows how we are formed. He remembers that we are dust"* (Psalm 103:14). He also knows that His Word will not return to Him void, but will accomplish what He desires (Isaiah 55:10). Therefore, He can entrust children into the care of human parents. So, Jacob became one of the patriarchs of God's chosen people, though he was raised by Isaac and Rebekah with all their problems and weaknesses.

And, yes, God allowed Jesus to come into this world and be raised to manhood by two fallible human beings. At the very time Jesus was leaving the ties of this earthly family for His unique ministry, God declared: *"This is my beloved Son, in whom I am well-pleased"* (Matthew 3:16). With all their human frailties, Joseph and Mary had done the job God required them to do as parents. Sometimes, only the Lord can bring about circumstances and teach our children — in ways that we are not able to do.

In His Word, God gives us specific instruction concerning how to raise our children. These areas include (1) protecting them, (2) teaching/training them, (3) disciplining them, (4) providing for them, and (5) loving them.

God can use all our failures and shortcomings as parents to bring our children to maturity pleasing to Him. Isaiah 54:13 (KJV) says: *"All thy children shall be taught of the Lord, and great shall be the peace of thy children."*

What are some of the personality traits and circumstances of your own upbringing that have an effect on your role as a parent?

_____

_____

If these are not appropriate, what can you do to change them?

_____

_____

Do you know and practice what the Bible says about disciplining your children?

_____

_____

How do you protect your children?

_____

_____

How do you provide for your children?

_____

_____

MODERN EXAMPLE

Susanna Wesley was the youngest of twenty-five children and bore nineteen of her own! But, like Isaac and Rebekah, Susanna and her husband, Samuel, had some parenting problems caused by their own personality flaws.

Samuel was a Rector in the Anglican Church in England. Very much an intellectual, he was frequently gone from home for various conferences, and engaged in long periods of study when he was at home. This meant that Susanna was often left alone to care for the children, nine of whom lived to be adults.

Between 1697 and 1701, five of the babies passed away. Yet, several of the children who lived had great impact upon the world. Their son John (the 15th child) was the founder of Methodism and wrote several books. Son Samuel became a preacher. Charles wrote over six thousand hymns, many of which are still used in churches today!

Six hours a day for twenty years, Susanna taught her children in her home school. She wrote some of their textbooks, and instilled in them a passion for learning and righteousness. In addition, she taught them to obey, to eat what was set before them, and to go to bed early.

Her high ideals and sublime faith possibly stemmed from the fact that she spent *two hours a day* in her own room alone with God.

Yet, the model of marriage that she and Samuel presented their children had its impact. In the attempt to escape the family's struggle with poverty, several of their daughters made unfortunate marriages. John, at age forty-eight, married a widow who publicly harangued him. This relationship lasted only a few months. She left him, and subsequently died. He never remarºried.

In 1735, burdened with debt, a disappointed Samuel Wesley died with his son John praying at his bedside. Seven years later, Susanna died on the premises of the foundry where the first Methodist Chapel was built. Still the instructing parent to the very end, her last words to the children standing around her bed were, "Children, as soon as I am released, sing a psalm of praise to God."

Jacob, Leah, and Rachel

Understanding Covenant Relationships

When you make a vow to God, do not delay in fulfilling it. He has no pleasure in fools; fulfill your vow. It is better not to vow than to make a vow and not fulfill it.

Ecclesiastes 5:4-5

SETTING THE STAGE

In the last decades of the 20th century attitudes toward marriage, commitment, and even toward taking wedding vows, have become very complacent. We have become self-centered, intent on pursuing personal pleasure. We're bombarded by Satan's lies, which exalt the idea of individual rights — that we should do whatever pleases us and meets our personal needs.

Though we may have been unaware of it at the time we married, God says we give up our rights to our own feelings when we marry. Scripture tells us that God sees marriage as a covenant (with Him and with each other) which He ordained; and He is committed to seeing that it is kept. This is the kind of love God demands in marriage.

In this lesson, we are studying Jacob and his relationship with his two wives, to illustrate the difference between a covenant relationship and a relationship that is based primarily on emotions.

INTRODUCING JACOB AND HIS WIVES, LEAH AND RACHEL

(Based on Genesis 29-31; 35:16-19; 49:31)

Jacob simply couldn't believe it! He'd been tricked! For seven long years, he had worked for his uncle Laban in order to have one of his uncle's daughters for a bride. And, now, Laban had deceived him!

The morning light was softly filtering through the slits in the tent. He'd barely slept all night, and already it was daybreak! A new day was dawning...the day he'd dreamed of for years!

He turned over to face the side wall of the tent. As he did, he could hear the measured breathing of the young woman who lay sleeping at his side. No...no...no...it simply couldn't be! He tried, unobtrusively, to get more comfortable. He certainly didn't want to waken Leah...he couldn't face her yet. Let her sleep. He had too much to think about.

Had it been only yesterday that the wedding feast had taken place? It had been such a happy occasion! And Rachel...Rachel...Where was Rachel? Did she know all that had happened? He must find her first thing! No, the first thing was to find Laban! He'd given him Leah and not Rachel! Leah was his wife...Leah, not Rachel...What would he do now?

According to the rest of the story found in Genesis, Jacob did find Laban, who reminded him that their custom was to give the oldest daughter in marriage first. And, Jacob had taken the wedding vow with Leah. Laban then made an offer to Jacob. Finish Leah's bridal week. Then Laban would give him Rachel, for whom he would work another seven years! Jacob agreed because *"he loved Rachel more than Leah"* (Genesis 29:30).

LESSONS FROM JACOB, LEAH AND RACHEL

Covenants Versus Emotions

If feelings were the basis for marriage, Jacob and Leah had no future. All of Jacob's romantic emotions were for Rachel. Yet, he knew that he had consummated the marriage with Leah, and because he had, he was bound in a covenant relationship with her. He knew he must keep this covenant in the fear of the Lord, with whom a covenant is serious business. Leah longed for Jacob's love, but, evidently, never received it. She had to learn, instead, to look to the Lord for fulfillment as she committed herself to her husband.

We can see her yearning, in Genesis 29:32-30:13, through the names she gave the children she bore to Jacob. From her first child to her last, Leah gave them names which described how she was trusting God as she committed herself to a husband who did not return her love. God gave them six sons and one daughter. He later used the sons as leaders of half of the twelve tribes of Israel. It was through one of these tribes, Judah, that He sent Jesus into our world. At her death, Leah was buried in the Cave of Macpelah in Hebron along with Abraham and Sarah, Isaac and Rebekah, and Jacob. God honored the covenant relationship between Jacob and Leah.

On the other hand, it appears that the relationship between Jacob and Rachel was based on emotions. Though we read several times of how Jacob loved Rachel, we never read that she loved him! We do see how other emotions ruled in their relationship. Genesis 30:1 tells us Rachel was jealous of Leah for bearing children when she could not, and she became so angry with Jacob she lashed out at him: *"Give me children, or I'll die!"* (Genesis 30:1) Then, when God later gave her a son, her ungrateful response was, *"May the Lord add to me another son"* (Genesis 30:24).

When Jacob decided to move his families back to his homeland, Rachel took her father's idols — making her trust in Jacob's God questionable. Rachel died after the birth of her second son. God would not even allow her to enter the land of promise where He was raising up Jacob to be the leader of His people and, thus, would want him to set the example of covenant relationship.

In a covenant (or testament), God binds (pledges) Himself to fulfill a promise to man. He will see that it comes to pass. As used here, the Hebrew word for "covenant" means "in the sense of cutting; a compact made by passing between pieces of flesh." We can see this in God's covenant with Abraham (Genesis 15:10, 17-18) when Abraham saw a blazing torch pass between halves of slain animals. In the New Testament (covenant), the covenant was sealed by the death of Jesus Christ, who shed His blood for the remission of man's sin. Because God has bound Himself in this covenant with man, we can have hope of salvation. He does not go back on His promise when He makes a covenant.

What covenant did God make with Noah? What is the sign that it will not be broken? (Genesis 9:7-17)

_____

_____

What covenant did God make with Abraham? What was the sign of this covenant? (Genesis 12:1-3 and Genesis 17:1-14)

_____

_____

_____

What covenant did God make with David? (Psalm 89:3-4; I Kings 8:16; Psalm 132:11-12; Revelation 22:16)

_____

_____

_____

What covenant did Jesus make with us? (I Corinthians 11:24-28; Hebrews 9:11-22)

_____

_____

_____

God's View of Covenant

What are the consequences of breaking a covenant? (Isaiah 24:1-6)

_____

_____

One enters into a covenant by making a vow. In God's sight, how important is making a vow? (Ecclesiastes 5:4-7)

_____

_____

Since it is impossible for man to keep his part of a covenant without God's help, how does God provide for this? (Jeremiah 31:33-34)

_____

_____

The Marriage Covenant

According to the dictionary, a covenant is a formal, binding agreement. Covenants can be made between men, but they are difficult to keep without God's help. God is a covenant God. He not only keeps His agreement with man, but also helps man keep the agreement with Him!

The use of symbols helps others understand what has taken place when a covenant has been made. Covenants might be symbolized by an exchange of clothing — especially belts — or cutting the flesh to intermingle blood. Covenant-makers might eat a special meal together, or give a blessing, or exchange names. Many symbols are used in the wedding ceremony to illustrate the fact that a covenant is being made. Consider how some of these wedding traditions symbolize this covenant:

White runner down the aisle

Walking on holy ground in the presence of a holy God.

White wedding dress

The purity of heart and life for which the husband will soon be responsible. He is to cleanse his wife by the Word of God as Jesus does the Church, according to Ephesians 5:25-28.

The wedding ring

The transfer of authority, strength, protection, and identification.

The veil

Modesty, respect, and the exclusiveness of the marriage covenant.

Food at the reception

One of the root meanings of the word "covenant" is "to feed." Entering into a meal is a form of covenant.

Bride and Groom feeding one another cake

Becoming one flesh.

Guest Book

Official witnesses to the covenant made.

Feelings Versus Faith

It takes faith, not feelings, to keep a covenant. Emotions fluctuate according to circumstances within or around us. Galatians 5:16 says to "*live by the Spirit, and you will not gratify the desires of the sinful nature.*" How do we do this? By accepting, in faith, God's Word, not acting according to how we feel.

We inherit God's promises through our faith, not our feelings. Consider the following:

Salvation comes through faith, not feelings.

Ephesians 2:8: *For it is by grace you have been saved, through faith...and this is not from yourselves, it is the gift of God...not of works, so that no one can boast.*

God does not ask us to pray or to love according to our feelings.

Matthew 5:44:   *I tell you; Love your enemies and pray for those who persecute you.*

God does not judge by His feelings, but by His Word.

John 12:48:   *There is a judge for the one who rejects me and does not accept my word; that very word which I spoke will condemn him at the last day.*

We are not healed according to our feelings, but by accepting God's Word.

I Peter 2:24:   *He himself bore our sins in his body on the tree, so that we might die to sins and live for righteousness; by his wounds you have been healed.*

We must not respond to others' evil ways according to our feelings.

I Peter 3:9:   *Do not repay evil with evil or insult with insult; but with blessing, because to this you were called so that you may inherit a blessing.*

We must not base our decisions on our feelings.

Proverb 14:12:   *There is a way that seems right to a man, but in the end it leads to death.*

SUMMARY

God is a covenant-making God. He wants us to be a covenant-keeping people in our relationship to Him and to one another in marriage. If we respond to His love and will for our life, through faith and commitment to Him, He will see our marriage through. He has bound Himself to the institution of marriage through a covenant. He wants us to do so, too!

Jacob's relationship with his two wives, Leah and Rachel, illustrate the difference between a covenant relationship and a relationship based on feelings.

CONSIDER THIS

Do you see your marriage as a covenant between each other and God?

_____

How do you deal with your feelings in the light of your commitment to each other? To God?

_____

_____

If you have not thought of your marriage as a covenant, what can you do to make that more real?

_____

_____

MODERN EXAMPLE

Clebe and Deanna McClary speak before thousands of people each year in churches, schools, businesses and military installations. Their books *Living Proof* and *Commitment to Love* have reached people all over the world. But they would not have had such a powerful message on commitment and the covenant relationship during their thirty years of marriage had it not been for their response to a tragedy that struck them as newlyweds.

Deanna was only nineteen when she married Clebe, who was on a brief leave from Marine Corps training. When he got orders for Vietnam, he was glad to be able to fulfill his patriotic duty, though it meant leaving his new bride. Almost every day, they mailed letters and audiocassettes back and forth. Then, on Clebe's last patrol in Vietnam — on Deanna's twentieth birthday — a grenade landed in his foxhole and shrapnel hit him in the back, neck and shoulder. After that, a North Vietnamese, strapped with explosives, fell into his pit. Before he knew what had happened, Clebe had lost an arm. And if that weren't enough, as he climbed out of that foxhole and started running to another one, he was shot in the neck.

Deanna received a telegram telling her that Clebe had lost an arm, was wounded in all extremities, and his prognosis was poor. Two months later, when he was sent to Bethesda Hospital in Maryland, Deanna hardly recognized him. Mustering all the strength she could, she rushed to his side, told him she loved him, and promised that they would always be together.

Although he was just scabs and scars and stitches, Deanna found herself falling more and more in love with him. It was then that she began to understand that love is commitment, a conscious decision to make the best of whatever comes along. When Clebe and Deanna made the decision to stay together, God helped them do so, despite some incredibly difficult years. The vows they made on their wedding day were "until death do us part." They have kept their vows, not because their love was based on emotions, but because they had a covenant relationship with each other and with God.

Amram and Jochebed
Manoah and His Wife

Raising "Special" Children for the Lord

Those God foreknew he also predestined to be conformed to the likeness of his Son, that he might be the firstborn among many brothers. And those he predestined, he also called; those he called, he also justified; those he justified, he also glorified.

Romans 8:29-30

SETTING THE STAGE

In this lesson, we'll look at two couples in the Bible who were given special children, children that God had foreordained for His unique timing and purposes.

Amram and Jochebed were given Moses. Not only did he become a leader of His people, he was raised under unusual circumstances. Manoah and his wife were given Samson to be used of God as the last Judge of Israel. He, too, was raised in a unique fashion, according to the instructions of God.

All children are special, both in the eyes of their parents and in God's sight. According to Isaiah 49:15-16, God does have a plan for each life. So it behooves us, as parents, to seek His wisdom as we raise each of our children on His behalf. Parents who are given physically or mentally disabled, terminally ill, or even specially gifted children, will have more than ordinary concerns and questions about God's plan for themselves and their offspring.

But, those who have their trust in a good and loving God will see that He can use every child, for His purposes as part of His plan, *if* we allow Him to do so!

INTRODUCING AMRAM AND JOCHEBED

(Based on Exodus 2:1-10; 6:20; Numbers 26:59)

Amram and Jochebed were the parents of Moses, Aaron, and Miriam, the three people God chose to lead Israel out of Egypt, across the Red Sea, and through the forty-year trek in the wilderness to the Promised Land. Moses was the leader, Aaron acted as High Priest, and Miriam led the people in worship and praise to God. Though most of what we know about Amram and Jochebed is contained in a few verses of scripture, we can assume they raised their children in a God-fearing home.

When Moses was born, the Hebrews had been slaves in Egypt for about 400 years. The Pharaoh lived in constant fear that they would multiply and become too mighty for him, so he inflicted them with heavy burdens. But this didn't keep the Hebrews from growing in numbers. So he decided to kill all the Hebrew boys at birth. But the Hebrew midwives feared God and spared the infants when possible.

Amram had married Jochebed, his father's sister. They already had two children, Aaron and Miriam, when sometime before the birth of Moses, a decree went forth concerning the slaughter of newborn males. As the story goes, after hiding Moses for three months, Jochebed put her little son in a basket and hid him among the bulrushes in the river. She stationed her daughter, Miriam, nearby to watch over him. When the Pharaoh's daughter came to the river to bathe, she found the baby — as well as Miriam, who offered to get a nurse for the baby. The nurse turned out to be Moses' own mother! Thus, Jochebed and Amram were able to influence their child in the ways of God, even though he had become part of Pharaoh's household!

INTRODUCING MANOAH AND HIS WIFE

(Based on Judges 13)

The angel of the Lord appeared to Manoah's wife and told her that, after years of barrenness, she would have a son. He was to be raised as a Nazirite, set apart to God from birth. She was even told his mission. He would begin the deliverance of Israel from the hands of the Philistines!

She then went to her husband, Manoah, and told him what the angel had said. Manoah's response was to pray that God would send the angel again to teach them how to raise this boy. God heard Manoah, and sent the angel to his wife a second time. She rushed to get Manoah so he could also hear the instructions. Manoah then had a conversation with the angel, who asked him to prepare a burnt offering. Manoah did. As the flame blazed up from the altar and the angel descended in the flame, Manoah and his wife knew for certain that they had heard from God Himself! Manoah's wife gave birth to the boy we know as Samson, the last Judge of Israel before Saul was anointed King.

LESSONS FROM AMRAM AND JOCHEBED AND MANOAH AND HIS WIFE

God's Special Children for Special Tasks

Though God knows every person before they are born, and has a special plan for each life (Psalm 139:13-16, Isaiah 49:15-16, and Ephesians 1:11), He does seem to bring certain children into the world for special tasks. Examples we can read about are found in Jeremiah 1:5 and Isaiah 43:1, 7. In the Bible, we find stories of several women who were barren until God, in His perfect timing, used them to bring special children into the world for something He wanted to do at that particular time. Look at the following scriptures and write the name of the child and the ministry to which God had called him — even before his birth!

Mother	Child	Special Task
Sarah	Genesis 17:15-19; 18:9-15; 21:1-8	
Rebekah	Genesis 24:60; 25:21-26, 33-34; 28:10-15	
Rachel	Genesis 30:22-24; 39:1-4; 41:38-46	
Manoah's Wife	Judges 13:2-5, 24-25	
Hannah	I Samuel 1:1-5, 10-28; 3:19-21	
Elizabeth	Luke 1:5-17, 57-66, 80	
Mary	Luke 1:26-38; 2:8-19	

Read the following illustration, then consider it in light of the above scriptures. What is your view on abortion?

The mother, pregnant with her fifth child, had tuberculosis. Her husband had syphilis. Their first child had been born blind. Their second child had died. Their third child had been born deaf. Their fourth child had tuberculosis. Should she have aborted the fifth child? We can be glad she didn't — for if she had, there would have been no Ludwig van Beethoven!

According to Psalm 127:3-5, children are

_____

_____

Children With Special Physical/Mental Needs

If God knows each person as he is formed in the womb, He must also know that some will have physical or mental disabilities which may result in great suffering for parents and child.

Caring for a child with a life-threatening disease, even for a limited time, causes parents to ask "Why?" or, "How can a good God allow this?" We forget how much it cost God to watch His own Son suffer, and then to see Him die a cruel death upon a cross — not for anything He did, but for our sin.

Since angels were often the messengers God sent to announce the birth of special children, let's imagine a conversation between such an angel and God after Jesus died upon the cross.

"How it must grieve you to see what has taken place. You sent your only-begotten Son to be raised as a man, by Mary and Joseph; now, He's dead. He was theirs…but He also was yours. What was the purpose of His life, anyway?"

The Father was silent. What words could He use to explain how such sorrow could, in the end, produce such joy? His ways were hardly ever understood. People even blamed Him when He was loving them the most! With utmost compassion, He replied, "I have an ultimate plan which overrides all sorrow and pain. It's truly exciting. You see, all people who accept what Jesus' shed blood has done for them in forgiving their sins, will become my family, my church, my kingdom. More than that…they'll become the Bride of Jesus Christ!"

"Jesus will have a Bride?" asked the angel. "When will the wedding be?"

"That's arranged, too," said the Heavenly Father. "I'm calling it the Marriage Supper of the Lamb. It will take place at the end of the age."

"Will the Bride be ready for such a magnificent occasion?" questioned the angel.

"Yes, she will. In fact, that will be the purpose of the Holy Spirit who will be sent to lift up Jesus, to enlighten my Word, and to prepare the Bride for the wedding. You see, I want a very beautiful Bride for Him, one without spot or blemish. The Holy Spirit will develop beautiful fruit in her…love, joy, peace, long-suffering, gentleness, patience…much like our nature."

"How will He do that?" asked the angel.

"Circumstances, problems, trials, afflictions, suffering. These are the best teachers," the Father responded.

The angel spoke with sudden insight. "I'm beginning to understand. People need trials and afflictions to become the perfect Bride of Jesus. The Holy Spirit will be sent to get them ready for the wedding! All their suffering will be for a purpose. Why, that means that all those special children born to certain parents can be used to mature those parents and children (and those who come in contact with them) into the beautiful Bride!"

"Exactly!" exclaimed the Father. "That's part of my plan. It's not necessarily my fault that children are born the way they are, but I can use every child for my purpose, even those who are disabled. It really depends upon whether or not the Holy Spirit is allowed to do His job."

"Perhaps they can, if they can get past the 'blaming' part and see what You have in store," responded the angel. "Wouldn't it be great for them! I would think they would be the very most beautiful part of the Bride."

Musing to himself, the angel spoke wistfully. "I almost wish I could be the parent of a special child…especially in the end times when the Bride is earnestly being made ready. I think I'd rather be part of the beautiful Bride of Jesus than just a messenger angel!"

Raising Children in the Fear of the Lord

Christian parents who want to raise their children to become followers of the Lord Jesus Christ, follow guidelines in raising their children, which are not part of the world's ways. Such as:

In Faith

Hebrews 11:23 tell us that_____

_____

By faith, because they saw that he was no ordinary child, not only did they risk their own lives to hide Moses, they also exposed Miriam to danger. As parents we, too, must have faith in God in what may seem to be impossible circumstances.

How are you raising your children in faith?

_____

_____

With Full-Time Commitment

Deuteronomy 6:4-7 says: _____

_____

_____

Evidently, even in Pharaoh's household, Jochebed took advantage of every bit of time she had with Moses and taught him of his Jewish heritage. It takes extra time for us to teach our children about the Lord and how to follow Him.

How do you take advantage of various times in your day to teach the children?

_____

_____

_____

By Training

Proverbs 22:6 says _____

_____

We train our children all the time by the examples we set for them. Our "walk" must coincide with our "talk." We need to be available for them, respect them, keep the lines of communication open.

What do you do to train your children?

_____

_____

_____

Through Prayer

Judges 13:8 says _____

_____

We must pray for our children, just as Manoah did before Samson was born. We are not left alone to raise our children. If we follow the instructions God has given in His Word, and pray for specific wisdom and guidance, He will teach our children as well.

How and when do you pray for your children?

_____

_____

SUMMARY

God gives us a each child to raise — either for something He has for that child in the way of ministry for Him, or for what He wants to do in the lives of parents or other family members — to form His child to the nature of Jesus Christ. We have the responsibility, as parents, to raise our children in the fear of the Lord.

CONSIDER THIS

Have you, or anyone you know, been given a "special" child to raise? If so, what difference has that made?

_____

_____

How does your relationship with the Lord, and being accountable to His Word, specifically help you in raising your children?

_____

_____

Raising "special" children requires more time, physical stamina, emotional support, finances, etc. Is there some way you do, or can, help such a family?

_____

_____

If you are raising a "special" child, what kind of help would you appreciate?

_____

_____

MODERN EXAMPLE

When David and Cindy Hooker started their family, they anticipated raising several children, but they didn't realize what God had in store for them. Their first baby died shortly after birth. Then, Cindy's second pregnancy ended in miscarriage. Both children had a chromosome disorder.

So, David and Cindy decided to adopt a baby. Sam came into their home when he was four days old, and they fell in love with him. When he was seven years old, he was diagnosed with dyslexia, an impairment of the ability to read. Although Sam was also found to be quite gifted, he is a challenge to home school.

When Sam was three years old, Cindy became pregnant again. David and Cindy were concerned enough to have some tests done to see if this baby, a girl, also carried the same genetic deficiency as the first two children. She did not; but doctors discovered that she did have Spina Bifida. Sara was born paralyzed from the waist down. She can walk around the house with braces, but she must use a wheelchair when outside the home.

After Sara's birth, Cindy had a tubal ligation. The couple had decided that they and their families had been through enough trauma. But when Sara was about a year-and-a-half old, Cindy wanted more children. David wasn't sure. Then, after a "divine dialogue" during a Sunday worship service, he came across a verse of scripture which seemed to confirm what the Lord was saying to him. It was Psalm 113:7-9: *"He raised the poor from the dust and lifts the needy from the ash heap; he seats them with princes, with the princes of their people. He settles the barren woman in her home as a happy mother of children."*

At first, the couple thought maybe God wanted them to establish an orphanage. They prayed about that. When nothing materialized, they began to think God wanted them to adopt international children. Yet when they looked in to it, they found the process very expensive and knew they couldn't afford it. Thus began a waiting period of just trusting God to bring whatever He had in mind, in His perfect timing.

Some time later, friends of theirs came into an inheritance which they wanted to use for what they called "life purposes." They asked David and Cindy if they were still interested in adopting international children. If so, they would like to help make it possible! Thus began a new search for children overseas who needed a loving home.

After much prayer and paperwork, they were told about Ben, a five-year-old boy in a Vietnam orphanage. Though they had also hoped to get a younger girl, no girls were available. So they decided to take Ben. David made the arrangements to fly to Vietnam to pick him up. Three weeks before his departure, they received a call that there was a ten-day-old baby girl, in another orphanage, who also needed adoption! David purchased a ticket for his sister, and while Cindy stayed home to care for Sam and Sara, they went to Vietnam to bring both Ben and Rachel, to California.

David and Cindy now have a very special family — all unplanned by them, but known to God. They believe God gave them these children as gifts to raise, and they are eager to see what else He has in store for them as they bring up these children in the fear of the Lord!

Lesson 7

Moses and Zipporah
Nabal and Abigail

Living in Peace

> *Rather, clothe yourselves with the Lord Jesus Christ, and do not think about how to gratify the desires of the sinful nature.*
>
> Romans 13:14

SETTING THE STAGE

Every couple must deal with conflicts in their relationship. Sometimes these conflicts arise because we are "unequally yoked." We have different personalities, backgrounds, beliefs, and goals. But most of the time, conflicts stem from the fact that we haven't dealt with the "flesh." We become overly sensitive, angry, or have a constant need to be right. We haven't "crucified the flesh" or "put off the old man."

An episode in Moses and Zipporah's relationship illustrates the need for "spiritual circumcision" in our lives — that God wants us to walk after the Spirit, not the flesh.

Abigail became an intercessor in a conflict between Nabal, her husband, and David, the king-elect. She illustrates the need to use spiritual weapons where the enemy is at work causing disharmony.

Both of these couples will help us understand why we don't always have the peace God desires for every marriage.

INTRODUCING MOSES AND ZIPPORAH

(Based on Exodus 2:11-22; 4:19-26)

Although Moses grew up in the royal court of Egypt, he had been cared for by his own Hebrew mother, who instilled in him his Jewish heritage. Identifying with his own people, he had compassion for them. So when, as a young man, he saw an Egyptian beating a Hebrew slave, he killed the Egyptian and buried him in the sand. When the Pharaoh discovered what had happened, he sought to slay Moses. But Moses had fled to the land of Midian.

It was here, at a watering trough, that Moses met Zipporah, the eldest of seven daughters of Jethro, the Priest of Midian. The family took him in, and sometime during the forty years Moses spent here, Jethro gave Zipporah to him in marriage.

Moses and Zipporah had at least one son, Gershom, before God confronted Moses from a burning bush and called him to return to Egypt to lead the children of Israel out of bondage. The only recorded conversation we have between Moses and Zipporah took place during the trip back to Egypt from Midian. This conversation appears to have been the result of

God dealing with them concerning their failure to circumcise their son. Because of a sudden confrontation by God, Zipporah took a sharp stone, cut off the foreskin of her child, and threw it at her husband, shouting *"Surely, you are a bridegroom of blood to me!"* (Exodus 4:25b). She was angry! And, Moses made no response.

We don't know when Zipporah and her two sons returned to live with Jethro, but we hear no more of her from the time of this incident until much later, when Jethro brought Zipporah and the two boys, Gershom and Eliezer, to visit Moses in the wilderness. Moses welcomed them all. During their stay, Jethro helped Moses organize the leadership of the people. After this, we have no further mention of Zipporah again. Curiously, the Bible tells us only that Jethro departed. Did Zipporah and the boys go with him? Or, did they stay with Moses? The Bible doesn't say.

INTRODUCING NABAL AND ABIGAIL

(Based on I Samuel 25)

The account of Nabal and Abigail begins just after Samuel died. David had been anointed king, but had not yet assumed the throne. Saul was still reigning and was extremely jealous of David. So, David often ran from Saul. It was between confrontations with Saul that David came from the wilderness of Engedi and asked Nabal for help.

David and his 600 men were moving to the wilderness of Paran when he heard that Nabal was shearing sheep in Carmel. They had often helped Nabal's men when they were in the area, so David sent a request to Nabal for some food for his hungry men. But Nabal refused to give them even a crumb, and insulted David in the process. This, of course, angered David, and he armed his men for battle. Meanwhile, one of Nabal's young men told Abigail what was happening and she decided that something had to be done immediately. Without telling her husband, she gathered food, packed it on donkeys and rode out to meet David before he came near their property. She knew that if David got close enough, there would be a bloody battle between him and a very angry Nabal.

Her intercession kept Nabal and David from a head-on collision. Not long after she returned home, Nabal died. David later recognized her wisdom and intercession. Abigail eventually became one of David's several wives.

LESSONS FROM MOSES AND ZIPPORAH, NABAL AND ABIGAIL

Unequally Yoked

Both couples appear to have been unequally yoked in marriage. Zipporah was a Midianite, a descendent of Abraham and Keturah, the wife Abraham had taken after Sarah died. This meant that Zipporah was not in the lineage of Isaac, the one through whom God chose His people. Moses, on the other hand, was the son of Amram and Jochebed, who were from the chosen lineage (Exodus 6:14-27). It is possible that the rite of circumcision, therefore, was not as important to Zipporah as it should have been to Moses.

The first few verses of I Samuel tell us that Nabal and Abigail had very different personalities. She refers to God and His power, which shows that she probably believed in Him and, thus, recognized David as His servant. Nabal seems to have had no belief or fear in the true God who, in the end, struck him dead.

What advice does II Corinthians 6:14-18 give to those considering marriage? (Other scriptural teachings, which are not being considered here, apply to those already married to unbelievers.)

_____

_____

First Corinthians 6:17 tells us that this is because

_____

_____

Therefore, if a Christian is one Spirit with God and the unbeliever is not, how can they have true intimacy? Colossians 1:13-14 reminds us that as those who share in the inheritance of saints, we

_____

_____

Spiritual Circumcision

God instituted circumcision when He told Abraham that this rite would be a sign of the covenant He would make between Himself and His people (Genesis 17:10-14). This external sign performed on the reproductive organ of the male symbolized cutting away fleshly dependence and signified that future posterity was not to rest upon man's ability.

God uses this analogy throughout scripture to show man's need for spiritual circumcision, the cutting away of flesh, which separates one from being led by the Spirit of God. "Self" must die that Christ so can live in us.

Moses and Zipporah's failure to perform the rite of circumcision on their son, as a baby, may have been caused either by Zipporah's abhorrence of the practice, or by observing the Midianite custom which called for males to be circumcised at puberty. God was displeased with Moses for not seeing that his son was circumcised on the eighth day according to His law. He used Zipporah to do what Moses should have done.

Significantly, it was to Moses that God first gave the insight on spiritual circumcision. In Deuteronomy 10:14-20, God tells His people, through Moses, to

_____

_____

Jacob was a man full of self. To deal with Jacob's flesh, God had to get him alone, so that they could wrestle (Genesis 32:22-32). What was the result in Jacob's life?

_____

_____

_____

God knew that man's heart is desperately wicked, so He told Jeremiah (in Jeremiah 31:33-34) that part of the covenant would be that He would

_____

_____

David knew that he alone could not change his own heart; so in Psalm 51:10-12, he asked God to

_____

_____

Dealing With Our Flesh

Galatians 5:16-17 tells us: "*Live by the Spirit, and you will not gratify the desires of the sinful nature. For the sinful nature desires what is contrary to the Spirit, and the Spirit what is contrary to the sinful nature. They are in conflict with each other, so that you do not do what you want.*" Then, the following verses name what some of these acts of the sinful nature (or flesh) are:

Sexual immorality	Anger/rage
Impurity	Selfish ambition
Idolatry	Dissension
Witchcraft	Envy
Hatred	Drunkenness
Discord	Jealousy

In summary, verse 21b says, "*those who live like this will not inherit the kingdom of God.*"

According to the following scriptures, how can we deal with our flesh?

Galatians 2:19-21 _____

_____

Colossians 3:10, 12-14 _____

_____

_____

Ephesians 4:22-32 _____

_____

_____

_____

Romans 6:11-14 _____

_____

_____

Romans 8:5-11 _____

_____

_____

Spiritual Warfare

Besides dealing with the flesh through spiritual circumcision, we must also use spiritual weapons against Satan, the enemy who also likes to cause conflict in marriages.

Abigail and Nabal were opposites in character and personality, much like the Church and Satan! As Abigail used special "weapons" of intercession, God vindicated her, and Nabal was defeated! Let's look at some of the weapons we can use in our battle with Satan. II Corinthians 10:3-5 tells us that we are not to use weapons of the flesh.

Put a check by the ones you use when doing spiritual warfare. Then, look at the ones not checked and determine how you can begin to use them so that you may be a well-equipped warrior in settling conflicts with Satan and his host.

We must wear the whole armor of God. (Ephesians 6:10-18)
We must be protected by the blood of Jesus. (Revelation 12:11; Hebrews 9:12, 14)
We can use the name of Jesus. (Philippians 2:9-11; Psalm 44:4-5)
We can use the Word of God. (Hebrews 4:12; Luke 4:4, 8, 12)
We can praise the Lord in song. (II Chronicles 20:22; Psalm 149)
We can watch what we say. (Mark 11:23-24; Revelation 12:11)
We can fast. (Isaiah 58:5-12)

We can wait in prayer for God's timing. (Daniel 10:2-20)

We can draw nigh to God and resist the devil. (James 4:7-8)

We can have faith in God. (Hebrews 11:6)

We can separate ourselves from the world. (II Timothy 2:3-4)

We can pray according to God's will. (I John 5:14-15)

We can accept the authority given us. (Luke 10:19; Mark 16:17f)

SUMMARY

Moses and Zipporah were handicapped when it came to dealing with the flesh. It takes the blood of Jesus and the power of the Holy Spirit to truly be spiritually circumcised. Though she was not fully able to use all the spiritual weapons we have available since Jesus defeated Satan at the cross, Abigail did intercede when a conflict arose between Nabal and David, thus helping David avoid further sin. It is probable that neither of these couples knew what it meant to be "unequally yoked," even though they experienced it.

As couples "crucified with Christ" and yielded to the Holy Spirit's work in our lives, we have the unique challenge and responsibility daily to "reckon ourselves dead" as we deal with our own flesh in relationship to our spouse. We also have the privilege to agree together in prayer and do spiritual warfare on behalf of our families, and for other needs. Working in agreement in both these areas will not only bring peace into our relationships, it will also benefit many others.

Consider This

If you were unequally yoked at the time of your marriage, what has God done to bring you together in Him?

_____

_____

Are you, as individuals, dead to self — no longer living by the flesh, but by Christ who lives in you? (To answer this question, ask yourself: "Am I sensitive when not recognized, angry when corrected, defensive when challenged? Do I always have to be right?)

_____

_____

What are some of the conflicts you face in your relationship? How do you presently deal with them?

_____

_____

Do you presently do any spiritual warfare together? If not, how can you?

_____

_____

MODERN EXAMPLE

John and Polly met when she was thirteen and he was seventeen, though it would be eight more years before they married. If they had become husband and wife any earlier, they would certainly have been unequally yoked and in conflict much of the time.

John had been born and raised in England. Though his Christian mother had taught him scriptures, poems and songs, before she died when he was six years old, he was an atheist by his own admission.

He lived much of his youth among sailors, since he often sailed with his father and other sea captains. But this only encouraged the lust, anger, pride, unforgiveness, and other "works of the flesh" which had become a major part of his lifestyle. When the ships carried slaves from Africa to other countries, John and the other sailors raped the young women aboard. He even lived in Africa for a while, where he kept a mistress and participated in many types of sordid activities.

Throughout these years, John wrote Polly from various ports and always arranged to visit her when he was in England. Polly's parents, aware of the kind of life John was living, were not happy with the situation. Polly, the oldest of six children, lived with her very proper family in England where she helped care for her brothers and sisters in their Christian environment.

On one of John's trips back to England, he had an experience that not only changed his life forever, but also allowed him to deal with the rampant works of the flesh which had become so much a part of his life.

While sailing along the coast of Africa, John mocked the Gospel and derided Jesus Christ to those around him. Then, in a drunken stupor, he nearly lunged overboard.

But one evening, while he was alone, he picked up a translation of *Imitation of Christ* by Thomas á Kempis. Its message pierced his spirit. Soon after, a fierce storm struck. When the ship began to sink, John suddenly recalled scriptures he had learned as a pre-schooler, and cried out to God for mercy. He was now barely twenty-three.

Though he backslid before becoming firmly established in his walk with the Lord, John was a devout Christian when he finally married Polly. Being equally yoked and able to live in a peaceful relationship was now possible.

And although he continued sailing for a while, John became a very compassionate pastor, preaching the gospel which he had so mocked previously. He was persuaded to put the story of his early life into a book, so that readers could see how God's power can, indeed, change lives and give one the strength to deal with the works of the flesh. John Newton also began to write poetry, one of which has become much-favored hymn which has brought hope to many people all over the world. It truly is his own story.

Amazing Grace

Amazing grace
How sweet the sound That saved a wretch like me!
I once was lost, but now am found
Was blind, but now I see.
'Twas grace that taught my heart to fear,
And grace my fears relieved;
How precious did that grace appear the hour I first believed!
Through many dangers, toils and snares, I have already come
'Tis grace hath brought me safe thus far, And grace will lead me home.

Lesson 8

Boaz and Ruth

Enjoying Extended Family

A father to the fatherless, a defender of widows, is God in his holy dwelling. God sets the lonely in families.

Psalm 68:5-6a

SETTING THE STAGE

The story of Ruth and Boaz contains beautiful parallels concerning the way we, as Gentiles, are grafted into the family of God. We see privileges and responsibilities that are ours and the blessings we derive from belonging to His family. This applies to both husbands and wives who have been born again into the kingdom of God. They are, in analogy, Ruth, the Church, the Bride of Jesus Christ.

INTRODUCING BOAZ AND RUTH

(Based on Ruth 1-4)

Famine had driven Elimelech to take his wife, Naomi, and their two growing boys into Moab to find food. It was difficult being separated from friends and family they had left behind in Bethlehem-Judah — especially for Naomi, after Elimelech died. But she stayed on, because by then Mahlon and Chilian had married Moabite girls. When both sons met untimely deaths, however, Naomi decided to leave her daughters-in-law and return to her native land. She knew that she had no way of providing more husbands for Ruth and Orpah, and she had heard that the Lord had visited His people by giving them bread once again.

With great sorrow, Naomi told Orpah and Ruth to go back to their families. But Ruth had made a commitment to her husband's family and to her new-found God. She was willing to leave her homeland because she believed God would set her into a new family that He would provide. Leaving Orpah behind, Naomi and Ruth set out for Bethlehem. They arrived at the beginning of barley harvest. Ruth immediately went to glean in the fields, a job always available to the poor and needy.

It so happened that she came upon the field of Boaz, a kinsman of Naomi. He was so impressed with Ruth that he told his young men to leave plenty of grain for her to pick up. When she returned home and told her mother-in-law of her good fortune, Naomi was pleased. She suggested the proper way for Ruth to claim Boaz as her own kinsman, something which had been provided through Levirite law. Ruth made her desire known to Boaz by the custom of lying at his feet. Another male more closely related than Boaz should have been the kinsman-redeemer, so Boaz bought the right from him. When the transaction was complete, Ruth became his wife. From their union came a son, Obed, who bore a son, named Jesse, the father of David, through whose seed Jesus was born!

LESSONS FROM BOAZ AND RUTH

The Analogy of Naomi, Ruth, and Boaz to God's Family

Symbolically, Naomi represents Israel, God's covenant people. She had left her homeland. A Gentile was grafted into her family (Romans 11:17) as her foreign-born daughter-in-law chose to accept her God and follow Him. By being joined into the same family, they had the promise of receiving the same inheritance as long as they obeyed the rules God had commanded. By law, it should have been Naomi who married Boaz; but, because she could no longer fulfill her obligation to bear children, she allowed her widowed daughter-in-law, Ruth, to take her place. So Israel, which forsook Jesus when He came as her Messiah, must now allow the Church to be the Bride of Jesus Christ.

Naomi wanted to return to her own country and come into closer relationship with her own people. When, at last, she arrived in Bethlehem, the entire city was moved and asked, *"Is this Naomi?"* She replied, *"Don't call me Naomi. Call me Mara, because the Almighty had made my life very bitter. I went away full, but the Lord has brought me back empty. Don't call me Naomi. Call me Mara, because the Almighty has brought misfortune on me."* (Ruth 1:20)

After Ruth had married Boaz and had a son, the women told Naomi that her life would be restored, since God had given her an inheritance. So, Naomi is found in direct lineage to the Messiah, a rightful place in the family of God. Thus, we have a picture of the Jews returning from the nations of the world and being restored in their own land. God, who has dealt bitterly with them, will bring them back into relationship with Himself as He uses the Gentiles to bring this about. Isaiah 54:1-8 describes Israel who, for a time, is barren, but will be restored as a married wife, the Lord Himself being her husband.

By the grace of God, Ruth ultimately became the bride of Boaz — not because she deserved it, but because he loved her enough to pay the price required for her hand in marriage. He welcomed Naomi into the household, but he married her "grafted in" relative. Boaz is a picture of the Kinsman-Redeemer of the Church (the people related to God's covenant people, the Jews). From the union of Ruth and Boaz came a son, Obed, who bore a son, named Jesse. Later, Obed had a grandson we know as David, through whose seed Jesus was born!

The Family of God

According to Galatians 4:1-7 and John 1:12-13, how do we become God's children? What rights that does give us?

_____

_____

_____

_____

What does Romans 8:12-17 say about the relationship God wants us, His children, to have with Him?

_____

_____

_____

If God is our Father and we are His children, then fellow Christians are our brothers and sisters. This is God's family.° After each scripture passage below, write down its specific instructions as to how we are to relate to God's family:

Romans 14:10-21

_____

_____

_____

II Thessalonians 3:6-15

_____

_____

_____

James 2:15-17; I John 3:17

_____

_____

_____

I John 2:9-11

_____

_____

_____

I Timothy 5:1-16

_____

_____

_____

According to I John 4:19-21, what does loving our brother have to do with loving God?

_____

_____

How does I John 3:10 describe the difference between a child of God and a child of the devil?

_____

_____

Proverbs 6:16-19 gives us six things that God hates. What does one of these say about how we treat our brothers?

_____

_____

(For Husband) Testimony of how you became a child of God, part of His family:

_____

_____

_____

_____

(For Wife) Testimony of how you became a child of God, part of His family:

_____

_____

_____

_____

The Salvation of Whole Families

Salvation for a whole household had its origin in the Old Testament on the night of the Passover as the Israelites were leaving Egypt. Just as a lamb was sacrificed for each house, Jesus can be the Lamb for each family member now. First Corinthians 7:14 indicates that children are brought into a relationship with God (made holy) by a believing parent. Job 1:5 is an example of a father interceding on behalf of his children. In Ezekiel 22:30, God said He was looking for a man who would stand in the gap so He would not have to bring destruction upon the people living in the land. Consider other examples in scripture where the whole family, or household, was saved:

- In Hebrews 11:7, we find that Noah prepared an ark, by faith, for the purpose of saving his family, not just the animals. Noah's righteousness was credited to the account of his wife, his three sons and their wives.

- In Genesis 19:29, we find that because God remembered Abraham's intercession, He spared Lot and his family from being destroyed when He rained fire and brimstone on Sodom.

- In Joshua 6:12, we find the harlot, Rahab, asking the spies to spare her whole family when they captured Jericho. Because she followed their instructions and let down a scarlet cord at the proper time, her whole household was delivered from death.

- In II Kings 4:26, we find the Shunamite woman as an example of one who claimed her son's life, even in the presence of death. And he was given life.

- In Acts 16:16-34, we are told of Paul and Silas' being imprisoned in Philippi when an earthquake occurred. As they sang praises and were spared, the jailer asked him what he could do. Paul told him to believe on the Lord Jesus Christ and he and his entire house would be saved. He did and they were.

- In Acts 10:1-2, 22-48 (especially v. 24, 44), Cornelius called together his relatives and close friends to meet Peter, whom an angel had said would come to his house. After Peter arrived and told them about Jesus, the Holy Spirit came upon all who heard the message and they were baptized in the name of Jesus.

From the above examples, what did the following people do to allow God to save the members of their family?

Noah was _____

Abraham _____

Rahab _____

The Shunamite woman _____

The jailor _____

Cornelius _____

Things we can do to help our family members find Jesus as their Lord and Savior:
Live righteous lives (I Timothy 4:12; I Peter 3:1)
Intercede on their behalf (Ezekiel 22:30-31; Job 22:29)
Obey God's instructions (Matthew 28:18-20)
Claim God's Word on their behalf (Acts 2:39; Psalm 102:28; Jeremiah 31:16-17)

Share the Gospel with them (Romans 10:14-15)

Take authority over Satan, who blinds men's eyes (II Corinthians 4:3-4)

Take the position of Priest, which is rightfully ours (Revelation 1:5-6)

    This includes:

        Offering the sacrifice of praise (Hebrews 13:15)

        Claiming the provision of the atonement for their sin by faith (Romans 4:7)

        Remitting sin on their behalf (John 20:23)

It is God's will that our loved ones be saved, for He wishes that no one perish, but that all should come to repentance. (See II Peter 3:9.) The Word of God also declares (in I John 5:14-15) that *"this is the confidence we have in approaching God; that if we ask anything according to his will, he hears us. And if we know that he hears us…whatever we ask…we know that we have what we asked of him."*

SUMMARY

The story of Naomi, Ruth, and Boaz is a beautiful picture of how the Gentiles have become part of God's people by being grafted into His family of the Jews. This was possible because Ruth became the wife of Boaz, her kinsman-redeemer from of Naomi's family.

We inherit certain benefits and relationships through our natural family simply because we were born into it. But when we are born again into God's family, we can have new brothers and sisters, a new "elder" brother, Jesus, and a Heavenly Father who wants only the best for us! We may — or may not — enjoy the relationships in our natural families. But because of our common belief in the Lord Jesus Christ, we can be blessed with many relationships in an extended family, the family of God.

CONSIDER THIS

How did you become part of God's family?

_____

_____

What, if anything, is the difference between how you relate to your earthly family and how you relate to members of the family of God?

_____

_____

How can you help members of your earthly family become part of God's family?

_____

_____

What responsibilities do you have to each other as brothers and sisters in God's family?

_____

_____

MODERN EXAMPLE

Because we were in the pastoral ministry for several years, we sometimes found ourselves living many miles away from our natural families — especially both sets of our girls' grandparents. We visited as often as we could during summer vacations and holidays, but we didn't have that continuing relationship that comes from frequently dropping in for the evening or occasional dinners together. We had to depend mostly on letters or phone calls to keep in touch.

When our oldest daughter was about two years old, we moved from Kentucky to central California, where our second girl was born. Though we were now in the same state, our parents still lived about 200 miles away.

Almost as soon as we arrived, an elderly couple, Roy and Stella, came to visit us. Not only were they members of our church, they also lived in our neighborhood. They lived on a small pension, so they couldn't give a lot to the church. And they didn't have a car, so they needed transportation to Sunday services and occasional church meetings. All of their grandchildren lived far away — some in India, where their daughter and husband were missionaries. So, they had a proposal for us: As their contribution to the church, they would baby-sit free for us for all church activities…and other times, too. Perhaps, they suggested, we could help them some with transportation when possible. It would give them a chance to be the grandparents they wanted to be.

Needless to say, we accepted the offer, and our two daughters had much loving care in the five years we lived there. When we moved away, we had to return to visit "Grandma Stella" and "Pop-pops."

When we moved to Phoenix, we had three girls, the oldest in the fifth grade. With our parents still in southern California, we were, once again, without grandparents nearby. That is, until we met Jack and Mary, members of our church who had three grandsons all living in southern California. So began a relationship with these "in-town" grandparents, as our girls called them. They lived in our neighborhood and often had us over for dinner, swimming, — everything families like to do together. To this day, our adult daughters remember the candy Jack used to carry in his pocket to share with them after church services!

Eventually, we lived closer to the girls' "real" grandparents and were able to see them quite often. But they, nor we, have ever forgotten the way God provided "in-town" grandparents in other places, and how He has blessed our family as part of God's extended family!

Lesson 9

Elkanah and Hannah

Agreeing in Prayer

The eyes of the Lord are on the righteous and his ears are attentive to their cry.
Psalm 34:15

SETTING THE STAGE

Unlike other Biblical couples to whom God sent a child to be used in a special ministry by Him, Elkanah and Hannah did not know that they would become parents of a son who would not only become a judge, prophet, and priest, but would anoint the first king of Israel. Rather, Samuel appears to have been born as a result of their petition to God.

In the Modern Example at the close of this lesson, you may learn for the first time of how much George Muller's wife Mary was involved with him. Just as most people know only of George's prayer life, so most think of Hannah as being the only one who petitioned God for a child. Though scripture doesn't specifically tell us of Elkanah praying, we must assume that he agreed with her in prayer. For in I Samuel 1:8, we find that they had a very close relationship as husband and wife. Then, in I Samuel 1:19, we find that they worshipped God together after Eli had assured Hannah that God had heard her as she poured out her soul to him for a child.

God still answers prayer. In His Word He tells what agreement in prayer does, as well as some of the things that will hinder our prayers from being answered. These are the instructions that we will consider in this session so that we, too, may be successful in receiving answers to prayer.

INTRODUCING ELKANAH AND HANNAH

(Based on I Samuel 1:1-2:11, 18-21)

The story of Elkanah and Hannah introduces the time of the Judges of Israel. God wanted Israel to look upon Him as their king (I Samuel 8:7). The Judges exercised God's authority both in military and civil matters. God used Elkanah and Hannah, ordinary people, to bear Samuel. Samuel became God's instrument for establishing the kingdom of Israel in a time of great national crisis, and laying the foundation of the prophetic office.

Unlike other couples to whom God sent special children to be used in particular ministries by Him, Elkanah and Hannah did not know they would be given Samuel. Their son appears to have been born as a result of Hannah's petition to God.

Elkanah already had children by his other wife, Peninnah; but he loved Hannah very much. Even so, it must have been very difficult for Hannah to see Peninnah blessed with the family she would like to have given Elkanah, especially when Peninnah gloated over the situation!

Elkanah was a God-fearing husband and priest of his household. He took his family to Shiloh regularly to worship and sacrifice to the Lord. He was very supportive of Hannah as she prayed for a child. When God answered their prayer and Samuel was born and weaned, they fulfilled Hannah's vow and gave him to Eli to raise in the fear of the Lord and for His use. They were blessed with three more sons and two daughters after that.

LESSONS FROM ELKANAH AND HANNAH

Hindrances to Answered Prayer

Before looking at how couples can agree in prayer, let us, first, look at some of the reasons why we may not get answers to our prayers.

I Peter 3:7
A husband's prayers may be hindered if

_____

_____

Psalm 66:18
God doesn't listen to our prayers if

_____

_____

Malachi 2:13-15
God may ignore our offerings or not accept them with pleasure if

_____

_____

Proverbs 28:9
If we do not hear what God is saying through His Word, our prayers

_____

_____

Prayers of Agreement

Would God have sent Samuel to Elkanah and Hannah if they had not prayed for a son? Do we miss receiving the desires of our hearts because we do not "agree" with Him in prayer?

Immature faith regards prayer as a weapon we must use to force God to make good His promises. But true prayer is not a human effort at persuading God. Rather, it is founded upon finding agreement with God's will. In I John 5:14-15, we find that we must ask according to His will, then stand in faith, confident that God hears us and will give us what we ask.

Matthew 18:19-20 says: *"Again, I tell you that if two of you on earth **agree** about anything you ask for, it will be done for you by my Father in heaven. For where two or three come together in my name, there am I with them."* What better agreement can there be than a Christian couple praying for the needs of their family, friends, church, and world…according to God's will!

Let us look at some scriptures and see what the result was when people prayed together in agreement. After reading the verses listed on the left, draw a line to the appropriate result listed on the right.

Acts 1:24	Brings peace when things are falling apart
Acts 1:14; 2:1-2	Opens doors for personal witness
Acts 4:31	Gives ability to make right decisions
Acts 12:5-11	Brings freedom
Acts 16:25-26	Allows the Holy Spirit to come in power
Romans 15:30-31	Gives the ability to speak boldly for God
II Corinthians 1:9-11	Protects from peril
Colossians 4:2-3	Provides for fruitful ministry

Philippians 4:6 tells us not to be anxious for anything, but, in everything, to present our requests to God. He delights to hear from us. He especially enjoys our prayers of thanksgiving not only for all He has done for us, but for who He is! Add to the following list of subjects that couples, especially, can pray for. Then, write in the name of a specific individual that goes with that subject, as well as an appropriate scripture verse to claim for the situation.

Subject	Specific Person	Scripture Verse
Children	_____	_____
Finances	_____	_____
Healing	_____	_____
Guidance	_____	_____
Deliverance	_____	_____
Protection	_____	_____

The Lord of Hosts

In the King James Version of the Bible, we find, in I Samuel 1:3, that Elkanah went up yearly to worship and to sacrifice *unto the Lord of hosts* in Shiloh and, in I Samuel 1:11, that Hannah vowed a vow *unto the Lord of Hosts*. This is the first time God is referred to in this way, though there are over 200 such references in the Old Testament after that. The Hebrew word for "hosts" is "tsbaah" which means "an army poised and ready for battle." Thus, in the first of the books of the kings, we find God now being lifted up as the mighty and powerful one, in charge of an unseen army assembled and ready for battle on behalf of His kingdom.

Because we live after Jesus' death on the cross, we can know the power of the Almighty God through Jesus and the power of the Holy Spirit. From history, we can learn of the supernatural acts of a mighty Lord of Hosts. And scriptures such as Psalm 68:17 tell us that the chariots of God are 20,000, even thousands of angels! That's quite an army at His command — and ours!

According to Ephesians 6:10-18 (and other scriptures), we can learn about the spiritual battle which we are in, and of the spiritual weapons at our disposal. But it's up to us to do battle under the conditions provided by God, commander-in-chief over Satan and his host. God is, indeed, the Lord of Hosts!

How, When, and Where to Pray

The positions of prayer as described in the Bible are as follows:

Prostrate with face to the ground	56 times
Facing toward Jerusalem	20 times
Kneeling	9 times
Hands up	10 times
Standing	5 times
Head bowed	8 times
Eyes closed	0 times!

Jesus' most common way to pray was lifting up His eyes toward heaven.

Couples today use some of the following times and places to get together for agreeing in prayer. Try each to see which works best for you.

- Arise early in the morning before the rest of the family is up, and spend ten to fifteen minutes praying about the events and needs of that day.

- Kneel together by the bed before retiring, bringing to the Lord all the cares of the day, as well as asking for guidance in the day to come.

- Set aside a certain time during the week to pray for special needs common to both.

- Take a prayer walk, and pray while getting some physical exercise.

- Take advantage of your times in the car together to lift up special needs.

- Saying grace at mealtimes helps the whole family come together in agreeing prayer.

- Couples really committed to spiritual warfare often find the middle of the night the best time to pray together — there's no telephone ringing or household chores clamoring for attention. Psalm 134:1 confirms this: *"Praise the Lord, all you servants of the Lord, who minister by night in the house of the Lord."*

What works for you as a couple?

_____

_____

_____

SUMMARY

Elkanah and Hannah received an answer to prayer. We can, too, as we:
- deal with any hindrances we might have
- persist in our petitions
- ask in the name and authority of Jesus
- take our place in spiritual warfare and intercession
- use the spiritual weapons at our disposal
- recognize God as the "commander-in-chief" or the "Lord of Hosts"

We just need to believe upon the One in whom *nothing* is impossible!

CONSIDER THIS

Do you pray together as a couple? If not, how can you make this a priority?

_____

_____

What may be some of the hindrances to your prayers being answered?

_____

_____

Have you seen any special answers to prayer because you have agreed together according to God's will?

_____

_____

MODERN EXAMPLE

Many have heard of George Muller, a man who, through prayer and faith in God, educated, housed, and trained over 10,000 children in his lifetime. What many may not have heard is that his wife, Mary, was very much his partner in prayer.

George was born in Germany in 1805, landed in jail at the age of sixteen, and became a playboy when he went away to school. His life was changed, however, when he gave his heart to the Lord Jesus Christ after being invited to a Bible study during his second year at the university. He later became a minister in the Plymouth Brethren Church in England, and there married Mary, when he was twenty-five and she was thirty-two. Within three weeks of their wedding, and with encouragement from Mary, George announced to his congregation that he would no longer accept a set salary. Thus began a lifetime of praying that God would supply their needs — not only for their own family, but also for the many orphans for whom they eventually became responsible.

During this time the few orphanages in England accepted only children from wealthy families. Poor children who were left on the streets began appearing at George and Mary's door for food. Before long, George and Mary opened an orphanage in Bristol for poor children. Accustomed to living by faith themselves, they began "praying in" every need. Many times, with no food in the house, George would go into the dining room to see a table fully set, and children standing behind their chairs. He would bow his head and ask God to supply the food needed for that very meal. And God did! Time and time again, food came in various, miraculous ways! Years earlier, George had decided that he would tell only God about his needs — and people about how God had provided!

Mary served in a variety of roles — business manager, auditor, overseer of the kitchens and dormitories — all the while raising their one daughter. George began his day at 5 a.m., alone in prayer, then joined with Mary to pray for the needs of the day. He concluded the time of prayer and Bible study at breakfast with his family. Then, at the last hour of the workday, while at one of the orphanages, George and Mary joined together in prayers of supplication, intercession, and thanksgiving on behalf of the children.

In the fortieth year of their marriage, Mary died. George preached at her funeral, which 1,200 orphans and hundreds of believers attended. Though he would remarry and be invited to speak all over the world, he never forgot Mary, his partner in prayer on behalf of thousands of children for whom they, and God, cared in the orphanages they had established.

One need not look far in scripture to find that providing for and ministering to the poor and needy (especially children), and bringing people into salvation is praying according to God's will.

David and Michal

Meeting Expectations

My soul, wait thou only upon God; for my expectation is from him.

Psalm 62:5 KJV

SETTING THE STAGE

Many times, trouble in the marriage relationship comes from the disappointment one spouse has in another, because the spouse doesn't live up to the other's expectations of what a husband/wife should be. David and Michal were such a couple.

Michal, as a daughter of King Saul, never seemed to fully appreciate what God was doing in David's life. She even mocked him as he joyfully brought the ark of the covenant back into Jerusalem from the land of the enemy. And David, no doubt, thought Michal would understand that if he were to someday be king, he would, indeed, be a God-fearing man.

What do we do when we fail to meet one another's expectations? Or, when our spouse doesn't meet our needs? In this session, we'll look at the importance of trusting God more than man and of not making idols of one another. We shall discover that our expectation is to be in God, not man.

INTRODUCING DAVID AND MICHAEL
(Based on I Samuel 18:17-29; II Samuel 6:12-23)

David was the youngest son of Jesse and was only a young shepherd when Samuel anointed him to be the successor to King Saul. It was several years before David actually became king. During this time, many things happened that caused both love and hate between the two.

When David slew the giant Goliath, Israel's dreaded enemy, he became an instant hero. But Saul became jealous of David. He offered to give David his oldest daughter, Merab, in marriage if David would become a soldier in his army. But when the time came for the wedding, Saul suddenly gave Merab to another man. He then offered David his younger daughter, Michal, for the dowry of one hundred Philistine foreskins — secretly hoping, because he still envied David, that David would be killed. David, much to Saul's surprise, was delighted to accept the offer to marry Michal. He brought Saul the one hundred Philistine foreskins.

After David and Michal were married, David often left her alone while he went into battle or was on the run from her father, King Saul. During one of these absences, Saul gave Michal to another man. David demanded that she be returned to him. Second Samuel 3:13-16 tells us that she came back, though we do not learn what her feelings were. Perhaps, in order to have the position that would be hers in court, she was willing to leave a man who obviously loved her. Perhaps she resented David for all that had happened.

The difficulties in David and Michal's relationship came to a head when David led a joyous procession bringing the ark of the covenant back into Jerusalem. The ark had been in enemy hands for many years and the Jews were very glad to have it in their possession once again. In demonstrative exuberance, David danced his way into the city, singing and praising God for what was happening. But as Michal watched from the window in the palace, she saw David, her husband and the king, leaping and dancing. The Bible says she "despised him in her heart." Although she had once declared her love for him, and even risked her life for his safety, she now hated him!

When David came home, she mocked him. The result was that their relationship came to an end. We read no more of them as a couple. God closed Michal's womb; she would never bear David an heir to the throne. She lived out her lonely life caring for her dead sister's five sons, while David, King of Israel, took other wives and concubines.

LESSONS FROM DAVID AND MICHAL

Basic Needs in the Marriage Relationship

Everyone has basic needs which marriage is intended to fulfill. These include physical, social, emotional, and spiritual needs.

Marriage partners need affection shown in ways other than a monogamous sexual relationship. This includes being attentive to one another's needs and accepting one another the way they are. Spouses should expect to do some things in common, especially when children come into the family. Unfulfilled basic needs are often the cause for unfaithfulness.

Unfulfilled Expectations

David and Michal's relationship had a rather fairy tale beginning. She was a beautiful young princess, and he was a handsome and daring hero soon to become king! We can imagine some of their expectations of each other:

"David's such a hero. I'll always be proud of him! Just imagine, I'll be queen someday."

"Michal loves me. Since I'm going to be king, surely Saul's daughter is the right one for me."

As in the initial relationship of most couples, David and Michal were full of expectations. Your dictionary defines expectations as things looked forward to. The Hebrew word for "expectation" as found in Psalm 62:5 means a "cord," an attachment or "thing longed for." Our expectations are our hopes and dreams, images we set up for ourselves of the way things will be. The problem is, unless our expectation is in the Lord, our sinful self, wanting to be "as god," begins to create rigid and unrealistic images. We then expect things to turn out as *we* imagine.

The first time we hear of Michal, we learn that she "loved" David. Since, at this point, she really didn't know David, we can assume her love was based upon an image she had of him — the eligible young hero anointed to be the next king. If she wanted to be the next queen, it would be even more accurate to say that she was really in love with a dream. Even then, she was forming a rigid expectation of David, attaching to him the things she longed for, thus using him to meet her needs.

On the other hand, we are never told of David's love for Michal. Perhaps, since Scripture never tells us that David loved anyone, he had never learned to express love — and this may not have met Michal's expectations. We can also assume that David thought Michal would rejoice when the ark was being brought back to Jerusalem, even that she might praise him for accomplishing such a task.

Because man is a sinner — and can never be perfect — people will always disappoint us, just as we will disappoint those who look to us with expectations. It is only through Jesus that we receive forgiveness and become new creatures — and that's a process we're in all our lives! God is the *only* One in whom we can put our trust. He is the *only* One who can fulfill our expectations. Even Jesus, as revealed in John 2:23-25, didn't trust man because he knew what was in man!

Check the following expectations you had before marriage. Should you have had them?

Marriages are made in heaven. There is only one right man for one right woman

Marriage will help me find my role, who I am to be in life

Marriage will make be happier than if I remain single

Being married will help fulfill my own personal needs

I can change the things in my spouse that I really don't like

Together, we can surmount any trial that comes our way

He/she will become a Christian after we get married

His/her family will accept me, even if they don't now

We have gone together so long, I feel I really know him/her

Having children together will give us a close relationship

Other_____

Trusting in God

Evidently, Michal didn't trust God. It is interesting to note that nearly every scripture mentioning her by name, refers to her as "daughter of Saul." She never completely forsook the former kingdom to which she belonged, a kingdom which God had rejected because of Saul's disobedience. Michal is a type of person who has never been delivered from the kingdom of darkness and transferred into the kingdom of God's dear Son, as described in Colossians 1:13. For us, the old kingdom is our old nature, our uncrucified flesh where Satan rules. As we accept Jesus and all He has done for us through His death and resurrection, we come into a new kingdom. As He comes to live in us as Lord and Savior, we then have power over our old nature to reckon it dead and made alive in the Spirit of God. We are thus able to live according to the ways of His kingdom and light.

It's too bad that Michal didn't know Ephesians 5:22 which, tells wives to submit to their own husbands *as unto the Lord*. She seems to have outwardly submitted to David, but not enough to submit also to God.

David, on the other hand, learned to put his trust in God. Weak in himself, he knew of God's mercy and forgiveness. In fact, though David was far from being perfect, the Word tells us that he was a man after God's own heart! (I Samuel 13:14)

Meditate upon some of the words that David wrote which can help us, too, to put our expectations in God — not our spouse.

"Some trust in chariots and some in horses, but we trust in the name of the Lord our God." (Psalm 20:7)

"In you our fathers put their trust; they trusted and you delivered them. They cried to you and were saved; in you they trusted and were not disappointed." (Psalm 22:4-5)

"To you, O Lord, I lift up my soul; in you I trust, O my God." (Psalm 25:1-2a)

"The Lord is my strength and my shield; my heart trusts in him, and I am helped." (Psalm 28:7a)

"Blessed is the man who makes the Lord his trust" (Psalm 40:4a)

"Give us aid against the enemy, for the help of man is worthless. With God we will gain the victory, and he will trample down our enemies." (Psalm 60:11-12)

Though not attributed to David, Psalm 118 is full of declaration of how God can be trusted. Verse 8 summarizes succinctly where man is to put his expectation: *"It is better to trust in the Lord that to put confidence in man."* (KJV)

Idolatry

One of the ways we put our expectations in men, instead of God, is by making people our idols. We expect a person, instead of God, to supply all of our needs. We fashion that person for our use, rather than letting God fashion that person for His use.

According to J. R. Miller, an idol is "anything which we keep in our hearts in the place God ought to have…whether it be an image of wood or stone or gold, or whether it be money, or desire for fame, or love of pleasure or some secret sin which we will not give up. If God does not really occupy the highest place in our hearts, controlling all, something else does, and that something else is an idol."

Scripture instructs us how to deal with idolatry. Look up the following verses, then summarize what God says about idols and how to deal with idolatry:

I Corinthians 10:14 _____

I John 5:21 _____

Colossians 3:5-6 _____

I Corinthians 5:11 _____

I Corinthians 10:19, 21 _____

Acts 14:11, 15 _____

God gives His final judgment on idolaters in Revelation 21:7-8. It is

_____

Serving One Another in the Grace of God

God designed most of us to need another person in order to feel complete. Yet the marriage relationship should not require either spouse to suppress his individuality. Marriage functions best when both people have an attitude of serving the other and allowing the grace of God to cover everything they say and do. This is the opposite of controlling each other and expecting the other person to meet all our needs. Marriage is not a 50-50 arrangement with each spouse keeping track to be sure the other person contributes exactly half — whether it's finances, emotional support, housework, yard work, child care, etc. A relationship based on God's grace gives expects nothing in return. Thus, expectations never fail to be met!

In a healthy marriage, each spouse depends on the other, yet each person maintains independence.

Read I Peter 3:8-12 and summarize what it says about relating to one another with sacrificial love and grace.

_____

_____

_____

The practical way to understanding each other's needs and values (and lessen the disappointment of unfulfilled expectations) is to discuss what is expected in the relationship. Sometimes the other person just needs to know what is expected of him/her and will respond in a positive way. But doing this in the heat of anger only intensifies the problem.

Each person is responsible for his/her own actions. As individuals we need to deal with our own anger, fears, and frustrations instead of blaming the other person.

Write down what you would like to tell your spouse concerning what you would expect him/her to do.

_____

_____

_____

Now write down some of your own anger, fears, and frustrations that you need to deal with, so that you don't blame your spouse for what is actually your own problem. (Example: You expect him/her to keep in touch with your extended family because you don't want to do it yourself because of some hurt or anger toward them.)

_____

_____

_____

SUMMARY

David and Michal were a couple whose expectations of one another were unfulfilled, and whose relationship as husband and wife had a sad ending. We, too, will have sad experiences in relationships where we have unrealistic expectations that are not met — whether it's with a spouse, friends, family, or even in a church situation. As long as we don't see people as sinners and thus, not perfect, we'll put them on pedestals and look to them to fulfill our needs. Whether or not we call it idolatry, we have put them above God, who is the only One we can truly trust, the only One who will never let us down.

We need to learn how to serve others and relate to them in the grace of God, even perhaps, dealing with some of our own anger, fears, frustrations, etc., instead of projecting on them our problems. The sooner we learn to trust in God, not man, the happier we will be in our marriage relationship.

CONSIDER THIS

What expectations did you have of each other before you were married? Did you marry an image, thinking that he/she would fulfill all your needs?

_____

_____

How do each of you react when you fail to meet one another's expectations?

_____

_____

How can you learn to put your expectations in God and only in Him?

_____

_____

How do you make idols out of your spouse, your friends, and even your church/pastor?

_____

_____

MODERN EXAMPLE

Tim Kimmel, author of *Powerful Personalities*, describes how he and his wife, Darcy, worked out some of their expectations concerning the roles of husband and wife. They actually started this process before they were married as they spent time discussing what each liked and didn't like to do. For instance, he discovered that she loved to cook; he didn't. She found that he enjoyed mowing the lawn; she would be most happy if she never did.

After they were married, they found that they still had some unrealistic expectations of one another. He had preferences for the clothes she wore when they were going out; and it wasn't such a happy scene when, after she was ready, he would say, "I think you should have worn …." They also discovered that neither one like to vacuum, so the house went for weeks until they would have a "discussion" on whose turn it was to clean it.

By working through their expectations during their twenty-five years of their marriage, they have concluded that three relational dynamics must be maintained simultaneously in marriage:

1. Dependence…because God designed us to need each other
2. Independence…because the uniqueness of each individual must be kept intact
3. Interdependence…which recognizes both the personal, dependent needs of the individual and the independent needs that put them both together

This only works because true love concentrates on what one can *give* to the relationship, regardless of what he or she gets in return. Tim and Darcy call it operating by grace. It takes a lifetime to fully learn to operate in grace and live with no unrealistic expectations of one another; but it is worth doing, and it makes for a happier marriage.

1. Dependence…because God designed us to need each other
2. Independence...because the uniqueness of each individual must be kept intact
3. Interdependence…which recognizes both the personal, dependent needs of the individual and the independent needs that put them both together

This only works because true love concentrates on what one can *give* to the relationship, regardless of what he or she gets in return. Tim and Darcy call it operating by grace. It takes a lifetime to fully learn to operate in grace and live with no unrealistic expectations of one another; but it is worth doing, and it makes for a happier marriage.

Ahab and Jezebel

Establishing God-Ordained Marital Roles

> *Youths oppress my people, women rule over them. O my people, your guides lead you astray; they turn you from the path.*
>
> Isaiah 3:12

SETTING THE STAGE

It's interesting to note the way God let judgment fall upon His people as the time of the Babylonian captivity drew near. Judah had rebelled against God by worshipping idols. God sent Isaiah to call people to repentance and warn them of impending judgment. He allowed another phenomenon to take place, something which probably went unnoticed by the majority of the people. Women and children began to rule over the people, oppressing them and causing them to err. Leadership roles became confused and Satan had his way.

We're now living in the last days. The devil knows his time is short. He's doing everything he can to encourage women to come out from under authority, and to get men to abdicate their responsibility. He's doing this through all kinds of "rights" movements, unisex clothing, and "gender-blending," so that there seems to be little difference between men and women. It's affecting the family, our nation, and even the church.

In Revelation 2:18-29, we have Jesus' words of warning to the church in Thyatira, one of the seven churches. He sees this church as one known for its faith and good works, and He recognizes their patience, love and service. But He also reminds them that He has a few things against them because they had allowed the false prophetess, Jezebel, to deceive them and lead them astray. She, like the Jezebel of the Old Testament, had seduced them into committing fornication and eating food which had been offered to idols. Jezebel manipulated people and situations and even as she controlled Ahab behind the scenes. Their marital roles were confused, as is the case in many couples' relationships today.

INTRODUCING AHAB AND JEZEBEL

(Based on I Kings 16:31-32; 21:1-25; 22:29-37; II Kings 9:30-37)

Ahab was one of the kings of the northern kingdom of Israel. First Kings 16:30 states that *"Ahab son of Omri did more evil in the eyes of the Lord than any of those before him."* He wasn't a God-fearing man, even before he married Jezebel.

Jezebel was the daughter of Ethbaal, the king of the Zidonians. Because of her allegiance to Baal, she tried to build altars to worship him in Israel. A very domineering woman, she tried to rule Ahab as well. In fact, when anyone crossed her will, she manipulated him or her into doing what she wanted.

We see an example of her manipulation in the story of Naboth's vineyard. Ahab wanted to buy this vineyard to expand his land holdings. When Naboth wouldn't sell it, Jezebel came up with a secret scheme. Without telling Ahab, she sent letters, in his name, instructing the elders and nobles in the city to proclaim a fast and to seat Naboth where all could see him. She then arranged for some men to tell everyone that Naboth had blasphemed God and the king. As a result of the lie, the people stoned Naboth to death and Ahab took possession of the vineyard, all according to Jezebel's plan.

Jezebel and Ahab complemented one another, but not according to God's divine order and plan. First Kings 21:25 sums up their relationship with each other and with God: *"There was never a man like Ahab, who sold himself to do evil in the eyes of the Lord, urged on by Jezebel his wife."*

Ahab, whose own father was a poor role model, was used to being indulged. He didn't take advice well, even from the prophet Elijah, whom God sent to counsel him. When he didn't get the vineyard he wanted, he became angry and pouted. Like other men who abdicate their God-given position of authority, Ahab made it easy for his wife to manipulate and control him.

The lives of Ahab and Jezebel ended unhappily. Ahab disguised himself as he and Jehoshaphat, the king of Judah, rode into battle. A random arrow hit the king between the sections of his armor and he died. Jezebel was killed, as prophesied by Elijah. She was thrown out of a window and her body was trampled by horses. When they later went to bury her, there was nothing left of her but her skull, her feet and her hands.

LESSONS FROM AHAB AND JEZEBEL

God's Divine Order for Husbands and Wives

What does it mean to be a man? For what purpose did God create a woman? How does blending sexual roles affect the marriage relationship?

In a sense, God doesn't regard our sexuality as important. Galatians 3:28 tells us

_____

_____

Our sexuality is only for the earthly realm. When we are born-again, we are not reborn male and female; our spirits, which are not sexual, are made alive with His Spirit. The Sadducees questioned Jesus as to which man would be a certain woman's husband in heaven. Mark 12:25 says He told them

_____

_____

_____

72

When God created the earth, He made us male and female. He fashioned Adam and Eve in His image, to have dominion over the fish of the sea, the fowl of the air, and the animals on the earth. God saw man and woman as one (Genesis 1:26-28) and it appears He gave them equal treatment. They were equal partners with shared, equal responsibility.

However, God did spell out the difference between male and female, whom He had made to complement one another. When, God created Adam a helpmeet, He put Adam to sleep, took a rib from his side, and made a companion for him. God fashioned this woman specifically for the man and brought her to him. In fact, I Corinthians 11:9 says

_____

_____

She was not only bone of his bone and flesh of his flesh, she was made uniquely for him! It wasn't long before Eve, tempted by Satan, disobeyed God; and Adam joined in her rebellion.

Because of this "fall" into sin, man lost his intimate relationship with God. As a result of Adam and Eve's disobedience, God punished each of them and banished them from the Garden of Eden. Adam would be required to work by the sweat of his brow and, according to Genesis 3:16, God told Eve

_____

_____

The purpose of the husband's rulership was not to diminish the woman's personhood or giftedness, but rather to assign to the husband responsibility for leadership in the marriage relationship.

I Corinthians 11:3 tells us

_____

_____

God has established a chain of authority. When the woman submits properly to her husband, she is "covered" and, therefore, protected from the attacks of Satan, just as the man is protected when he submits properly to his head, Jesus Christ.

In addition to understanding covering, we must also understand what it means to truly submit to authority. Submission is not an outward act whereby one submits for appearance's sake but is really determined to do what he wants! Nor is proper submission allowing oneself to be treated like a doormat, taking no personal initiative. To properly submit, the one under authority should tell the one in authority their thoughts or feelings, so that the one in authority has all the facts and, thus, can make the best decision. Failing to communicate at all allows deception and manipulation. So, in marriage, the wife submits to her husband's authority after she has shared her thoughts, views, etc. with him — as long as he doesn't ask her to do anything contrary to God's Word. He, then, is responsible to his authority, Christ Jesus, for the decisions he makes.

Because submission is frequently misinterpreted, women often think they must submit to an abusive spouse. But a person's first submission is to God and His Word. An example of this is found in Acts 5:27-32 when Peter and some other apostles were told not to teach and preach about Jesus. See Acts 5:29 for Peter's response.

_____

_____

No one under human authority is required to submit to anything contrary to God and His Word. Our first allegiance belongs to Him!

Write the instructions found in I Peter 3:7 for the husband.

_____

_____

Write the instructions found in I Peter 3:1-6 for the wife.

_____

_____

_____

Because of economic necessity, and to fulfill educational pursuits, many women today work outside the home. Some have found the way to blend jobs, household responsibilities, and parenting. Others have, or can, not. In such cases, one question to be settled is whether the wife can blend these areas and still be submissive to her husband. Another is whether the husband can share the housework and child care and still assume the spiritual leadership of the home.

The following questions are for couples with both the husband and wife working outside the home.

Husband: Write down what you see as your present role in the relationship you have with your wife and children. Do you see yourself as the spiritual head of your family, even though your wife may work outside the home?

_____

_____

_____

_____

Wife: Write down what you see as your present role in the relationship you have with your husband and children. Do you see yourself in submission to your husband, even though you may work outside the home?

_____

_____

_____

_____

Servant Leadership

Matthew 20:25-28 gives the definition of the role of a leader (even a spiritual leader in the home): *"You know that the rulers of the Gentiles lord it over them, and their high officials exercise authority over them. Not so with you. Instead, whoever wants to become great among you must be your servant, and whoever wants to be first must be your slave...just as the Son of Man did not come to be served, but to serve, and to give his life as a ransom for many."* To rule over others is to be responsible for their welfare, not to control or manipulate them. It is caring *for* those under your authority, not using them for your own pleasure or benefit. This is exemplified in scriptures that inform church elders how they are to assume their leadership role.

First, Hebrews 13:7 tells them how they are to set an example.

_____

_____

Next, Hebrews 13:17 tells us to obey our leaders and submit to their authority. It then goes on to say what the responsibility of the leader is.

_____

_____

Summarize the qualifications of a spiritual leader, as found in I Timothy 3:2-7.

_____

_____

_____

_____

_____

_____

Co-Dependent Relationships

With the rise in the number of dysfunctional families comes an increase in the number of people who marry because of unfulfilled needs. Perhaps a wife unconsciously expects her husband to take the place of a father she never had; or the husband hasn't dealt with repressed anger from events in his childhood, and thus has not become mature emotionally. So, one or the other — or both — take on roles such as the rescuer, the martyr, an enabler, etc. This is often seen in marriages where one is an alcoholic. The spouse becomes an enabler — and thus out of divine order — because he/she is trying to protect their image as a couple/family. This does not allow consequences to occur, so that the problem can be dealt with. Co-dependent relationships also confuse the marital roles.

SUMMARY

As couples in the Word, we have great challenges, as well as great responsibility, to be the examples God intended in our roles as husbands and wives. We also are accountable to God for teaching our children the ways of the Lord in a world that is trying to form them into its image. Satan was nearly able to destroy God's people through the weakness of Ahab and the manipulation of Jezebel, who were out of God's divine order. It behooves us, as Christians, to know what God says in scripture concerning sexual roles, what it means to be a "servant" leader, and how to deal with emotions and our pasts. Only then can we truly be the persons He designed us to be, even in our marriage.

CONSIDER THIS

Are you, as husband and wife, in divine order? If not, what can you do to be so?

_____

_____

Have you dealt with past actions and reactions, so that you can live the marital roles God has ordained for you?

_____

_____

How are you, as parents, passing on to your children principles from God's Word concerning sexual and marital relationships?

_____

_____

How do you deal with the confusion of roles which our society bombards us with?

_____

_____

MODERN EXAMPLE

One of the best selling Christian books was one written in 1874 by a forty-three-year-old housewife, Hannah Whitall Smith. Ironically, *The Christian's Secret of a Happy Life* has made a big impact upon the lives of thousands of people, even though the author didn't have the secret for a happy marriage.

When they married in 1851 in Philadelphia, Hannah Whitall and Robert Smith, both Quakers, seemed to be the perfect match. She was the daughter of a prosperous glass manufacturer. He came from a highly-educated family and was just beginning a career in publishing.

The first six years of married life seemed normal. Children were born into their family. Robert was working hard to build up his business. But Hannah was spiritually restless and eventually began looking outside her Quaker beliefs. She associated with Plymouth Brethren assemblies, was baptized in a Baptist Church, and studied the Bible with the Methodists. Eventually Robert also left the Quakers and became a Presbyterian. When his publishing business went bankrupt, he suffered an extreme sense of failure and became manic-depressive. While Robert was in and out of sanatoriums, Hannah assumed his responsibilities. She also began to immerse herself in writing. Her first book chronicled the life of their oldest son, who had died while a sophomore at Princeton. Between nervous breakdowns, Robert did some preaching in England, where he made the headlines because of an alleged affair with a young woman who had come to him for counsel. As a result, he was no longer allowed to preach. On his way back to Hannah in America, he suffered a breakdown in Paris. Thus began a spiritual slide from which he never was able to recover.

Though they remained married, their lives drifted apart. Robert spent much of the time away from home. The more he abandoned his spiritual leadership in the home, the more Hannah withdrew emotionally and took charge of the family — which resulted in him feeling less and less the man, husband, and father he wanted to be. It was a vicious cycle, which had consequences in the lives of their children. Their oldest daughter renounced her belief in God at age nineteen. Eventually she left her husband and two children for another man and had several affairs after that. A son claimed that he had lost his faith in God at age eleven. And, their youngest daughter was married (for eight years) to the British philosopher and noted atheist, Bertrand Russell.

Did Robert's abandonment of spiritual leadership, which resulted from his overwhelming sense of failure, cause Hannah to assume the role of head of the family? Or, did her assertive personality and unsubmissiveness to his faults and lacks cause him to withdraw from the role he could have taken? We don't know — nor do their biographers agree. What we do know is that their marriage was unhappy to the end.

Lesson 12

Naaman and His Wife

Keeping the Marriage Vows

> *This God is our God forever and ever; he will be our guide even unto death.*
>
> Psalm 48:14

SETTING THE STAGE

On their wedding day, most couples look forward to spending a lifetime together in relatively good health. No one wants, or expects, to become the other's caretaker in a lingering illness. Nor, does either eagerly anticipate caring for the other in a short-term major illness or disability such as results from an accident. Perhaps they haven't even discovered how a simple cold affects relationships!

What do we do when our spouse becomes ill, sustains injuries in accident, or faces death due to a devastating disease? How do we relate to one another, then? Are we truly committed to each other in sickness and in health…until death do us part? Or, will we be like Job's wife who encouraged her husband to curse God and die? Naaman's wife found a way to help her husband regain physical health. In the process, he became spiritually alive.

INTRODUCING NAAMAN AND HIS WIFE

(Based on II Kings 5:1-18)

In the Old Testament book of II Kings, we find the story of a couple whose marriage was tested because of an illness. Naaman was captain of the host of the king of Syria. As such, he had great influence over the king. He was a mighty man of valor, but he had been stricken with the dreaded disease of leprosy. With rotting flesh and running sores, he would become an outcast. He and his wife were greatly concerned for his health, his job and his future.

By God's divine appointment, a little Jewish maid was brought into their household to serve Naaman's wife. Young though she was, she shared her faith in God and told her mistress of a prophet in Samaria who performed miracles of healing. Intrigued, Naaman's wife listened and shared the news with Naaman. He then went to the king of Syria and told him what the servant girl had said. King Aram not only gave him a letter to give to the king of Israel, but also gave Naaman gifts to take with him, too. When Naaman arrived, the king of Israel was frustrated because he didn't know how to help him. Elisha heard of the situation and asked the king to send Naaman to him. When Naaman arrived at Elisha's house, Elisha's servant came to the door and gave him a message from Elisha — go to the Jordan River and dip yourself in it seven times! Enraged and humiliated, Naaman, refused to go do what seemed like a foolish thing. Finally, one of his servants convinced him to go. Naaman's flesh was restored and became clean like that of a young boy! He was elated. He told Elisha that he would never again worship any god other than the Lord of Elisha!

LESSONS FROM NAAMAN AND HIS WIFE

Healing According to God's Word

Naaman's wife, in the process of helping her husband find healing for his body, helped him find God, the source of all healing, both physical and spiritual! Our goal, when we're faced with physical infirmities, should be to receive the healing that God has provided — through whatever means He chooses — for both our body and our spirit. Even though dipping himself in a dirty river seemed a foolish thing to do, Naaman's body was healed as he obeyed God's word given to him through Elisha.

Scripture has some specific instructions so we can be healed, both physically and spiritually:

Through Prayer and Intercession

According to James 5:14-16, the first thing Believers should do is

_____

_____

If God does not heal instantly, He will give guidance on how to obtain healing. Sometimes He uses doctors; with Naaman, He used a muddy river!

Through Laying on of Hands

Mark 16:18b tells us that

_____

This is especially fitting for the husband/father to do as priest of his household.

Through Spiritual Warfare

Perhaps the illness is Satan's way of harassment. If so, according to Ephesians 6:10-18 and James 4:7, spiritual warfare is in order — putting on the whole armor of God and submitting to Him and resisting the devil. In any case, remind Satan of I John 3:8: that Jesus came to _____

_____

Through Faith in God's Word

Build your faith by meditating upon the Word of God. According to Romans 10:17, it is the Word that gives us faith to claim the promises we have in God. First Peter 2:24 is such a promise: _____

_____

Proverbs 4:20-22 emphasizes the need to trust in what God says, not in what others say. These verses remind us to

_____

_____

_____

By Obeying God's Word

Many illnesses are caused by emotional stresses which are the result of anger, resentment, unforgiveness, or bitterness. This is of special concern to couples, because offenses especially come with those we live closest to. We must learn to give, and receive forgiveness — with others as well as with God. The great love chapter, I Corinthians 13, tells us in verses 4-7 that part of love is to

_____

_____

_____

Through Medical Advice

Paul knew what would help some of the stomach problems in his day. He advised Timothy, in I Timothy 5:23 to

_____

_____

Through Proper Nutrition

Paul recognized that those with him on board ship needed nourishment to survive. So, he encouraged them, in Acts 27:35-38, by

_____

_____

_____

As a result, they were able to

_____

_____

Until Death Do Us Part

Because more people are living into their 80's and 90's, couples today face a whole new set of problems not common even a generation ago. With the longer life span comes the possibility of long-term illnesses needing specialized care, or even the need for assisted living. This requires some couples to care for one another under very difficult circumstances, and can force the aging to give up their homes because heavy financial burdens, and/or to have to watch a spouse's health deteriorate before their very eyes. Other stresses common today include children whose own marriages/families are falling apart, raising grandchildren, and perhaps even at the same time, caring for elderly parents. Sometimes, depression sets in when we realize that our own body is wearing out and we aren't able to do the things we once took for granted.

The key to being able to live life in real peace, abundant joy, and a sense of fulfillment is to recognize who we are in Jesus Christ. If we've been born again, we've already begun to live in eternity. Our transition from this earthly life to eternal life is a process of graduation. To the saved, the "golden years" can be a blessed time of preparation and service. With less responsibility, we have more time to pray, especially to intercede for the many needs of our family, our nation, and the world. There can be more opportunity for personal Bible study, as well as time to share the Word of God with others.

Should the Lord tarry, what are some of the things you would like to do or accomplish during your "golden" years of "retirement"?

_____

_____

_____

_____

Facing Death and Eternity

Though we may experience many healings throughout our lifetime, Hebrews 9:27 reminds us that everyone is appointed to death. (Except those Jesus is coming for as described in I Thessalonians 4:16-17!) We need to be prepared, not only by having our earthly affairs in order, but by believing in the promises regarding eternal life in heaven with Him for those who have accepted the atoning work of redemption which Jesus accomplished for us when He died upon the cross. Write down — and memorize if possible — some of these promises.

Romans 6:23 _____

_____

John 3:16 _____

_____

_____

I Corinthians 15:52-54 _____

_____

_____

II Corinthians 5:6 _____

_____

_____

I Peter 5:10 _____

_____

Hebrews 5:8-9 _____

_____

_____

Hebrews 9:15 _____

_____

SUMMARY

Phrases such as being faithful in sickness and in health and until death do us part are often included in wedding vows. These responsibilities will vary with each couple. Because Ecclesiastes 9:12 tells us that no man knows when his hour will come, it behooves each of us to be ready to pass from this earthly existence into the heavenly realm. Meanwhile, we can remain faithful to the one we have committed ourselves to throughout the remainder of this life, though it may mean having to do things we never even imagined. But God can give the provision for what He has allowed.

CONSIDER THIS

How do you interact when one of you is not in good health?

_____

_____

Have you experienced a supernatural healing in your family due to obedience to God's Word?

_____

_____

How are you preparing for your own "golden" years?

_____

_____

What responsibility, if any, do you have concerning your aging parents?

_____

_____

What is your attitude toward death…personally, and concerning your spouse?

_____

_____

MODERN EXAMPLE

What do you do if God doesn't supernaturally heal, doctors can do no more, and you must live the rest of your life with a debilitating disease?

George and Caroline would say, "You still live every day committed to each other and trusting in God." And, they have, for fifty-six years. For forty of those years, Caroline has moved from crutches to braces to a wheelchair, due to polymyositis, a disease which causes the muscles to atrophy because of the way it affects the nerves attached to them. Not a lot is known about this disease, which is one of the reasons she has had to go to various doctors, several clinics, and a teaching hospital, up and down the state of California. She was treated for polio and even took arthritis medication for eleven years before doctors realized the true nature of her disease.

Since the couple had four children (the youngest only four years old) when Caroline began having trouble with her legs, she had to continue in her role as mother and wife, despite the handicaps and pain. She gives much credit to her husband, his mother, and her own mother for all the help they gave her while the children were still living at home.

Those who attend the same church as George and Caroline have, many times, seen George lift Caroline in and out of the car, her wheelchair, and the church pew.

Lifting her, coupled with all his years of walking as a mail-carrier, has made George strong for a man in his 70's! Yet George, too, has a physical disability. He is unable to see well due to an eye disease. So the "pay-back" is that Caroline reads to him and tells him about the things he needs to see more clearly. In addition to caring for Caroline, George is the Salvation Army's representative in his city, so his caring attitude extends to others as well.

When asked to describe what has kept their relationship going over the years, despite handicaps, they said: respect and acceptance of one another, a cheerful attitude, a sense of humor, recognizing each other's strengths and weaknesses, perseverance despite frustration, and most of all, God's grace.

When George and Caroline began dating soon after high school — now nearly sixty years ago — they talked of values important to each of them and of their belief that the marriage vow was until death do us part. They have been faithful in both. But what amazes those of us who know them is their ever-positive attitude. Many times they have given testimony in church for the goodness of God in their lives!

Lesson 13

Ahasuerus and Esther

Sharing Mealtimes

Here I am! I stand at the door and knock. If anyone hears my voice and opens the door, I will go in and eat with him, and he with me.

Revelation 3:20

SETTING THE STAGE

God's people are always in His hands. The book of Esther shows how Divine Providence rules over all things. The story of Esther is usually associated with a special fast, as well as the Feast of Purim, which proved to be significant in Jewish history. Through the Fast, Jews were miraculously delivered out of the hands of their captors. Today, they celebrate this event with the Feast of Purim, to remind themselves of God's power and mercy toward them.

Though things do happen spiritually as a result of fasts, much also happens to change lives when people eat together. This seemed to be especially true in the story of Ahasuerus and Esther. In fact, the book of Esther revolves around seven banquets and one great fast.

God has ordained a year of feasts and fasts for the Jewish people. Our lesson will look at what He has accomplished through these, and how they have been fulfilled in the life of Jesus.

Most importantly, we will consider the significance of our sharing meals with others and how lives can be changed as a result!

INTRODUCING AHASUERUS AND ESTHER

(Based on the book of Esther, particularly 1:1-12; 2:1-18; 4:16-5:14; 7:1-10; 8:17; 9:18-28)

The book of Esther begins with the proclamation of a feast to be given by King Ahasuerus, ruler of Persia. His kingdom, which stretched from India to Ethiopia, was the greatest kingdom of its day. But the king wasn't satisfied. He wanted to conquer Greece. So he invited all of his princes and military advisors to his palace in Shushan where he hosted a feast, which lasted a full six months. At the end of that time, he held a seven-day feast, this one, for all the people of the land.

On the last day of this second feast Ahasuerus, somewhat drunk from his own wine, asked that his wife, Queen Vashti, be brought in so that he could show her off. When she refused to come, the king became angry. He issued a decree that she could no longer come before him. He also declared that her position would be given to someone else.

A beauty contest was held and, after a period of time, Ahasuerus chose Esther to replace Vashti. He made her queen and celebrated the occasion with another feast.

However, Ahasuerus didn't know that Esther was a Jewess. Nor did he know that Mordecai, a man who had risked his own life to prevent an assassination attempt on the king's life, was Esther's uncle.

Mordecai refused to bow down to Haman, the king's chief advisor. This angered Haman, who then wanted to get even by annihilating all Jews. When Esther heard of this, she called a three-day fast by all Jews, believing that she had come into her place in the kingdom for such a time as this. Through this special fast, she believed that God would protect and deliver His people.

She prepared a banquet and asked both Ahasuerus and Haman to attend. The king was pleased and, at this meal, told her that he would give her whatever she desired. She chose not to give him an answer then, but invited both him and Haman back the next day for another banquet.

Between the two banquets, events took place that set in motion certain actions, by both Ahasuerus and Haman. After the banquet, Haman, with encouragement from his wife, decided to demand Mordecai's death, and ordered the gallows built.

But that night the king couldn't sleep. So, he ordered some of the palace records to read and, in the process, found that Mordecai had never been honored for his valiant efforts to save his life. So, he called Haman in to ask what honor would be appropriate. Haman jumped to the conclusion that the king wanted to honor him, and suggested that the person be dressed in royal garments and ride through the streets of the city for all to see! Of course, when he discovered that the king was referring to Mordecai, and that he, Haman, would be the one to lead Mordecai through the city, Haman was humiliated.

While he was discussing this later, with his wife and friends, the king's men arrived to escort him to the second banquet with Esther and the king. At this banquet, Esther asked the King for the deliverance of her people, the Jews. When he discovered what Haman had done, the king ordered that he be hung on the very gallows he had prepared for Mordecai! Thus, as a result of Esther's two meals, and a fast, the Jews were spared, Mordecai was honored, Haman was hung, and Esther was used by God to save His people!

LESSONS FROM AHASUERUS AND ESTHER

Meals in the Bible

A search through God's Word reveals a number of significant mealtimes, and how things changed when people shared them together.

Genesis 3:1-6 — Soon after creation, man's fall was due to the fact that Eve yielded to Satan's temptation to eat that which God had forbidden. What did Satan ask Eve to do? With whom did she share her food?

_____

_____

What was the result? _____

_____

Genesis 18:1-15 — Who shared in this meal? What important announcement was made?

_____

_____

Genesis 19:1-13 — Who shared in this meal? What happened soon after?

_____

_____

Genesis 25:29-34 — Who shared in this meal? What was the result?

_____

_____

Genesis 43:17-34 — Who shared in this meal? What was the result?

_____

_____

Luke 5:27-29 — Who hosted this meal? What event did it follow?

_____

_____

Luke 7:36-50 — With whom did Jesus share this meal? What of significance took place at this meal?

_____

_____

Luke 15:11-32 — What was the occasion for this meal? What took place at this time?

_____

_____

Luke 22:7-23 — Who participated in this meal? What happened during it?

_____

_____

Luke 24:13-25 — Who was present at this meal? What happened as they broke bread together?

_____

_____

_____

Luke 24:36-43 — What is unusual about this breakfast on the beach? What purpose did it serve?

_____

_____

_____

First Corinthians 11:23-30 — What meal are we instructed to partake of? What are the instructions concerning it?

_____

_____

_____

Revelation 19:6-9 — Following Jesus' coming again for His Bride, there will be a Marriage Supper of the Lamb which will culminate the relationship the Church has with her Bridegroom, Jesus Christ. What an awesome event that will be! What do these verses say about those invited to this supper?

_____

_____

_____

Purim and the Other Feasts of Israel

Purim, meaning "lots," refers to the lots cast by Haman who believed the gods would use them to show him the right day to make his move against the Jews. Purim, one of the minor holidays in the Jewish calendar, is celebrated in an atmosphere of merriment. Plays called Purimspiels enact the story of Esther. Young Jewish girls participate in Queen Esther beauty pageants. During the reading of the book of Esther in the synagogues, children drown out the mention of Haman with noisemakers, while adults hiss and boo. Some people send gifts to the poor, and everyone enjoys the traditional three-cornered poppy seed or prune pastries, which represent Haman's three-cornered hat.

God has revealed many of His truths for His people through the Jewish Feasts. These include:

Passover
Exodus 12;
Leviticus 23:4-5

With foods symbolic of their deliverance this special meal commemorates the deliverance of the Jews from Egyptian slavery.

Jesus ate the Passover meal with His disciples to establish the new covenant and our deliverance from bondage. I Corinthians 11:23-26

Feast Of Firstfruits
Leviticus 23:9-14

With the offering of the firstfruits of the barley harvest, God reminded His people of His ability to provide.

Jesus was the "firstfruit" to rise from the dead. I Corinthians 15:20

Pentecost
Leviticus 23:15-22

This feast, which takes place fifty days after the Passover Sabbath, commemorates a harvest festival. During this feast, priests offer two loaves of bread made with newly harvested grain and baked with leaven.

After Jesus ascended into heaven, the Holy Spirit was given in fullness to the Church. Acts 2:1-4

Feast Of Trumpets
Leviticus 23:23-25

Rosh Hashanah marks the beginning of the Jewish New Year. It begins ten days of introspection and repentance.

Day Of Atonement
Leviticus 23:26-32

Yom Kippur is a day of fasting, prayer, and repentance.

Feast Of Booths°
Leviticus 23:33-43

Also called Feast of Tabernacles, and Succoth, this is the final fall festival. Jews build temporary booths to live in during this feast as a reminder of the temporary dwellings the Israelites had in the wilderness.

Jesus fulfilled the spring feast days during the time of His first coming. Many Bible scholars believe that He will fulfill the fall feast days at the time of His second coming!

How Mealtimes Can Change Us

Physically

The obvious benefits of family mealtimes are physical. If we are concerned about the health of the family, meals will be nutritious — which is not always the case when people are left alone to grab a bite to eat. If pleasant conversation accompanies the meal, each person will come away refreshed, and will experience good digestion! Eating alone, especially under stress, encourages us to focus on our own problems and, thus, also affects the body.

What physical benefits have you observed in your family when you share mealtimes?

_____

_____

_____

Socially

Eating together also has social benefits. We take time to consider another's needs as we pass the food, as well as when we help in the preparation and clean-up of the meal. As we converse, we come to know each other a little better. Sharing happy mealtimes brings a family into a oneness hard to come by in any other way.

What social benefits have you observed in your family when you share mealtimes?

_____

_____

_____

Spiritually

As we say grace at the beginning of the meal, we are not only acknowledging God as the source of our food, but we are allowing Him to sanctify our food so that it will bless us! (See I Timothy 4:4-5.) If we begin our mealtimes with prayer, or share scripture at the beginning or end of the meal, we'll also find it more natural to share the things of the Lord with each other.

What spiritual benefits have you observed in your family when you share mealtimes?

_____

_____

_____

SUMMARY

Just as sharing meals served a purpose in the story of Ahasuerus and Esther, so mealtimes were turning points in the lives of a number of other people and situations in the Bible. Family mealtimes can also be important in our individual and family lives physically, socially, and spiritually. It is interesting to note that one of the last invitations of Jesus (in Revelation 3:20) is *"If anyone hears my voice and opens the door, I will go in and eat with him, and he with me."* He wants a relationship that comes from sharing spiritual food, of communing with Him in prayer and in the Word. He wants us to allow His strength, love, and power to flow into our lives as He indwells us. If we'll do this, we'll lose our lukewarmness and return to our first love, Jesus Christ! Yes, something happens when we share in mealtimes with others!

What, if anything, has happened because you have shared meals as a family?

_____

_____

Do you have family devotions around the table? If not, how can you?

_____

_____

How have your lives changed because you have shared meals with others outside your family?

_____

_____

What should your attitude be when partaking of the Lord's Supper?

_____

_____

MODERN EXAMPLE

Vicky and Bob picked up their cups of coffee and settled in the family room recliners to discuss a topic of much concern to them both — the decreasing number of whole-family mealtimes. It had been another evening of sitting at the table with two empty chairs and two dinners waiting to be eaten after a soccer practice and a band performance. As parents of four growing children, they knew they couldn't always do everything as a family forever, but they felt they needed to take charge while the children were still under their roof. They weren't only missing the daily communication which mealtimes provided, but Vicky especially, was concerned about the family's nutrition. She was a nurse, which was also part of the problem. To help out financially, she worked two evenings a week at a nearby convalescent hospital.

Both of them reminisced about their own childhood mealtimes. For both, breakfasts and evening meals had usually been eaten together as a family, with lunches eaten at school or work.

The family mealtimes were usually a time for sharing events of the day, as they ate the good food their mothers had prepared. But, this was not the case now in their own family. Though lunches were still seldom eaten at home together, breakfasts were more often than not, eaten individually and on the run. Microwaves had made this particularly easy! And evening meals were more often than not interrupted by various sport-school-church activities as well as phone calls, television programs, and work schedules. Not only had they allowed many secular commitments to take over, they no longer had time for family devotions at any meal.

They discussed their various options: changing jobs, not allowing the children to participate in extracurricular activities, controlling the television (including news), and requiring everyone to get up earlier for breakfast together. Vicky shared how she had read in a magazine about one family who not only did the latter, but even changed the menus to have traditional dinner food (casseroles, salads, etc.) for breakfast, and breakfast food (cereal, eggs, etc.) for the evening meal!

It didn't seem possible, at this time, to change jobs, but they did believe they could limit the children's outside activities and control the television and incoming phone calls. Fortunately Bob didn't have a long commute to and from work. Though it would be more difficult for Vicky, they finally decided to try getting everyone up earlier, which meant, of course, that bedtimes would be earlier.

How has it worked? Vicky admits to being very tired the two evenings she works. It hasn't always been easy to get every one up early five mornings a week, either. And they haven't started fixing spaghetti, fried chicken or casseroles for breakfast, but they do eat more omelets, pancakes and muffins.

On the other hand, it has been great being able to start the day with the whole family thinking about each other's needs and plans. And they have been able to have a devotional time, as well.

Bob and Vicky are satisfied. They believe the Lord will honor this new commitment to each other and to Him.

Job and His Wife

Overcoming Trials and Suffering

> *In this you greatly rejoice, though now for a little while you may have had to suffer grief in all kinds of trials. These have come so your faith...of greater worth than gold, which perishes even though refined by fire...may be proved genuine and may result in praise, glory and honor when Jesus Christ is revealed.*
>
> I Peter 1:6-7

SETTING THE STAGE

What have we done wrong? Why do the wicked prosper? Why do those of us trying to follow God have to go through trials and suffering?

Most people ask these questions at some time in their life. We find ourselves in various circumstances that we didn't choose, and don't know how to easily resolve. We suffer — physically, emotionally, mentally, or spiritually — and we're misunderstood by those around us. When any one of these trials overtake us, we may become depressed and want to lash out at God and/or others.

Job and his wife faced many calamities in one sudden blow. What was the result for them? Did they learn anything from going through the trials and suffering that ensued? What do (or can) we do when we're faced with situations beyond our control, through which we may have to suffer? Is there anything God may be trying to teach us in the process?

INTRODUCING JOB AND HIS WIFE,

(Based on the book of Job, especially chapters 1-3; 19; 23; 40; 42)

Job crouched down, settling himself gently among the heap of cool ashes. Perhaps, here, he could get some relief. Pus was oozing out of the boils that covered his whole body, from the crown of his head to the bottom of his feet. Spreading infection racked his frame with pain. As he sat, scraping his rotting flesh with a piece of broken pottery, he wondered if he was going to die.

He thought about the events of the previous days. It was hard to believe that only a short time ago he'd had seven healthy sons, three lovely daughters, many servants, great flocks of sheep, 3,000 camels, 500 yoke of oxen, and 500 asses — in addition to all the money that it took to support his family and keep such an operation going! He had been known as the wealthiest man in his part of the world. Now, here he was sitting in a heap of ashes with his family, herds, and possessions gone. Everything had been destroyed in one short day. Yesterday he'd had it all; today, he had nothing — nothing, that is, except a bewildered wife who couldn't even begin to understand the calamity that had befallen them.

The story of Job actually took place in the time span covered in the book of Genesis. We read, in Genesis 46:13 (KJV), that Job was a son of Issachar, one of Jacob's twelve sons. At the beginning of the book of Job, we find God and Satan having a discussion concerning the perfect and upright Job, a man who feared God and avoided evil. Satan had noticed Job and suggested to God that Job was only a righteous man because all was going well for him. To disprove that, God allowed Satan to do whatever he wanted to Job, except kill him. So, with God's permission, Satan caused all of Job's children to be killed, most of his servants slain, and his animals stolen or consumed by fire. Eventually, Job lost his own health.

Job's wife suffered along with him, though she wasn't afflicted with illness as he was. She, too, lost her children, her livelihood, and her wealth. What's more, she probably lost the respect of friends and neighbors because her husband no longer held a prestigious position. Finally, she became so overwhelmingly frustrated that she told Job to curse God and die!

Three friends came to comfort Job. For the first seven days, they said absolutely nothing as they watched Job in his terrible grief. They really didn't have any answers to his "why's," so they began to think of explanations for the suffering he was experiencing. They talked to him about sin, trying to get him to confess something so that God would stop punishing him. Through both these conversations and Job's own dialogue with God, God began to reveal Himself to Job. After a time of testing (which was probably no more than a year) and insight on Job's part, Job was given twice what he'd had before! So the Lord blessed the latter part of Job's life more than the first.

LESSONS FROM JOB AND HIS WIFE

Job's Response to Trials and Suffering

What was Job's response to the great catastrophe which took everything in a single day? Job 1:22 tells us that as he fell to the ground in worship, *"Job did not sin by charging God with wrongdoing."* This response irritated Satan more, so he then talked God into allowing him to touch Job's physical body with disease. Even at this point, it wasn't until Job's wife had encouraged him to "curse God and die" and his friends had sat silently with him for seven days, that Job cried out, cursing the day he was born. Job was able to trust God because he believed that all that happened to him was in God's hands. *"The Lord gave and the Lord has taken away; may the name of the Lord be praised"* (Job 1:21b). Evidently Job had no thought of Satan and the part he had in all that was going on.

Job's Wife's Response to Trials and Suffering

Like many people today who are faced with sudden calamity and trials that don't seem to go away, Job's wife questioned her husband's trust in God. Her advice was for him to curse God and die. This attitude not only undermines our belief and trust in God, it also shows that we don't understand that Satan is the "god of this world" (II Corinthians 4:4).

God never promised justice in this life. In II Timothy 3:12, His word says, *"In fact, everyone who wants to live a godly life in Christ Jesus will be persecuted."*

The Benefits of Trials and Suffering

We Find That God's Ways Are Not Our Ways

Isaiah 55:8-9 says _____

_____

_____

When trials come our way, our first question is usually "why?" It seems as though they always come as a surprise, as something we don't expect a kind and loving God to allow in our lives. We may even feel abandoned by God. But we have a choice: We can either embrace the suffering for what God has for us in it, or we can become angry and turn away from Him.

Through all of Job's suffering he knew that there was a God, and he worshipped Him though all was taken away. Though he couldn't think of any way he had sinned, he did recognize that as God put him through this testing, he would come forth as gold (Job 23:10). More than that, he said, *"I have treasured the words of his mouth more than my daily bread"* (Job 23:12b). Job depended upon God and trusted Him, but he didn't really see all that God was and is. Man never will; and when we think we do, we'll will find ourself in a very self-righteous position. This was Job's problem.

God began to reveal Himself to Job in a very interesting way. He asked Job sixty questions, such as: "Were you present when I created the earth?" "Have the gates of death been opened to you?" "Where does light and darkness dwell?" "Who makes the birds to fly?"

Job, who seemingly had it all together, now began to see his self-righteousness and pride. He began to see an awesome God, one who was so great and powerful that no man could ever figure Him out, even to understanding His creation. Just as important, Job began to see himself as finite and obnoxiously self-righteous — and he abhorred himself and repented in dust and ashes.

If we, like Job, can get past blaming God in our suffering, and can turn to Him, He will show us things about Himself that we would never discover while busy with people and the cares of this life.

Like Job, we want reasons for the things which happen to us. It's very hard to accept the fact that there are some things God just does not reveal. (See Deuteronomy 29:29.) Sometimes, we later discover why we went through particular trials. But for others, we may understand and have the answers only in eternity — and then it probably won't matter!

We Find Jesus Revealed in Suffering

Job lived long before Jesus lived on earth. Yet, somehow, he was given insight into Him as His Savior. He never called Jesus by name, but was can recognize what he said as referring to Jesus, because we know Him and what He has since done for us. Let's took at the progression of revelation given to Job.

In Job 9:32-35, Job recognized his need for a mediator who would be able to present his case to God. According to Hebrews 9:15, who is the mediator between man and God?

_____

In Job 13:15-16, Job stated his devotion to God: "Though He slay me I will still trust Him." We can see Job had some thought of being in touch with God after death, because he said he would "*surely defend my ways to his face*" (v. 15b). According to John 3:16, 36; 5:24; 6:40, who came to give us hope of life after death?

_____

In Job 19, we find Job in the depths of self-pity because of all that had happened. In the midst of this, he had an amazing revelation and proclaimed (in verses 25-26) "*I know that my Redeemer lives, and that in the end he will stand upon the earth. And after my skin has been destroyed, yet in my flesh I will see God.*" In the worst of his suffering, Job saw what some people never see in their whole lives. He saw that he had a Savior, that this Savior lives, and that He will reign on the earth to the end. More than this, Job knew that he would be resurrected and stand before God.

We can also find Jesus in the midst of suffering, because He identifies with those who suffer. Suffering brings us to that lowly, humble position before God, a position that Jesus took as He made Himself of no reputation and became obedient unto death. It's as Hebrews 2:9 says:

_____

_____

_____

In Philippians 3:7-11 Paul counted everything loss except knowing Jesus, and he was willing to suffer that _____

_____

First Peter 4:12-19 tells us what our attitude should be when we are required to suffer as a Christian. _____

_____

_____

We Learn to Trust God, Not Man

Job must have had many acquaintances; he was the wealthiest man in his part of the country. He probably had many friends, for he was good and kind and did no evil. But where were they when tragedy struck? Only four came to comfort him, but they didn't really understand Job's plight. At one point, even Job's wife turned against him.

It's significant to note that the middle verse of the whole Bible is Psalm 118:8-9 which says:

_____

_____

Even Joseph, in Genesis 50:20, realized that God often has other purposes than men have when we're allowed to go through trials and suffering. He says _____

_____

_____

Sooner or later, we all must learn this lesson. Job found this out through trials and suffering.

We Learn to Appreciate Spiritual Warfare

In the first dialogue between God and Satan in the book of Job, Satan recognizes (in Job 1:10) that God had supernaturally put a hedge of protection around Job. We can ask God to do the same thing for us and for others. Psalm 34:7 reminds us that _____

_____

_____

Psalm 91 is good to memorize — to have in your heart and mind when you feel any kind of anger because of what you are going through.

The Word plainly states that it was Satan (with God's permission) who had brought all the calamities upon Job. We don't know that Job knew how to wage spiritual warfare against his enemy although Job did remind God, in Job 6:23, that he had never asked for deliverance from the hand of the enemy.

We, who live this side of the cross, have a privilege that Job didn't have. We have the written Word, the knowledge of Jesus' victory over Satan, and the Holy Spirit to give us power in spiritual warfare. Sometimes it takes a crisis to show us our need for becoming soldiers in battle over an enemy who is already-defeated yet tries to make us believe that he is all-powerful. According to Ephesians 6:10-18, as we stand against the wiles of the devil, how are we to be prepared with armor?

_____

_____

_____

_____

We Learn to Deal With Our Fleshly Lusts

As Job conversed with his friends and with God, all former lusts and worldly matters became unimportant. His only goal became to see what purpose there was for his life. His actual "turn around" came when, in Job 42:10, he _____

When he did this, the Lord _____

According to I Peter 4:1-2, he who has suffered in his body is _____

_____

As a result _____

We Learn to Have a Grateful Attitude in All Circumstances

Even at the outset of his time of suffering, Job recognized the sovereignty of God and did not blame Him. Job 1:20-22 says _____

_____

In I Thessalonians 5:16-18, Paul admonishes us to _____

_____

For _____

He will use our trials for His purposes.

SUMMARY

And, so, God, Jesus, Man, and Satan all come into sharper focus when we are suffering through trials that come our way. We see more clearly who each is and what our relationship to each one should be. Job's time of great suffering came to an end. When Satan saw that Job and his wife were still trusting God through all their trials, when he saw Job repent of his self-righteousness, and when he heard Job pray for his friends, he gave up on Job. God then restored the hedge around Job and blessed him doubly for all he had gone through.

God never tells us that we won't experience suffering. In fact, the Bible tells us that we, as God's people, should expect trials and afflictions. Second Timothy 3:12 says, *"In fact, everyone who wants to live a godly life in Christ Jesus will be persecuted."* Second Timothy 2:12a (KJV) says *"if we suffer, we shall also reign with him."* Job and his wife came to know the Lord better through trials, and to trust in Him instead of man. God blessed them in the end. He can do the same for us.

What have you learned about God in the trials you have gone through?

_____

_____

How has Jesus' suffering for you become more real as you go through suffering?

_____

_____

What have you learned about spiritual warfare in the midst of your trials?

_____

_____

How has man failed you when you needed him the most?

_____

_____

How can/do you minister to your friends when they are going through trials?

_____

_____

MODERN EXAMPLE

It's one thing to have trials and suffering come upon you; it's another to choose them as a way of life. But Adoniram and Ann Judson (also known as Don and Nancy) did just that as America's first missionaries to the Far East! In fact, in a letter to Ann's parents after proposing to her, Adoniram asked for permission not only to marry Ann, but to take her to a heathen land with every distress, degradation, persecution, and, perhaps, violent death. It turned out to be a prophetic letter — they suffered most of these things.

Adoniram and Ann were married in Bradford, Massachusetts on February 5, 1812, and sailed for India the next day. After a four-month trip, a short time in India, and the death of their first baby during the voyage to Burma, they finally settled down in Rangoon. There, they began their work by learning the language. It was a very lonely time; it took three years for the first packet of letters to arrive from the United States. Ann frequently suffered from jungle fevers; they lost another child, a boy, at age eight months. Yet Ann wrote in her journal that God is the same when He afflicts us, as when He is merciful — He is always worthy of our trust and confidence.

In her sorrow, Ann launched a school for Burmese girls, wrote a simple catechism in Burmese, and began translating the book of Jonah. Five years went by with no converts.

After developing a liver ailment which grew progressively worse, Ann returned to the States to receive treatment and recuperate. After two-and-a-half years, she was reunited with Adoniram in Burma. He had spent the time translating the whole New Testament and part of the Old Testament into Burmese. During the first nine years in Burma, they had made only eighteen native converts.

When war between England and Burma broke out, Adoniram was imprisoned and Ann was made a prisoner in her own home. She did manage to sneak him food and clothing…and his Bible translation, which she had hid in a pillow. But when a prison guard confiscated the translation and threw it into the garbage, Adoniram was in despair. (Much later, after Adoniram was released, a Burmese Christian brought it to him saying he'd found it on a garbage heap.)

Ann was expecting during this time, and after their little girl was born, she took her to see Adoniram in prison. Then followed months of him being moved from prison to prison and her trying to find out where he was. All the while, she not only had the baby to care for, but she had her own health to be concerned about, too. She had contracted smallpox and other tropical fevers.

In February 1826, Don and Ann were reunited in Rangoon, and subsequently moved to lower Burma where they started a new work. But Ann was stricken with cerebral spinal meningitis and died in October at age thirty-six. Not long after that, Adoniram buried their two-year-old daughter as well.

Although Ann did not live to see the realization of all her dreams, her husband's translation of the Bible into Burmese provided for the establishment of fifty-three churches in Burma.

Hosea and Gomer
David and Bathsheba

Committing Adultery

You have heard that it was said, "Do not commit adultery." But I tell you that anyone who looks at a woman lustfully has already committed adultery with her in his heart.

Matthew 5:27-28

SETTING THE STAGE

Adultery, the sexual unfaithfulness of a married person, was a problem in Bible times. It's still a major problem in our society today. No one is immune. It has caused difficulties in our government, in the military, in churches, and in families. (Some statistics say that more than one-third of married Americans are guilty of adultery.)

Unfaithfulness by either marriage partner causes great pain to the other. And as in the case of David and Bathsheba, the guilt which accompanies adultery may lead to other sins as well — sins such as deception, lying, even murder.

God used the story of Hosea and Gomer as an illustration of the consequences of both physical and spiritual adultery and how He can, nonetheless, forgive when repentance is sincere. This lesson focuses on what God says about adultery and how marriages can be restored through repentance and forgiveness, rather than what society teaches about its acceptance. We will also look at the difference between adultery and fornication, as well as what the Word says about divorce and remarriage.

INTRODUCING HOSEA AND GOMER

(Based on Hosea 1-3)

The Lord told Hosea to marry Gomer, a beautiful young woman much attracted to the ways of the world. Hosea followed God's instruction because he loved Him, and he continued to preach fiery sermons to the people for whom he was greatly burdened.

Soon after their marriage, Gomer gave birth to a son, Jezreel, so-named to remind Israel that God's judgment was surely coming. Before long, she had borne two other children, a girl and a boy, though Hosea wasn't sure that they were his because Gomer had enjoyed the pleasure of other men. And so, he was deeply grieved.

Hosea then watched his wife give herself to prostitution, as she served as a priestess of Baal. He prayed for her daily, knowing all the while that she was committing adultery. He was heartsick; but he continued to love her, and he continued to care for their children while she was away from home.

The picture of God's unfathomable love comes clearly into focus when we see Hosea standing in a slave market and watching his once-beautiful wife be put on the auction block. He paid the required price for her release and, in great mercy, took Gomer home and nursed her back into the relationship he had so desired with her in the beginning.

INTRODUCING DAVID AND BATHSHEBA

(Based on II Samuel 11:1-12:25)

While reigning as king over all Israel, David decided to remain in Jerusalem when he sent Joab out with the army to war against the Ammonites. Unable to sleep one evening, he got out of bed and took a walk on his rooftop. From there, he saw a beautiful woman, and immediately sent messengers to bring her to his palace. As a result of sleeping with him that night, she became pregnant. When he heard the news, he quickly sent word for Joab to send Uriah, her husband home. Uriah was a good soldier, so when he came back to Jerusalem, he slept on guard at the entrance to the palace instead of going home to his wife. The next day, David got Uriah drunk and tried to get him to go home. But he would not. Frustrated, David told Uriah to return to the battle and gave him a letter, which he was to give to Joab. In this letter, David told Joab to put Uriah on the front lines. Joab did as he was instructed, and Uriah and was killed. David was relieved until confronted by the Lord through the prophet Nathan, concerning both the adultery and murder he had committed. Repentant, David confessed his sins to Nathan and to God. God forgave him and later even called David a man after His own heart. Though David and Bathsheba were married and later became the parents of Solomon, the king who succeeded David, they had to suffer the consequences of this sin. This baby died soon after its birth and David's household was plagued with murder and sexual immorality from then on.

LESSONS FROM HOSEA AND GOMER
AND FROM DAVID AND BATHSHEBA

Lustful Eyes and Deceitful Hearts

As grievous sin as adultery is, Jesus says that there are other sins that precede it. In the Sermon on the Mount, in Matthew 5:27-28, Jesus says that adultery takes place in the heart before the act is even committed. This happens when one looks lustfully at another. Looking at someone lusfully is one of the ways sin gets into the heart, and then, into actions. God's Word gives specific instructions on how to deal with lust. According to the following scriptures, what are we to do?

Galatians 5:24 _____

Titus 2:12 (See KJV.) _____

II Timothy 2:22 (See KJV.) _____

Colossians 3:5 _____

_____

When we look at someone lustfully, adultery takes place in the heart, which Jeremiah 17:9 tells us is *"deceitful above all things and beyond cure"* — unless it is given over to Jesus Christ and the work of the Holy Spirit.

If we sincerely want God to change our heart, we will obey the following scriptures:
Believe with your heart. (Romans 10:10)

Above all else, guard your heart. (Proverbs 4:23)

Love God with all your heart. (Matthew 22:37)

Set apart Christ as Lord in your heart. (I Peter 3:15)

Observe God's decrees and laws with all your heart. (Deuteronomy 26:16)

Trust in the Lord with all your heart. (Proverbs 3:5)

Don't cherish sin in your heart.(Psalm 66:18)

Do God's will from your heart. (Ephesians 6:6)

Adultery

From Genesis through Revelation, the Bible tells us that God sees adultery as a grievous sin. Write what the following scriptures say about adultery.

Exodus 20:14 (Deuteronomy 5:18) _____

_____

Leviticus 20:10 (Deuteronomy 22:22) _____

_____

Numbers 5:12-31 _____

_____

_____

Judges, Kings, and Prophets

Throughout the Old Testament history, we find stories of adultery and its consequences — from the sons of Eli to King David. Ezekiel 16 graphically describes Israel as a harlot, and says this was an abomination to the Lord.

Job 31:9-12 _____

_____

Proverbs 7:10-27 _____

_____

Malachi 3:5 _____

_____

Matthew 5:27-28 _____

_____

Romans 7:1-3 _____

_____

I Corinthians 6:9-10 _____

_____

Hebrews 13:4 _____

_____

James 4:4_____

_____

Revelation 21:8 _____

_____

Adultery and Fornication

Sometimes the words "adultery" and "fornication" are used interchangeably. Even the NIV uses the term "marital unfaithfulness" where the King James Version uses "fornication." (See Matthew 5:32 and 19:9.) The word "fornication," used in the King James Bible, is "porneia" and refers to all sexual immorality. It is not restricted to marital unfaithfulness. The word "moichos" (adultery) would have been used if Jesus meant only marital unfaithfulness. Fornication has a broader meaning, such as sexual relationship prior to marriage — for which, according to Deuteronomy 22:13-21, a marriage could be dissolved. "Fornication" (porneia) is also used in I Corinthians 5:1 in referring to an incestuous relationship (which is also condemned in Leviticus 18). Simply stated, adultery is unfaithfulness by a married partner. Fornication also includes premarital sex.

Divorce and Remarriage

Nowhere does the Bible teach that a person must or should get a divorce because his/her mate has committed adultery. Some say that Matthew 19:8-9 allows for this. Yet, as noted above, the King James Version used the word "fornication," which could imply that divorce was allowable because there was evidence of *pre*marital sex.

A second scripture, I Corinthians 7:15, is also used to support remarriage after divorce. Yet the very spirit of I Corinthians 7 is to encourage singleness, not remarriage.

Study verses 7-8, 10-11, 27, 32-40 and summarize what is said.

_____

_____

_____

_____

Consider the following verses, which came from the mouth of Jesus Himself.

For the Woman

Matthew 5:32 (KJV) *"But I say unto you, That whosoever shall put away his wife, saving for the cause of fornication, causeth her to commit adultery; and whosoever shall marry her that is divorced committeth adultery."*

For the Man

Mark 10:11-12 (KJV) *"Whosoever shall put away his wife, and marry another, committeth adultery against her. And, if a woman shall put away her husband, and be married to another, she committeth adultery."*

God permitted divorce for those who were backslidden in heart. Our belief in and obedience to a holy, covenant-keeping God requires that our lives reflect the same kind of commitment and holiness toward each other as toward Him. *"Be perfect, therefore, as our heavenly Father is perfect."* (Matthew 5:48)

Forgiveness

God wants us to see sin for what it is, to confess it, repent of it, and receive His forgiveness for it. The only way we can do this is through the mercy of God and the blood of Jesus Christ. Jesus shed His blood to cover our sin. As great High Priest, He then sprinkled it upon the Mercy Seat in heaven so that we can have access to the presence of God. As we recognize that this sacrifice was made personally for us, and accept the atoning work of Jesus' blood for our sin, we will experience the forgiveness of God. To accept this forgiveness, we must first confess our sin and repent of it.

David, with a broken and contrite heart, repented as he confessed his sin — and God forgave him. We can read about this, and David's own thoughts, in Psalm 51. Scripture doesn't tell us anything about Bathsheba's repentance. It appears that she did repent, because she was allowed to bear the son whom God chose to be the one who would succeed David as king. We assume, too, that since she married David, she must have forgiven him for killing her husband.

The story of Hosea and Gomer ends the way it does because of Hosea's willingness to forgive Gomer, undeserving though she was. Their story is a picture of God's mercy towards His wife, Israel, who was committing spiritual adultery when she determined to have a relationship with the world and its idols instead of the one true God who loved her very much. Gomer had to depend upon Hosea's great mercy — given to him by God — before her heart was even open to reconciliation with him. Israel will have to do the same.

In John 8:1-11, we have a story of an adulteress who was brought to Jesus by the scribes and Pharisees to see what Jesus would say. By law she should have been stoned; but Jesus suggested that anyone without sin should throw the first one — and they simply walked away. He then told her that He did not condemn her, but that she was not to sin anymore.

Forgiveness is not only the greatest gift man can receive from God, it's also the greatest gift couples can give one another. In fact, according to Matthew 6:12, we cannot receive God's forgiveness unless we forgive one another first!

Because any close relationship is bound to have offenses, we, as couples, will have daily opportunity to forgive each other. To forgive major offenses, like adultery, may take more time. But it's possible, with God's help. The way we'll know the transaction has been completed is when we can truly do what I Peter 3:9 says:

_____

_____

_____

SUMMARY

The story of Hosea and Gomer shows us God's everlasting mercy and unending grace toward the sinner. It shows that He is always willing to forgive, always willing to take us back and restore the relationship He wants us to have with Him, even when we've committed spiritual adultery. God is as Hosea, suffering because of our sin and yet paying the price so we can be reconciled to Him. Gomer represents Israel, the wife of God's bosom, who was often tempted by other lovers into committing adultery. We don't know the end of the story of Hosea and Gomer, we only know that a remnant of God's people chose to remain faithful to Him and He continues to love and woo them back to Himself. He has already paid the price for their redemption.

David and Bathsheba, though they committed the sin of adultery, repented and were forgiven by God. Today, many people are looking for the supernatural — for signs, wonders, and miracles. Yet, the greatest gift of all is the miracle that often goes unnoticed because it's so unspectacular to those not involved. It's the gift of forgiveness — of God's forgiveness toward us and of our forgiveness toward one another. It not only causes the God of the universe to forget our sin, but it also creates a new spirit within us and gives us a new relationship with Him as well as with others, including our spouse.

Have either of you ever committed adultery? If so, have you repented of it and received God's — and your spouse's — forgiveness?

_____

_____

What effect does unbridled lust — such as through pornography — have in your life, or the lives of your family and friends?

_____

_____

What do you do when you know of others — especially fellow Christians — having adulterous relationships?

_____

_____

What is spiritual adultery? Are you guilty of it?

_____

_____

MODERN EXAMPLE

Sheri and Scott had met in their early twenties. She was a paramedic when Scott, a seminary student, met her during an internship program which introduced prospective pastors to various services in the community. They married after Scott's graduation and began serving a church in a metropolitan suburb in California. Within the next few years, they became parents of a boy and a girl. Sheri, busy as mother and pastor's wife, occasionally longed for the freedom and adventure she had once known.

Scott enjoyed being pastor. He had a special gift for reaching the hurting — which included Melanie, a young woman whose husband had been killed in a motorcycle accident. Melanie was part of the worship team and Scott always tried to encourage her whenever she came to the church for music practice. When he discovered she needed some practical help, a well as spiritual ministry, he began stopping by her apartment to do little tasks. Though to himself he justified his need to help her out, he also began to realize that he was physically attracted to this beautiful, lonely young woman.

As living on one income became increasingly difficult, Scott and Sheri decided that she would return to work, part-time, for a local ambulance service. Although she loved her children, she was glad for the break from being "tied down" at home. She found herself eagerly anticipating the conversations with adults at work — especially with Chad, a single man who seemed to be able to engage her in conversation about a variety of things — something she and Scott rarely had time for anymore.

Oblivious to how far apart they were growing, Sheri and Scott were soon relating to one another just enough to keep family and jobs intact.

Then, without warning, their three-year-old son was diagnosed with leukemia. Sheri had to quit her job to care for him. It was then that Scott realized anew how important his children, and Sheri, were to him. In the shock of Bobby's illness, both Sheri and Scott had to come to terms with the direction their lives had been going. Though Sheri missed her work, and especially Chad's attention and humor, she knew deep inside that it had been God's mercy to keep her from an ongoing relationship with him. Scott, already convicted of the feelings he was beginning to have for Melanie, was relieved when he and Sheri finally admitted to each other what had been going on in their hearts and lives. Though neither had been sexually unfaithful, they realized how each of them had committed adultery in their heart. Though they considered themselves spiritual overseers to others, they discovered that they, as human beings, had the same temptations as those to whom they ministered.

Lesson 16

Zechariah and Elizabeth

Communicating With Each Other and With God

I tell you that men will have to give account on the day of judgment for any careless word they have spoken. For by your words you will be acquitted, and by your words you will be condemned.

Matthew 12:36-37

SETTING THE STAGE

In the course of a day's communication, a husband and wife exchange a variety of words — words of affection, criticism, accusation, gossip, encouragement, forgiveness, and hopefully, even the confession of God's Word. Since marriage is a means of communication in close relationship over a period of years, it becomes a unique opportunity for God to conform us to His nature, as we allow Him to bring our words in line with His Word.

The way we use our tongue becomes a major factor in the success or failure of marriage when fluctuating emotions cause us to say things that surprise even ourselves. It can also be something to consider when we look at how we communicate with God.

As we look at the story of Zechariah and Elizabeth, a couple who endured nine months of silence because God did not allow Zechariah to speak, we'll consider what God says about the tongue and communication.

INTRODUCING ZECHARIAH AND ELIZABETH

(Based on Luke 1:5-25; 57-80)

We find the account of this godly couple in the first chapter of Luke, where they are described as *"upright in the sight of God, observing all the Lord's commandments and regulations blamelessly"* (Luke 1:6).

Zechariah was a priest. One day, as he was burning incense in the temple, the angel Gabriel appeared at the side of the altar and told Zechariah that he and Elizabeth would have a son — that not only had their prayers been answered, but that many people would rejoice at this child's birth. The angel went on to say that their son (who later became known as John the Baptist), would be set apart unto God for the special task of preparing the way for the coming of the Messiah.

Undoubtedly, Zechariah was shaken. It had been four hundred years since God had spoken through a prophet. Now, an angel was telling him that he and his wife would have a special child to carry out God's plan! Feeling that he needed a sign, he asked, *"How can I be sure of this? I am an old man and my wife is well along in years"* (Luke 1:18). Apparently, because of the unbelief this question implied, God chose to take away Zechariah's ability to speak until after the baby was born. Only after proclaiming the name of his son at the circumcision ceremony eight days after the baby's birth, was Zechariah able to speak again!

It is interesting to note that immediately after Zechariah wrote that the child was to be named John, his tongue was loosed and he praised God. He was filled with the Holy Spirit and began to prophesy as he praised the Lord for all that He had done.

LESSONS FROM ZECHARIAH AND ELIZABETH

The Tongue and How We Use It

One cannot help but wonder why God bound Zechariah's tongue for nine months, especially when he was known to be a God-fearing, even blameless man. But God knows that our tongue is the most unruly member of our body. He has much to say about it in the Bible. James 3:5-10 tells us that though the tongue is a small part of the body, it boasts great things. It is like a fire, a restless evil full of poison. It can corrupt the whole person. It can be used to bless God or to curse men. Psalm 64:3 says that the tongue can be sharpened like a sword. Its use can cause all kinds of irreparable damage. In fact, according to Proverbs 18:21, death and life are in the power of the tongue!

Match the scriptures below with the adjective that describes the tongue:

Psalm 5:9	a boastful tongue
Psalm 12:3	a deceitful tongue
Proverbs 10:31	a perverse tongue
Proverbs 15:4	a lying tongue
Proverbs 1:19	a healing tongue
Psalm 10:7	an evil tongue
Proverbs 25:15	a gentle tongue

Communicating With Each Other

According to Psalm 139:4, there is not a word on our tongue that God doesn't know! Thus, He gives instruction as to how to speak and how to bring our communication in line with the truth of His Word.

Ephesians 4:25-32 tells us _____

_____

_____

_____

One of the reasons for watching our speech so carefully is that, according to Mark 11:23, we have what we say! Perhaps it was for this reason that God didn't allow Zechariah to speak during the nine months of Elizabeth's pregnancy. Can't you hear him now? "But Elizabeth's too old to have a healthy child and safe delivery!" "Maybe it wasn't an angel of God who spoke to me!"

Colossians 4:6 says _____

_____

Psalm 39:1 says _____

_____

Since our speech shows where our heart is, we need to pray what David prayed in Psalm 51:10. _____

_____

_____

In the fear of God, we need to remember the words of Matthew 12:36-37.

_____

_____

_____

One way to control our tongue is to know God's Word and the truths He wants us to apply to our life. We can come to know His Word through Bible studies, books, tapes, church services, etc. But we must also take time daily to be alone with God...to meditate upon scripture and to communicate with Him in prayer. In Ephesians 5:22-32, and John 15:3, we find that Jesus, as the husband of the Church, wants to cleanse and sanctify His Bride *by the washing of water by the Word.*" As we allow ourselves to be immersed in God's Word, our heart and mind are cleansed. This corrects our tongue, because it is out of the heart that the mouth speaks (Matthew 12:34). Knowing God, and being in His Word, helps bring our tongue into conformity with God's Word and the nature of Jesus. That, in turn, helps us say the right things...even to our spouse!

Communicating With God

After nine months of not being able to speak, Zechariah confirmed that his baby was to be named John. Luke 1:67 also tells us that Zechariah was also filled with the Holy Spirit and prophesied. Thus, He was able to both communicate with others and to speak for God...all with a voice that had been silent for many months.

First Corinthians 12:7-11 outlines the manifestations of the Spirit given to people.

Included in verse 10: *"to another prophecy...to another speaking in different kinds of tongues."* These are supernatural gifts given to men to speak forth God's Word.

In Genesis 11, we find the story of the tower of Babel when all the people of the earth were *"of one language and of one speech."* They had no difficulty understanding one another as they were united in rebellion against God. They wanted to build a tower to heaven so they could obtain the knowledge and power rightfully belonging to God. However, God could not allow this, so He came down and confounded their language. With the resulting confusion of speech, they were unable to work together. God then scattered the people abroad over the face of the earth and, from that time on, they had difficulty communicating with each other — and with Him.

Many centuries later, following Jesus' death, resurrection, and ascension, another group of people were found "in one accord." This time, it was Jesus' followers, in an upper room in Jerusalem. They weren't trying to build a tower to heaven. They were waiting for the Holy Spirit to descend upon them as God had promised. It was the Day of Pentecost, and God had chosen this day to come down from heaven to man again — this time, to reverse the experience of the tower of Babel. Instead of giving diverse tongues so that man would be separated by speech, God gave men new languages to bring about a oneness through His Spirit. To accomplish this, He purposed that man be immersed in His Holy Spirit so that the Spirit could give utterance...bypassing man's mind and intellect. Thus, as God poured out the Holy Spirit on the Day of Pentecost, men were able to speak languages which those present could understand, even though they, themselves, perhaps did not. (See Acts 1:4-5; 21-13.)

Yet according to I Corinthians 14:4, even if one speaks in an unknown tongue with no one else around, he edifies himself. For as he yields the most unruly member of his body to the Holy Spirit, he is able to speak mysteries unto God (I Corinthians 14:2). In fact, the Spirit will make intercession for him with groanings which cannot be uttered (Romans 8:26). This is particularly helpful when one is uncertain how to pray in specific situations.

In I Corinthians 14:18-19, Paul tells us that he spoke in tongues more than anyone else. Yet, in church, he would rather speak five words with understanding than 10,000 words in tongues. Therefore, most of his speaking in tongues must have been what is called "praying in the Spirit."

Jude 20 tells us, *"But you, dear friends, build yourselves up in your most holy faith and pray in the Holy Spirit."* By praying in tongues (or in the Spirit) when speaking to God, we allow Him to build us up, increase our faith, and give us His words of wisdom, knowledge, interpretation, and prophecy.

Praying in the Spirit allows us to pray unceasingly, for it can be done even while we're thinking about other things. Out of our mouth, then, will more likely come truth, encouragement, and blessing as we manifest the fruit of the Spirit.

Perhaps the greatest purpose for "tongues," however, is that it represents an act of utmost surrender to God. For when we yield our tongue, the primary expression of self, we are essentially saying to God: "You are the Lord of my life. I allow You to have Your way...even though it seems utterly foolish to me."

Scripturally, speaking in tongues comes along with the baptism (or infilling) of the Holy Spirit. How did this baptism take place in the following settings?

Acts 2:4 _____

_____

Acts 10:44-46 _____

_____

Acts 19:6 _____

_____

This baptism is available to all who have repented of their sins and believed on the Lord Jesus Christ (Acts 2:38-39). But to enjoy the full benefits of the gifts of the Spirit, we should allow the Holy Spirit to have full control over the most unruly member of the human body — the tongue. This does not make us a better class Christian; it only opens the way for us to come into full provision of God's Word.

SUMMARY

Each person speaks millions of words during their lifetime, many of these in communication with a spouse. Matthew 12:36-37 tells us that we will be accountable for every careless word not repented of. (Verbal abuse happens not only in marriage, but in relationships between family members, and employers and employees as well.) What great motivation to spend time in God's Word — to be edified and cleansed by it. And what great grace, to know the provision God has given through His Holy Spirit — that our unruly tongue can be yielded to Him so our words can come into line with His Word! Zechariah and Elizabeth had to allow God to deal with them in an area of communication. Perhaps, we need to do so as well.

CONSIDER THIS

How can you improve your communication as husband and wife?

_____

_____

What do you do when you are in the presence of people who use their tongues to curse or blaspheme God? How do you respond when someone takes God's name in vain?

_____

_____

How can you make your tongue a blessing and not a curse?

_____

_____

What are some of the ways you have experienced verbal abuse? What was the result?

_____

_____

What do you believe about speaking in tongues? Is it for today?

_____

_____

MODERN EXAMPLE

Over two million men have attended Promise Keepers' rallies across America the past few years to make, or renew, a commitment to seven promises, including that of building strong marriages and families through love, protection, and Biblical values.

The organization was founded in 1990 by Colorado University's head football coach Bill McCartney. God used these rallies to do a work in Bill and Lyndee's marriage, and in the area of their communication with each other.

Indeed, Bill was a busy man, both as the Buffaloes' football coach and Promise Keepers' leader. But even when he was at home, he was so preoccupied that he did not even see what was happening to his own wife and family…let alone share his own needs and desires. He was a great communicator…to everyone but them. Lyndee was becoming very depressed and was losing weight as she suffered his rejection and lack of intimate communication. On the other hand, she was also hurt by what he did say to her — that he had had an affair early in their marriage.

In the summer of 1994, a guest speaker came to their church and challenged their men by saying, "When you look into the face of a man's wife, you will see just what he is as a man. Whatever he has invested in or withheld from her is reflected in her countenance." Looking into Lyndee's face, Bill was devastated. He knew, without a doubt, that he was not the husband that he pretended to be. This eventually led to his resigning from his dream job of coaching to give his time to Lyndee and his family…and to Promise Keepers.

When interviewed in the fall of 1997, Bill and Lyndee told how God had restored their marriage. Part of this process has been to frequently look each other in the eyes while holding hands and repeating their marriage vows aloud. Their relationship — and communication with each other — has not only been restored, but it is better than ever!

Lesson 17

Joseph and Mary

Receiving God's Guidance

> *Whether you turn to the right or to the left, your ears will hear a voice behind you saying, 'This is the way, walk in it.'*
>
> Isaiah 30:21

SETTING THE STAGE

Those who are acquainted with the events surrounding the birth of our Savior, Jesus Christ, will know most of what is recorded about his parents, Joseph and Mary. The story begins with supernatural encounters — a dream for Joseph and an angelic visit for Mary — as God informs them of what is about to take place in their lives. He gave them details. He not only let them know that His Son would be born to them, but that this child would be conceived by the Holy Spirit. He told them to name the child Jesus, that he would save His people from their sins, and that He would not only be given the throne of His father, but that He would reign over the house of Jacob forever. They had not asked for this information; God simply visited them.

To guide us today, God can visit through supernatural encounters. But most of the time, He wants us to seek Him, to have open ears, and to be sensitive to the leading of the Holy Spirit. In this lesson, we'll look at some of the ways God can guide us, as He guided Joseph and Mary.

INTRODUCING JOSEPH AND MARY

(Based on Matthew 1:18-25; 2:13-23; Luke 1:39-45; 2:1-7)

Joseph and Mary were the earthly father and mother that God chose to raise His Son, Jesus Christ, when He came to earth to live in the flesh. We first hear of Joseph in Matthew 1, where we are given the genealogy of Jesus through Joseph, His legal human, but not natural, father. Matthew's genealogy of Joseph goes back to Abraham and shows that Jesus was related to the Jews. In Luke, when Mary is first introduced, the genealogy goes back to Adam, showing that Jesus is related to all human beings.

Joseph and Mary were betrothed when the angel of the Lord appeared to Joseph in a dream and told him that Mary was pregnant. Because betrothal was as binding as the marriage vows, it would have been natural for him to think he had two options: divorce Mary quietly or have her stoned. Instead, he chose to receive God's guidance and marry her. Through other dreams, God guided Joseph and his little family, even after Jesus was born.

Mary was a young woman living in the humble village of Nazareth. She was so open to the Lord that when the angel Gabriel visited her and gave her the news that she would bear the Son of God, she simply responded: *"May it be to me as you have said"* (Luke 1:38).

Because many people were going to Bethlehem for a census, there was no room for Joseph and Mary in an inn and Jesus was born in an animal shelter in Bethlehem. After a while, the family had to flee to Egypt to escape King Herod. They later returned to Nazareth, where Jesus spent His childhood. Scripture doesn't tell us anything about Joseph after he and Mary took Jesus to the Temple when He was twelve years old. According to Matthew 13:55-56 and Mark 6:3, Joseph and Mary had other children after Jesus — James, Joseph, Judas, Simon and some daughters. We do hear more of Mary. She stood beneath Jesus' cross watching Him die. At that time, Jesus gave her into the hands of John to be cared for. She also had the privilege of being among the members of the early church, for she is the only named woman waiting in the upper room until the day of Pentecost when the Holy Spirit descended and the Church came into being.

LESSONS FROM JOSEPH AND MARY

How Joseph and Mary Received Guidance from God

While Joseph seemed to be attuned to God's voice in his dreams, Mary spoke directly with an angel who had a word for her. Like Joseph, Mary accepted the word of God, as spoken in dreams and visions, and was obedient to it. Note that the message the angel gave to Joseph lined up with what the prophets, in Isaiah 7:14, had foretold — that a virgin would conceive and bring forth a son who would be called Immanuel. Joseph's second dream fulfilled God's word through the prophet Hosea, *"Out of Egypt I called my son."*

Another principle of guidance, which so aptly fits with the story of Joseph and Mary, has been called the "wise-men principle." Just as the wise men followed the star and, in so doing, were all led to the Christ child, so God will use two or more persons or circumstances to confirm His Word to us. Second Corinthians 13:1, tells us God will confirm His Word by *"two or three witnesses."* In the process, He can "fine-tune" the guidance, just as He did when the wise men first went to Jerusalem and, then, were led to go to Bethlehem. Simeon and Anna each recognized Jesus for who He was when Mary and Joseph brought Him to the temple as an infant, again confirming that He was "The Lord's Christ, " "God's Salvation," "The Light to lighten the Gentiles" and "The Redeemer of Israel."

Not only is God's guidance and perfect timing evident in the events already mentioned, it is no coincidence that the same shepherds who received the announcement of Jesus' birth from the angels, were probably tending the very sheep that would be used for temple sacrifices and were also the first to see the Lamb of God, the ultimate sacrifice for our sins.

Receiving Guidance From God

We don't hear from God may for some of the same reasons we don't hear one another:

We don't allow enough time.

We aren't close enough in proximity.

We have our attention on other things.

We want to hear something else.

We don't understand what we hear.

Our ears are too dull of hearing.

Our hearts are too hardened to receive.

We cannot predetermine when God may supernaturally guide us through a dream or vision or other encounter. If, however, we are seeking His guidance, we can:

Call Out to God	Jeremiah 33:3 says that if we call out to God, He will answer and show us great and mighty things.
Ask, Seek, Knock	Luke 11:9-10 says that if we ask, we will receive, if we seek, we will find, and if we knock, it will be opened to us.
Fast	Isaiah 58:11 tells us that if we fast properly, God will guide us always.
Delight in the Lord	Psalm 37:4 says that if we delight ourselves in the Lord, He will give us the desires of our heart.
Repent of Sin	Psalm 66:18 says that if we want God to hear us, we are not to pray with sin in our heart.
Believe God	Matthew 21:22 says that if we want to receive, we must believe when we pray.
Pray in Jesus' Name	John 14:13 says we must pray in the name of Jesus, so that He will do what we ask.
Ask According to God's Will	First John 5:14 says we must ask according to God's will and He will hear us.

Ways God Can Guide Us

Read the following scriptures. On the left, write down who received God's guidance. On the right, state what the guidance was and how it was given.

Example:

Through	**Scripture Reference**
Dreams and Visions	*Matthew 2:12*
Mary and Joseph	Through a dream, were told to go home another way
	Acts 16:9-10
Circumstances	*Genesis 24:10-26*
	I Samuel 10:1-16
Prayer	*Acts 13:1-3*
	Acts 12:1-19
	I Samuel 1:1-20
Gifts of the Spirit	*Acts 21:10-11*
	Acts 10:19-20
An Audible Voice	*Numbers 12:1-9*
	Acts 9:1-18

Colossians 3:16-17

Inner Peace of God

If we are in God's will, He promises peace within. See Colossians 3:15; Jeremiah 33:6; and Isaiah 26:3.

SUMMARY

Though they may not have actively been seeking God's guidance, Joseph and Mary were given supernatural guidance from God. God may speak to us in this way as well. However, if we truly want to hear from Him, so that He can guide us not only on special occasions but also in everyday life, we must do certain things — such as fast, pray, and cry out to Him — as we keep our hearts clean and our ears open to His voice. He wants to guide us. We must be open to His leading all the time.

CONSIDER THIS

What are some of the ways you can see God's guidance in your life in the past?

_____

_____

How, and for what, are you seeking His guidance now?

_____

_____

Have either of you ever had a dream or vision (or other supernatural encounter) that you felt was truly a way God was guiding you?

_____

_____

Have you known of any dreams or visions that were not of God? How did you know?

_____

_____

MODERN EXAMPLE

As Elizabeth Sherrill experienced car trouble and pulled off an unfamiliar freeway to find a mechanic who would possibly be on duty in the "wee hours" of a Sunday morning, she recalled how she and her husband, John, had learned the importance of turning to God for direction even in small matters.

What is now a way of life for John and Elizabeth Sherrill, founders of "Guideposts" magazine, began over forty years ago when they interviewed men of great faith in order to write various articles and books. They learned how David Wilkerson, founder of Teen Challenge, sought God for every move as he began his work among the gangs in New York City. They listened to Brother Andrew, of Open Doors Ministry, tell how he prayed for specific guidance and then was supernaturally led to underground churches when going behind the Iron Curtain to deliver Bibles.

Even so, Elizabeth and John had a difficult time believing that God would turn from a world on the brink of war to advise human beings on relatively inconsequential matters. But they had opportunity to put God to the test in when they and their three young children visited East Africa and found themselves constantly in unfamiliar situations. They began to benefit from their prayers for specific guidance, and soon found themselves praying over many decisions — what places to visit, what water was safe to drink, what food to eat, etc. When they returned home, they realized a new dimension of reality had been opened to them. To ask God into moment-by-moment living is to act out the faith that He cares for us intimately, individually.

Did God hear Elizabeth's inquiry for direction concerning her disabled car? Three miles after turning from the ramp off Interstate 80 on that rainy night, she pulled into a lit Shell station where a teenage boy, after a five-second glance under the hood, replaced a broken fan belt. Yes, she had been traveling in the company of the One who knows every road and every traveler, and delights in directing His children's every path!

Lesson 18

Zebedee and Salome

Changing Parental Roles

Until we all reach unity in the faith and in the knowledge of the Son of God and become mature, attaining to the whole measure of the fullness of Christ.

Ephesians 4:13

SETTING THE STAGE

Most obstetricians and hospitals provide prenatal courses for potential parents as they await the birth of a child. The soon-to-be mother and father learn how the baby grows in the womb and what to expect in the process of delivery. When the child is finally born, they receive advice from grandparents, friends, neighbors, and yes, even mere acquaintances!

In the years that follow, a variety of programs are provided parents of the pre-schooler. And, in the elementary school age, teachers and other group leaders give parents further help. During the teen years, parents are afforded all types of information to guide them through these critical times.

Then, all too soon, a special moment arrives which everyone knows is coming, but for which no one is fully prepared — the time when the child leaves the nest of home and family. Perhaps it takes place on the day the child leaves for college, or takes his first job, or gets married or simply moves into an apartment with a friend. Whatever the occasion, the parent-child relationship changes.

While those outside the immediate family probably don't notice, parents are suddenly put into the position of reordering their personal lives, as well as reevaluating their relationship with one another. And, the child finds himself faced with new decisions, new experiences, new relationships — all the while unsure how his parents fit into them. Each family is unique, and it's not always easy to understand the parent-child relationship, especially while it's in transition.

It appears as though Zebedee and Salome came to this particular time in their lives on the day their sons were called, by Jesus, to follow Him. Using them as example, we will now look at the changing parental roles each of us can expect as our children mature and set their own life course.

INTRODUCING ZEBEDEE AND SALOME

(Based on Matthew 4:18-22; 20:20-28; Mark 15:40-41; 16:1-2)

Salome was one of the saintly women who followed Jesus in Galilee and ministered to Him. She appears to have been one of His followers from the beginning of His public ministry, and her devotion continued to the very end of His earthly life.

Zebedee was a fisherman. As was the custom, his sons worked with him in the family trade. This meant that they spent many hours huddled together, sharing close quarters in their fishing boat. Whether in storms at sea, or mending nets on land, they had, no doubt, shared many conversations as they worked long hours day after day.

They were together on the shore when Jesus walked by and called James and John to follow Him. Matthew 4:22 says that they *"immediately left the boat and their father and followed him."* Evidently, Zebedee did not hinder their sudden departure; he simply let them go. We can hope this was because he, too, wanted his sons to follow Jesus. Regardless of his feelings, he suddenly found himself experiencing a major change in the parent-child relationship he had known for many years. And, like most parents, he knew that it would never be the same again.

Salome, however, seemed to have had a little more difficult time letting her sons go. As an ambitious mother, she continued to try to do things for them — even asking Jesus for honored positions in the kingdom for them. Though we hear no more of Zebedee after the day his sons left to go with Jesus, we know that Salome continued to follow the Lord. She was among the women who watched the crucifixion from afar, as well as those who went to the tomb and found that He had risen from the dead. She was later privileged to share her own place of motherhood with Mary, the mother of Jesus. For from the cross, Jesus put Mary into the care of John, Salome's son.

LESSONS FROM ZEBEDEE AND SALOME

The Changing Parental Role

Like Zebedee and Salome, we, as parents, will face a similar dilemma, if we haven't already. How does one let a child go, especially after having been involved so intimately over the years? Each family situation is different, yet parents at this stage need guidance nearly as much as when they brought children into their lives!

Relinquishing parental control and allowing children to become adults with their own value system is no easy process. But God wants us, and our children, to come into full maturity in Him. Maturity in Christ involves change and growth. Note an interesting illustration of this in the lives of James and John. In Mark 3:17, Jesus calls them the "Sons of Thunder." This probably came from the incident when they asked Jesus if they could call down fire from heaven to consume the inhabitants of a Samaritan village that had refused them permission to pass through on the way to Jerusalem (Luke 9:54). Jesus squelched their impetuous request by reminding them that He had come not to destroy, but to save the lost. Years later, as mature men, James and John were willing to suffer persecution. James became the first martyr among the disciples when King Herod Agrippa I had him put to death (Acts 12:2). John underwent much suffering before receiving, in his old age, what we now know as the book of Revelation. Full maturity in Christ should be the true goal of every believer and should also be the highest desire of all Christian parents for their children.

The following verses are guidelines to help us relinquish our children to the care of the Lord, as well as help them come into the full maturity we desire for them in Christ.

Isaiah 54:13 _____

_____

A most important first step is to lay our children upon the altar before God. Abraham and Sarah had to do this literally; we need to do this symbolically, in our hearts, knowing that God has a plan for their lives, because He loves them more than we do.

Proverbs 22:6 _____

_____

Parents who have already made the choice of Joshua 24:15b, *"But as for me and my household, we will serve the Lord,"* will have tried to train their children in the ways and fear of the Lord. God's promise to them is that these children will, ultimately, not depart from the training they have received.

II Timothy 1:5-6 _____

_____

Here we find that Eunice and her mother, Lois, passed on their faith to Timothy as he was being raised in their home. When he later left to work with Paul, the apostle saw that he had been given faith, and admonished him to stir up the gift within him. Sometimes, as we let our children go, others are able to say things to them that the child will never "hear" from us.

Galatians 4:19 (KJV) _____

_____

If our children have not made a personal commitment to the Lord, we travail until that day when Christ is born in them. Then, as they come into that new birth, we travail again until Christ is formed in them. This may take the rest of their lives, and ours!

Job 1:5 _____

_____

Job was a father who took his responsibility seriously, even on behalf of his grown sons who had homes of their own. As priests of our households we, like Job, can continue to cover our children with prayers and intercession — lest they have sinned and cursed God in their hearts.

Job 1:10 _____

_____

We can also wage spiritual warfare for the sake of our children, pleading the blood of Jesus over them and asking God to put a hedge of protection about them. We can continue to remind Satan that we, as believers in the Lord Jesus Christ, have claimed the salvation of our whole household (Acts 16:31). We can bind Satan who blinds the eyes of our loved ones to the truth of God's Word (II Corinthians 4:3-4) .

Parents may also need to deal with guilt and disillusionment when children do not turn out as they had hoped. Even godly parents don't always grasp the ways of the Lord. Manoah and his wife were unhappy when their son, Samson, wanted to marry a Philistine girl. But, Judges 14:4 says *"his parents did not know that this was from the Lord."* God had a purpose beyond their understanding. God will work everything for His good and His purpose, and in His time, if we trust in Him!

Unplanned Parenthood

Many parents who have adult children are facing a phenomenon which was not as common in past generations — that of having to raise their own grandchildren.

The 1990 U.S. Census reported that 4.2 million children under the age of eighteen live in the home of their grandparent. No doubt that number is much higher now. This definitely calls for a change in the lives of senior citizens who, having worked hard to enjoy their retirement years, find they must be involved in school activities, settling childhood disputes, and just coping with stressful schedules without the energy of their youth. Much of the necessity for parenting grandchildren today is due to divorce, drugs, pornography, and the general increase in the number of single parents who cannot make it financially without help in childcare and support in other practical areas.

Care-Givers

Another change in the parental role takes place because people are living longer. This means that "children" in their sixties and seventies are now "parenting" their own parents. The role of caregiver can also become necessary due to lingering illnesses in the elderly — such as Alzheimer's, strokes, and cancer. This definitely changes the lives of everyone involved!

Character Traits

In the changing role of parenting, whether it's learning to let our maturing children go, or resuming the role as parent to our grandchildren, or becoming caregiver to elderly parents, God can work in our lives to develop the character traits He desires. Look over the following list, read the accompanying scriptures, and check the ones you think need to be further worked out in your life. Then, look at the ones you've checked and think about how God might want to use some of the present situations — even your changing parental role — to work these out in your life. (The definitions of these character traits are taken from material developed by Institute in Basic Life Principles, Oak Brook, and Illinois and are used with permission.)

Availability (vs. Self-Centeredness) Adjusting my personal responsibilities around the needs of those whom I am serving. (Philippians 2:20-21)

Alertness (vs. Unawareness) Being aware of the physical and spiritual events taking place around me so that I can have the right responses to them. (Mark 14:38)

Attentiveness (vs. Unconcern) Showing the worth of a person by giving undivided attention to his words and emotions. (Hebrews 2:1)

Compassion (vs. Indifference) Investing whatever is necessary to heal the hurts of others. (I John 3:17-18)

Dependability (vs. Inconsistency) Fulfilling what I consented to do, even if it means unexpected sacrifice. (Psalm 15:4)

Endurance (vs. Giving Up) The inward strength to withstand stress to accomplish God's best. (Galatians 6:9)

Flexibility (vs. Resistance) Learning how to cheerfully change plans when unexpected conditions require it. (Colossians 3:2)

Forgiveness (vs. Rejection) Clearing the record of those who have wronged me and allowing God to love them through me. (Ephesians 4:32)

Gentleness (vs. Harshness) Showing personal care and concern in meeting the needs of others. (I Thessalonians 2:7)

Hospitality (vs. Loneliness) Cheerfully sharing food, shelter, and spiritual refreshment with those God brings into my life. (Hebrews 13:2)

Loyalty (vs. Unfaithfulness) Using difficult times to demonstrate my commitment to God and to those whom He has called me to serve. (John 15:13)

Orderliness (vs. Disorganization) Preparing myself and my surroundings so that I will achieve the greatest efficiency. (I Corinthians 14:40)

Patience (vs. Restlessness) Accepting a difficult situation from God without giving Him a deadline to remove it. (Romans 5:3-4)

Responsibility (vs. Unreliability) Knowing and doing what both God and others are expecting from me. (Romans 14:12)

Sensitivity (vs. Callousness) Knowing by the prompting of God's Spirit what words and actions will benefit the lives of others. (Romans 12:15)

Tolerance (vs. Prejudice) Viewing every person as a valuable individual whom God created and loves. (Philippians 2:2)

SUMMARY

How sad it would have been if Zebedee and Salome had not allowed their sons to leave their childhood home and follow the Lord Jesus Christ! We can rejoice, also, when we let go of our children, putting them into the hands of God, who can complete what He has begun in each of them, so that both we and they can follow Him and come into the full maturity He desires. As our parental role changes, whether due to having to raise grandchildren or becoming caregivers for our own parents, we can, again, try to see from God's perspective what He wants to do. Perhaps it is putting us in situations to form character traits in us that will make us more like Him!

CONSIDER THIS

Have you had to let go of your children? How has this changed your life and theirs?

_____

_____

What can you do, as parents, to prepare your children for their future independence?

_____

_____

How can you prepare yourselves for the time when all your children will have left the nest?

_____

_____

How can you relate to your grown children as individuals?

_____

_____

If you are having to raise your grandchildren, or be caregivers to your parents, do you see anything God is trying to do in your life through this experience? If so, what?

_____

_____

MODERN EXAMPLE

Many churches and individuals participate in Operation Christmas Child, a program through which shoe boxes filled with gifts are distributed at Christmas time. These gifts are sent to hurting children in refugee camps and other poverty stricken places around the world. The president of Samaritan's Purse, the organization which sponsors this program, is Franklin Graham, son of Billy and Ruth Graham.

Many people everywhere have been blessed as Franklin has been faithful in attending to physical needs of the world, while also helping his father in his ministry of evangelism to meet people's spiritual needs.

Yet, Franklin has lived the life of a rebel, obvious even from the title of his autobiography, _Rebel With a Cause_. In this, he tells of various tactics his parents used to discipline him throughout his youth and young adult years — and of how their parental role had to change when, after having three girls, they became parents of two wayward-prone sons. Though they tried everything from putting him in a boarding school under strict discipline to allowing him freedom to investigate various places around the world, they never preached to him — even about his drinking smoking and long hair, because they knew the Lord would have to deal with him on these things.

Ruth and Billy's prayers, patience and relinquishment finally paid off, as they allowed God to parent Franklin and bring their prodigal home. After various episodes of moving out and then returning to the family home, his turning point came in the summer of 1974 in Switzerland. After lunch to celebrate his birthday, Billy took Franklin for a walk during which he confronted him by saying, "Franklin, your mother and I sense there's a struggle going on in your life. You're going to have to make a choice either to accept Christ or reject him. You can't continue you play the middle ground....We love you no matter what you do in life, and no matter where you go. The door of our home is always open, and you're always welcome. But you're going to have to make a choice." Franklin says that, despite the most beautiful and inspiring scenery in the world, and being near the man he loved and wanted to please the most, he felt joyless, empty, lonely and dirty.

Several weeks later, through some God-ordained circumstances, Franklin committed his life to the Lord (and threw away the last of his cigarettes) while alone in a hotel room in Jerusalem.

God had been faithful to his parents' prayers as they had allowed God to adjust their parental role for His use and His glory!

Lesson 19

Jairus and His Wife

Accepting God's Perfect Timing

Do not throw away your confidence; it will be richly rewarded. You need to persevere so that when you have done the will of God, you will receive what he has promised. For in just a very little while, He who is coming will come and will not delay.

Hebrews 10:35-37

SETTING THE STAGE

Jairus and his wife seem to have a unique place in the Word of God. They are the only named couple who, together received ministry from Jesus. Their daughter was dying and Jairus, a ruler in the synagogue, had heard that Jesus had come to his town. He had heard the reports that Jesus had done many miracles, including healing people. Desperate for a healing miracle, Jairus ran to find Jesus to urge Him to come to his home where his daughter lay near death. But, not only was Jesus busy with the crowd surrounding Him, a woman who had been ill for many years delayed Him as He made His was to Jairus' house. So while Jairus waited, he received word that his daughter had died. He probably thought that, for sure, it was too late now for a healing. And, if Jairus was like us, no doubt he decided that Jesus had missed it this time. In this lesson, we'll look at others in Scripture who experienced "divine delays," and we'll see how God's timing is always perfect.

INTRODUCING JAIRUS AND HIS WIFE

(Based on Mark 5:21-43)

Jairus was a ruler of the synagogue, a man of worldly, as well as religious, status. As a group, the Jewish leaders were hostile to the claims of Jesus Christ. Some even accused Jesus of having a devil because He didn't fit their ideas of obeying the law relating to the Sabbath, hand-washing, associating with sinners, etc. For these reasons, it took great moral courage for any Jewish ruler to approach Jesus with a need. Yet, in desperation, Jairus was willing to do just that because his daughter was dying.

Thus it was, when Jesus' boat arrived on the Galilean shore that day and a large crowd gathered, Jairus, willing to risk his own position, made his way through the mass of people until he fell at Jesus' feet, and implored Him to come to his house where his daughter lay dying. As Jesus started to follow, He stopped, for He felt healing virtue leave His body. He turned to see a frightened woman lying prostrate at His feet. She had wanted a touch from Jesus, for she had suffered hemorrhaging for twelve years and the doctors had given up on her. Jairus, no doubt happy to see the woman healed, was worried that this delay might mean that it would be too late for his daughter's healing. His fears were confirmed when one of his servants ran up to him with the news that she had already died.

After what seemed like an eternity, Jairus, Jesus, and His disciples — Peter, James and John — finally reached the bedside of the little girl. Here they found not only Jairus' wife, but also many mourners who had come to wail and lament over the child's death. Jesus asked the mourners to leave the room and, in the presence of the girl's parents and the disciples, He took the twelve-year-old by the hand and simply said, *"Little girl, I say to you, get up!"* (Mark 5:4b). Immediately, she got up and walked around the room, while Jesus told her parents to get her something to eat. What praise and thanksgiving Jairus and his wife must have experienced as they witnessed the resurrection of their little daughter!

LESSONS FROM JAIRUS AND HIS WIFE

Divine Delays

We live in an instant society — fast foods, microwaves, the Internet, pagers, minute-by-minute TV news coverage, etc. We don't like to wait for anything, even in spiritual matters. We complain because it seems as though God is never going to answer our prayers concerning a spouse's lingering illness, a child's deliverance from drugs, or salvation for our friends.

The story of Jairus and his wife, and what seemed like an untimely delay, is only one of many incidents in Scripture where a lapse occurred between the request or promise and its fulfillment. The story of Jesus raising Lazarus from the dead is another example. Jesus seemed to have purposely delayed in responding to the sisters' request to come and heal their brother, until Lazarus had been dead for four days! Yet, when He asked them to roll the stone away from the tomb, Jesus said (in John 11:40), *"did I not tell you that if you believed, you would see the glory of God?"* Once again, the result of Jesus' delay was that God's glory might be more fully realized!

The whole episode of the children of Israel wandering in the wilderness must have seemed like one big forty-year delay! But, Deuteronomy 8:2 says that God used this experience to humble and prove them and to know what was in their hearts. It was a time of testing to see if they would continue to believe Him when it appeared that He had forsaken them.

Sometimes a delay has nothing to do with our faith or our readiness to receive an answer to prayer. Instead, there may be a spiritual battle in the heavenlies, such as in the case of Daniel, who experienced a twenty-one-day delay in answer to his prayer because the prince of Persia was standing in the way (Daniel 10:12-14). Perhaps we must take a stand against Satan and his hosts before God can fulfill His Word.

Thus, answers to our prayers may be delayed for several reasons. Perhaps God wants to bring about a greater revelation of His glory. Perhaps He is using the delay to test us in our faith. Perhaps the delay is an opportunity for us to wage spiritual warfare against the enemy. Only God knows; but His timing is perfect.

God's Ways Are Not Man's Ways

Moses was not always the leader of the Israelites. David was not always the king of Israel. Matthew was not always a disciple of Jesus Christ. They, and others, had no idea of how God was going to use them, how He would get them from where they were to where He wanted them to be, or how long the process would take. Neither they, nor we, know what all God is doing, especially when, according to our timing, He seems to be late.

If we knew God's timing, we would probably get ourselves to where we thought He wanted us to be at a specific time. But His thoughts are not our thoughts, nor are our ways His ways, according to Isaiah 55:8. To see this in the lives of some major Bible characters, look up the scriptures below and write where each of the individuals were when God called them. Then, write down what God called them to do.

Character	*Place*	*Ministry*
Joseph (Genesis 41:14, 39-43)		
Moses (Exodus 3:1-5, 10-12)		
Gideon (Judges 6:11-16)		
King Saul (I Samuel 9:1-3, 6, 13-17)		
Elijah (I Kings 17:1-9, 22-24)		
Peter and Andrew (Matthew 4:18-20)		
James and John (Matthew 4:21-22)		
Matthew (Matthew 9:9)		
Paul (Acts 9:1-16)		

People Who Waited for God's Perfect Timing

We think of many Biblical couples who had no children because the wife was barren until the time that God was ready to open her womb. Abraham and Sarah, Isaac and Rebekah, Jacob and Rachel, Manoah and his wife, Elkanah and Hannah, Zechariah and Elizabeth — none understood why they could not conceive. Yet, God, in His perfect timing, had special plans for Isaac, Jacob, Joseph, Samson, Samuel and John the Baptist!

After reading the appropriate scripture, write down what the following people were waiting for:

Joseph of Arimathea (Mark 15:43)

Anna (Luke 2:38)

_____

Elizabeth (Luke 1:24)

_____

Joseph (Matthew 1:20-21)

_____

Zechariah (Luke 1:20)

_____

Paul (Acts 17:16-17)

_____

Ezekiel (Ezekiel 3:22-27)

_____

Waiting For Jesus to Come Again

As Believers in Jesus Christ, we are given instructions in the Bible as to what we are to do as we wait for His Second Coming:

- Eagerly wait for Jesus to be revealed. (I Corinthians 1:7)
- Look for that blessed hope and glorious appearing of our great God and Savior, Jesus Christ. (Titus 2:13)
- Watch and be ready — for we don't know at what hour He will come. (Matthew 24:42-51)
- Long for His appearing. (II Timothy 4:8)
- Take heed of our conduct, watch and pray. (Luke 21:34-36)
- Not give up on meeting together, rather encourage one another. (Hebrews 10:25)
- Pray, love one another, be hospitable, minister grace, be faithful stewards, rejoice even in suffering, commit our souls to God, be prepared for the judgment of the church. (I Peter 4:7-19)
- Understand that there will be many scoffers in the last days who will continue to do evil. (II Peter 3:3-7)
- Continue in Him so that we will not be ashamed before Him. (I John 2:28)
- Refrain from judging others. (I Corinthians 4:5)
- Proclaim the Lord's death as we partake of communion. (I Corinthians 11:26)
- Relate to one another in love and allow God to strengthen our hearts. (I Thessalonians 3:12-13)
- Preach the Word, be committed to ministry. (II Timothy 4:1-2)
- Be patient and remain steadfast. (James 5:8)
- Keep ourselves in God's mercy and be merciful to others. Also, "snatch others from the fire." (Jude 21-22)

SUMMARY

We may not understand divine delays in our life. Surely Jairus and his wife didn't understand why Jesus delayed in coming to minister to their daughter. But, from other examples in scripture, we can be assured that God has His reasons for delays. Thus, we can heed the instructions, given in scripture, until He fulfills His Word — even to the timing of His Second Coming!

CONSIDER THIS

What can you do to maintain trust in God when you, seemingly, receive no answer to your prayers?

_____

_____

Can you recall incidents in your life when a divine delay resulted in your benefit or gave God special glory?

_____

_____

How are you using the time now as we wait for Jesus' Second Coming to earth?

_____

_____

MODERN EXAMPLE

Julie and I met at an interdenominational Christian women's breakfast. Almost immediately, we discovered that we had two things in common: we had been married in the same city in Southern California, and neither of us were sure why we were now lining in a small town on the central coast. The jobs each of our husbands had come for had not worked out, even though both had felt God had led them here for specific positions of ministry. And so, we were questioning "Why?" and "What do we do now?"

The four of us began getting together, and before long we were meeting nearly every Sunday afternoon to talk, to pray, to share a meal. During these visits, our friendship grew, as we also became better acquainted with each other's families. We can recall serious conversations as we shared experiences and hurts in ministry, and then prayed for one another. We can also recall both laughing and crying at some of the temporary jobs the men found. Don, who is an ordained minister, dug graves at the local cemetery. And Wayne, a Christian school administrator, drove the garbage truck from the state fair grounds to the city dump.

In time, Wayne began teaching in the public schools, and then in the educational program of the California Youth Authority. He and Julie began home-educating their own children and were excited when a door opened for them to take over a small Christian home education program. In the years since, they have developed this into a large covering organization for about eighty home-schooling families in our area.

Meanwhile, Don worked at some secular jobs while meeting regularly with a group of pastors for prayer and involvement in various interchurch programs. When, during a bad winter, they were inundated with requests for food, shelter, etc., they asked Don to formulate a plan to minister to these needs on a city-wide, interchurch basis. Thus, he became founding director for Loaves and Fishes, a ministry which has subsequently served thousands of homeless, transients, and those experiencing emergency needs of all kinds.

Why did God take a while in answering our prayers? *Now* we can see some of the reasons He may have had for His "divine delay." He would be using both men to pioneer new ministries, and they needed to become acquainted with, and gain the respect of, leaders in the various churches and community, since they would be serving the whole Body of Christ in this area. God would also be teaching patience and trust in Him and His Word when He seemed to be silent — character traits needed in the work they would be doing. No, God's timing was not ours. He had a bigger plan than either of us ever imagined!

Lesson 20

Herod and Herodias Samson and Delilah

Avoiding Unlawful Relationships

> *It is good for a man not to marry. But since there is so much immorality, each man should have his own wife, and each woman her own husband.*
>
> I Corinthians 7:1b-2

SETTING THE STAGE

We now look at unlawful relationships that are so prevalent today. To do this, we will study two couples in the Bible whose relationships were unlawful. Though both relationships could also be considered adultery, we'll look at them from the standpoint of other kinds of unlawful relationships.

The relationship of Herod and Herodias was considered a type of incest, because Herodias had been married to Herod's brother, Philip. Though Samson and Delilah are often thought of as a couple, scripture only says that he fell in love with her. He already had a wife, according to Judges 15:1.

As we have noted throughout this Bible study, marriage is a divine institution. In the beginning, God sanctioned monogamy. He desired husbands and wives to covenant with each other and with Him so that He could fulfill His purpose in the marriage relationship — to give man a companion with whom he could share his life, just as He has destined the Bride of Christ to reign with His Son, Jesus.

As civilization developed and sin increased, man perverted the ideal marriage relationship by marrying more than one woman at a time. By the time of Noah, man had become so full of lawlessness that he found himself in all kinds of illicit relationships. Because of this, God chose to destroy all the inhabitants of the earth except Noah and his family.

Even after this, polygamy returned, though God still did not approve of it. He reminded the people of this in the Mosaic Law (Leviticus 20:10). The Old Testament contains many stories of multi-marriage relationships and the problems that come with them. By the time of the New Testament, monogamy had returned as the more accepted norm, and Jesus reinforced it as ideal. Through the ensuing gift of the Holy Spirit, man has been given the means to be faithful to the monogamous marriage covenant if he so desires.

INTRODUCING HEROD AND HERODIAS

(Based on Matthew 14:1-12)

We first hear of Herod and Herodias' unlawful relationship in Matthew 14:1-4, when John the Baptist accused Herod of being unlawfully married to the wife of his own brother.

This confrontation led to imprisonment for John; and Herodias later saw to it that he was beheaded.

Other sources tell us that Herodias, the granddaughter of Herod the Great, had first been married to Herod's brother, Philip. During one of Herod's visits to Rome, he was entertained by his brother and sister-in-law. He became enamored with Herodias and abducted her, then divorced his own wife.

Herodias was probably afraid to have Herod listen too closely to John's preaching for fear he would repent and she would lose her position as queen. This couple chose not to heed John's message, and they continued to live together unlawfully. Eventually, Herod was banished from rule, and he and Herodias ended their days in shame and exile.

INTRODUCING SAMSON AND DELILAH
(Based on Judges 16:1-22)

Samson is commonly associated with Delilah, but we are never told that they were married. In fact, we know that Samson had previously married a woman of Timnath. We also know he had also slept with a prostitute in Gaza. His relationship with Delilah seems to have been for personal gain. She used him for financial reasons; he used her for sexual satisfaction. As we know from their story, found in Judges 16:4-31, not only did their relationship come to an end, Samson's life ended tragically because of Delilah's betrayal.

Many "Samsons and Delilahs" live together today simply for the advantages they each receive, not because of real commitment. This is increasingly true for the elderly who want companionship, but cannot afford to let their Social Security income be altered. Some people enter a relationship for financial gain, others for sexual satisfaction, for physical protection, or to give their children surrogate parents. There is no true love, no commitment, no fear of God or His Word; and, when the relationship has accomplished its purpose, each person moves on to other relationships hoping, sometime, to find fulfillment for his or her own lusts. Of more consequence today, many people suffer from AIDS and other sexually-transmitted diseases. It is as if God allows a plague to come upon those who disobey His laws.

LESSONS FROM HEROD AND HERODIAS
SAMSON AND DELILAH

Unlawful Sexual Relationships

Read the following scriptures under the various headings. First, write down what the verse(s) says. Then, at the end of each section, summarize what you find God saying in His Word about that subject.

Adultery (Sexual unfaithfulness of a married person)

Exodus 20:14 _____

_____

Matthew 5:28 _____

_____

Mark 10:12 _____

_____

Numbers 5:20-27 _____

_____

Deuteronomy 22:22-24 _____

_____

Proverbs 6:32 _____

_____

I Corinthians 6:9-10 _____

_____

Hebrews 13:4 _____

_____

Summarize _____

_____

_____

_____

_____

_____

_____

_____

Fornication (Sexual intercourse outside of marriage)

Deuteronomy 22:20-22 _____

_____

Acts 15:20 _____

_____

I Corinthians 6:13 _____

_____

Ephesians 5:3 _____

_____

I Thessalonians 4:3 _____

_____

Summarize _____

_____

_____

_____

_____

_____

Incest (Sexual relations between persons so closely related that marriage is illegal)

Deuteronomy 22:30 _____

_____

Leviticus 18:6-18 _____

_____

_____

_____

_____

I Corinthians 5:1 _____

_____

Summarize _____

_____

_____

_____

_____

_____

_____

Homosexuality (Sexual relationship between members of the same sex)

Leviticus 18:22 _____

_____

I Corinthians 6:9-10 _____

_____

Romans 1:26-28 _____

_____

Leviticus 20:13 _____

_____

Summarize _____

_____

_____

_____

_____

_____

_____

SUMMARY

Unlawful relationships make for many difficulties — both in the relationship with one another, and in one's relationship with God. They are contrary to His plan. The sin brings with it many consequences, not only for the couple involved, but also for all with whom the couple is associated, including their children.

The two couples in this lesson — Herod and Herodias and Samson and Delilah — found that their unlawful relationships brought neither all the happiness they expected, nor the approval of God.

God, in His enduring mercy, still offers the message of repentance. If man recognizes his sin, repents of it and confesses it, God will forgive him. He can become a new creature in Christ.

Long ago, Israel, the wife of Jehovah, found herself in unlawful relationships with other nations. God sent Hosea to speak to His people. These words of God can also be His words to those who now find themselves living in unlawful relationships:

Come, let us return to the Lord. He has torn us to pieces but he will heal us; he has injured us but he will bind up our wounds. After two days he will revive us; on the third day he will restore us, that we may live in his presence.

Hosea 6:1, 20

CONSIDER THIS

Is there some past unlawful relationship that either of you need to repent of to God, so that you can have His forgiveness and a clear conscience?

_____

_____

Do you use your spouse for your personal gain, even in your lawful marriage?

_____

_____

What have you observed to be the consequences of unlawful relationships?

_____

_____

What can you do to help friends or family members, who are living together unlawfully, to see what God's Word says?

_____

_____

MODERN EXAMPLE

When I was in high school, many years ago, a close friend of mine became pregnant through a relationship with her boyfriend. As soon as the discovery was made, she had to drop out of school and out of public view, because it was a disgrace to her family.

Today, as I reflect upon the many "unlawful relationships" with which I am acquainted, I am amazed — not only at the number, but at the variety. And all are taken for granted in the society in which we now live. Some of these include:

- a young couple in the neighborhood, who have been living together and recently got married, just four months before their baby is due

- a single man, also a neighbor, who frequently has his girlfriend in to spend the night or weekend

- a man down the street, who is a homosexual

- older friends of ours, who are living together because if they were legally married they would jeopardize their social security benefits

- a significant number of friends our age, who are surrogate parents for their grandchildren because their own sons/daughters had children out of wedlock and are now finding it tough to be financing single parenthood

- an out-of-state friend, who calls upset because her daughter is moving in with her boyfriend in another city, where both are in college

- a dear friend, whom I've been trying to comfort since she received word that her nephew Larry is now Laura, due to a sex-change operation

- a local church, as we've watched it go through the trauma of letting a well-liked, talented pastor go, because he admitted to an adulterous affair with one of the members

And, I am only one person. How many "unlawful relationships" can you name?

Pilate and His Wife
Ananias and Sapphira

Doing What Is Right

> *The cowardly, the unbelieving, the vile, the murderers, the sexually immoral,*
> *those who practice magic arts, the idolaters and all liars...their place will*
> *be in the fiery lake of burning sulfur. This is the second death.*
>
> Revelation 21:8

SETTING THE STAGE

The verse quoted above is one of the most awesome verses in Scripture. In it we discover the fate of murderers, and those who practice magic arts, and people who are simply cowards or liars. They will have their place in the final death, the eternal lake of fire!

Pilate was a coward who refused to heed his wife's warning because he feared the crowd that wanted to put Jesus to death. Ananias and Sapphira were a couple who twisted the truth and were struck dead because they lied to the Holy Spirit and to Peter. If this lesson does nothing else, it should put the fear of God in us as to how seriously He deals with unrepentant sin.

INTRODUCING PILATE AND HIS WIFE
(Based on Matthew 27:1-2,11-26; Luke 3:1a; John 18:28-19:22)

Scripture does not tell us what happened to Pilate and his wife after that fateful day when he delivered Jesus into the hands of the Jews to be crucified. In John 19:20-21, we read that Pilate had words inscribed on the cross, declaring: *"Jesus of Nazareth, the King of the Jews."* Perhaps it was his way of continuing to ease his conscience, just as he had attempted to do when he washed his hands in front of the crowd. The historian Eusebius tells us that after several years of depression and despair, Pilate took his own life.

Most of the Governors would have dreaded this dry, barren outpost, but Pilate had found delight in tormenting the Jews. Josephus tells us that he hung golden shields inscribed with the names and images of Roman deities in the temple itself. Once, he appropriated some of the temple tax to build an aqueduct. Luke 13:1 mentions the horrible incident concerning the *"Galileans whose blood Pilate had mingled with their sacrifice,"* recalling the time when Roman soldiers slew some of the men who were making sacrifices in the Holy Place. Pilate had often antagonized the Jews, who no doubt then complained to Rome. Perhaps because of this, Pilate didn't want to incite the wrath of the Jews any further at Jesus' trial.

He might have been fearful as to what they might report to Caesar, as well as what they might do to him if he didn't give them what they wanted. His reputation and position were at stake, and since Jesus didn't try to defend Himself, it was just easier to let the Jews have Him. Even his wife's appeal didn't sway his decision. She had had a dream, which had led her to warn Pilate not to have anything to do with Jesus. But, Pilate feared the crowd more than his wife's message and he allowed Barabbas — rebel, murderer, and robber — to live, and Jesus to die.

LESSONS FROM PILATE AND HIS WIFE

The Problem of Cowardice

Cowardice is the opposite of boldness, courage, and fearlessness by which people are willing to stand, even when it requires personal sacrifice. Cowards are fearful and unbelieving. They aren't able to trust God, because they fear men.

Abraham

In Genesis 12:10-20, Abraham evidenced cowardliness when he was driven to Egypt by a famine and told everyone that Sarah was his sister instead of his wife. He did this because

_____

_____

Aaron

In Exodus 32:22-24, Aaron showed signs of cowardice when Moses questioned him as to who had made the golden calf for the people to worship. Why was Aaron afraid to admit his part when he said to Moses: *"So I told them, whoever has any gold jewelry, take it off. Then they gave me the gold, and I threw it into the fire and out came this calf!"*

_____

_____

Caleb and Joshua

In Numbers 13:17-33, Caleb and Joshua were the only ones who came back from spying out the promised land and encouraged Moses to take the people into it. Who were afraid to do this? Why?

_____

_____

_____

The Parents of the Blind Man

In John 9:22, the parents of the blind man evidenced cowardice when they refused to say how their son was healed, because they

_____

_____

Read the following scriptures and write down what they say about being bold, fearless, confident, and courageous.

Proverbs 28:1

_____

_____

Ephesians 6:19

_____

_____

Acts 9:27-28

_____

_____

Philippians 1:14

_____

_____

Hebrews 4:16

_____

_____

I John 4:17-18

_____

_____

Now, write down how you believe you can become bold, fearless, and confident instead of being a coward. _____

_____

_____

INTRODUCING ANANIAS AND SAPPHIRA

(Based on Acts 4:32-5:11)

We find the account of Ananias and Sapphira in the first part of Acts, as the story of the early church unfolds. Jesus had already risen from the grave and ascended to Heaven to be seated at the right hand of the Father. Following the outpouring of the Holy Spirit fifty days later at Pentecost, believers were filled with new faith and power, as well as a new expectancy for the soon return of Jesus. Peter had new boldness as he preached to thousands of people. The Lord added many daily to the church. New converts were hungry for the Word and needed discipling. Believers, new and old, worshipped in the temple, and fellowshipped from house to house.

Because of the heightened reality of God's love and power, believers experienced a unity and concern for one another and began sharing all things. Those who owned land or houses sold them and brought their money to the apostles who, in turn, distributed it according to each person's need. In this way, no one lacked for any provision, and those who couldn't work, because of their involvement in ministry, had their needs met as well.

Ananias and Sapphira, however, secretly agreed to withhold some of the profit from the sale of their property, and pretended to give the whole sum of it to the apostles. Through a word of knowledge, Peter confronted Ananias about this deception when Ananias brought him the money. Upon hearing Peter's words, Ananias fell to the ground and died. Three hours later, Sapphira came in, not knowing what had happened. When Peter questioned her about the price they had received for the land, she also lied — and dropped dead immediately.

Great fear came upon the entire church when they saw the swift judgment that came to this couple, who without repenting, suffered immediate consequences for inventing and acting upon a lie.

LESSONS FROM ANANIAS AND SAPPHIRA

Lying

Scripture does not say why Ananias and Sapphira allowed themselves to be deceived. We only know that when they lied, God brought their sin to light, and swift judgment fell. They had fallen into Satan's trap and had to pay the consequences.

Many people tell lies — including "white" ones — and seemingly, get away with it. But what is God's attitude toward those who lie? What punishment does He have for all liars?

God's Attitude Toward Lying

Proverbs 6:16-19 _____

_____

_____

Ezekiel 13:8-16 _____

_____

Psalm 101:7 _____

_____

God's Punishment for Liars

Proverbs 19:5 _____

_____

Psalm 63:11 _____

_____

Psalm 31:18 _____

_____

Revelation 21:8-27 _____

_____

How Do We Keep From Being Deceived?

It's scary to think of the judgment received by Pilate and his wife for allowing cowardice to rule in their lives, and for Ananias and Sapphira who were immediately struck down when it was discovered that they had lied.

And well it should be, for the day of judgment is approaching when each person will give account of himself to God. Equally frightening is the fact that we are living in the end of the church age, when Satan, in all his fury, will be out to deceive even the elect. With so many people actively pursuing the supernatural and seeking answers to life's basic questions, false teachers and cults are increasing every day.

- John 5:22 says *"the Father judges no one, but has entrusted all judgment to the Son, that all may honor the son just as they honor the Father."*
  The Father has given "judgment" to His Son. His Son has given "judgment" to His Word.
- John 12:48 says *"there is a judge for the one who rejects me and does not accept my words, that very word which I spoke will condemn him at the last day."*
  Judgment will take place before the Son, according to what one has done with His Word.
- Romans 14:10b says *"for we shall all stand before the judgment seat of Christ."* (KJV)
  God has provided judgment — either now or later — for both believers and nonbelievers, and it is all according to His Word.

How can God's judgment take place in our lives now, so that we can repent while we have time?

_____

_____

Meditate upon the following verses and answer the questions concerning God's Word, His Truth.

Joshua 1:8   Do you read it, study it, meditate upon it, do it?

Psalm 119:11   Have you hid it in your heart, so that you won't sin against God?

Ephesians 5:26   Are you allowing Jesus to cleanse and sanctify you by the daily washing of water by the Word?

Psalm 107:20   Are you letting God's Word heal and rescue you from the grave?

Romans 10:17   Are you allowing the Word of God to produce faith in you?

II Timothy 3:16   Are you giving God's Word the chance to reprove you, correct you, and instruct you…even by others who know and understand His Word and share it with you?

Hebrews 4:12   Do you use it as a sword, so that it may divide asunder the soul and spirit and be a discerner of the thoughts and intents of your heart — so you can discern what is of God and what is of Satan?

I John 4:1-6   Do you test the spirits, which must be in accordance with God's Word?

SUMMARY

All cowards and liars will pay severe consequences for unrepentant sin. Pilate and his wife did, even while they lived. Ananias and Sapphira received immediate judgment. God does give us instruction in how not to become deceived. It comes from being so immersed in His Word, that it becomes such a part of our lives it becomes *life* to us. Then, we will live in God's strength, courage, boldness, fearlessness, and righteousness…and we won't need to fear man! Nor, eventually, pay the penalty of the second death.

CONSIDER THIS

Have you feared what people might think of you as individuals, as a couple, as a family? If so, why?

_____

_____

Have you ever been deceived? If so, how did it happen?

_____

_____

How are you allowing the Word of God to judge you now?

_____

_____

Do you know someone who has been deceived? Is there any way you can share the truth with them?

_____

_____

MODERN EXAMPLE

Friends had invited Marge and Frank to attend their church. They had enjoyed the Sunday morning worship service and attended a few special programs at other times as well. They had not, as yet, become involved in any of the several Bible Studies, which the church offered.

After only a few weeks, Frank suddenly died of a heart attack and Marge, not having been a part of any other church, called the pastor to ask him to have the funeral. When she went to meet with him to make the arrangements, she asked if the Masons could have a part in the service, since Frank belonged to the local Masonic Order and she, to the Eastern Star.

At first, the Pastor suggested that she have the Masons do the entire service. After some discussion, he agreed to have the actual funeral service, and the Masons would be in charge of the internment at the graveside.

When she asked the why they couldn't do this together, he explained that he believed there are many things in the Masonic beliefs and practices that are contrary to Christian beliefs and practices. He didn't see them compatible at all, even though Masons use spiritual terms and many Christians belong to their organization. The pastor went on to tell her that Albert Pike, author of *Morals and Dogma* (the "bible" of Freemasonry) believed that Christianity is just one religion among many equally good ones. The pastor believed it was his duty to remind people that Acts 4:12 says that *"salvation is found in no one else, for there is no other name under heaven given to men by which we must be saved."* And this name is *Jesus*.

The pastor agreed with her that many Christians are part of the Masons; even that sixteen of our Presidents have been Masons. And, that Masons do many good works. He just believed that people have been deceived into thinking Christianity and Freemasonry are compatible.

Marge agreed to the compromise and found support of friends in both groups. But after things began to settle down once again, she began a search to discover the truth, asking questions of both the pastor and friends in the Masonic Order, as well as doing her own private research. She had to know whether or not she had truly been deceived. She didn't want to live a lie, and then have to pay the consequences.

Lesson 22

Aquila and Priscilla

Serving the Lord Together

I planted the seed, Apollos watered it, but God made it grow. So neither he who plants nor he who waters is anything, but only God, who makes things grow. The man who plants and the man who waters have one purpose, and each will be rewarded according to his own labor. For we are God's fellow workers.

I Corinthians 3:6-9a

SETTING THE STAGE

Many of the cults so prevalent today deceive people into believing that it is necessary to do certain works in order to be saved. Our human nature responds to these demands because we like to think that we can earn acceptance in this life. That's why the busiest worker in the church is often considered to be the most devout Christian!

The relationship between our faith and our works is clearly described in James 2:14-25. Here we find that it is *after* we have been saved by faith in Christ and *because* of His mercy toward us, that we will want to show Him our gratefulness and love by doing His works. This is reaffirmed in Ephesians 2:10, which says *"we are God's workmanship, created in Christ Jesus to do good works, which God prepared in advance for us to do."*

After looking at Aquila and Priscilla, a couple who faithfully served the Lord in working with the Apostle Paul, we will see how each scriptural passage about them reveals one of the types of crowns which may be received by those who do God's work.

INTRODUCING AQUILA AND PRISCILLA

(Based on I Corinthians 16:19; Romans 16:3-5a; Acts 18:18-28; II Timothy 4:19)

Aquila and Priscilla were contemporaries and friends of the Apostle Paul. They were Jews, probably expelled from Rome by the Emperor Claudius. They had moved to Corinth, where Paul met and worked with them in the trade of tent making. Not only did they work together in a practical way to earn a living, no doubt they also shared much about the Lord and His Word as they spent many hours together in this trade. We know that this couple often followed Paul on his missionary journeys, helping in the ministry of the early church. They worked well as a husband and wife team, as they shared in ministry with Paul as fellow-laborers together with God. In scripture, one is never named without the other…and their names are interchangeable. Thus, they have always been known as a couple; one does not dominate the other.

Priscilla and Aquila took their oversight of the flock seriously enough to want to feed them the whole truth; but they were also concerned about other teachers, wanting them

151

to teach the full counsel of God. One of these teachers was Apollos, an eloquent speaker who seemed to be lacking in some knowledge of God's way. Aquila and Priscilla took him aside, in a kind and loving way, and explained some doctrine to him. They encouraged and supported church leaders. They were laborers with others in the work of the Lord.

Priscilla and Aquila didn't always remain in Corinth, but their home was open to others wherever they lived — whether in Corinth or Ephesus (Acts 18:18-22) or in Rome (Romans 16:3-5). They had a long continuing relationship with Paul; the greetings he sent them covered at least sixteen years — from the time he met them in Corinth to the time he wrote them from prison in Rome. Paul even sent them greetings in the last hours of his life. He wrote, in II Timothy 4:19, *"Greet Priscilla and Aquila and the household of Onesiphorus."* This couple, who worked well together, also helped and encouraged Paul in his ministry by serving the Lord with him.

LESSONS FROM AQUILA AND PRISCILLA

Aquila and Priscilla as Co-Laborers With God

Read the following scriptures, and write how Priscilla and Aquila served God as they lived out their commitment to Him.

Commitment to God's work — I Corinthians 16:19

_____

_____

Commitment to God's truth — Acts 18:26

_____

_____

Commitment to God's servants — Romans 16:3-4

_____

_____

Commitment to each other— Acts 18:2-3

_____

_____

Ways We Can Serve the Lord Together

From their story, we can see some of the ways Aquila and Priscilla served the Lord together:

Hospitality…hosting churches in their home

Teaching…giving correct doctrine to Apollos

Assisting leaders…even risking their lives for Paul

Earning a living together…so they could be free to minister

Growing together in the Word…as they shared in Bible study with Paul

Other possible ways couples can serve together in ministry:

Teaching a Sunday school class or weekly Bible study

Visiting the elderly, homebound, or the hospitalized

Leading youth groups

Volunteering for various para-church groups, i.e. ministry to the poor, prisoners, etc.

Working in the church nursery

Being part of music in a worship team

Evangelizing through visitation, street ministry, etc.

Leading or assisting in camps, retreats, seminars

Discipling other couples, families

Entertaining individuals and groups at home

Other _____

Crowns as Rewards

First Corinthians 3:13-15 tells us that we will have different kinds of works to be judged by God. The "wood, hay and stubble" will be consumed by fire. The works considered "gold, silver and precious stones" will be put through the fire also, but they will survive intact. And, as for the works that endure, rewards will be given. Scripture refers to these rewards as "crowns." Let's look at some of these "crowns" and see how the works of Aquila and Priscilla qualify for some of them.

The Crown of Life

Write James 1:12.

_____

_____

_____

From Acts 18:2, we can assume that Aquila and Priscilla had experienced some trials because of their love of God. They were Jews who had been deported from Rome and had come to live in Corinth. Separated from their homeland, they were recognized by Paul, for their continuing commitment and courage, when he wrote in Romans 16:3-4, *"Greet Priscilla and Aquila, my fellow-workers in Christ Jesus. They risked their lives for me. Not only I, but all the churches of the Gentiles are grateful to them."* They were willing to give up the luxury of a home so they could travel and minister with Paul. The Crown of Life is given to those who are willing to endure such trials.

An Everlasting Crown

Write I Corinthians 9:25.

_____

_____

_____

The incorruptible crown (or everlasting crown) is given to the man who has brought his body under subjection so that he can be fully committed to Christ. In order to obtain such discipline, we must find our strength in the Lord, and place our all on the altar before God. We cannot be a spiritual spectator in the game of life. Paul calls Aquila and Priscilla his helpers in Christ Jesus. We know that to earn this title, they had to deny their flesh. There would have been no room for self-indulgence and laziness in working with Paul!

The Crown of Rejoicing

Write I Thessalonians 2:19-20. (See KJV.)

_____

_____

_____

_____

The greatest joy is to bring another person into the knowledge of Jesus as Savior and Lord. First Corinthians 16:19 tells us that a church met in the home of Priscilla and Aquila. In Romans 16:3-4, Paul also refers to the church in their home. Those who hosted the "house churches" were, no doubt, involved in bringing souls to Christ.

The Crown of Righteousness

Write II Timothy 4:6-8.

_____

_____

_____

_____

This crown is given to those who are sanctified, prepared as a Bride without spot or blemish. Paul wrote two letters to his young protègè, Timothy, in which he urged him to keep the faith by the Holy Spirit, which dwelt in him. We know Priscilla and Aquila were in Ephesus with Timothy at the time, for Paul sent greetings to them through Timothy. So they must have heard the instructions in holy living directed to the leaders of the church. And they must have heeded Paul's instructions to allow the Holy Spirit to sanctify them, and thus, prepare them for the Crown of Righteousness.

The Crown of Glory

Write I Peter 5:2-4.

_____

_____

_____

_____

This is a special crown for the faithful, obedient God-called pastor, as well as for the believer who shares the work of the pastor by supporting him, praying for him, and encouraging him in the work of the Lord. The pastor earns this crown by feeding the flock (II Timothy 4:2-5), taking spiritual oversight of the church (I Timothy 5:17) and being an example to the church (I Timothy 3:1-7).

Our Crowns

Perhaps we like to picture ourselves wearing several crowns as we reign with Christ. But, it's quite possible that we'll do as the twenty-four elders, described in the fourth chapter of Revelation, did. Here, they're sitting around the throne of heaven, from which proceeded lightnings, thunderings and voices, saying: *"Holy, holy, holy Lord God Almighty, who was, and is, and is to come"* (v.4). Soon, they were so overcome with a desire to worship the One on the throne that they took off their crowns of gold and cast them all before Him saying: *"You are worthy, our Lord and God, to receive glory and honor and power, for you created all things, and by your will they were created and have their being"* (Revelation 4:11). Perhaps we won't wear our crowns for very long. But, how wonderful it will be to have some to cast before Him as He is seated in all His glory, recognized, at last, as King of Kings and Lord of Lords!

SUMMARY

Though we may have various motives for serving the Lord, our greatest desire should be that our works are gold and silver, not wood, hay and stubble. For the ones pleasing to God will also be rewarded with various crowns, as described in scripture.

Priscilla and Aquila can be role models for couples, as they complemented one another in ministry to the Lord. Their love of God helped them put their priorities in order and be available for service wherever and however the Lord led them.

CONSIDER THIS

Do you, as a couple, work together in any kind of ministry for the Lord? If so, what?

_____

_____

Will the works you are doing be the kind to stand the test of fire, or are they wood, hay, and stubble?

_____

_____

How can you better labor together with God?

_____

_____

MODERN EXAMPLE

William Booth and Catherine Mumford were married in June of 1855. As newlyweds, they were out in the streets preaching, teaching and praying among the poor and needy in London, England. They believed that to save people from evil and teach them about Christ, they needed to do more than just feed and house them. So, they formed a mission and organized it as if they were in battle against the enemy. Their leaders were known as "officers," Christians were "captives," and outreaches into new cities or countries were called "invasions." We know this organization as The Salvation Army.

While raising eight children, and with no one place to call home, Catherine and William were a ministry team that few can surpass. Catherine was beside her husband in every aspect of the work, helping to forge this "army" into the militant and triumphant Christian force it has become today.

She designed the women's uniform, including the "Hallelujah" bonnet, and she preached the message of salvation to crowds. When she died of cancer in her sixties, it took five days for 50,000 persons to file past her casket in London's Congress Hall where she lay in state wearing her bonnet, tunic and blouse, with her Bible in her hand and her flag by her side.

William lived twenty-two more years, continuing the ministry of the Salvation Army. Before he died, he had traveled around the world and preached 60,000 sermons. Not only have hundreds of thousands been ministered to in food and housing and in other practical ways, but, through this couple working together in service to the Lord, many thousands will live eternally in heaven with the Lord Jesus Christ.

Jesus and the Glorious Church

Fulfilling God's Plan for Marriage

For this reason a man will leave his father and mother and be united to his wife, and the two will become one flesh. This is a profound mystery...but I am talking about Christ and the church.

Ephesians 5:31-32

SETTING THE STAGE

The Wedding of the Ages! The culmination of His-story! A great Mystery of God! The Marriage of the Lamb and the Glorious Church! The perfect couple…at last!

How can we begin to describe the consummation of the marriage of Jesus Christ, the Son of Almighty God, and the Body of Christ, which has become a Glorious Church and Blameless Bride? Even the thought of it defies our imaginations, and yet, God has said that it will be — and His Word endures forever! And, if that is not enough, the wedding is near at hand — the invitation is out! We may well be the last generation of people living before this great event takes place!

In this, the concluding lesson, we will share insights on how we, as members of Christ's Body, will be also His Bride. We will also discover what that should mean to us as we are waiting in preparation for the Marriage Supper of the Lamb!

LESSONS FROM JESUS AND THE GLORIOUS CHURCH

Comparison of the "First" Couple and the "Last" Couple

To look at the final couple in God's plan, we must first look at His first couple, Adam and Eve, and see how they were a type of Jesus and the Glorious Church. To do this, we will look at the comparison as found in I Corinthians 15:45-50.

First Man, Adam	**Last Man, Jesus**
Called first man	Called second man
From the dust of the earth	From heaven
Became a living being	Is a life-giving spirit
Came first, as natural	Came after the natural, as spiritual

Paul goes on to explain that, as we have borne the likeness of the earthly man, Adam, so shall we have the likeness of the man from heaven, Jesus. For, flesh and blood, the perishable, cannot enter the kingdom of heaven, the imperishable. The reason that we must be born again, born of the Spirit, is so that we can inherit and participate in that which is imperishable.

Other Parallels

Adam and Eve	Jesus and the Church
God made Adam a helpmeet	God is fashioning a Bride for His Son
Eve was taken from Adam's side while he slept.	The Church came into being because Jesus' side was pierced while He hung upon the cross.

The Church — The Bride of Christ

As the Holy Spirit is allowed to do His work of sanctification in us, we begin to see our relationship to Jesus as that mysterious union — the Church as the bride of Jesus Christ.

We have a description of this Bride in Revelation 21, where she is pictured as the Holy City, the New Jerusalem. God will have completed a work in her, clothing her with His righteousness, adorning her with jewels which have come through fire. Former things will have passed away; she will be a new creation and He will dwell with her. Pictured as this city — its very infrastructure being God Himself — she will have no need of the sun or moon, for the glory of the Lord, the Lamb, will be her light.

According to Ephesians 5:22-33, the Glorious Church will be without spot, wrinkle, or blemish. She will also be an overcomer in the battle against Satan, as she follows the instructions in Ephesians 6:10-18. Jesus stated, in Mark 12:25, that there will be no need of marriage in heaven. Our relationship with Jesus will be so all-glorious and complete that any other relationship would be unnecessary or desirable.

A bride — including the church — may be a beautiful woman, a very capable homemaker, and have all the character attributes that one would desire. Yet, a groom would want something more. He would, most of all, desire her *love*. In fact, he really wants her *first love* — that exciting, fresh, joyful expression of her feelings, which are only toward him and no one else. Though he wants her commitment, her submission, her obedience, and her faithfulness, he does not want just her "duty love;" rather, he wants a real, whole-hearted affection for him. He wants her to love him for who he is, not just for what he has done for her!

The Song of Solomon, a love-song depicting Jesus and His Bride, begins with the maiden saying, *"Let him kiss me with the kisses of his mouth...for your love is more delightful than wine. Pleasing is the fragrance of your perfumes; your name is like perfume poured out"* (Song of Solomon 1:2-3). She wants the kisses of his mouth, not just a kiss on the cheek! To her, his love is better than even the best fruit earth can produce. She wants to tell him of her love and have him share his love with her.

One of the ways the Church can, even now, share her love with Jesus is through the experience of praise. And what we do now is only preparation for what we will be doing through all eternity. Imagine the scene in Revelation 5:11-13:

> *Then I looked and heard the voice of many angels, numbering thousands upon thousands, and ten thousands times ten thousand. They encircled the throne*

and the living creatures and the elders. In a loud voice they sang:
'Worthy is the Lamb, who is slain, to receive power and wealth and wisdom
and strength and honor and glory and praise!' Then I heard every creature
in heaven and on earth and under the earth and on the sea, and all that is in
them, singing: 'To him who sits on the throne and to the Lamb to praise and
honor and glory and power, forever and ever!'

We know, from the events of our day, that Jesus is coming soon for His Bride! The invitation is out…the Wedding Day draws near. The Gospel is being preached all over the world. Translators are continuing to publish the scripture in every known language. Radio and television can beam the Good News of God's love into places where no missionary has ever gone. Believers are learning to praise and to do spiritual battle. The Holy Spirit and the Church are calling the thirsty to come and partake of the Water of Life freely. We do not know *when* Jesus will come for His Bride and the Marriage Supper of the Lamb will take place. We do know, however, that we must be ready!

Couples in the Bible Can Help Fashion the Bride of Christ

Our marriages, now, can be a workshop that God uses to prepare us for that ultimate relationship as a Bride for His Son. As we come to the close of our look at couples in the Bible, we realize more fully the plan that God has had for marriage all along. We can begin to see that some of the couples are types of Jesus and the Church. We can also see how understanding them and their problems in the light of God's Word can help us in our relationship as couples here and now. Listed below are the names of the couples we have studied. Think back to what you learned from each one, and then write down something that you can apply to your life that is helping you to become the beautiful Bride, ready for the coming of our groom, Jesus Christ!

Adam and Eve, who failed to maintain oneness in the marriage relationship

_____

_____

Abraham and Sarah, who walked by faith in God

_____

_____

Lot and his wife, who failed to be separated from the world

_____

_____

Isaac and Rebekah, who failed in some areas of parenting

_____

_____

Jacob and Leah/ Jacob and Rachel, who show us what a covenant relationship is

_____

_____

Amram and Jochebed/ Manoah and His Wife, who raised special children

_____

_____

Moses and Zipporah/Nabal and Abigail, who lived in conflict with each other

_____

_____

Boaz and Ruth, who enjoyed the extended family

_____

_____

Elkanah and Hannah, who received an answer to their prayer

_____

_____

David and Michal, who had unrealistic expectations of each other

_____

_____

Ahab and Jezebel, who failed to keep the marital roles God ordained

_____

_____

Naaman and his Wife, who kept the marriage vow in sickness and in health

_____

_____

Ahasuerus and Esther, who saw lives changed through shared mealtimes

_____

_____

Job and his Wife, who overcame trials and suffering

_____

_____

Hosea and Gomer/David and Bathsheba, who failed to keep God's Word concerning adultery

_____

_____

Zechariah and Elizabeth, who were not always able to communicate

_____

_____

Joseph and Mary, who received guidance from the Lord

_____

_____

Zebedee and Salome, whose parental roles changed

_____

_____

Jairus and his Wife, who had to wait for God's perfect timing

_____

_____

Herod and Herodias, who failed to keep God's Word concerning unlawful relationships

_____

_____

Pilate and his Wife/Ananias and Sapphira, who did not do what was right, because of cowardice and deception

_____

_____

Aquila and Priscilla, who served the Lord together

_____

_____

SUMMARY

Soon, all husband-wife relationships will be no more. The earthly institution of marriage will have served its purpose. The covenant between God and His people will have been fully realized. And, all the couples of His written Word, together with all the couples who have been in His Word through the ages, will find their ultimate relationship with Jesus, the Bridegroom at the Marriage Supper of the Lamb and the Glorious Church.

And so, it is with great excitement and joy of anticipation that we hear Jesus' very last words, spoken to us through John in Revelation 22:20: *"Yes, I am coming soon."* As the Bride-in-preparation longs for her husband-to-be and the consummation of their relationship, we respond: ***"Even so, come, Lord Jesus!"***

> *May he (the Lord) strengthen your hearts so that you will be blameless, and holy in the presence of our God and Father when our Lord Jesus comes with all his holy ones.*

I Thessalonians 3:13

WE WANT TO KNOW WHAT YOU THINK ABOUT THIS STUDY!

Please share your comments about this study by posting your review on our website. From the menu bar at the top of the Hensley Publishing home page, select **Our Products**. On the Products page, scroll down the page until you see the cover of the Bible study. Choose the study by clicking on the cover image. On the next screen, select **Write a Review** in the right column. Write your review and click on **Submit**.

You can see our complete line of Bible studies,
post a review, or order online and save at:

www.hensleypublishing.com

HENSLEY
PUBLISHING

6116 E 32nd St.
Tulsa, OK 74135

Toll Free Ordering: 800.288.8520
Fax: 918.664.8562
Phone: 918.664.8520

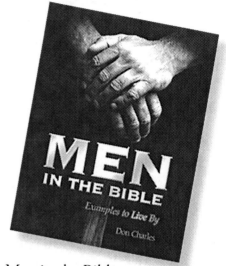
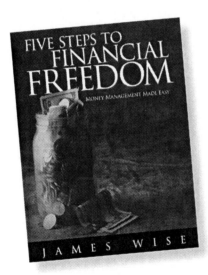

Printed in the United States
104694LV00003B/33-106/A

DIPLOMACY LIBERATED

THE GOLDEN TREASURY OF
T. P. SREENIVASAN

Edited by WG CDR RAGASHREE D. NAIR (R)

KONARK

Konark Publishers Pvt. Ltd
206, First Floor,
Peacock Lane, Shahpur Jat,
New Delhi 110 049
Phone: +91-11-41055065
e-mail: india@konarkpublishers.com, us@konarkpublishers.com
website: www.konarkpublishers.com

ISBN: 978-81-973432-3-0

Edited by Ranjana Narayan
Jacket design by Sanjeev Kumar
Cover image © T.P. Sreenivasan
Cover image enhancement by Vishnu Ramachandran
Icon© Shutterstock
Section image © Freepik.com
Typeset by Saanvi Graphics, Noida
Printed and bound at Saurabh Printers Pvt. Ltd, Greater Noida

*Dedicated to the memory of my wife,
the late Chandralekha Sreenivasan, who suggested
such an anthology for my eightieth birthday*

Contents

P. PERSONAL MEMOIRS

Foreword

Ambassador T.P. Sreenivasan is a person I admire greatly. He is one person who never allowed retirement blues to get to him. He continued to work, writing multiple books, article after article, in many of our best newspapers and periodicals. He writes with equal fluency in both English and Malayalam. He attends functions galore, teaches civil service aspirants, and travels across India and abroad. He is today one of the best-known faces in the cultural and intellectual world of Kerala, a sought-after speaker, a man whose views matter.

After returning from Delhi, we worked together in the Government of Kerala; he was the Vice Chairman of the Kerala State Higher Education Council, and I was the Vice Chairman of the Kerala Planning Board. Though we had not met before, we had many familiar friends and shared diplomatic experiences, and therefore, we were able to establish a personal rapport and a working relationship. We worked with other prominent educationists on a plan to reform higher education. He worked energetically on those ideas in the next four years and produced several ground-breaking reports, which could have transformed the education scene in Kerala. But his proposals for liberalising education, such as granting autonomy to several colleges, the establishment of private universities, collaboration with foreign universities and others, ran into rough weather because of the accusations made by the opposition of commercialisation and commodification of education, and his term ended soon after student protests led to a physical attack on him at the opening of a Global Education Meet in Thiruvananthapuram.

However, some of his ideas were later accepted by the subsequent government, though they have not been implemented yet.

Even during this period and the subsequent years, his first love was foreign policy and geopolitics, and he maintained a prolific writing career, resulting in 10 books and nearly 1,500 columns in prominent journals in India and abroad. He also popularised international affairs through the Kerala International Centre, where he is the Director General, and his weekly programme on international affairs on the leading television channel, *Asianet*. He taught at various educational institutions, including the Central University of Kerala, Kasaragod, and delivered lectures on multiple topics. He introduced a course in international relations to some leading business schools in Kerala, such as the SCMS, Rajagiri, and DC Business School. He also worked nationally as a member of the National Security Advisory Board member and participated in national and international conferences. Side by side, he directed the NSS Academy of Civil Services and encouraged many youngsters to join the Indian Foreign Service. At the global level, he was a Senior Fellow at the Brookings Institution in Washington, where he worked on the India-US Agreement on civil nuclear cooperation.

I am glad that on the threshold of turning an octogenarian, TPS has chosen to produce this volume of his significant and timeless essays, selected and edited by Wing Commander Ragashree D. Nair (Retd) and Gokul K., a research scholar working under his guidance for a PhD at the Somaiya Vidyavihar University, Mumbai, where TPS is a Mentor and Professor of Eminence in International Relations.

Believing that journalistic writings constitute the first draft of history, TPS not only preserved his columns published in such publications as *The Asian Wall Street Journal, The New York Times* (India Ink), *The Hindu, The Indian Express, The Tribune, The Times of India, Rediff.com, The PenNews, The Quint, The Lede* and others but also updated them and collated them for posterity in this volume. The breadth and depth of his oeuvre are awe-inspiring, and we should appreciate his effort in placing this Golden Treasury on our bookshelves.

TPS is the most experienced multilateralist in the IFS, with Ambassadorial postings in our UN missions in New York, Vienna and

Nairobi and as the head of the UN Division in the Ministry. His work at the UN and his writings on the organisation are highly respected.

He writes about decolonisation, disarmament, human rights, the environment, and other issues, commanding attention from the world body itself. His knowledge of UN reforms from 1979 to this day has been of value to our present practitioners. He has no illusion that India will become a permanent member of the UN Security Council soon, but he has articulated our case very well in various international forums. An article in *The Asian Wall Street Journal* on the possible conditions the world would like to impose on us to qualify for permanent membership made waves in the UN corridors. He said that unless we signed the Nuclear Non-proliferation Treaty and solved the border issues with Pakistan and China, we would not be able to occupy the horse-shoe table. Another of his essays, discussed in the UN fora, was his proposal to set up a Health Keeping Force on the lines of the UN Peacekeeping Forces to combat pandemics. A column he wrote for *rediff.com* on a revelation made to him by a White House official that the US would never have nuclear trade with India even after the signing of the nuclear deal shook the nuclear markets around the globe. Many manufacturers of nuclear material wanted to know his source. The source was never revealed, but till today, the US has not cleared trade in atomic material or reactors to India. They were willing to facilitate Indian trade with others but did not want to contribute to India's nuclear capability.

It is not easy to pick and choose the writings of TPS that are of interest and importance. He is as much at home with foreign policy as with humour, as he demonstrated in his book in Malayalam titled *Humour in Diplomacy*. His sense of humour and irony shows up in all his writings, bringing smiles to the readers of serious issues. His obituary note for his wife, Lekha, a lady of many parts, gracious and friendly, humble to the core, a gifted dancer, charity organiser and a close family friend, particularly touched me. All of Trivandrum mourned her sad demise, even in other parts of India and in countries in which her kind hand had touched many.

I'm confident that *Diplomacy Liberated* will be read with interest by scholars and the general public alike for its value as a chronicle of diplomacy in the last 20 years. While his writings in the previous 37 years in the Foreign Service will remain in the Ministry of External Affairs archives, this anthology in which he has given free rein to his imagination, innovative thinking and even flights of fancy will remain in the public domain for years to come.

17 May 2024   **K.M. Chandrasekhar**

Former Cabinet Secretary and author

Prologue

A collection of my essays written over a period of 20 years of retirement is presented here in an effort to save some of my writings from fading into oblivion by preserving them on the bookshelf in the belief that some of them deserve to be read even after the circumstances that prompted their creation have changed. Journalistic writings serve as the first draft of history, said B.G. Varghese.

I trust that my narration and observations of the time will be beneficial to some historians in the future. I have been both a witness to and a participant in a number of game-changing developments nationally and internationally, and my recollections may one day throw light on some inexplicable decisions made on both scales. My judgements may not withstand the scrutiny of future analysts, but they are objective and based on my own ringside view of events and personalities. Many of the essays have been updated to make them as contemporary as possible.

A seamless approach to ease the burden of retirement is to continue to do the kind of work one has been doing for many years. A career change may appear attractive, but the risk of failure may be intimidating. Having written for the archives of the Ministry of External Affairs for 37 years from different corners of the world, the sudden liberation from the shackles of the government became an inspiration to engage in flights of fancy with no fear of responsibility for implementation.

With sufficient time to research and rich experience to provide the backdrop, retired diplomats can be interpreters of world events and effective advisers to the Government. Most former diplomats follow this path by sheer force of habit. The result is a new genre of professionals designated as Ambassador-Professors. Unlike pure academics, they can recall the circumstances that led to particular decisions and also the expectations at that time.

I shared my intention to write columns, and even some books with friends, and all of them encouraged me to do so, albeit with the cautionary advice that the Official Secrets Act should not be violated. The Government will not give any prior clearance, but if there is any embarrassing revelation then you should be ready to face the music, I was told.

I had already started my work on a memoir, *Words, Words, Words,* and spent quite some time on it in my early months of retirement. It was released by my former boss in New York, Vice President Hamid Ansari, at his residence in the presence of a large number of colleagues and friends. A reviewer called it a gentleman's book and suggested that I should write a sequel to be more revelatory. The publisher, Shri K. P. R. Nair, published most of my books subsequently and was an influencer in making choices of themes and formats.

The thrill of producing a book was immense, and the positive reviews in various publications encouraged me to pursue a writing career. One person who put me on the track of writing op-eds was Shri Suresh Prabhu, former Minister, who called up his friend at *The Times of India* and said that I would have interesting things to say. That was a big opening, and I continued writing for *The Times of India* for several years till Shri H.K. Dua persuaded me to write for *The Tribune*. The rumour in Delhi was that the first paper the then Prime Minister Dr Manmohan Singh read was *The Tribune*, and that writings in the paper might catch his attention.

But despite the twists and turns in my journalistic career, the one person who was a constant inspiration was Shri Nikhil Lakshman of *Rediff.com* till now. As it happened, it was Shri Lakshman who published my first essay on the follies and foibles of the United Nations in *The Illustrated Weekly of India*.

The reach of the web and the possibility of seeing the articles printed in *India Abroad* were a great attraction even as I wrote for *The New Indian Express* and *The Hindu*. Shri Siddharth Varadarajan was the first to invite me to write for *The Hindu* about the Italian Naval officers who killed two Indian fishermen off the Kerala coast in February 2012.

I wrote several important articles for *The Hindu*, but its practice of keeping writers in limbo for days together was rather disheartening. *The New Indian Express* was very prompt in publishing whatever I wrote, but its editor wanted to know the source of an article at one point, and it ended my writing in the paper. I thought it was unethical of him to have asked me to name one of his own editors who revealed a story to help me in my writing career. Afterward, I switched to the original *The Indian Express* for a while.

Then there was Shri K. Gopalakrishnan, formerly the Editor of the iconic *Mathrubhumi*, who asked me to write regularly for his *PennNews* and a mother and daughter duo, Sundari and Sandhya Ravishankar of a web newspaper, *The Lede*, who invited me to write a regular column for several months. I also wrote for *The Sunday Guardian* for a time.

I was happy when Shri S. Prasannarajan carried my unsolicited philosophical pieces in *Open The Magazine* and I wrote frequently for him. I wrote several essays for *The Quint* and other web magazines as and when I was requested to do so. A number of my articles were carried by the UAE newspaper, *The Khaleej Times*.

I wrote in English for *Manorama Online* and in Malayalam for the *Mathrubhumi* newspaper. When the TKM institutions in Kollam started their glossy monthly magazine, *Prabhatha Rashmi*, its editor, Shri S. Nasser insisted that my column should be there in every issue of the magazine. This chain has not been broken till today. Shri Nasser's indefatigable pursuit of his favourite writers to get their writings has been phenomenal, and that explains why many prominent writers write for it. My first Malayalam book, *Narmam Nayathanthrathil*, consisted of a collection of light essays published in *Prabhatha Rashmi*. The book was released at the Kerala Literary Festival in January 2024.

Then there were many start-up journals that invited me to write for them, but most of them did not last long. Dr D. Babu Paul, former Additional Chief Secretary of Kerala, told me a way to evade these fortune seekers. He said that he would inform them that he would write for them in the fourth issue of the journal. Most of them did not survive that long!

My writing for foreign journals began soon after my first book was published. It was released at the Indian Consulate General in New York and quite a few of the Indian writers were present. Among them was Shri Tunku Varadarajan, already a well-known writer for *The Wall Street Journal*, who was struck by an answer I gave someone who asked about the prospects of India becoming a permanent member of the UN Security Council.

I had told the questioner that apart from the opposition of the five permanent members, India suffered from the handicap of having major border disputes with China and Pakistan. Moreover, India's refusal to sign the NPT (Treaty on the Non-Proliferation of Nuclear Weapons) and CTBT (Comprehensive Nuclear-Test-Ban Treaty), which had become fundamental documents of a global disarmament regime and have been endorsed by the majority of nations, added to its complexities.

Shri Varadarajan came up to me and said that he found my answer fascinating and asked me if I would write on the subject, which he could get published. I sent him a piece, which appeared in *The Asian Wall Street Journal*, much to my delight. Even more importantly, the Journal asked me to write a monthly column for it, which I did for about a year.

Several journalist friends of my son kept encouraging me to write for American journals, but I was not very optimistic. One of them had just begun a publication for *The New York Times* called 'India Ink' and he asked me whether I could write for it. I really enjoyed writing for the NYT! After some months, the publication ceased to exist, and I began concentrating on Indian publications. But I kept writing for some prestigious journals like *The Washington Quarterly* off and on.

My assignment as the Vice Chairman of the Kerala State Higher Education Council brought in a new challenge to study the education system in India, particularly Kerala, and writing on education became a necessity. I edited a peer-reviewed journal and also contributed occasionally to it. Four years as a member of the National Security Advisory Board of the Government of India meant constant study of security issues and writing on them, but those writings were not for publication.

My work on the Board related to nuclear issues, and one of the major events of the time was the Fukushima nuclear accident in March

2011, which caused a setback to the nuclear industry. Suggestions were made that India should slow down its nuclear expansion plan, but India proceeded to do business as usual. However, the Indian legislation on compensation in the event of accidents led to the Americans backing out of their commitment to build reactors for India. The Indian law contradicted the international practice of placing the liability on the operator, not the supplier. Several formulae were considered even after the change of government, but no solution was found.

One of my most celebrated columns during that period was "The US may have no nuclear trade with India" (21 August 2009) based on a briefing by a senior White House official, who revealed to me in one of his conversations that the US was not keen to have nuclear trade with India. He said that the India-US nuclear deal had opened up nuclear markets for India, but the US did not want to be responsible for India's nuclear capability. An article I wrote for *Rediff.com* became sensational as many companies in the US and India were preparing for nuclear trade.

Several US companies contacted me directly to find the source of my information, but I could not oblige them. Indian officials maintained that the nuclear deal was intact and announced several measures, such as identifying the location for US reactors. But till today, no foreign nuclear reactor has been set up in India, except the Kudankulam Russian reactors, which preceded the India-US nuclear deal.

The advent of Shri Narendra Modi as Prime Minister and his extraordinary rise nationally and internationally made for a rather fascinating tale, which I narrated continuously and objectively in different publications. At the request of my publisher, K. P. R. Nair, the essays written during the first term of Narendra Modi were published in a book titled *Modiplomacy*. The technique I used was to explain and analyse the story of Prime Minister Modi through the prism of a Shakespearean play. Watching his epic journey around the world, I felt that it had the flavour of the Aswamedha Yagna, in which a ceremonial horse was dispatched to conquer new territories by goodwill or force. His rise as a global player and a man of action was spectacular, and it had many Shakespearean dimensions.

This was brought out by the structure of a play in five acts—the first act is exposition, which introduces the characters and the setting, the second is the rising action section, which has a series of events, leading to the climax which in itself is the third act. The fourth act is the part of falling action, or resolution where the final outcome of the conflict begins to unravel. All of this culminates in the fifth and final act which is the denouement, tying up the loose ends and presenting the consequences of the resolution. The structure provided an ideal platform to bring out the hero's struggles and his eventual victory in the elections.

The Covid-19 pandemic prevented a proper release of the book and its promotion. The book was positive about the many accomplishments of Modi, but not without criticism of some of the steps taken. As a result, neither the Government nor the Opposition championed the book. But it was the first objective analysis of the first term of Narendra Modi as Prime Minister. I continued in the same vein about his second term in several journals and newspapers.

A selection of my quintessential essays was made by my editor, Wing Commander Ragashree D. Nair, and my research scholar, K. Gokul, from more than about 1,500 essays on a multiplicity of topics published in a variety of journals to mark my turning into an octogenarian. They did a marvellous job of choosing my writings, which may be of lasting value. Only time will tell how creations of a particular generation will prove valuable. Since they represent two generations beyond mine, they will live to see the wisdom of their choice. I remain eternally grateful for their work. This collection represents a large volume of writings written over 20 years. But I hope that it will remain a legacy of my effort to understand and interpret global events after my Foreign Service career.

United States of America

I have a mass of material on the USA, with my three assignments in the US, but only some of my writings find a place here. My articles on the nuclear deal themselves will fill several volumes. Some of them, like the one on the American way of appointing Ambassadors, the memorial for 9/11, the installation of a Gandhi statue on federal land in Washington, and how racial inequality fanned the pandemic fire, lobbying on the Hill and the right to carry arms have been chosen. They do not belong to the beaten track and contain interesting information, which may be new to many readers.

Multilateralism

Multilateral diplomacy has fascinated me ever since I first entered the UN building in 1979 and joined the Indian mission in 1980. Most of my postings since then were related to multilateral work—New York, Nairobi, New Delhi and Vienna at the Ambassadorial level, setting a record as the most experienced multilateral diplomat in the Indian Foreign Service. I have also written extensively on the UN, particularly on its reform. I also chaired two Committees of the UN General Assembly on reform. Considering the body of literature I have generated, the 11 essays included in this collection may be inadequate.

But the article on "Red Berets", the voting system, India's image in the UN and the G-20 as a dream Security Council are seminal, and were debated even in the UN corridors at the time. While some of the points in these essays were considered valid, the feeling was that the time for such reforms had not yet come. The lighter essay on the UN gaffes has been included for comic relief.

The transformation of the Non-Aligned Movement (NAM) after the Cold War has been fully explained. The emergence of the Quad (USA, India, Australia and Japan) in the face of challenges from China brought the four major democratic countries in the region together. It was an important development, even though the Quad has not developed into a military alliance.

The 75th anniversary of the UN on 21 September 2020 was marked by several analyses of the successes and failures of the UN, one of which has found a place in the volume. In one essay, I have argued that India should be more selective about joining multilateral groupings, some of which are only alphabetical soups. Ironically, India is a member of the Shanghai Cooperation Organisation (SCO), but not of the Asia-Pacific Economic Cooperation (APEC). We were reluctantly dragged into the multilateral export control regimes, the Wassenaar Arrangement and the Australia Group, even after the promise of membership of the Nuclear Suppliers Group (NSG) never fructified. India also became a member of the Missile Technology Control Regime (MTCR). The American package of four agreements was unravelled by China by denying NSG membership to us.

China

The concerns over China's expansionism and its attacks across the Line of Actual Control (LAC) grew in recent years, culminating in its occupation of several posts in Ladakh, which still remain under Chinese control. Although contacts have continued, the disavowal of the seminal agreements by China has resulted in a vacuum in the relationship. A few of the articles of the period have been included here to give a flavour of the times.

Some of them touch upon the internal situation in China and the relevance of the Dalai Lama, which give diverse signals on Beijing's stability, economic, and environmental concerns. President Xi Jinping has secured a third term, but there are reports of purges at high levels, indicating chances of instability. The new alliance between China and Russia has major implications for India, as our relations with China deteriorate.

The concerns over China have only increased after New Delhi hosted the 18th G20 Summit in September 2023, which Xi did not attend and sent several signals regarding the emergence of the Global South. The selected articles reveal an uncertain horizon in India-China relations. The complete rejection of the seminal mutually-agreed principles beginning from Panchsheel to the agreements of 1988 and 1993, signed by Prime Ministers Rajiv Gandhi and P.V. Narasimha Rao respectively, has altered the fundamentals of India-China relations.

Cuba

Havana was my second home during my first tenure in New York because of the Cuban Chairmanship of the NAM. The Havana Summit of NAM in 1979 was a turning point in history when Cuba became a credible spokesperson of the developing world. Though hated by the US and the West, Fidel Castro held the position with dignity. I noticed that there was a semblance of mutual admiration between the US and Cuba. The Cuban cigar and rum held sway in the American market despite trade sanctions, and I suspect that they played a role in Barack Obama's ill-fated normalisation with Cuba. I watched Castro closely whenever

I had the opportunity to be the note-taker for meetings between him and Indian leaders. He was a living legend already, and he lasted long in that capacity. He was fond of India and very tolerant of the antics of some of our Ministers.

Gorkhas became his heroes after the Falklands war (1982) which brought victory to the British, though Castro was on the side of Argentina. The furore over the hug he gave to Indira Gandhi while handing over the NAM gavel to her astonished him. "What else do you do when you congratulate your sister?" he asked a squeamish Indian audience. Asked by Mrs Ansari about the rumours about his women, he answered, "I was lucky in that respect!" I remember expressing my admiration for Castro to a Cuban American Senator and getting virtually thrown out of his chamber!

Japan

My first posting was in Japan and the country has been an all-time favourite. There was hardly any substance in India-Japan relations at that time, but the 1966 film, *Love in Tokyo*, the "Sayonara, Sayonara" song and Subhas Chandra Bose inspired the Japanese and Indians alike. Our bilateral relations have come a long way since then, and Japan, which was the most critical of India's nuclear capabilities, has now formed a nuclear cooperation agreement with India. Some essays on Japan appear in this volume, particularly the one dealing with the various strands of India-Japan ties, another on Shinzo Abe, the architect of the new relationship between India and Japan.

A piece on Netaji Subhas Chandra Bose touches upon the controversy about Netaji's ashes, which are still in Japan. The Japanese view this as a case of India's lack of trust in Japan, which arose out of India's disbelief in Bose's death. It is high time that the ashes were brought back after a scientifically done DNA examination of the ashes. Having been part of an investigation into his death by Justice G.D. Khosla, I recall how genuine the people were who testified that denying Netaji a final return to his homeland was a great injustice to his memory, as well as the trustworthiness of those who were witnesses to the accident.

South Asia

South Asia has remained in turmoil as the articles on Pakistan, Afghanistan and Sri Lanka show. Sri Lanka almost became a failed state as its economy nearly collapsed till India extended support and the IMF stepped in.

Terrorism from across the border in Pakistan has prevented any kind of dialogue between the countries and the SAARC (South Asian Association for Regional Cooperation) is in suspended animation. My visit to Bangladesh was pleasant, as described in my column on the subject. The electoral victory of Sheikh Hasina is a victory for India also.

The Pakistan-Iran clash over Baluchistan was surprising, but we have not heard the last of it yet. The suicidal moves of Maldives will hurt the island state more than India. Nepal and Bhutan may have their grievances, but our policy of firmness with flexibility seems to be working with them. Chanakya's dictum that close neighbours cannot be good friends has been proven right time and time again.

The dramatic improvement in relations with the countries of Southeast Asia and the Gulf illustrate the value of ancient wisdom. Neither the reciprocity principle nor the Gujral Doctrine has been effective and irritants keep arising in Nepal, Myanmar, Bangladesh and even Bhutan.

Some specific issues relating to South Asia such as the Sri Lankan debt crisis, abrogation of Article 370, developments in Afghanistan, Pakistan's political and economic crisis, my impressions of Bangladesh, including a memorable trip to Dhaka to present the Dr Kalam Smriti International Excellence Award 2019 to Sheikh Hasina are also included here.

Russia-Ukraine War

Some of my columns on the Russia-Ukraine war have been included to show how wrong I was to think that such a war would not take place. The David and Goliath story is on display again when Ukraine is fighting a battle for survival, while Vladimir Putin persists with his grand vision of the glory of the Russian empire. India's masterly tightrope walking has helped maintain its ties with Russia, but history may be harsh on the Indian tactics to insulate itself from the consequences of the war. In the event of a lining up of democracies against autocracies in a new global order, India should be able to side with democracies.

Nuclear Disarmament

My assignment to the First Committee of the UN General Assembly and as India's Governor of the International Atomic Energy Agency (IAEA) kept me close to nuclear matters throughout my career. Our peaceful nuclear explosion of 1974 when I was in Moscow made India a suspect in the world and it was a tough journey for India till the India-US Nuclear Agreement of 2008. My article, written on the request of *The Washington Quarterly* in April 2010, has been included here as a comprehensive piece on India's position on nuclear disarmament. The other essays deal with the issues that arose from time to time in our nuclear journey from 1974 to 2008.

The stunning freeze in Indo-US relations following the 1998 tests took a long time to resolve. President Bill Clinton's visit to India in March 2000 and Prime Minister Atal Bihari Vajpayee's visit to Washington in September of that year were important milestones in bilateral relations. The hard reality is that as a non-signatory of the Nuclear Non-Proliferation Treaty (NPT), we still remain away from the nuclear mainstream. Pakistan and Israel are in the same boat, but their positions are considered negotiable if India signs the NPT. As for the nuclear danger, the threat of a nuclear attack has become more real today than at the dawn of the 20th century because of the ongoing wars in which nuclear weapon states are involved. The attainment of Global Zero—a world without nuclear weapons—has become more distant. The denial of NSG membership to India, even after the Indo-US nuclear deal, was part of a diabolical strategy by China to block us from the nuclear mainstream. However, major advances in space cooperation have been registered in 2023 and after.

Indian Foreign Service

The Indian Foreign Service has been undergoing several changes since I retired in 2004, most of them in the right direction. But there have also been efforts to reduce the involvement of the IFS in specialised negotiations falling under the purview of different technical Ministries. Lateral entries of professionals from time to time were also being proposed. I have written a number of articles stressing that the integrity of the IFS should be preserved.

As it is, the popularity of the IFS has been eroded among the candidates and the plans to dilute the importance of the service will make the service even less popular. I have also noted that, as it was demonstrated in a recent celebration of the IFS Day, there is a resurgence of interest in the Indian Foreign Service.

Prime Minister Modi has been very supportive of the Foreign Service, and the appointment of Dr S. Jaishankar as the External Affairs Minister has boosted the morale of the Service. Some of my writings on the subject in the last few years find a place in this collection, such as new challenges to diplomacy, a comparison between journalists and diplomats, and the need for having IFS specialists of Blue Economy.

Environment

Having been involved in the environmental negotiations since 1989, notably at the COP 1 in Berlin, where I was the Vice Chairman of the conference and the spokesman of G-77 in 1995, I had taken a keen interest in environmental negotiations even after retirement. I wrote on the great betrayal in Copenhagen (COP 15, in 2009), where the Kyoto Protocol was abandoned and a system of voluntary reduction of greenhouse gases was adopted, followed by the 2015 Paris Agreement, which created an impression that it was a panacea.

Subsequent COPs (Conference of the Parties) and other meetings, including the COP 28 in Dubai in 2023, have proved that the world will not be able to accomplish the 1.5 degrees Celsius target for global warming or the net zero carbon emission targets fixed by various countries. A realisation is growing among nations that only a scientific solution like carbon capture can tackle the global warming issue.

What the governments cannot do may be done by scientists, though there is no evidence of a scientific breakthrough yet. A selection of some of my essays in this volume, particularly on the tough transition away from fossil fuels, may be of interest to the readers.

Covid-19

The biggest existential threat to humanity, which came in the form of Covid-19, broke out in China and spread far and wide from the end of 2019 to early 2023. The death and devastation caused by it were unprecedented. Moreover, no one is certain that no mutations of the virus will emerge. But one silver lining of the pandemic was that the leisure offered by the lockouts led to a literary renaissance. The mood was extremely gloomy, but the creativity blossomed.

I had written another book titled *IFS: Charms and Challenges*. A number of articles written by me during that period are available here. The spirit of optimism prevailed in many writings of the time, together with the fear of an apocalypse. A sense of mortality for those above the age of 65 was palpable, with rumours of old people infected with the virus being forcefully quarantined and even killed in China.

Indian Diaspora

Next to multilateral matters, my postings gave me an exceptional exposure to the diaspora in Myanmar, Fiji, Kenya, the United States and Austria. I was expelled from Fiji in 1989 because India supported the Indo-Fijians' struggle to restore their democratic rights, and I was hurt in an armed attack because of the clash between the Indians and the Kenyans on account of the disparity in income between the two communities.

The Fiji episode paved the way for a new Indian policy on the diaspora that India would intervene diplomatically if Indians were denied their democratic rights. Prime Minister Rajiv Gandhi convinced the Commonwealth leaders that Fiji should be suspended from the Commonwealth on account of "reverse apartheid". The articles selected for this volume do not describe those developments, but share a futuristic exploration of both India and the diaspora.

A narration of how I was invited back to Fiji after the subsequent restoration of democracy 25 years after my expulsion, and how the coup leader gave me his whole perspective on the Fiji situation may be seen in one of the articles. Interestingly, today the same coup leader, Sitiveni Rabuka, is the elected Prime Minister of Fiji with the support of the Fiji Indians. Other articles on diaspora issues may also be of interest.

Higher Education

My tenure as the Vice Chairman of the Kerala State Higher Education Council gave me an opportunity to study the education system in Kerala and to interact with educationists across the country. My focus was on reform of higher education in Kerala, but it was the time of the formulation of the National Education Policy. I was happy to find that many of the ideas which I had advocated for in Kerala found their way into the National Education Policy. Some of the key articles I wrote at that time are included here, but my book, *Education of an Ambassador: Reflections on Higher Education Reform in Kerala*, tells the whole story. Ironically, the same political groups, which opposed reform, now talk about the need for reform.

Kerala

Living as I did in Kerala after retirement, I actively followed the developments in Kerala. My family and I were involved in the first election campaign of Shashi Tharoor, who was virtually unknown in Kerala and his Malayalam was inadequate for a campaign. My book on Tharoor, *Mattering to India: The Shashi Tharoor Campaign* tells the whole story. I have written several essays throughout the campaign, one of which is included in this collection as a sample. A nasty rejoinder he wrote to my *Rediff* article analysing the diminished majority he secured in the second campaign is best forgotten.

A number of columns on different aspects of Kerala may be seen here. Of particular interest are the stories on the treasures in the Sree Padmanabha Swami temple, a major scandal of a seller of fake antiquities, including the magic wand of Moses in which several celebrities were trapped, the Mullaperiyar Dam dispute, the global attention received by a tiny island and political satire in Kerala. Most of my writings in Malayalam were on international issues.

For over 15 years, I have been hosting a weekly show on international affairs. With the enhanced capabilities of Zoom, I am able to bring experts from around the world to my show. My writing time is reduced on account of the preparation needed, but my show reaches many more people than my newspaper audience in Kerala.

Around and Aside

This section comprises a collection of fascinating, yet isolated articles. Among them are the discovery of Slovenia, allegations of Afrophobia in India, Davos Diplomacy and the Perils of Apparel. These pieces include occasional observations from travels across continents and reflections from reading books on various subjects.

Personal Memoirs

Having written a full autobiography and recalled many personal experiences in my columns, there is really no place for personal memoirs. What is given here are some poignant tales penned on special occasions. Some throw light on childhood and college memories, one bemoans the lost glory of my alma mater, which has been turned into a red fort, another mourns the first diplomatic martyr of India, who was destined to rise to the highest level of diplomacy, and finally witnessing the tragedy of my wife, Lekha's breath turning into air. I cannot write anymore…

T. P. Sreenivasan

Editor's Note

Encapsulating a journey through the vista of diplomacy and global affairs for half a century, Ambassador T.P. Sreenivasan's anthology of essays, written in the last 20 years, is a captivating odyssey. As we traverse the pages of this remarkable collection of articles, which take us back and forth in history, we witness the intricate tapestry of international relations, painted with his strokes of wisdom, experience, and foresight. Diplomacy, however liberated, will bear the stamp of its erstwhile practitioners.

Throughout his illustrious career, Ambassador Sreenivasan has been a steadfast beacon of diplomacy, navigating the tumultuous waters of geopolitics with unwavering dedication and astute discernment. His writings reflect the essence of diplomacy in its myriad forms, from the intricate negotiations of statecraft to the subtle nuances of cultural diplomacy.

In this compendium, readers will find a treasure trove of thought-provoking analyses, incisive observations, and poignant anecdotes, each offering a unique perspective on the complex interplay of global forces. From the corridors of power in New Delhi to the bustling streets of Beijing, from the tranquil shores of Kerala to the hallowed halls of the United Nations, Ambassador Sreenivasan's insights transcend borders and illuminate the universal truths that shape our world.

The collection includes reflections on key moments in India-China relations, from the strained dynamics encapsulated in 'Broken Promises in India-China Relations' to the significance of the Dalai Lama in Chinese politics as explored in 'The Dalai Lama's Political Influence'.

Ambassador Sreenivasan's keen analysis delves into geopolitical crises such as the Doklam standoff in 'Elusive Peace: The Doklam Crisis' and the enigmatic nature of the Chinese state in 'Deciphering China: The New Kremlinology'.

Readers are also treated to a deep dive into the rise of Xi Jinping and his policies in 'Xi Jinping: Architect of China's Ascendancy', as well as an examination of India-China agreements in 'Panchsheel Revisited: India-China Agreements'. Meanwhile, 'China's Communist Resurgence: Lessons from Economic Reform' sheds light on contemporary developments.

The book further explores diverse topics ranging from the Covid-19 pandemic, with insightful articles such as 'Global Pandemic Pact: Toward a Unified Response' and 'Aging in the Pandemic Era: Life Beyond 65'to personal reflections on diplomatic encounters and experiences in articles like 'My Nobel Moments: Recollections on the Stockholm Ceremony' and 'Settling Down: A Diplomat's Quiet Retreat'.

As we journey through these pages, we are reminded of the words of Robert Frost, who famously wrote:

"Two roads diverged in a wood, and I—
I took the one less traveled by,
And that has made all the difference."

Indeed, Ambassador Sreenivasan's career has been marked by a steadfast commitment to charting the path less travelled, to seeking out new perspectives, and to championing the cause of peace and diplomacy in a world often fraught with conflict and discord.

It is with immense gratitude and humility that I pen this editor's note, acknowledging the privilege of being entrusted with the task of introducing the remarkable legacy of Ambassador Sreenivasan to readers around the world by editing the anthology. His contributions to diplomacy and scholarship are truly unparalleled, and it is an honour to celebrate his remarkable achievements through this collection of articles.

As a defence officer, I find myself deeply moved and honoured to have been chosen to edit this book. Ambassador Sreenivasan's astute observations and profound insights resonate deeply with me, as they offer a nuanced understanding of the complex geopolitical landscape that shapes our world. His dedication to diplomacy and his unwavering commitment to the pursuit of peace are a source of inspiration to me and to countless others who serve in defence and security roles. This book serves as a beacon of wisdom and guidance, illuminating the path forward in an ever-changing and challenging world.

This book stands as a testament to Ambassador Sreenivasan's unparalleled expertise and invaluable contributions to the field of diplomacy. It is a must-read for anyone seeking a comprehensive understanding of international relations and domestic policies through the years. As we journey through the pages of this remarkable collection, we are reminded of the enduring importance of diplomacy in shaping the course of history and the critical role that individuals like Ambassador Sreenivasan play in advancing the cause of peace and understanding on the global stage.

Wing Commander Ragashree D. Nair (R)
Co-Chair & CEO, Medicaid Ethos Private Limited
Director, Nuttmeg Products Private Limited

Gratitude

A book, however personal, has many influencers, editors, designers, typists, typesetters, publishers and printers, but the author has to take the blame. My late wife, Lekha, ignited the spark that inspired not only this book but all of my literary endeavours. Ragashree, an accomplished Air Force veteran and management expert, graciously accepted the challenge of debuting as the book's editor, demonstrating her remarkable abilities. Additionally, young K. Gokul, a diligent research scholar at Somaiya Vidyavihar University, Mumbai, took on the brunt of the responsibility to build the book, brick by brick. My secretary at the NSS Academy of Civil Services, Resmi Nair, dedicated herself to this project, unaware of the transformative impact it would ultimately have. Despite the challenges, my family, relatives, and friends stood by me, even as the prospect of another book release seemed daunting. My unwavering publisher, K. P. R. Nair, embraced the manuscript with trust and confidence, a testament to our enduring professional relationship. To each and everyone of them, particularly the Konark team led by Jiza Joy, I extend my heartfelt gratitude.

T. P. Sreenivasan

Praise

This book is a collection of some of the finest insights into foreign policy and international relations over the last two decades. While we, as younger diplomats, were truly fortunate to have the benefit of Ambassador T.P. Sreenivasan's advice and wisdom while in service, the public at large were fortunate that he took to writing soon after his retirement and got the benefit of his experience and understanding of geopolitics in a changing world.

This book covers a wide spectrum of issues, both past and contemporary, giving us insights into what continues to motivate India's policies and decision making, at a time when geopolitical challenges are only getting more complex and diverse – ranging from bilateral to the multilateral, from the Ukraine war to Artificial Intelligence and from the local to the civilisational.

—Ambassador T.S. Tirumurti (Retd)

Former Permanent Representative of India to the UN in New York

In this diverse and delectable anthology, Ambassador Sreenivasan ranges effortlessly across a wide geographical, historical and thematic landscape to provide us with some breathtaking reflections, analyses and insights on events, policies and decisions that have shaped the world during the past half century. *Diplomacy Liberated* is a sumptuous, elegantly written and often deeply thought-provoking volume where the author deconstructs some of the inbuilt habits of nations, both big and small as well as the foibles of their leaders while also evoking the charm and charisma of professional diplomats across the world, a tribe he so ably exemplifies.

—Ambassador Vijay Nambiar (Retd)
Former Permanent Representative of India to the UN in New York

Diplomacy Liberated: The Golden Treasury of Ambassador T.P. Sreenivasan brings back my memories of my husband's and my visit to Tokyo, where he and Lekha began their foreign sojourn and to Vienna, where they completed their Diplomatic Odyssey. Their return to Thiruvananthapuram gave me an opportunity to watch them using their knowledge and experience for the benefit of their homeland. Seeing his writings, 10 books and hundreds of articles, I feel that Sreenivasan never retired. Lekha, whom we lost last year, was also full of life with her charity and a book on the better half of diplomacy.

This anthology of essays written over 20 years reveals the breadth and depth of his experience and vision. It is a chronicle not only of international affairs, but also of matters around and aside for us to savour at leisure. His TV shows in the last 20 years have been a source of knowledge and enlightenment for us all. I wish him many more years of productive and purposeful life.

—Princess Aswathi Thirunal Gouri Lakshmi Bayi
Author and Member of the erstwhile Travancore Royal family

Ten years ago, I had the privilege of editing an anthology of Ambassador T. P. Sreenivasan's essays to mark his 70th birthday, titled *Applied Diplomacy Through the Prism of Mythology*. It was a resounding success, particularly because of the link I established between diplomacy and mythology. Now the foreign policymakers use mythology to trace the evolution of Indian foreign policy.

I am glad to see that another anthology is being published on the occasion of his turning an octogenarian. How time flies! This anthology, like the previous one, is quintessential TPS, insightful analysis, based on his diplomatic experience and his research, inimitable style with humour and wit and study material for his civil service students. Since I have been as good as a member of his family for more than 15 years, during which he was my great influencer and shaper of my destiny, what I write here will be seen as blind admiration. I shall just say that this 'Golden Treasury' will illumine the lives of many.

—Dr Divya Iyer IAS

Administrator, author, singer and dancer

This volume was very much needed—a cogent, coherent, comprehensive and with a lot of clarity—I prefer to call it "Diplomacy Unveiled". The "Personal Memoirs" section in the volume has captured the essence of what a diplomat is expected to do while leveraging one's own country's national interests. The essays on almost every area relating to India's foreign policy and its strategic choices have been very well covered. Full of anecdotes and personal reflections, which have added value to the volume. Essential reading for everyone, especially those who are interested in knowing about India's foreign policy and diplomacy.

—Dr Arvind Kumar

Professor of United States' Studies, School of International Studies, Jawaharlal Nehru University, New Delhi

A. USA
A ROLLER COASTER RIDE

Mahatma in Washington:
Symbolism in Diplomacy

Mahatma Gandhi has a special appeal to overseas Indians, as he is considered one of the greatest "pravasi" (expats) of all time. Being the most prosperous community in the United States, the Indian diaspora has installed several statues in various parts of the country even during the Cold War. But surprisingly enough, the Mahatma could not find a place in Washington, even though the Chanakyapuri of Washington, the "Embassy Row", was littered with statues of various historical figures, big and small, of men and women who may not be recognised today even in their own countries.

Though the Indian Embassy was located on Embassy Row since 1946, when the Embassy purchased two buildings, there was no statue of Mahatma Gandhi there till the year 2000. It's not that the idea had not struck anyone, but the only available land in front of the Embassy was a triangular traffic island with some trees and shrubs, and categorised as Federal Land. Doing anything on that land was a Herculean task, and several generations of Indian diplomats and Indian Americans found it hard to get a Congressional approval for a Gandhi statue. Apart from the anti-colonialist and anti-imperialist sentiments that Gandhi evoked, India-US relations were also not particularly smooth during the Cold War years.

It was as early as 1949 when the US Congress first resolved to authorise the India League of America, or any other organisation which may have been organised for the purpose of erecting a memorial to both celebrate and testify to the great wisdom and leadership of Mohandas K. Gandhi, as a philosopher and statesman, in the city of Washington, D.C. While the resolve was there, nothing much was done till Ambassador Naresh Chandra decided to make a Gandhi statue his legacy. He dedicated himself to this monumental task with unbreakable will and resolved to move heaven and earth to bring the project to fruition.

Ironically, most of the work on the statue was done during the extremely difficult phase of India-US relations, following the nuclear tests of 1998. The US Congress enacted HR 4284, authorising the Government of India to erect a memorial to Mahatma Gandhi on October 26, 1998 and President Bill Clinton signed it into law on May 19, 1999, in the midst of the Jaswant Singh-Strobe Talbott talks on nuclear disarmament and non-proliferation, which lasted two years. The talks were showing signs of progress and President Clinton felt comfortable enough to visit India in early 2000.

This was followed by a return visit to the US by Prime Minister Atal Bihari Vajpayee, when he went to visit Washington D.C. in September 2000. The statue was then unveiled on September 16, 2000 jointly by Vajpayee and Clinton. Clinton had indicated that he would spend only 10 minutes at the venue but felt inspired enough by the Gandhi magic to stay for a full hour, interacting with both the PM and the guests, much to the joy of the participants.

We discovered to our horror that the Congressional approval was just the beginning of a bureaucratic rigmarole involving several committees and offices, which had to consider the size and nature of the statue, such as its posture, its pedestal, and its likely impact on the traffic around it.

Short of asking for changing the face of the Mahatma, they altered every plan we put forward for one reason or another. The most objectionable condition that they put forward was that the Gandhi statue should not be taller than the statue of Winston Churchill installed in the compound of the British Embassy, a few blocks away from our Chancery. Since the statue was already made and sent from India, the only way to reduce the height of the statue was to make the pedestal lower.

The sculpture of Mahatma Gandhi was cast in bronze as a statue with a height of 8 feet 8 inches. It showed Gandhi in stride, as a leader and man of action, evoking memories of his 1930 protest march against salt tax, and the many *padyatras* (long marches) he undertook throughout the length and breadth of the Indian sub-continent. The statue was a gift from the Indian Council for Cultural Relations (ICCR).

The pedestal for the statue was crafted from a block of New Imperial Red Granite, also known as Ruby Red, which are available in various parts of the country, including Karnataka, Tamil Nadu, Rajasthan, and Andhra Pradesh. These states are world famous for their granite, giving India the first ranking in the export of granite blocks. This particular block was excavated from a quarry in Karnataka and gifted by Sree and Ambika Nair, originally from Kerala but now settled in Omaha, Nebraska.

The pedestal was shaped from a block originally weighing 25 tons-reduced to a size of 9'x7'x3'4" with a weight of 16 tons. The block was largely rough-hewn and polished in parts to provide suitable surface for the inscriptions. This was done to provide a natural earth-like surface to serve as the base for the statue, as befits Gandhi's personality.

Ambassador Naresh Chandra personally selected the quotations from Gandhi and others and supervised the inscription. The funding was provided by a large number of donors, mostly Indian Americans, some of whom had been collecting money for the project for many years. Some individuals were prepared to pay for the statue entirely, but we insisted that there should be wide participation and received small donations to make the amount.

The tensest moment came when a Congressional Committee, which was to accord final permission to erect the statue, called a meeting two days after India's nuclear tests, which President Clinton had severely criticised to the point of imposing comprehensive sanctions against India.

We thought that the statue would be the first casualty of the tests. Ambassador Naresh Chandra and I were holding our breath when the first Congressman began speaking. He started with a harangue about the tests by saying that India had forgotten the very precept of non-violence that Gandhi had propagated.

He continued to say that it was very necessary to remind the Indians of the teachings of Mahatma Gandhi by setting up the statue as fast as possible. Every speaker who followed repeated the argument and the approval was given in record time.

A prayer went up from our lips to the Mahatma, whose magic had worked at the right moment. His statue on Mass Avenue is neither gigantic nor an ornamental one, but just like him. Small in stature, but also simultaneously huge with its impact on humanity.

Published: October 11, 2019

Capitol Hill Lobbying:
Influencers in US Politics

As more and more videos of the presidential insurrection of January 6, 2021 emerged, the horror of the attack and vandalisation of one of the citadels of democracy, Capitol Hill in the heart of Washington DC, became evident.

The domestic terrorist attack was a truly vicious and carefully planned incident, one with the collusion of some members of the law enforcement agencies.

The attackers had the upper hand throughout and it appeared that the police were simply watching the proceedings as they rummaged through documents and possessions of the Congressmen, while a man with horns occupied the Speaker's chair.

In total contrast, two weeks later, Joe Biden and Kamala Harris were sworn in with minimum ceremony, but abundant hope.

Biden declared victory for democracy and unity, but admitted in a sombre mood that both appeared fictional at the moment.

A nightmare was over, but the pangs of change had just begun.

The wisdom of hindsight after four years showed the tragedy of lost years.

Finally, it appears that democracy has overcome one of its severest threats.

While the Congress is primarily concerned with internal matters, it also directs the administration on foreign policy, and therefore, diplomats in Washington fight their own battles on the Hill to win support from the Senators and Congressmen.

Lobbying on Capitol Hill is one of the main responsibilities of the diplomatic missions in Washington.

The grand and elegant long corridors of the Capitol and the well-appointed suites of the Senators and the Congressmen are often frequented by diplomats of countries who compete with each other for American attention, some for assistance and others for political and military support.

The easy accessibility to Capitol Hill for both the public and diplomats is striking.

There was no visible presence of security forces and a simple identity card was all that was required to enter the corridors.

The main hazard in going to meetings on the Hill was the long walks involved to reach the various offices.

For some architectural reasons, exits and entrances were only at the two ends of the corridors.

Our shoes got worn out every time we had to lobby hard for a particular cause on the Hill.

I do not know how many diplomats, particularly ambassadors, seek out members of the Indian Parliament.

I guess not many, because the individual MPs do not take initiatives in foreign policy and the treasury benches follow Government policy and the opposition opposes the Government blindly.

On the other hand, US lawmakers are loyal to their parties, but not necessarily to every action of the President.

Senators and Congressmen alike are often ahead of the government in formulating policies, and they apply their mind to every decision that is presented for their approval.

For this reason, lobbying with the Senators and Congressmen was more productive than lobbying with officials.

Diplomats, with or without professional lobbyists, frequent Capitol Hill to seek support from traditional supporters and even those who oppose us.

During the years that I was in Washington (1997 to 2001), we happened to have one issue or another to lobby for on the Hill.

Ambassador Naresh Chandra and I met every key Congressman and Senator several times, either together or individually, because of the several issues which came up one after the other.

The present Ambassador to the US, Taranjit Sandhu, a young diplomat at that time, carefully planned our schedules with his intimate knowledge of the Congress calendar and the staffers, some of whom have risen to high positions in various administrations.

We had to either reinforce the moves of the President or counter his actions through friendly Congressmen.

Unlike now, there were not many Congressmen of Indian origin and we had to depend on influential Indian Americans or the lobbyists to get attention.

Professional lobbyists or personal friends were essential to have social meetings, as the Congressmen are not allowed to accept hospitality from diplomats and they have to pay for their own meal when they break bread with diplomats.

But there is no restriction on entertainment by 'close friends' even if diplomats are invited.

This is how the lobbyists and Indian Americans become catalysts for discussions with the Senators and Congressmen.

Once we select the guests, we choose appropriate Indian Americans or lobbyists to organise the rest. They generally remain silent, except during exchange of courtesies.

The first issue which took us to the Hill many times was the Burton Amendment.

The biggest headache for the Indian embassy in Washington at that time was the annual Burton Amendment, moved by Republican Congressman Dan Burton from Indiana, an inveterate critic of India, seeking a cut of 25 percent in the US development aid to India.

Burton wanted to 'punish' India for what he called its 'unsatisfactory' human rights record, particularly in Kashmir, and treatment meted out to the minorities in the country.

A majority of the members did not share his view.

He maintained a steady flow of correspondence with the President, the Senators and the Congressmen about human rights violations in India with the help of lobbyists provided by Pakistan.

Over the years, the Burton Amendment became a litmus test of India's popularity on the Hill and the effectiveness of Indian diplomacy.

We did not hesitate to meet many Congressmen, who supported the amendment and Burton himself.

In 1998, Burton decided to drop the amendment as he could line up only two lawmakers to speak in his favour.

In sharp contrast, at least 21 Congressmen, led by Congressional Caucus on India and Indian-Americans Chairman Gary Ackerman (Democrat) took the floor to successfully resist the anti-India proposal.

They included the House International Relations Committee Chairman Benjamin Gilman and its Asia and Near-East Panel Chairman Douglas K Bereuter (both Republican), and Frank Pallone (Democrat).

It was the result of our active diplomacy on the Hill, as against heavy lobbying by Pakistan.

Congressmen used to say that India and Pakistan cancelled each other by their competition on the Hill.

What followed after our nuclear tests in May 1998 was much more serious.

President Clinton imposed the Glenn Amendment sanctions against India, which virtually choked trade and even normal cooperation in various areas.

We had marathon meetings on the Hill for several weeks.

Even the traditionally friendly Congressmen turned against us and gave lectures on Mahatma Gandhi and the Bhagavad Gita.

The Indian community exerted considerable pressure on their Senators and Congressmen to lift the sanctions against India.

Senator Sam Brownback (Republican) came up with a number of amendments to the sanctions law, citing the losses sustained by the US economy, business, and education.

That started the end of the sanctions' regime, which was gradually withdrawn by the US government.

The Kargil War was another occasion for us to fight against Pakistan on the Hill. Initially, there was an impression that India had started the war. But after we met a number of Congressmen, the wind changed in our favour, particularly since we did not cross the LoC to stage counterattacks.

Our effort on the Hill finally resulted in a meeting between President Clinton and Pakistan Prime Minister Nawaz Sharif, ultimately leading to Pakistan's withdrawal from Indian territory.

Our embassy may have been even more active on the Hill during the long negotiations on the nuclear deal (2005-2008), as it involved several legislative measures as part of the deal.

American lawmakers are generally polite in their discussions with diplomats, but some of them demonstrate righteous indignation when they speak on nuclear or human rights issues.

"Do what we tell you to do, not what we do," is the general refrain in these matters.

In such cases, we have no option but to strike a retreat.

But most of them gave a patient hearing, even if they were not convinced.

Lobbying on the Hill is a time consuming and cumbersome process, but nonetheless very effective when it comes to the subject of influencing the US government policies.

The place is iconic in many ways and the events of January were truly shameful and purposeless.

For those of us, who walked those artistic and polished corridors frequently, the insurrection was traumatic to the say the least.

Donald Trump had no possibility of preventing the Joint Session of the Congress from verifying the election results. The blood and dirt left behind by the attackers may have been wiped clean, but the world will long remember the reckless behaviour of a serving President.

The insurrection on the Hill may well have hit the last nail on Trump's political future.

Published: January 28, 2021

Ambassadorship Ethics: Examining Political Appointments

I magine this conversation.

U.S. Senator: "Good morning, Ambassador-designate. I see that you have been nominated as our Ambassador to Sri Lanka. Have you ever been to Colombo?"

Ambassador-designate: "Yes, Senator. But I am going to Sri Lanka, not to Latin America."

U.S. Senator: "Colombo happens to be the capital of Sri Lanka. Have you heard of Bandaranayake?"

Ambassador-designate: "No, Senator. But I assure you, as soon as I arrive in Sri Lanka, I shall visit that place."

Money Counts

This conversation may be apocryphal. But given the way that US Presidents appoint ambassadors out of those who have paid big financial contributions to the Democratic Party, even more bizarre conversations may take place during the Senate confirmation hearings; the qualification is not knowledge of history or geography, but the weight of the money bags deposited. This is part of the "spoils system", except that over the years, a price tag has been fixed for ambassadorships. U.S. President Richard M. Nixon had once even suggested that a floor price of $250,000 should be suggested for ambassadorships.

Now that U.S. President Joe Biden is in the process of filling up thousands of high-level posts, and the Senate has begun considering various names for confirmation, the ambassadorial aspirants who had paid money to the party, have also begun to assert their claims.

Making the right appointments is crucial for the Biden administration in order to clean up the mess created by his predecessor, Donald Trump.

Mr. Biden has appointed Linda Thomas-Greenfield, a retired career diplomat as the US Ambassador to the United Nations and she has been confirmed by the Senate, but many heavy contributors are waiting in the wings.

Anticipating that Mr. Biden will offer ambassadorial positions to some of his major donors—most of who are not particularly suited for such assignments—a member of the editorial board of *The New York Times*, Michelle Cottle, has made a fervent plea to Mr. Biden, in an article (March 18, 2021, 'Stop letting rich people buy ambassadorships') to "jettison the skeezy practice of rewarding big campaign contributors with Ambassadorships".

Entrenched as a "Tradition"

This is not the first time that a torch is being shone on this unfair practice. A study, some years ago conducted by some legal experts had recommended that rich people buying ambassadorships should be stopped.

In 1980, a decision was taken that most ambassadors should be career foreign service officers. Still, succeeding Presidents have filled from a minimum of 30% to a maximum of 57% (under Mr. Trump) of the posts with donors.

Since such a tradition has been established and is deeply entrenched, Mr. Biden may not be able to stop it either. The crucial question would be on what to do with those who had made donations for diplomatic stardom.

The appointments have solid backing of the U.S. Constitution, with Article II providing that the President "shall nominate, and by and with the Advice and Consent of the Senate, shall appoint ambassadors".

The President enjoys wide latitude in selecting a nominee and the Senate is comparably free to choose whether to advise and consent. The onus for the quality and integrity of the nominees rests on the President, but the Senate has the right to hold back confirmation of any nominee, including career diplomats.

Complicated Process

The path to ambassadorships for donors is not at all smooth. The Senate confirmation is quite a complicated process in which the investigating agencies examine their entire past to see whether they have ever been guilty of any misdemeanour, which disqualifies them for the high appointment.

Anything adverse that comes to the notice of the agencies will be conveyed to the nominee concerned. It is then up to him to decide whether to face the charges or quietly withdraw his candidature. There is an example of an Indian-American having been considered as Ambassador to Fiji and some other Pacific Island states, but he had to withdraw his nomination after the Federal Bureau of Investigation had communicated to him that it would be in his best interest to withdraw rather than face an investigation into his past.

There was another example of a donor ambassador, a rich businessman from Buffalo, who had apparently paid a huge sum for the U.S. Presidential campaign. He made no secret of his having been appointed on the strength of his financial contribution. He had his own grievances, such as being denied permission by the State Department to bring his own private aircraft to Fiji.

When he figured out that he would be accredited to six island states from Fiji and that there were only weekly flights from Fiji to the other capitals, he thought his own plane would be a great asset.

The ambassador spent his own money to refurbish the Embassy residence and to entertain well, with the choicest food and wines flown in from the U.S. He did not bother much about the politics of the South Pacific as he knew that he was there not to pursue a career but to enjoy a well-earned holiday.

He went to an island state called Tuvalu, which has a total population of 5,000, to present his credentials. He saw a little store at the airport which sold local handicrafts and asked the owner how much it cost. The bewildered owner asked which item he was looking for to which he said "The whole shop". The owner said that he would not be able to sell the whole shop as it would take several months to get the stock replenished and there would be no handicrafts shop at the airport.

The Indian Way

India has a more sophisticated system of appointing "political" ambassadors, not for donation to political parties, but as an avenue to recognise and reward talent. Till very recently, career diplomats could not aspire to ambassadorial posts in London, Washington or Moscow as distinguished people from different walks of life were appointed to add weight to the positions.

In the early years, Maharajas were appointed to several posts. And later, politicians were sent abroad when they had to be kept away from the country. The Government apparently has the discretion of appointing political ambassadors in up to 30% of the posts. But now, the number of political ambassadors is small, if at all, and the senior posts are open to career diplomats.

India has had some very distinguished and successful political ambassadors, who had access to the Prime Minister back home and to high levels in the host countries. Examples are three political ambassadors in Moscow (Dr. K.S. Shelvankar, D.P. Dhar and I.K. Gujral) and one in Washington (Naresh Chandra); all of them fulfilled certain criteria set by the Government, which included greater acceptability of political ambassadors in major capitals. Senior career diplomats were assigned to these posts as Deputy Chiefs of Mission, often with ambassadorial rank, to do much of the work, leaving the political ambassadors to deal with high policy.

The most celebrated political ambassador was Kushok Bakula Rinpoche, a Buddhist monk from Ladakh, who was appointed to Mongolia. He is credited with reviving Buddhism in Mongolia.

The Head of State himself used to pay obeisance to him as the Mongolians followed the same Mahayana Buddhism practised in Ladakh. Even after he completed his diplomatic assignment (January 1990-October 2000), Kushok Bakula Rinpoche retained strong ties with Mongolia till he died in his eighties.

False notion

In recent years, career ambassadors are occupying those posts which were considered political in nature. But the practice continues in many countries because of the general feeling that long careers in the Foreign Service are not necessary to be effective ambassadors.

In other words, diplomacy is not considered a profession for specialists, a notion as ridiculous as appointing a politician as the Surgeon General or a General.

We do not know whether Mr. Biden will heed the advice not to appoint donors as ambassadors. But if he does, there will be many frustrated donors in Washington and one source of political funding will dry up. On the other hand, the credibility of Biden diplomacy will increase and career diplomats will have better prospects.

Published: April 2, 2021

9/11 Museum Visit: Reflections on a Tragic Legacy

Someone had once suggested, that instead of killing Osama bin Laden, the United States should have made him walk in and out of the security zone of an airport in the country for the rest of his life.

That would be worse than hell for the architect of 9/11. He could be humiliated, strip-searched, x-rayed and be in perpetual tension as to what to expect next.

That is what every US citizen and foreign visitor undergoes 13 years after the plane missiles ripped through the World Trade Centre twin towers and wounded the psyche of the United States beyond redemption.

I heard a recent quip in New York that no terrorist attack took place after 9/11 because the US authorities were constantly terrorising their own people enough.

I was looking for any sign of relaxation in security procedures during my travels in the US earlier this month. I was pleasantly surprised when I presented myself for security screening for an early morning flight from La Guardia airport to Raleigh just a day after my arrival in New York.

The agent stopped me from taking off my jacket, belt and shoes and just waved me through the security arch, with my metal rod intact in my leg. I thought for a moment that the paranoia had ended.

But things were back to normal the next day on my return journey, when I had to take everything off and also explain why I had reinforced my leg with a metal rod.

Soon after, I read about a new regulation from a tweet that in future, you should make sure that any electronic device you carry is fully charged. If you fail to turn on the device, the device itself would be confiscated and you will be subject to special procedures.

It was clear that there would be no end to the restrictions which can be imposed on citizens by a state that still lives in fear.

The height of irony here is that security is at its peak in the newly opened National 9/11 Memorial Museum and the areas around Ground Zero, the place where the twin towers stood. The security checks are more rigorous than those at the airports, as though the terrorists are likely to strike even the museum that commemorates the tragedy they inflicted on the nation.

One wished that the museum had been left open for friends and foes alike to seek a deeper understanding of what it means to be a human being living in the beginning of the 21st century. But even this museum has become a monument to the fear that has gripped the nation, and visitors are constantly reminded of the perils that threaten them.

The footprints of the two towers are now vibrant pools with the names of the victims inscribed on their walls. Next to it is the giant new tower, getting ready for occupation.

The Memorial Museum, which was opened on May 21 this year near the new tower, has become a place of pilgrimage for those who were affected by the terrorist attacks in one way or another and an important stop for tourists that throng New York city throughout the year.

The mission of the museum is "to bear solemn witness to the terrorist attacks of September 11, 2001 and February 26, 1993". It honours nearly 3,000 victims and all who risked their lives to save others. It further recognises the thousands who survived and all who demonstrated extraordinary compassion in the aftermath of the tragedy. The museum attests to the triumph of human dignity and affirms an unwavering commitment to the fundamental value of human life.

What strikes the visitor most is the vast area of the museum at different levels and the small number of exhibits, which have been judiciously selected and displayed. The most important exhibits are located seven storeys below the ground and the walk prepares the visitor for an awesome encounter with history.

The planners obviously resisted the temptation to build a museum around the debris of the towers, or to present a ghastly picture to create aversion or sympathy. Only very few significant pieces of the building are exhibited and the most memorable is the Survivors' Stairs, a few stone steps that survived the blast to provide some support to the fleeing survivors.

Equally impressive is the mangled communications antenna, which adorned one of the towers, showing the multitude of cables and wires, which were built with care and precision at the time of its construction.

The atmosphere is certainly sombre, but not melodramatic. The exhibition conveys a sense of peace and optimism, not frustration and despondency.

Needless to say, the primary emphasis is on those who perished in the attack, but the proven heroism and sacrifice of the rescue workers receive equal attention in the museum.

In a sense, those who perished in the process of rescuing innocent victims evoke stronger feelings of admiration, which is reflected. A partially burnt fire engine is as prominently displayed as the telltale remnants of the towers, which are embedded in the walls.

A fine selection from among the very many artifacts and memorabilia created for the victims in different parts of the globe also find place in the display. A gleaming, seemingly new Honda motorcycle appears a little out of place among the exhibits, but on close examination, it turns out that it is an old prized possession of one of the victims, which was refurbished with care in accordance with the unfulfilled desire of the owner.

The pictures of the victims are tiny, but each is identified and displayed. There are also photographs taken by a French photographer, who captured the early moments of the bombing from a nearby home. These images are displayed with an account of how he stopped taking pictures and heroically began rescue work for several days.

A sense of peace and tranquillity overwhelms the visitors as they walk out into the gardens outside after taking in the enormity of the tragedy and the limitlessness of human depravity.

Visitors to the museum have the facility to write their remarks on an electronic board or record their impressions on camera. The planners seem to have taken into account the instinctive desire of visitors to the monuments to become their part.

In place of the graffiti that visitors create on old monuments around the globe, the museum has the facility to record comments and put signatures, which will be preserved for posterity.

My thoughts as I left the museum to merge into the traffic and crowds of lower Manhattan were about a nation living in fear even years after the attack of 9/11, though it is armed with the capability of destroying the world many times over.

No one can forget the moment when the first plane hit the tower. I heard about it first at a meeting of the Board of Governors of the International Atomic Energy Agency in Vienna. In the midst of the severe shock that reverberated in the board room, the chairman suggested an adjournment, but the Ambassadors took the floor to request that the meeting should continue "as though nothing had happened".

The meeting continued, but most delegates left the room to watch the news on the screens outside. Can the world ever move on as though nothing had happened on 9/11? The museum elegantly captures what happened on that fateful day and the continuing impact of those events on the US and the rest of the world.

The immortal line from Virgil's *Aeneid* engraved on the hall reminds us: "No day shall erase you from the memory of time".

Published: July 21, 2014

Racial Inequality:
A Persistent Pandemic

"I can't breathe," gasped an able-bodied black man, George Floyd, as he was pinned down on the ground by a white policeman. It was a brutal killing of a human being, whatever his crime may have been. Another white policeman was seen standing close by without any reaction. Passers-by kept pleading to let the man go, but the matter ended only when the man was sent to the hospital where he was declared dead on arrival.

This is not the first incident of racial tension and conflict in recent US history, but the deadly combination of a pandemic and racial violence, coupled with an insensitive and unpredictable president mismanaging the crisis, is an apocalyptic cocktail. After a week of violence in more than forty cities, it reached Washington and the White House precincts, forcing President Donald Trump and his family to take shelter in a nuclear bunker.

Even worse, he threatened to deploy the military if the law and order deteriorated any further. In the middle of all this, the president walked to the church nearby with the Holy Bible in hand for a photo-opportunity as tear gas kept the protesters at bay. Nothing could be more bizarre than that at a critical moment in history.

There is an old saying that sums up the disparities in the US with a health metaphor: "When white America catches a cold, black America gets pneumonia". But now, white America is not just catching a cold. Rather, it is getting ravaged by the coronavirus on nearly every front.

The virus has claimed the lives of over 106,000 Americans, accounted for over 1.7 million positive cases and cost the country 40 million jobs. Resultantly, the brunt of the pandemic is borne by those black Americans, who do not have the required medical cover or live in unhygienic conditions, which do not permit social distancing or quarantine.

The proportion of black Americans in the long list of deaths proclaims the tragedy. The blame is put on them as they invariably indulge in alcohol, tobacco and drugs. The sustained racial inequality is fanning the pandemic fire.

The president, blinded by racial hatred, is determined to fight the protests by harsh words and provocative action. He described the white-armed anti-lockdown protesters as "very good people", but called the multiracial Minneapolis protesters as "thugs".

"When the looting starts, the shooting starts," he tweeted with reference to an infamous phrase from an era of an eye for an eye and a tooth for a tooth. Twitter, which has been the greatest beneficiary of the president's tweet diplomacy, objected to the tweet for "glorifying violence".

The Irony

The irony of the whole situation is that it was not long ago that a black Nobel Laureate president was in the White House for two successful terms just before the present incumbent. The first black president was a symbolic victory for the black people of the US and the underdogs everywhere.

But Barack Obama did not want to come across to the public as a black president. It was as if he was trying to position himself as a neutral arbiter in racial matters, though one sensed his preference was for not intervening at all. But it was clear as time went on, that he was passionate about improving race relations. He spoke out more passionately and more intimately.

Telling reporters that his son would have looked like Trayvon Martin, the unarmed high school student shot dead in Florida by a neighbourhood watch coordinator, was a big change.

During the funeral of a black preacher, alongside eight other deceased worshippers, by a white supremacist, he spoke with a cadence that echoed Martin Luther King Jr.

Obama wanted to be a transformational president not only in race-relations but also in Medicare, nuclear policy, relations with Cuba and Iran. Trump ended all these hopes and became the symbol of a "white lash" against Obama.

Obama was fond of paraphrasing Martin Luther King's famed line that the arc of history bends towards justice, but it veered off into an altogether different direction. In the final days of the Obama presidency, the more accurate descriptor of race relations is a "fault-line"—the angriest fault-line in US politics. The world had expected seismic changes from Obama.

The presidency that began atop a mountain ended in something of a valley. It is not surprising that the race relations deteriorated, as other matters, during the Trump presidency. The US had already become a divided nation even before the pandemic arrived, but Trump wished everything away to prove his invincibility. The cry that "I can't breathe" comes not just from a suffocated African American but also from patients without ventilators and the economy in distress, while Trump fiddles away into the distant horizon.

The protests have reverberated in many countries, either in the form of statements by leaders or sympathetic protests. In India, there has not been any reaction either from the government or from any political/human rights groups. We seem to be in a different world, oblivious to the gathering clouds.

Published: June 3, 2020

Gun Violence in America: Addressing a National Crisis

President Joe Biden, like many of his predecessors, spoke in agony and desperation when a mad man shot and killed innocent children in a school. He said "When in God's name are we going to stand up to the gun lobby?" He was bewildered that the gun lobby was more powerful than him.

In an ironic twist, the most powerful country in the world cannot discipline its own citizens against the uncontrolled spread of guns across the country, leading to many such cases of gun violence.

Parents, whilst sending their kids to school in the US, cannot help but fear for their children's lives, with the prevalent gun culture in the country robbing them of the confidence that their children will come back alive. To make matters worse, the President can only pray "God bless America," while citizens believe they are safe only if they are armed.

Constitutional Right

The Second Amendment to the U.S. Constitution is one of the US' most important laws, as it gives Americans the right to bear arms; over one third of American adults have claimed to personally owning a gun.

There was a lack of clear federal court ruling defining the right, until the US Supreme Court ruled that the law protects any individual's right to keep and bear arms unconnected with service in a militia for traditionally lawful purposes, such as self-defence within the home.

In the latest incident a few days ago, an 18-year-old boy, Salvador Ramos, opened fire and killed at least 19 children—most of them under 10—and two teachers at a primary school in Uvalde, Texas.

A week prior to that, another 18-year-old killed ten people at a supermarket in Buffalo, New York. The scenes were familiar as it had happened many times before in different parts of the United States. Every time, everyone is agitated and determined to legislate new gun laws, and every time it fails; even before the last dead body is buried and the last blood stains are washed away, another corpse arrives.

The next reminder comes when another group of innocent children fall victim to another gun in another corner of the country.

Futile Anti-Gun Lobbying

Much has been written about the matter of gun legislation in the US, and how and why it is stuck in various Congressional gridlocks, and why nothing much will come out of all the anti-gun lobbying anytime in the near future.

It is very clear, however, that the failure to implement gun control-laws only shows that this is a scourge that will only spread further, unless there is a strong legislation banning firearms outside the law enforcement community.

Stark Divisions on Gun Policy

The ridiculous arguments against gun control are based on a false sense of absolute freedom expressed in the opposition to wearing masks, or vaccination even when there were grave risks to the whole community. The polarisation in the society on this subject is unbelievably strong.

There are differences in gun ownership rates by political party affiliation, gender, geography and other factors. For instance, 44% of Republicans and Republican-leaning independents say they personally own a gun, compared with 20% of Democrats and Democratic supporters. Men are more likely than women to own a gun (39% vs 22%). And 41% of adults living in rural areas report owning a firearm, compared with about 29% of those living in the suburbs and two-in-ten living in cities.

The gun sales have risen in recent years, particularly during the pandemic. At the same time, more than half of the US population (53%) favours strict gun control laws. But the population is divided as to whether gun-control will reduce shootings at all, because it is generally believed that those indulging in shootouts are mostly deviants and mentally deranged people, who respect no laws.

Arms for Safety, says Trump

President Trump was unmistakably on the side of the gun lobby and even President Obama could not push any legislation through. But both of them initiated legislative measures, which were abandoned for no good reason. After the latest shootings, Donald Trump said that the response to the shooting should be arming the people, not disarming them.

Rejecting calls for stricter gun controls at the National Rifle Association's (NRA) event, Donald Trump said that the existence of evil is one of the very best reasons to arm people. He said that Americans should be allowed the use of firearms to defend themselves against "evil." As for schools, he recommended a strict security system to prevent shooting incidents.

Biden's Words Ring Hollow

President Biden spoke movingly and blamed the gun lobbies for inhumanly preventing legislation. He kept saying that the time had come for action, but did not promise anything except rhetoric.

"And the gun manufacturers have spent two decades aggressively marketing assault weapons which make them the most and largest profit. For God's sake, we have to have the courage to stand up to the industry.

"Here's what else I know: Most Americans support common sense laws—common sense gun laws." And he left it at that. A mix of passionate attachment to personal liberty, profit making by gun-makers, fear of fellow human beings, passion for hunting and sheer lethargy and negligence were evident in the US reaction to the Texas school shootings.

For God's sake, how many more innocent children will be sacrificed before the laws are changed?

Sadly, the only superpower stands bewildered without an answer as the rest of the world watches helplessly.

Published: May 29, 2022

B. MULTILATERALISM
COMPULSION FOR REFORM

NAM Revisited: Principles for a Changing World

From all accounts, the Cold War is breaking out again. The United States has identified both China and Russia as adversaries, whose leaders, Xi Jinping and Vladimir Putin, are strong and determined to stand up to a faltering Donald Trump, who is desperately clinging on to the doctrines of ultra-nationalism and nuclear hegemony.

The Russia Dare

Mr. Putin has just announced that Russia has invincible doomsday machines like an underwater drone armed with a nuclear warhead powerful enough to sweep away coastal facilities, aircraft carriers, and a hypersonic vehicle impossible to intercept as it flies in a cloud of plasma "like a meteorite".

Cuba is in the dog house again and the "axis of evil" has emerged once again under Iran's leadership. This time it is a three-cornered Cold War, without any corner having committed countries to act together as military allies.

Potential allies are hedging with no viable grouping to protect the interests of the weak and the poor. If the Cold War is here in a new form, can a reincarnation of the Non-Aligned Movement (NAM) be far behind?

NAM is an anathema today even to those who helped shape it and revelled in it for years. India was one of its leaders, if not *the leader*. India had a stake in its integrity and toiled tirelessly to keep it on the middle road, not to be hijacked by Cuba to the left or Singapore to the right. We fought to keep Egypt within it when every Arab country wanted it to be ousted in 1979 after the Camp David agreements. Prime Minister Indira Gandhi risked a bear hug from Fidel Castro as she took the NAM gavel to save it from the uncertain leadership of Iraq. Had it not been for India, NAM would have been wound up at a ministerial meeting in Ghana in 1991 soon after the collapse of the Berlin Wall. It was characterised as the "last gasp of the old-style radicals".

India argued vehemently against those who felt that NAM had outlived its utility. Since the essence of nonalignment was freedom of thought and action, India insisted that it was valid whether there was one bloc or no bloc. Even while building alliances with others, we availed of the NAM umbrella to promote our national strategies when it suited us.

The very lack of homogeneity and unity in NAM enhanced its utility for us. One forum where we effectively used the NAM constituency was the Working Group on UN Reform, where we blocked an effort by the U.S. and others to add Germany and Japan as permanent members and close the doors for further expansion.

Hit Refresh

An effort was made in 2012 to craft a 'Nonalignment 2.0' in the context of the new global situation, amid India's growing global importance and the increasing rivalry between the U.S. and China. The report, 'NonAlignment 2.0: A foreign and strategic policy for India in the 21st century', moved the concept of nonalignment away from its origins. It reiterated that India needed to move quickly to extend its global role and influence. But the authors said India's big challenge would be to aim at not just being powerful but to set new standards for what the powerful must do.

India's legitimacy in the world will come from its ability to stand for the highest human and universal values and at the global level, "India must remain true to its aspiration of creating a new and alternative universality."

In a situation where the world is no longer bifurcated between two dominant powers, nonalignment today will require managing complicated coalitions and opportunities in an environment that is not structurally settled, the report said. The policy of "strategic autonomy" recommended that India should not take sides in the rivalry between China and the U.S. The report further emphasised that for its strategic and foreign policy to be successful, India must sustain domestic economic growth, social inclusion, and democracy.

Coming as it did in the wake of a strategic partnership with the U.S., the revival of NAM, even with caveats of various kinds, did not seem to appeal either to the Manmohan Singh government or the opposition Bharatiya Janata Party. For Prime Minister Narendra Modi too, NAM was nothing but a relic of the Nehruvian past and it did not form part of his vocabulary.

As Mr. Modi pursued his priorities of development, security, neighbourhood and the diaspora, there was no room for maintaining a constituency of the poor nations of the world. In his transactional foreign policy, it is easier to act alone rather than as the spokesperson of a group. It was no wonder, therefore, that he did not find it necessary to attend the NAM Summit in Venezuela in 2016. India, which conceived and nursed the concept, was ready to cast it into the dustbin of history. We began a journey from the leadership of the super poor to become a super power on the rise.

Where We Stand Today

Into the second half of his term, Mr. Modi's balance sheet shows an altogether different scenario. As a close defence partner of the U.S. and a member of the "Quadrilateral", India is right in the U.S. camp. As the baton of the orchestra passed into the hands of a wayward conductor, the new symphony of India-U.S. relations promised in 2016 has not quite materialised. Both China and Russia, which have been identified as adversaries in the U.S. world view, have their problems with India.

Doklam and the Maldives have shown that China is in no mood for a compromise. In fact, China has attributed the increase of its defence budget to the formation of the Quadrilateral, which is being seen as a direct threat to China.

An obvious way to revive NAM is by breathing new life into it and making it fit to deal with the new norm. But it has baggage which may be difficult to unload. A movement conceived in the context of a bipolar world may not suit the new emerging global order of a multipolar world. A partnership of near equals like IBSA (India, Brazil and South Africa) with similar interests without any ideological conflict is probably the best model to follow. Something on the lines of the G-15 organised by India and other like-minded countries some years ago could be put together with the objective of dealing with the kind of issues identified by Mr. Modi at Davos—climate change, terrorism and protectionism. The members may have links with the U.S., China and Russia, but they should be able to work together without the undue influence of the three.

Mr. Modi is not someone who will hesitate to think out of the box to achieve his objectives. Given the present impasse in international relations with little leeway for game-changing initiatives, India will do well to move away from being a camp follower of one of the emerging poles to create our own fourth pole.

Published: March 8, 2018

Need for Selectivity in Choosing Economic and Political Groupings

The current ruckus over AUKUS—the trilateral security pact between Australia, the United Kingdom, and the United States, which was announced on September 15, 2021—has revealed the hazards of group diplomacy, which Prime Minister Indira Gandhi had anticipated when President Ziaur Rahman of Bangladesh proposed a regional organisation for South Asia.

The SAARC Years

Apart from its reservations about the reference to security in the draft charter for SAARC, or the South Asian Association for Regional Cooperation, India was in a dilemma—that not joining the forum would look as though India was against regional cooperation. And if it joined, it faced the possibility of its neighbours ganging up and using the SAARC institutions to pressure India on various regional issues. One other concern was that the proposer of such a group would be suspected of aspiring to the leadership of a region.

On balance, India joined the Association with a number of conditionalities such as the exclusion of bilateral issues, decision-making by voting, and holding of meetings without all members being present. But despite the imperative for cooperation in vital fields, SAARC became an arena for India bashing, particularly by Pakistan. It was bilateral diplomacy in the guise of multilateralism and it became moribund as India did not attend the last summit. SAARC became a liability as it was clear that the region was not mature enough to have a regional instrumentality.

Today, the world has a whole spectrum of groups—from the European Union at one end to the African Union at the other—with varying shades of cooperation. Groups with acronyms such as North Atlantic Treaty Organization (NATO) and the Association of Southeast Asian Nations (ASEAN) and numerical groups from a notional G-2 to a real G-77 which has more than a 100 members, exist.

Many of them do not have regional, ideological, or thematic homogeneity to lend them a reason for forming a group. The time, the money, and the energy spent on convening not only summits but also a whole paraphernalia of ministerial, official and expert level meetings do not seem justified.

Bureaucracies with United Nations salaries and perks grow around these bodies, developing vested interests to perpetuate them. Such groups which do not have "sunset" clauses continue even after they diminish in importance

Searching for an Agenda

Finding the agenda for these organisations and groups is another difficult exercise. The growing agenda of the United Nations includes everything from peace on earth to celestial bodies and even UFOs. When India decided to remain in the Commonwealth even as an independent country, the nature of the affinity to the British Crown changed and its agenda expanded beyond the concerns of the former British colonies.

The only way it could survive after Zimbabwe became independent and apartheid disappeared in South Africa, was by duplicating the agenda of the United Nations and repeating pronouncements of member-States made in other organisations. The role of the Commonwealth was reviewed, but the members reached the conclusion that it had continuing relevance.

The rationale of some of the other new groups was unclear even when they were formed. A Goldman Sachs economist found similarities among fast-growing economies such as China, Russia, India, and Brazil, and recommended massive Western investments in these countries. The countries concerned formed an intergovernmental group called BRIC and later BRICS, with South Africa added as a representative of the African continent.

At that time, it was feared that, with the presence of China and Russia in it, it would be construed as an anti-American group. As expected, China quickly assumed the leadership of BRICS and tried to seek changes in the international economic system by establishing a bank, with the possibility of credit for its members. The result of this development was undermining the relevance of another, less ambitious, group of India, Brazil and South Africa (IBSA), which had several common interests. As candidates for permanent membership of the Security Council, they had specific ideas on UN reform and on South-South cooperation.

On Afghanistan

The recent BRICS summit had Afghanistan on its agenda and the diverse group was able to reach a conclusion only with different caveats. Russia and China were more sympathetic to the Taliban than the others. At the Shanghai Cooperation Organisation (SCO) summit, delegations found some common elements of concern with dramatically different approaches.

The SCO started off as a friendly group of China and some of the former Republics of the Soviet Union, but with the addition of India, Pakistan and Iran, it became a diverse group and it could not reach agreement. Pakistan naturally sounded triumphant, but even Pakistan Prime Minister Imran Khan could not gloat over the unshackling of the Taliban in the face of a looming humanitarian catastrophe in Afghanistan.

Whether the Chinese presence in these summits and the meetings between Wang Yi and S. Jaishankar (the Chinese State Councillor and Foreign Minister and India's External Affairs Minister, respectively) made any difference to the stand-off in Ladakh is yet to be seen. But we know that frequent meetings with the leaders of China do not necessarily mean a meeting of minds as Beijing's trajectory of thoughts and actions are highly unpredictable.

Those who saw China's President Xi Jinping and Prime Minister Narendra Modi in conversation in Mamallapuram (Mahabalipuram), near Chennai, at the second informal summit between India and China, in October 2019, would never have thought that they would ever be in an armed conflict.

India and Other Groupings

India has also had experience of taking initiatives to encourage groups without the participation of Pakistan, knowing well that their presence is a sure recipe for trouble. One of them is the Bay of Bengal Initiative for Multi-Sectoral Technical and Economic Cooperation (BIMSTEC), an international organisation of seven South Asian and Southeast Asian nations which are dependent on the Bay of Bengal: Bangladesh, Bhutan, India, Nepal, Sri Lanka, Myanmar and Thailand. The group remained dormant for many years till it was revived a few years ago as an alternative to SAARC. Though it has an ambitious agenda for sectoral cooperation, it has not gained much momentum.

Another group which India has championed is the Indian Ocean Rim Association (IORA). The organisation was first established as the Indian Ocean Rim Initiative in Mauritius in March 1995 and formally launched on March 6-7 1997 (then known as the Indian Ocean Rim Association for Regional Co-operation). It also drags on without any significant progress.

On the other hand, the two active groups—Asia-Pacific Economic Cooperation (APEC) and Nuclear Suppliers Group (NSG)—have eluded us even though we have major stakes in them. We campaigned actively for membership of these two bodies but gave up when we made no headway. In the process of working with the U.S. on a bouquet of groups such as Missile Technology Control Regime (MTCR), NSG, the Wassenaar Arrangement and the Australia Group, we ended up with membership of Wassenaar and the Australia Group, in which we were not interested.

The Quad and AUKUS

The Quad had a chequered history of India flirting with it for years till the Chinese threat became real in 2020, but New Delhi's reluctance to call a spade a spade has driven the U.S. to new alliances such as a second Quad and then AUKUS as the U.S. wanted to fortify itself with allies against China.

But the reaction of France to AUKUS has raised the issue of loyalty among allies even though AUKUS has made it clear that it was meant only to enable the U.S. to transfer nuclear propelled submarine technology to Australia. The proliferation of alliances and groups will be a matter of close scrutiny by many countries in the light of the new trend initiated by the U.S.

Collective bargaining is the strength of group diplomacy but it cannot be effective without commitment to a common cause. It stands to reason that India should also reconsider the plethora of groups we are in and rationalise them after a reality check.

Published: October 4, 2021

G20 for Global Peace:
Leveraging Summit Dynamics

The outcome of the two recent ministerial meetings of the G20 in India this month is open to diametrically opposite assessments. For those who believe that no item on the agenda of G20 is as important as ending the Russia-Ukraine war, without which no amount of consensus on economic issues will resolve the gigantic issues facing the world today, the entire exercise was in futility.

On the other hand, as the Russian Foreign Minister Sergey Lavrov pointed out, G20 had not addressed political and security issues ever since it was established in 1999, and there was no reason why the G20 should now be judged on the basis of its performance in dealing with the war.

India being the host of the event appeared to be inclined to consider the meeting of G20 foreign ministers as a resounding success, with the outcome document reflecting the concerns of developing countries and the Global South. This was evident when the member countries discussed other issues of great global import, such as terrorism and reliable supply chains.

G20 countries condemned terrorism in all its forms and manifestations, noting that the growing threat from the misuse of new and emerging technologies for terrorist purposes presented a great danger globally. As such, they pitched for a more inclusive and reinvigorated form of multilateralism and reform.

The Delhi G20 foreign ministers' meeting was one of the largest such gatherings hosted by any G20 presidency. The outcome document at the end of it said supply chains of both food and agricultural products including fertilisers should be kept reliable, open, and transparent.

G20 foreign ministers had met at a time when the world faced multi-dimensional challenges ranging from insufficient progress towards Sustainable Development Goals (SDGs), climate change, pollution and biodiversity loss to economic slowdown, debt distress, uneven pandemic recovery, growing poverty and inequality, food and energy insecurity, and global supply chain disruptions which were further aggravated by geopolitical tensions and conflicts.

"Meeting under India's G20 Presidency, with the theme 'Vasudhaiva Kutumbakam'—'One Earth. One Family. One Future'—the G20 foreign ministers deliberated upon current global challenges. They brought focus on strengthening multilateralism, food and energy security, ambitious climate and environmental action, deepening cooperation on sustainable development, counter-terrorism, counter-narcotics, global health, global talent pool, humanitarian assistance and disaster risk reduction, as well as gender equality and women's empowerment," the outcome document said.

It added that the global order has undergone dramatic changes since World War II due to economic growth and prosperity, decolonisation, demographic dividends, technological achievements, emergence of new economic powers, and deeper international cooperation.

"The United Nations must be responsive to the entire membership, faithful to its founding purposes and principles of its Charter and adapted to carrying out its mandate. In this context, we recall the Declaration on the Commemoration of the 75th anniversary of the United Nations (UNGA 75/1) which reaffirmed that our challenges are inter-connected and can only be addressed through reinvigorated multilateralism, reforms and international cooperation," it said.

G20 foreign ministers said the need for revitalised multilateralism to adequately address contemporary global challenges of the 21st century, and to make global governance more representative, effective, transparent and accountable, has been voiced at multiple platforms.

As for the paralysis of the UN over the fight against the pandemic and stopping the war on account of the veto, the outcome papered over the issue by calling for a more inclusive and reinvigorated multilateralism and reform aimed at implementing the 2030 agenda. It made pious declarations about making the forthcoming multilateral conferences a success and working with the African partners.

The meeting recalled the Bali Leaders' Declaration where leaders had reaffirmed that the rules-based, non-discriminatory, free, fair, open, inclusive, equitable, sustainable and transparent multilateral trading system, with the WTO at its core, is indispensable to advancing our shared objectives.

These include the need for inclusive growth, innovation, job creation and sustainable development in an open and interconnected world. Furthermore, they involve supporting the resilience and recovery of a global economy strained by Covid-19 and global supply chain disruption.

The document was, however, silent about the way these can be accomplished even as a devastating war was raging, affecting the vitals of the entire world.

On climate change and biodiversity, the foreign ministers reaffirmed the steadfast commitments of their leaders, in pursuit of the objective of UNFCCC, to tackle climate change by strengthening the full and effective implementation of the Paris Agreement and its temperature goal; reflecting equity and the principle of common but differentiated responsibilities and respective capabilities in light of different national circumstances. It appeared as though a mere reiteration of these principles would be enough to give momentum to the international effort to reverse climate change.

The pandemic also received the attention of the ministers, yet there was no formula to deal with the present and future dangers of a pandemic. The helplessness of humanity to work together in the face of a permanent member of the UN Security Council being suspected of creating the virus still haunts the world. It called for support for a new mechanism to negotiate and adopt a new pandemic instrument, an idea which was not yet accepted.

Indian External Affairs Minister S Jaishankar claimed that there was a considerable meeting of minds on the bulk of the issues concerning the Global South—the developing countries. He added that if we had a perfect meeting of minds on all issues and captured it fully, then it would have resulted in a collective statement.

He made light of the fact that "it is just on two paragraphs that we were not able to get everybody on the same page." Answering a query on the impact of the Ukraine conflict, Jaishankar said it is impacting the Global South, adding that for a year, India was stressing the need to end the war.

But the fact that G20 could not collectively demand an end to the war was a matter of regret. The G20 failed to rise to the occasion to deal with the most pressing issue of the moment.

In composition and structure, G20 is better suited than the Security Council to deal with existential issues as members have no veto. A reformed Security Council will never materialise within the framework of the present Charter and all that the G20 can do is to arrogate to itself the right to demand the end of the war for the sake of humanity.

The little gain that it made in Bali by producing two consensus paragraphs could have been the basis of a larger consensus later in the year, if it was not frittered away at the ministerial meeting. Hopefully, the G20 summit will act as a force for peace later in the year and demand an end to the war.

Published: March 13, 2023

Yoga at the UN: Promoting Health and Harmony

Among the many rabbits that Prime Minister Narendra Modi has produced out of his hat, the one that has multiplied fastest is yoga as part of the Indian smart power, which has the potential to influence the world.

As author Manil Suri has observed in his *New York Times* column, "A practice with Vedic origins that has nevertheless attained such secular popularity is the perfect vehicle to create a shared national consciousness." The proposal that such a seemingly innocuous exercise of the body and the mind should be given an International Day by the United Nations was a masterstroke in itself.

There is no automaticity about any Indian idea getting accepted at the UN and, therefore, Modi chose an irresistible concept; one which had already been recognised around the world. But it took some efforts by our mission to the UN to find 175 countries to sponsor and to get it adopted without a vote.

Though 175 countries co-sponsored the relevant resolution, 16 countries refrained from doing so for one reason or another. Perhaps to ensure wide support, India is not even mentioned in the relevant resolution.

Any proposal to declare a new International Day at the UN meets with resistance because many such Days have been declared already at the instance of various member-States and the secretariat normally maintains that there is a ban on declaring more Days. It was almost 10 years ago that the idea of a Yoga Day was mooted by some NGOs, but it had no takers till Prime Minister Narendra Modi realised its potential, probably at the instance of Sri Sri Ravi Shankar.

Among the Days declared so far, only the most significant ones such as UN Day, Human Rights Day, Women's Day, etc. are celebrated, while many others, like World Toilet Day, are easily forgotten. Yoga was accepted because of the general familiarity it had acquired in the West, particularly at the UN.

Yoga was introduced to the UN in the early 1970s by a humble junior clerk in the Indian consulate in New York, who later became a yoga and meditation guru to many celebrities in the state. The roster of big names who became his disciples includes the former Secretary-General of the UN, U Thant. With the assumed name of Sri Chinmoy, he himself became a celebrity by the time he passed away in 2007.

Chinmoy established his first meditation centre in Queens, New York, and eventually attracted thousands of students in 60 countries. Since April 1970, he began giving meditation lessons in a room assigned to him. A prolific author, artist, poet, and musician, he advocated, in addition to meditation, athleticism to achieve spiritual enlightenment, including distance running, swimming, and weightlifting.

Towards the evening of his life, he began a project of "lifting" many celebrities, who visited the UN, using a special contraption. Among the hundreds he "lifted" were presidents, prime ministers, foreign ministers, and ambassadors. One of the most prominent names here is the former, and last President of the erstwhile Soviet Union Mikhail Gorbachev. I too had received an invitation to be "lifted", but I was not too sure that it was safe. Even today, we can see many members of the UN staff coming to work in white kurtas and saris, identifying themselves as the disciples of Sri Chinmoy.

Though there is no record of Sri Chinmoy being remembered in the context of Yoga Day, his views on yoga were very much in tune with the interpretation offered by the Indian representatives. He had once said, "Yoga does not interfere with any religion. The real aspirant who has launched into spirituality and yoga will find no difficulty in remaining in his own religion. I have disciples who are Catholics, Protestants, Jews and so forth. I tell them not to give up their own religion. It is always easier and safer in the beginning for one to remain in his own religion while he practises yoga.

"But once he realises God, he transcends all religions. When one goes deep within and realises God, he sees that the whole universe belongs to him, and this realisation transcends all religions. Religion is inspiration. Yoga is aspiration. Divinity is perfection. Inspiration, aspiration and perfection can easily and fruitfully blossom here on earth in transcendental harmony."

In a letter to Sri Chinmoy in April 1972, U Thant wrote, "You have indeed instilled in the minds of hundreds of people here the moral and spiritual values which both of us cherish very dearly. I shall always cherish the memorable occasion of our meetings at the United Nations."

The foundations laid by Sri Chinmoy over a lifetime will now come to India's help in propagating yoga at the UN. Ban Ki-moon may already know that he is not the first UN Secretary-General to practice yoga. But the UN itself will move on to celebrate another Day, having done its duty to mental and international peace, and incidentally, to a rising India.

In the old days, yoga had its opponents in the East and the West. When we wanted to introduce a series on yoga in the *India Magazine*, published by the Indian embassy in Moscow, the Soviet government objected to it, labelling it as "anti-Communist".

We were told that the spirituality propagated by yoga would promote capitalism. Not wanting to propagate capitalism in the Soviet Union, we finally settled for projecting yoga as a form of exercise sans spirituality! It was only after the Indo-Soviet Treaty that the USSR embraced yoga.

In the US, Christianity found an enemy in yoga and protested against its introduction in schools in New York and California. Many Muslim and Christian nations voted for the Yoga Day for political reasons, but they should not be expected to switch to yoga either as an exercise for the body or the mind.

Yoga is sure to become a fad in the short term both domestically and internationally, but it is not likely to be sustained as a way of life. Prime Minister Modi will find another rabbit soon to bring India and himself on the centre stage once again. Given the experience of promoting yoga, which is a part of Sanatana Dharma, he will do better to find something more secular.

Published: June 24, 2015

India at the UN: Balancing Principles and Pragmatism

Mohamed ElBaradei, a former director general of the International Atomic Energy Agency and a Nobel laureate for Peace, who describes himself as "a friend of India who holds it in high esteem and who is keen to see India adhere to its admirable long held principles, even if it is necessary to calibrate its policies with changing circumstances", wrote to me recently that "India's votes recently have not been great on matters of principle."

He said it in the context of the UN seeking an opinion of the International Court of Justice on the Israeli occupation of Palestinian lands for five decades. He also had made a reference to the upholding of international law in Ukraine.

Such sentiments have been on many lips since 2014 either to denigrate the foreign policy of the Modi government or out of nostalgia for the Nehruvian view of the world, which determined India's foreign policy even during the Vajpayee government. Initially, the concern was about India getting too close to the United States, when India became a close defence partner of the US by signing some fundamental defence agreements, which the previous governments had declined to do. Changes in policy towards Israel, which necessitated some changes in our position on Palestine, were also causes for concern among many supporters of the Palestinian cause.

Then the neighbourhood policy was in question when Prime Minister Narendra Modi went the extra mile to normalise relations with Pakistan and China in the initial phase. Many negative developments in relations with the neighbours resulted in India reverting to taking a harder stand on its neighbours.

Foreign policy became an election issue in 2019 and it was the surgical strikes and the resolute rejection of talks with Pakistan, as long as terrorism remained an instrument of policy, that the tide turned in favour of the government. The massive mandate Modi received for his second term was largely on account of his handling of India's neighbours, particularly Pakistan.

For the second Modi government, challenges came "not in single spies, but in battalions" in international relations. The pandemic, the Chinese incursions in Ladakh, the advent of the Biden administration and the Russia-Ukraine war raised unprecedented issues in foreign policy. The international reaction to the removal of Article 370, the Citizenship Act, the farmers strike and actions by 'overzealous Hindus' was hostile, and Indian democracy itself was downgraded by the likes of Freedom House. The India bashers basked in the negative coverage of events in India in the Western press.

The Russia-Ukraine war pushed us into a deeper dilemma, with our commitment to sovereignty of nations on the one hand and our legacy relationship with Russia on the other. India's position of neutrality all the way puzzled people in India and abroad, particularly as our votes in the Security Council and the General Assembly were identical to the Chinese position.

Even after the new security treaty between Russia and China on the eve of the Russian invasion of Ukraine, we remained steadfast in our neutrality, leading to concern in the world that India was abandoning its principles for the sake of the stakes we have in maintaining mutually beneficial relations with Russia. The economic and defence ties with Russia were so vital that India closed its eyes to Russian transgressions in Ukraine.

The way Modi's trusted External Affairs Minister S Jaishankar circumnavigates the Earth whilst fighting so many fires is testimony to the fact that India is facing criticism from friends and foes alike. Many are not convinced about our compulsions to follow our present policy on Ukraine.

The Prime Minister himself travels much less than before, as he knows that Jaishankar has the right mix of firmness and flexibility to tackle the hardest of the critics, and to be reasonable to well-wishers. However, the tide has not turned in our favour as a vast majority of nations condemn President Putin and wonder why India is not on the side of democracies against a dictator.

We can certainly deal with our detractors by defending our national interests, but there is a vast multitude of people like ElBaradei, who wish us well and genuinely expect that there is not enough justification for India to do business as usual with Russia when the global system itself is being challenged by it.

Russia cannot expect to derive the benefits of the fixed deposits of the Soviet Union made in India till eternity. The US has made it clear that it has no objection to nations buying oil from Russia at cheap prices. What our friends object to is that India is not taking into account the massive killings and destruction of a nation, which was once a part of the same union as Russia.

Our Prime Minister's outright declaration that this is not an era for war and that what we need today is diplomacy and democracy was welcomed worldwide. But Putin's fulsome praise for India and the presence of a huge delegation of senior officials with Jaishankar when he visited Russia recently have shocked many.

It appeared that it was business as usual for India even when the war was raging. It was ominous that Russia had to withdraw from Kherson within days after the Russia-India conclave. The threat of using tactical weapons in the war by Russia was an added element in the criticism against India.

Suggestions have been made that this is the time for India to offer mediation in the war. Nothing will be more unwise than that as we have no credibility with the US and NATO. Any move will be misconstrued as an effort to rescue Putin from disgrace. Furthermore, Biden has become stronger after the midterm polls and we may have to deal with him for some more years.

In my response to ElBaradei, I said: "India's votes appear different from before, but a little dose of pragmatism is necessary in these changing times." But like many other friends of ours, he is not convinced that we should be pragmatic to the extent of moving away from our principles.

By reiterating his call for a ceasefire, followed by negotiations, Modi has maintained in Bali his position of exploring the possibilities for peace rather than take sides. But many friends of India still feel that India should condemn the aggressor on the basis of the principles we uphold rather than adopt a pragmatic policy of neutrality.

With the likelihood of the world being divided into democracies and autocracies in the near future, our allegiance lies with the former. Our friends feel, therefore, that it is time for India to adjust its policy on Ukraine to make it principled on the values we hold, however pragmatic it may be to remain on the side of peace, democracy and negotiations, rather than on either side.

Published: November 23, 2022

UN Special Forces Proposal: Addressing Future Pandemics

The World Health Organisation (WHO) is not equipped to fight a pandemic of great proportion. Its responsibility is to monitor threats to public health and inform and advise the member states. The fight against Covid-19 had to be on a war footing. For this we need a composite force that has the capabilities of massive sanitisation, testing, hospitalisation, and providing adequate support systems.

Even the most powerful nations are not able to cope with the effort, and there are signs of conflict on account of shortages of equipment and trained personnel. The only UN body which has the training for assembling fighting forces for such emergencies is the Department of Peace Operations.

A Force under Chapter VII

The UN Security Council (UNSC) stands paralysed because of petty battles on the name of the pandemic, its origin, and the need for transparency. It should hold an emergency meeting and authorise the UN Secretary-General to put together a force under Chapter VII of the UN Charter.

The mandate of the Charter should be interpreted to emphasise that this is the greatest threat to international peace and security. Moreover, conflicts are possible on account of the fragility of the international system. Member states should be requested to send not only troops but also police, health workers, and equipment.

In war situations, the Secretary-General is able to put together a force in about four months. This operation requires even greater speed and emergency mobilisation. There is some delicacy about deploying the army internally in different political systems, but the UN forces have been acceptable in most countries.

As for the cost, the responsibility for the deployment of forces for peacekeeping, peacebuilding, and peace enforcement is that of the permanent members. Instead of competing with each other for leadership of the post-Covid-19 world, let them help create a post-Covid-19 world.

So far, Covid-19 has spread in relatively prosperous regions of the world, which have both stable, advanced infrastructure, and health systems. We cannot trust that it will not spread to less equipped states, in which the devastation will be much more. Only a UN force which can enforce social distancing and lockdowns on the dot can prevent a catastrophe.

Most Chapter VII resolutions determine the existence of a threat to the peace, a breach of the peace, or an act of aggression in accordance with Article 39, and make a decision based explicitly under its dictation. A UNSC Resolution is considered to be 'a Chapter VII resolution' if it makes an explicit determination that the situation under consideration constitutes a threat to the peace, a breach of the peace, or an act of aggression, and/or explicitly/implicitly states that the UNSC is acting under the mandate of Chapter VII in the adoption of some or all operative paragraphs.

Many Resolutions

Chapter VII resolutions are very rarely isolated measures. Often the first response to a crisis is a resolution demanding that the crisis be ended in swift fashion. This is later followed by an actual resolution detailing the measures required to secure compliance with the first resolution. Sometimes dozens of resolutions are passed over time to modify and extend the mandate of the first Chapter VII resolution.

The UN stands discredited today as the UNSC has not been able to meet. It may take place, now that China has vacated the Security Council chair and Dominican Republic has taken over. Several resolutions are in circulation, but none under Chapter VII. The first step will be to pass a resolution to take action to end the crisis and authorise the Secretary-General to request member states to make personnel available. Meanwhile, another resolution must spell out the modalities of the operation.

The UN peacekeeping forces are called Blue Berets because of the colour of the caps that they wear. The health force can have caps of another colour, probably red. The launch of the Red Berets will be a historic action to be taken at a critical moment. The UN's relevance will be established and there will be concrete action taken to end the pandemic.

Published: April 8, 2020

QUAD's Role: Strengthening Democratic Cooperation

The deteriorating global situation and the continuing Ukraine war have transformed the Quad from a security dialogue to a formal partnership of four countries, Australia, Japan, India, and the US, with a broad agenda to confront the looming political and economic crisis. The Quad has agreed upon the fundamental principles that will determine its approach and launched several initiatives, which will strengthen their defence and economic capabilities. With its expanded agenda, the Quad has become a "force for good", as said by Indian PM Narendra Modi.

However, there is no doubt that the Chinese threat was the reason for the Quad to become a robust partnership. After China and Russia declared an alliance without boundaries and Russia attacked Ukraine, Russia also became a matter of concern for the Quad. Russia raised objection even to the name Indo-Pacific and preferred to continue to call it Asia-Pacific.

The Western countries in the Quad were interested in turning the Quad into a democratic force, but India's neutrality in the Ukraine conflict prevented the Quad from uniting against Russia. Both China and Russia issued warnings just before and during the Tokyo summit against the Quad becoming an adjunct of NATO. Chinese and Russian jets are reported to have flown over Tokyo while the Quad was in session.

Concerns over Ukraine and Russia were voiced by the US, Japan and Australia, but India maintained its position that the focus should be on ending the conflict and the tragic humanitarian crisis and its negative impact on the Indo-Pacific. The differences between India and the rest of the Quad were narrowed and a common agenda was agreed upon.

The visit of PM Modi to Europe before the Quad summit may have prepared the ground for the new approach. At the same time, the Quad announced several measures to counter China, without naming them, to enable the partners to monitor the Indo-Pacific region to ensure peace and stability there.

The Joint Statement issued by member nations states that the countries "strongly support the principles of freedom, rule of law, democratic values, sovereignty and territorial integrity, peaceful settlement of disputes without resorting to threat or use of force, any unilateral attempt to change the status quo, and freedom of navigation and overflight, all of which are essential to the peace, stability and prosperity of the Indo-Pacific region and to the world.

"We will continue to act decisively together to advance these principles in the region and beyond. We reaffirm our resolve to uphold the international rules-based order where countries are free from all forms of military, economic and political coercion."

The reiteration of these principles makes it clear that the Quad does not approve much of what is happening in the world and the criticism of some of the actions of China and Russia is implicit in the Joint Statement.

One of the measures adopted was the Indo-Pacific Maritime Domain Awareness (IPMDA). It will offer a real time, integrated, cost-effective maritime domain awareness picture, and it will transform the ability of the Quad countries themselves and their partners in the Pacific Islands, Southeast Asia, and the Indian Ocean region to fully monitor developments.

The leaders reaffirmed their commitment to a free and open Indo-Pacific that is inclusive and resilient, and vowed to work tirelessly to deliver tangible results for the region.

Going further afield, the Quad supported the complete de-nuclearisation of the Korean Peninsula and condemned North Korea's destabilising nuclear and missile tests. It also called for the immediate end to violence in Myanmar and the restoration of democracy there, even though India has been more patient with the military junta and given humanitarian assistance to the people.

The Quad took a strong position against terrorist attacks including cross-border attacks and named the Mumbai and Pathankot terror attacks. As for Afghanistan, it demanded that the Afghan territory must never again be used to shelter or train terrorists.

Global health and combating Covid-19 have been assigned a high priority in the activities of the Quad. Infrastructure development and addressing of debt issues figure prominently among its concerns.

The Quad will steadfastly implement the Paris Agreement and deliver on the outcomes of COP26. It launched the "Quad Climate Change Adaptation and Mitigation Package (Q-CHAMP)" with "mitigation" and "adaptation" as its two themes. Advancing cyber security has also been identified as a priority for improving the defence capabilities of the partners.

The Quad today has a comprehensive agenda, going beyond security dialogue as non-conventional threats to human security have been on the rise. The Quad, with a shared vision for a free and open Indo-Pacific, has emphasised the importance of fundamental values and principles, and committed to work tirelessly to deliver tangible results to the region. It has also agreed to maintain a continuous dialogue among themselves, including a summit in Australia next year.

Published: May 29, 2022

UN Reflections: Past Mistakes and Future Imperatives

UN Gaffes are not Rare

No wonder only the Indian ambassador realised that our minister of external affairs was reading the wrong speech at the UN Security Council. The others were not listening, not even the Portuguese delegate who authored the text.

In the UN, delegates develop selective hearing because no one can listen to the millions of words spoken every day. Everyone knows that the first few minutes of the speeches in the Security Council will be devoted to congratulating the current President on his assumption of the position even though it is by rotation and thanking the previous President for his accomplishments, even if they did not achieve anything during their month-long presidency.

The members of the Council were waiting for our minister to come to the substance of the debate to give him some attention. If he had said anything new or original, it would not have gone unnoticed. But what happened to the practice in our Permanent Mission in New York of one officer being assigned to every politician to keep a copy of the speech and to make sure that every word is delivered correctly?

In the case of the minister of external affairs, this used to be done at the level of the Deputy Permanent Representative himself. How could the officers occupying the four chairs behind the minister not know he was reading the wrong speech for full three minutes? Has the good custom of having a heading and even a separate cover sheet for the speeches of the ministers been abandoned? Did the Portuguese mission also circulate the speech without a heading or a cover? We need to have answers to these questions if we have to understand where the system went wrong.

Such things are too important to be left to the minister himself. After all, ministers have too many things on their mind to check whether the text placed before them is the right one or not. The topic of the debate was also a motherhood issue, development, not any controversial matter.

One Minister Read 'Namibia' as 'Nambiar' Repeatedly!

I have had some experience of gaffes by our political delegates misreading or mispronouncing words. One distinguished minister of state read 'Namibia' as 'Nambiar' repeatedly from the podium of the General Assembly. Unlike in the Security Council, no one sits or stands behind the speaker when he speaks and there is no way to communicate with him quickly to correct any mistake.

Another delegate—this time a lady—accustomed as she was during the decolonisation days to condemnations of various policies of imperial powers, decided to 'condemn' UNESCO for helping a non-self-governing territory to preserve its cultural heritage. The text, of course, meant to commend the UN agency!

Speaking of pronunciation, my Indonesian colleague, sitting next to me in the General Assembly Hall, asked me once what language our delegate was speaking in. Normally if a delegate does not speak in any of the six languages of the UN, someone would read the English text from the booth. My Indonesian friend could not catch the English version as our delegate was actually speaking in his version of English.

On one occasion, we had a truly sick external affairs minister, who should have stayed at home without taking the strain of travelling to New York. In fact, the minister of state was also sent to New York at the same time in case the minister needed any help. But our minister insisted on doing everything that the ministers were expected to do, like making speeches and holding bilateral meetings. He resented any suggestion that he might want to rest after a few meetings.

That was one occasion when I had smuggled myself behind the podium with the permission of the chair when the minister spoke to help him, if necessary.

In replying to the minister's comments on Jammu & Kashmir, a particularly vicious Pakistani delegate referred to India as "the sick man of Asia", hitting somewhat below the belt. The same minister left us in a quandary when he called on the Secretary-General. The minister described all the problems we were having with Pakistan and repeatedly asked the Secretary-General to intervene in some way. The Secretary-General, who was very keen to intervene, knew the Indian policy too well to take the request seriously.

Still, we did not feel comfortable till we wrote a letter to the Secretary-General on our return to the mission, that the minister did not really mean to request for mediation.

India is Not the Only Country that Generates Such Gaffes at the UN

We also had political delegates, who wanted to change policy when they were at the UN. A very senior delegate was convinced that our policy on Afghanistan was wrong. He was inclined to support the resolutions which criticised the Soviet invasion of Afghanistan, but our policy was to abstain on them. We had abstained on the main resolution already, but in one of the committees, a similar resolution was introduced.

Knowing his views, I tried to send him for coffee to the delegates' lounge when the vote came up. He was not interested in shopping or sightseeing. He was also very conscientious and did not leave the chair in the committee.

When a roll call vote was announced and India's name was called, he said, "yes", but I shouted loudly "abstention" from behind him. The secretariat official, who knew the Indian position well, recorded our vote as abstention and our delegate was not any wiser. He was hard of hearing.

We had another delegate, who was convinced that our policy on East Timor was faulty. He was seen hobnobbing with the Portuguese delegation in the lounge occasionally. He tried to persuade me to change our position on East Timor and denounce Indonesian colonialism.

I explained to him the rationale of our policy and said that he could take the matter up with Delhi, which he was not inclined to do. He watered down the language of the speech I gave him, but as long as the speech conformed to the established policy of the government, I had no problem.

I kept a close watch on him as he read the speech and, sure enough, he deliberately changed a phrase to dilute it further. The statement that the people of East Timor had already exercised their right to self-determination was changed to suggest that we were not convinced that it was so.

I was astonished by his dishonesty, but without saying a word, I went to the secretariat and handed over a copy of the speech and said that it should be reflected faithfully and the electronic recording should be ignored. The secretariat normally obliges in such cases, but it does insist occasionally on showing the original and the correction. If a delegation votes wrongly on a particular resolution, the original vote will be recorded together with the amendment submitted subsequently.

In the case of the Security Council, I do not know whether the secretariat will insist on recording the pleasure of our minister in seeing two countries of the Portuguese-speaking community in the Security Council.

UN Archives have Plenty of Faux Pas Recorded for Posterity

India is not the only country that generates such gaffes in the UN. Uganda had a big problem once when no Ugandan delegate was present in the General Assembly Hall. When Uganda's name was called, someone walked to the podium and made a speech denouncing the reigning President of Uganda, Idi Amin. By the time the official delegates heard about it and rushed to the hall to challenge him, the damage was done and the news was already in the air. The whole Ugandan team was recalled and a new team was sent with instructions that the Ugandan chairs should never be left vacant.

Pakistan had to contend with a politician, a member of the official delegation, who denounced the regime in Islamabad. Knowing his views, the mission had refused to print out his speech, but he managed to type it on the teleprinter.

Once, when the Iraqi delegate referred to the Kuwaitis as "small people", the interpreter translated it as "pygmies". The Zaire delegate protested and the Iraqi delegate did not know why. "Pygmies" is not a politically correct word in Zaire! Another delegate was asked to repeat his vote four times till the secretariat was convinced that he was acting as instructed.

Gaffes in the UN create some red faces and send a few chuckles around, but they generally do not harm anyone, as each country's position is well-known, and the situation can be easily rectified. These incidents add some entertainment to the otherwise dull proceedings and go down to the archives, which have plenty of faux pas recorded for posterity.

Published: February 14, 2011

G-20 as Security Alternative:
Expanding Diplomatic Horizons

As India begins its presidency of the G-20 (Group of Twenty), there is a certain reluctance on its part to take the bull by the horns and try to end the Russian invasion of Ukraine. India has gone out of its way to say that Ukraine will not be the centrepiece of the G-20 this year. This position is because of the fear of failure, especially because of the position India has taken not to condemn Russia; it is not because the Russian invasion is not the most urgent issue for the world to resolve.

But after the G-20 summit in Bali, Indonesia, in November, there is greater understanding of the Indian position—as articulated by U.S. President Joe Biden himself. Considering that the Bali declaration was virtually drafted by India, New Delhi has been recognised as a potential honest broker who may be able to end the devastating war.

The Right Place and the Right Time for India

The alphabetical rotation of the G-20 presidency has brought India to the right place at the right time, especially when the world is looking for an alternative to the United Nations Security Council (UNSC), which has been paralysed by the veto. Most recently, during the Covid-19 pandemic and the Russian invasion of Ukraine, the UNSC's credibility hit rock bottom. Any reform of the UNSC, particularly the expansion of its permanent membership, will be strongly resisted by the permanent members and a large majority of the General Assembly because it does not benefit anyone except those who aspire to be permanent members.

Every candidate has a strong opponent waiting to pounce the moment there is any serious proposal to make the candidate country a permanent member. Among the proposals made in the last three decades, there is none that can command the votes of the five permanent members as well as two-thirds of the members of the General Assembly.

Although the G-20, which consists of 19 countries and the European Union (EU), was set up by the G-7 countries in 1999, and upgraded to the level of Heads of State/Government in 2008 to address "major issues related to the global economy, such as international financial stability, climate change mitigation and sustainable development", its composition is such that it looks like it is an expanded Security Council.

It is representative of all the significant countries of the 21st century and is balanced between developed and developing countries. The present permanent members and declared aspirants have been included while Africa and Latin America have also been represented. The EU represents a very important segment of the global power structure. A consensus decision of G-20 should be universally acceptable.

The Platform of the Bali Declaration

A gradual transformation of the G-20 from an economic body to a political body can be initiated on the basis of the Bali Declaration, which constitutes the consensus in the group on the Russia-Ukraine war. If the G-20 emerges as peacemaker in Europe, it will attain legitimacy as a group to promote international peace and security; it can gradually become an alternative to the UNSC.

The most important difference will be that no one can prevent its meetings by use of the veto. Care should be taken not to isolate anyone and promote a solution, which is acceptable. Russia will have to reason out its behaviour rather than threaten the use of the veto to intimidate the international community. The grave danger of a permanent member waging a war and vetoing every resolution against it is a reality that the UN should address.

The first step for India to take is to highlight the Bali Declaration and to present a road map during the preparatory process for the G-20 summit and persuade the sherpas to take it on its agenda. The response cannot be negative except by Russia as it has to negotiate as an equal with the other members of the G-20. If Russia is looking for an escape route, even Russia will accept India's role as an honest broker in the process. This will enhance India's capacity to deal with the crisis in a formal way within the G-20. It will accomplish India's ultimate goal of securing the reform of the UNSC. Once the basic work is done, the UNSC can formalise the decision and implement it for international peace and security.

Not a New Role

Being an honest broker in international peace and security is a role that is not new to India. Although it has taken strong positions on crucial issues such as decolonisation and rights of the developing countries to play a role as a leader of the non-aligned world, it kept the conversation going among the protagonists and promoted a balanced outcome.

India was the author of several landmark resolutions of the UNSC on the question of Palestine, and administered the healing touch whenever confrontation developed in multilateral fora. India was a part of efforts made to prevent the expulsion of Egypt from the Non-Aligned Movement at the Havana summit, when the Arab nations turned against Egypt.

Flexibility in negotiations even while being principled in its national position gave India a role in many situations. As the President of the G-20, the fund of goodwill that India has earned in the UN will be an asset at this critical moment.

The legitimisation of the G-20 as a global arbiter in international affairs will create a multilateral instrument where all members are equal. Though it may take a very long time for it to replace the UNSC, a beginning will have been made in making the UN an effective instrument in stopping wars and building cooperation. Such an opportunity comes, but rarely in history. It will be worth the effort even if it only plants the seeds for the beginning of a new UNSC.

Published: December 9, 2022

UN@75: Celebrating Milestones, Facing Challenges

This is the time when all roads lead to New York for the annual global festival of words. Manhattan turns into the world capital where there is a permanent quorum of world leaders for taking majority decisions on peace and war. A visit to New York at this time is like visiting 193 countries at the same time because their capitals are empty and the decision makers are in a huddle, making deals, both official and personal, behind the camouflage of the United Nations (UN).

Normally, the halls are empty and the streets are jam-packed. Gourmet food and the best of wines are upper most in the minds of delegates, not the Charter of the UN and the resolutions awaiting deliberations and approval, even if they do not matter to the world. It is a fantasy world rooted in traditions and protocol, but totally free in spirit. The constraints of time and money melt away under the arc lights and golden ceilings of banquet halls.

Today the UN is desolate, delegates are in their homes or hotel rooms and most discussions are online. Many governments may not have sent delegations to New York at all. The world has become smaller through technology. The newly renovated and equipped halls of the UN building remain unused. The exceptional communication skills and personal linkages of delegates go waste. The new norms are not quite established, but the systems, which have evolved over the last 75 years, have suddenly become outmoded.

The New Yorkers, who tolerated the UN as a cash cow, find its diplomatic population with its privileges and immunities increasingly troublesome. Their concerns have increased about the Israel-hating, Arab-loving, Communist-leaning UN which brought the likes of Fidel Castro, Yasser Arafat, and the tinpot dictators of Latin America as honoured guests to their city.

The present plight of the UN is attributed to the pandemic, which has turned the world upside down in every way. The attractions of diplomacy, like international travel, haute cuisine, fashionable clothing, luxury hotels all at government cost are fast disappearing as conferences move from the real world to the virtual. This makes diplomacy less attractive as a profession, as it is not just about hard negotiations from home to home, but which demands much social contacts, building of bridges and developing complementarities. The setting and atmosphere are as important as logic and arguments in the meeting of minds.

The pathetic state of the UN today on the occasion of its 75th anniversary, however, is not entirely because of Covid-19. Having worked with the UN for nearly 20 years in different capacities in different UN capitals and in Delhi since 1980, I have seen its gradual and steady erosion. The fault lay in its creation itself as the victors' conclave with non-democratic features, like the veto and designating of enemy countries.

The Cold War that erupted soon after its inception brought about a plethora of its own complications when the allies during the war became feuding superpowers. A kind of balance for fear of mutually assured destruction prevented a Third World War, but the UN could not save the succeeding generations from the scourge of war. But its finest hour was when the UN fought a war to liberate Kuwait with rare unanimity among the permanent members.

The UN had its critics throughout its history, but it survived essentially because it was different things to different member states. For the major powers, it was an instrument of their foreign policy, the middle powers created their own space in international power games and the least developed countries saw it as a guarantor of their sovereignty.

For India, it has been a forum to set standards of international behaviour and to share its own experience with the rest of the world. None was satisfied with its performance, but they relied on the lowest common denominator to justify their involvement. But all of them zealously guarded their sovereignty and fought to protect it. When Secretary-General Boutros Boutros-Ghali suggested after the Cold War that the days of absolute sovereignty were over, members, big and small, rejected it decisively.

Those who criticise the UN for inaction forget that if the UN took action against them, they would prefer inaction. In effect, the extreme caution exercised by the UN due to conflicting interests has ensured its survival for 75 years.

Everyone wants reforms, but they should be consistent with their own vision. But one man's vision is another man's nightmare. An expansion of the Security Council is a mirage that recedes every time it appears near, and there is no proposal today which can muster the requisite support. A confrontation on this issue will be suicidal for the UN.

The UN had its successes and failures and it has proved its resilience. But it reached the rock bottom when it failed to respond to Covid-19, the biggest threat to peace and international security it ever faced. To characterise it as a health issue to be left to the WHO and to refuse even to hold a Security Council meeting to discuss it, was the unkindest cut of all. Even the iota of hope that humanity had that the UN might prevent a catastrophe evaporated in March 2020, when China prevented a meeting to consider preventive and combative action.

The Security Council should have created a 'Health Keeping Force' to reach the far-flung corners of the world where the danger still lurks. Multilateralism was already on its last legs, following its rejection by President Trump, but now it lies crippled and paralysed. The world has begun to look away from the UN for alternatives, be it G-20 or any 'G' with a numeral attached to it.

The celebration of the 75th anniversary of mankind's biggest hope will be muted and the desolate streets of New York will bear testimony to its failure. Many trends of the first two decades of the 21st century have been accentuated by Covid-19. If we go by the message of Covid-19 that life beyond 65 is dispensable, then the UN at 75 has fulfilled its mission. Only a miracle can bring about its resurrection.

Published: September 19, 2020

UN Voting Dynamics: The Complexity of Decision-Making

The green, red and yellow buttons at the desks of delegates at the United Nations (UN) General Assembly and related conferences indicate only some of the options available when resolutions are put to vote. Over the years, the voting options have gone beyond 'Yes', 'No' and 'Abstention'. It is possible to be 'present and not participating' or 'absent at the time of the vote'. This makes it possible for member states to nuance their positions to suit their needs. The history of the UN shows that innovative use has been made by member states on several occasions. Some diplomats have often used these provisions to diverge slightly from their instructions to do a favour to some friendly delegations.

Voting System

The voting system in the UN Security Council is rigid. Every vote counts because the resolutions adopted by the Security Council are mandatory for all members of the UN. Their solutions adopted under Chapter VII of the UN Charter, 'Action with Respect to Threats to the Peace, Breaches of the Peace, and Acts of Aggression', are even more significant as they involve even war, as it happened in the case of Iraq.

In fact, the provisions of the UN Charter on voting have already been 'tweaked'. The Charter provision requires the "concurring votes of the permanent members; provided that, indecisions under Chapter VI

[Pacific Settlement of Disputes], and under paragraph 3 of Article 52, a party to a dispute shall abstain from voting". It would seem therefore, that an abstention by a permanent member would amount to a veto. But it is now agreed that if a permanent member does not fully agree with a proposed resolution, but does not wish to cast a veto, it may choose to abstain, thus allowing the resolution to be adopted, if it obtains the required number of nine favourable votes.

An additional provision to add conditionalities to the vote is the explanation of vote before and after the vote. The explanation of the vote before the vote acts as canvassing for votes of others and the explanation of the vote after the vote can even amount to taking with the left hand what has been given with the right, as it happened in the case of India's abstention on the Russian invasion. All the principles were stated in the explanation of the vote, but the vote itself was prompted by political expediency.

India's Vote

In the recent vote on the Russian invasion of Ukraine, the impression is that China and India voted together to indicate neutrality. But the impact of the vote of China is more nuanced than India's. If China had voted against the resolution, it would have amounted to a veto, which would not be in keeping with the cultivated image of China as a country which opposes foreign intervention in sovereign states. But the Chinese abstention reflected the new understanding between Russia and China. Intriguingly, the requirement of compulsory abstention by the affected parties in cases relating to Chapter VI does not apply to other resolutions and thus permanent members can veto resolutions against them even under Chapter VII.

The Indian abstention in cases relating to the Soviet Union at the UN was institutionalised by Indira Gandhi in 1980, when India became the only country outside the Soviet bloc to abstain in the UN General Assembly after the Soviet Union had vetoed a Security Council resolution against its intervention in Afghanistan. The world and India have changed since then, but the compulsions for India to abstain today are as valid as they were in 1979, regardless of the emergence of the Quad.

Technically, India could have abstained only in the substantive vote in the UN General Assembly, as the resolution contained references to invasion and other strong words, but it also abstained in the UN Security Council on an earlier procedural vote to refer the matter to the General Assembly. The same applied in the case of the Human Rights Council.

The U.S. criticism of India's vote was as expected in the context of the Quad. But it should be remembered that its criticism was even more severe in 1979, when India's relations with the U.S. were not so close. The U.S. took stern actions like denying fuel supply to Tarapur nuclear plant and supporting the jihadis in Afghanistan at that time.

The carefully crafted voting regulations in the UN General Assembly have created comic situations. Once, the Chinese delegate went out of the hall when a vote was in progress. When he returned, he realised that he could not follow the instructions given on that particular resolution. He took the floor to say that, instead of his being marked absent, it should be recorded that he would not have participated in the vote if he was present.

In roll-call votes, some delegates often vote wrongly, but the Secretariat, which knows better, records a vote as it should have been cast. On one occasion, a senior politician, who came from India as a delegate, wanted to change India's vote on Afghanistan. When India's name was called out, he said 'Yes' and I had to shout from behind, 'Abstention!' Fortunately, the delegate did not hear the correction. Such events are legion at the UN.

The UN regulations and practices on voting are designed to enable the delegations to express their national opinions, taking into account their vital national interests. In the ultimate analysis, delegations do not vote for or against other countries; they vote for themselves. In the case of India, votes in the Security Council, the General Assembly, and the Human Rights Council reflect its current national concerns in the light of the situation in Ladakh, Afghanistan, the increasing ties between Russia and China, and its membership of the Quad.

Without naming or blaming anyone, India has expressed its fundamental position that war is not a solution and diplomacy should be the only option to prevent war. This stance may have caused ripples in some countries, but India aims to remain relevant in the emerging global order by keeping its options open.

Published: March 16, 2022

C. CHINA

A MAJOR CHALLENGE

Broken Promises in
India-China Relations

India today stands bewildered, like a young teenager in front of a heap of hundreds of pieces of a jigsaw puzzle, not knowing where to fit them in to create the charming castle pictured on the box.

Patience, perseverance and imagination are required to complete the picture and it is not clear even where to begin. What we have are a few disjointed pieces of information, like the sighting of Chinese military movements in the Ladakh region in the vicinity of the Line of Actual Control (LAC), India's immediate response that the matter would be resolved through dialogue at the military and diplomatic levels, reports of meetings, and an announcement of disengagement by both sides.

Then there was a sudden clash in which there were 20 confirmed deaths on the Indian side and unconfirmed and uncounted deaths, including that of the Commander on the Chinese side and reports of withdrawal.

The whole episode, however blurred, brought back memories of nearly 60 years of Chinese betrayal, aggression, deception, and blackmail against India.

The Chinese behaviour revolved around the border between the two countries, which has remained un-delineated and un-demarcated because of China's stubborn rejection of the historical border.

The Chinese aggression of 1962 took place at a time when the two sides were discussing the realignment of a border on the basis of historic treaties and evidence. The war resulted in China occupying the Aksai Chin area in the west and the Chinese claim over the whole of Arunachal Pradesh in the east.

India remained steadfast in its demand for the occupied areas to be vacated, even while working bilaterally and multilaterally to find areas for cooperation as neighbouring developing countries.

India-China relations over the last 58 years were marked by efforts at settlement of the border, normalisation of relations, signing of various agreements to develop economic relations, occasional clashes on the border, summit-level meetings, and clashes in international bodies on account of China's solidarity with Pakistan.

China grew rapidly after it established relations with the United States and became Asia's largest and the world's second largest economy. China also became India's largest trading partner, next only to the United States.

China's exports to India far exceeded its imports from India, leaving a huge deficit in trade. The leaders of the two countries met at different places and kept a semblance of dialogue and understanding. But the border dispute remained acute and no formula emerged to solve it.

The conflict goes back to at least 1914, when representatives from Britain, the Republic of China and Tibet gathered in Shimla to negotiate a treaty that would determine the status of Tibet and effectively settle the borders between China and British India.

The Chinese did not like the proposed terms that would have allowed Tibet to be autonomous and remain under Chinese control and refused to sign the deal. But Britain and Tibet signed a treaty establishing what would be called the McMahon Line, named after a British colonial official, Henry McMahon, who proposed the border.

India maintains that the McMahon Line, a 550-mile frontier that extends through the Himalayas, is the official legal border between China and India. But China has never accepted it on the ground that it was a colonial legacy.

When India became independent and China became the People's Republic within two years of each other, they found themselves at odds over the border. Tensions rose throughout the 1950s.

The Chinese insisted that Tibet was never independent and could not have signed a treaty creating an international border. There were several failed attempts at peaceful negotiations. China sought to control critical roadways near its western frontier in Xinjiang. China took control of Tibet and the ruler, the Dalai Lama, sought asylum in India, which provoked China.

In 1962, Chinese troops crossed the McMahon Line and took up positions deep in Indian territory, capturing mountain passes and towns. The war lasted one month and resulted in more than 1,000 Indian deaths and over 3,000 Indians taken prisoners. The Chinese military suffered fewer than 800 deaths, as per Chinese estimates.

By November, Premier Zhou Enlai of China declared a ceasefire, unofficially redrawing the border near where Chinese troops had conquered territory, and the so-called Line of Actual Control (LAC) was established and the two countries confronted each other across an ill-defined border that ran through the bleak and inaccessible Himalayan peaks.

Tensions came to a head again in 1967 along two mountain passes, Nathu La and Cho La, that connected Sikkim—then a kingdom and a protectorate of India—and China's Tibet Autonomous Region. A scuffle broke out when Indian troops began laying barbed wire along what they recognised as the border. The scuffle soon escalated when a Chinese military unit began firing artillery shells at the Indian troops. In the ensuing conflict, more than 150 Indian soldiers and 340 Chinese were killed.

The clashes in September and October 1967 in those passes were later considered the second all-out war between China and India. India prevailed, destroying Chinese fortifications in Nathu La and pushing them farther back into their territory near Cho La. The change in positions, however, meant that China and India each had different and conflicting ideas about the location of the Line of Actual Control. In 1987, an Indian military exercise on the border provoked clashes on the LAC.

The term "LAC" gained legal recognition in the Sino-Indian agreements signed in 1993 and 1996. The 1996 agreement states, "No activities of either side shall overstep the line of actual control."

However, clause number 6 of the 1993 Agreement on the Maintenance of Peace and Tranquillity along the Line of Actual Control in the India-China Border Areas mentions, "The two sides agree that references to the line of actual control in this Agreement do not prejudice their respective positions on the boundary question".

The Chinese troops continued to illegally enter the area several times every year to nibble Indian land to fortify their positions, while the boundary discussions dragged on. In 2013, there was a three-week standoff between Indian and Chinese troops 30 km southeast of Daulat Beg Oldi.

It was resolved and both Chinese and Indian troops withdrew in exchange for a Chinese agreement to destroy some military structures over 250 km to the south near Chumar that India perceived as threatening.

In October 2013, India and China signed a border defence cooperation agreement to ensure that patrolling along the LAC does not escalate into armed conflict.

In June 2017, the Chinese began building a road in the Doklam Plateau, an area of the Himalayas controlled by Bhutan. The plateau lies on the border of Bhutan and China, but India sees it as a buffer zone that is close to other disputed areas with China.

Indian troops carrying weapons and operating bulldozers confronted the Chinese with the intention of destroying the road. A standoff ensued, soldiers threw rocks at each other, and troops from both sides suffered injuries.

In August, the countries agreed to withdraw from the area, and China stopped construction of the road. But it is suspected that the Chinese are stationed in the area, waiting for an opportunity to construct the road again.

The sudden and unexpected confrontation in the Galwan area in June 2020 at the time of a pandemic has raised suspicion that the Chinese action went beyond the border question. China, while on the defensive against the charge that the Coronavirus was created by it, has become assertive in different parts of the world. China flexed its muscles not only against India but also Hong Kong, Taiwan, and in the South China Sea.

China has ambitions to step into the perceived vacuum created by the health and economic disaster in the United States and it may have decided to "teach a lesson" to India again as a rival in Asia.

China has deliberately moved away from the "Wuhan Spirit" and the "Chennai Understanding" to ensure that India does not gain any advantages in the forthcoming changes in the global order in the post Covid-19 era.

This quick recap of history over 60 years establishes that the only answer to the India-China border dispute is an intensification of the dialogue on the border to delineate and demarcate the border in a time-bound manner.

The present situation of a notional LAC leaves the possibility open for minor and major clashes. The Indian Army has orders to retaliate and the present convention of not using firearms could be violated any time. We shall have to live with "a no-war no-peace situation" for a long time to come.

The meeting of the commanders from both sides on June 23 seems to have succeeded in finalising the modalities of withdrawal by the two sides, though details are not available.

If the status quo is being restored, it is only relief and not a solution and the shadow of the death of our soldiers will remain on India-China relations.

Published: June 24, 2020

The Dalai Lama's Political Influence

Sixty years after his arrival in India, when he is about to celebrate his 84th birthday, His Holiness the Dalai Lama, the spiritual and temporal leader of Tibet, is on centre stage again as his mortality and reincarnation have become matters of international concern.

The future of the Tibetan refugees in India and abroad is also in focus. With his characteristic wisdom, vision, and diplomatic skills, the Dalai Lama has begun to apply the healing touch to avoid any complication or conflict on account of these issues.

According to Tibetan tradition, the Dalai Lama is found, rather than chosen, as the next Dalai Lama is believed to be a reincarnation of the current Dalai Lama.

The search for the reborn Dalai Lama is the responsibility of the high Lamas and the Tibetan government. It took four years to find the current Dalai Lama.

The present situation of the Dalai Lama and a Tibetan government in exile in India make the exercise complicated. Both India and China have major stakes in where the next Dalai Lama will be found, and China has already stated that only someone born in Tibet and accepted by China can become the next Dalai Lama.

The issue is likely to add another point of contention between the two countries, particularly if the new Dalai Lama is found within the Indian territory like Arunachal Pradesh or Dharamsala.

The search for the Dalai Lama begins when the high Lamas have a vision or dream. If the previous Dalai Lama was cremated, they watch the direction of the smoke to indicate the direction of rebirth.

They often meditate at Lhamo La-Tso, central Tibet's holy lake, and wait for a vision or indication of the direction in which to search. This relates to a belief that the female guardian spirit of the lake promised the first Dalai Lama that she would protect the reincarnation lineage.

When a boy is found by following the stipulated procedures, there are a series of tests to ensure that he is the reincarnation. There is a secret set of criteria with which the child is assessed.

In addition to this, the main test consists of presenting the boy with a number of items to see if he can select those which belonged to the previous Dalai Lama.

If only one boy has been found, the high Lamas confirm their findings with eminent religious and secular figures before reporting to the Central Government.

If more than one boy is found, a public lot is drawn by officials and monks. The boy and his family are taken to Lhasa, where the boy can study the Buddhist sutra to re-learn knowledge accumulated in previous lives in preparation for spiritual leadership.

The whole process, which may last years, is likely to have major consequences.

Taking these factors into account, the Dalai Lama has raised doubts about the whole question of reincarnation. He has promised that he will leave detailed instructions on the succession issue.

He has said that the Buddha himself and the high Lamas of Nalanda were not reborn to assume any positions in Buddhism. By diminishing the importance of reincarnation, the Dalai Lama may have set the stage for a peaceful and immediate assumption of office by a selected successor for himself.

The other issue is the future of the Tibetan community, which has settled in India and abroad and grown over the last sixty years. The Dalai Lama had engaged in a long struggle to return to Tibet and secure its autonomy by peaceful means.

His representatives had held several rounds of discussions with the representatives of the Chinese government. But these have been suspended recently.

Though India does not formally recognise it, there is a Tibetan government in exile in India. Having realised that his dream to return to Tibet is no more practical, the Dalai Lama has said recently in an interview to 'The Week' that preserving the Tibetan culture and traditions is more important than seeking independence.

Independence will give the Tibetans happiness, but there is greater happiness in maintaining their culture, he has said. Here again, his purpose is to defuse the situation for his successor.

A privilege that the Indian Ambassador in Vienna enjoys is the opportunity of meeting His Holiness the Dalai Lama at least once in a three-year term, as he is a regular visitor to Austria and he makes it a point to touch base with the Indian Ambassador whenever he is there.

He invited us to his 'Kalachakra' programme in Graz and he not only received us warmly but also gave us a private audience for an hour. Years later, I met him again in Delhi for the release of my book, *Venkat Forever*, a collection of tributes to the former Foreign Secretary AP Venkateswaran, who was close to him.

I cherish those meetings as my encounters with divinity in human form. His demeanour, graciousness for even those who have sought to harm him, his simplicity, his open mind, and his good humour make it clear that he is no ordinary human being.

The Dalai Lama has stated that he is nothing more than a Buddhist monk and his manners and conversation are those of a monk and not of a spiritual leader or a head of state. He can oversimplify matters and laugh off important issues as though they do not matter. He does not try to give everything he says an aura of authenticity or moral authority.

He does not even seem obsessed with his political problems with China. He is sadder about the suffering of his people in Tibet than about the inconveniences of his people who have come to India. He believes that a dialogue with the Chinese that he initiated will eventually bear fruit and the Tibetans will be able to preserve their distinct culture even if they are not able to return to Tibet.

In the meantime, he is grateful to India for the reception accorded to him and for the facilities afforded to the Tibetans. He has no bitterness even against the Chinese. They are also human beings, pursuing their own path to happiness and they deserve our compassion, he has said.

His address to those being initiated into 'Kalachakra' was very simple and pragmatic. He did not quote from the scriptures to make his points, but used analogies from ordinary life in the West to illustrate his ideas.

No matter where we come from, we are all human beings. We all try to seek happiness and avoid suffering. We have the same basic human needs and concerns. All of us want freedom and the right to determine our future. Nothing could be simpler than that.

To a question as to what the meaning of mandala was, he surprised the whole audience by saying: "We monks like to make a mess of any place we see!" and laughed loudly at his own joke before explaining the meaning of the shapes and colours of the mandala.

Again, the explanation was simple. During meditation, it is important to have something to contemplate on. Mandalas are imaginary palaces with deities and inanimate objects. They represent some aspects of wisdom and indicate some guiding principles. There were no further questions on such a complex concept, on which treatises have been written.

The position the Dalai Lama has taken recently on his reincarnation and liberation of Tibet is in anticipation of the problems that may arise in the future. As a man of peace and reconciliation, he does not want to leave a legacy of confrontation or conflict.

Published: July 31, 2019

Elusive Peace: The Doklam Crisis

Commentators are at a loss to choose the right Shakespearean title to describe the end of the Doklam standoff. The tempting ones are *Measure for Measure, Love's Labour's Lost, As You Like It, and Comedy of Errors*. But the most appropriate thing to say, particularly when the details of the deal are not known, is that *All's Well That Ends Well*. We can even go one step further and console ourselves with Robert Browning's line, "God is in his heaven and all is right with the world".

Of course, all is not right with the world and the threat from China will not go away. India must be ready to deal with the Chinese menace for a long time to come. Incidents like Doklam will continue to take place and there will be no single approach to each of them. This time, the *deus ex machina* was the BRICS summit, which put a time limit on the standoff. After the Indian boycott of the BRI summit, a similar step by India on the BRICS summit was quite possible.

China's stake in BRICS is high as it is turning out to be a major political and economic instrument for it. After Brazil and South Africa have become minor players, China needs India and Russia to carry on the show. Knowing this fully, India made its moves cleverly and brought China to end the situation to pave the way for a trouble-free BRICS summit. If BRICS was not around the corner, the situation would have been different.

Surprisingly, even some former Indian diplomats have challenged the basic premise of India that the Indian Army moved to Doklam at Bhutan's request on the basis of the treaty that requires India to defend Bhutanese territory. It is difficult to imagine that India will lie on such a fundamental issue. Such a request will not be in the public domain as of now, but it does not mean that there is not even a verbal request.

According to Mani Shankar Aiyar, the last time there was such a threat to Bhutan, Rajiv Gandhi went to Bhutan to assure the king that India would intervene if necessary. Should we distrust the government so much to believe that the Bhutanese invitation is a cock and bull story? Another point being raised by the pro-China lobby is that India did not respond at all when China reportedly informed India about its plans to construct a road in the area. If China was building a road on its own territory, why should they have informed India? Even if they had, why should India have responded without consulting Bhutan, knowing well that the area in question is disputed between Bhutan and China?

Moreover, isn't there a public statement from Bhutan that the building of the road was violative of the understanding reached that the tri-junction should be settled only at a later date? Those who believe that they have a monopoly over all wisdom refuse to acknowledge that their successors are as good in diplomacy as them, if not better.

The theory of evolution supports the premise that mankind is becoming superior in intelligence. Till a few days ago, the situation was that India had expressed willingness to withdraw simultaneously with China and China had insisted that there would be neither simultaneous withdrawal nor talks till India withdrew. Such an impasse had to be resolved without loss of face and now the withdrawal has taken place, perhaps because the civilisational wisdom of both countries prevailed. It does not matter now as to who took the first step. Let both sides look for their own face-saving devices and gloat over them.

Those who are nit-picking on the modalities seem to forget that India has accomplished its objectives. What India wanted was the restoration of the status quo, which essentially meant China discontinuing road construction. China has admitted that it will only patrol the region and not continue the road construction. Nothing succeeds like success and let us not grudge the Indian side their sense of victory.

If the Chinese violate the understanding, it will be another ball game, which has to be faced. At the same time, this is no time for celebration as some ruling party activists seem to believe. Military and diplomatic victories are to be savoured, not proclaimed. How some of them turned a success in anti-insurgency operations in Myanmar and the surgical strikes against terrorist camps in Pakistan into victory parades and made matters worse should be remembered.

Any celebration of victory is a blow to the other party. Victory can turn into defeat if it is unduly celebrated. Moreover, trust and confidence are important ingredients of successful negotiations. In the coming years, India will face such difficult situations as long as the list of grievances on both sides grows. The list is not shorter today than what it was in 1962.

Doklam had novel features because it was a test of India's bonds with Bhutan. China kept claiming that Bhutan had no problem with the road it was building, but Bhutan kept its customary silence in public. Now that we have overcome the present challenge, let us savour the moment and move on. Peace and tranquillity on the China border will remain a distant dream. The only choice we have is to strengthen ourselves militarily and economically and develop friendships with others without alarming our neighbours.

Published: August 29, 2017

Deciphering China:
The New Kremlinology

The world has long recognised that China behaves in enigmatic ways and has accepted that we do not know enough to explain its actions. Such a reputation gives China the freedom to do what it wants, without having to explain itself. The onus is on others to fathom its true intentions.

China merely carries on, asserting its rights as the Middle Kingdom, trampling on the rights of its own citizens and of other countries. The world awaits a handshake here, a smile or an aphorism there to figure out the real meaning of China's words and deeds.

The Sinology industry has assumed the dimensions of Kremlinology of the past. The constant refrain from Sinologists is that there should be more Confucius centres, Chinese language institutes, and China chairs to learn about China. The secret of Chinese actions, they say, lies in the unravelling of its history, language and philosophy.

Many years of Chinese studies have not made us any wiser, though. We have still not analysed fully the purport of the Chinese claim that it was merely teaching India a lesson in 1962. The phrase came up again recently when the Dalai Lama was about to visit Arunachal Pradesh. Does it mean India has not yet learnt the Chinese lesson?

If so, we need to fathom the lesson before hoping to have normal relations with China. The lesson was administered when India was at the forefront of the struggle to secure for China its rightful place in the world. The lesson we should have learnt was that China's pursuit of domination is not tempered by any atmosphere of friendliness we create.

Many more events in Sino-Indian relations remain unexplained, and we accept that the Chinese will never explain them. Our response is generally bewilderment first, self-accusation second, and then finding a temporary solution that fits the Chinese agenda. Nothing is resolved finally, but we pursue our friendship moves in the expectation that an atmosphere of trust will prevent unfriendly moves. We make common cause with China at the UN, not on our priority of reform of the Security Council but on trade and environment, where China gains from our partnership. We open up our markets for their consumer goods, intrusive IT tools and boast of huge trade figures, all in favour of the Chinese. Our comfort zone is not disturbed till we come across another unfriendly act.

We do not know why China invaded Vietnam when the Indian external affairs minister was on Chinese soil. A.B. Vajpayee's sudden departure made no impact on the Chinese and no explanation was offered. We do not know why China decided to take nearly 2,000 km off the length of its border with India or why the residents of Kashmir, including an army general, were discriminated against in matters of visa.

We still wonder why there was much sabre-rattling when the Indian PM visited Arunachal or when the Indian envoy decided to attend the Nobel Prize ceremony for a Chinese dissident. No explanation was offered for violating NSG guidelines to supply nuclear reactors to Pakistan. For our part, we anticipate Chinese sensitivities and do everything possible not to provoke.

We seem to have accepted the Chinese proclivity to see issues not in terms of months or years but centuries when it comes to the border. We do not rush them in the hope that the Chinese have their own ways of dealing with such important issues left behind by the colonialists. The fact that an unsettled border is a sure recipe for trouble does not seem to trouble us. The deafening Chinese silence on the Brahmaputra issue at the Durban summit did not seem to disturb us. Our patience is proverbial; our acceptance of the Chinese mystery is incredible.

When the Chinese Army decided in April to move deep into the Indian side of Line of Actual Control and set up tents, we sought no explanation and the Chinese gave none. We went on to give them the benefit of the doubt as though we had unwittingly provoked them by building bunkers in our own territory. We characterised it as a localised incident, mere acne to be healed by an ointment. The media noise was drowned out by soft words of perfect understanding from the government. Finally, victory was declared when we withdrew from the enemy positions in return for the Chinese withdrawing from our side. The easiest way was to attribute the whole episode to the inscrutability of the Chinese.

Some analysts even celebrated the episode as a welcome change in China's approach. The "non-threatening, but provocative military action" was apparently a benign signal of new activism on the border issue, which should be resolved as soon as possible, as set out in the new "Panchsheel" unveiled by the new Chinese president.

We see the Chinese action as a response to our own activities to strengthen the defences on our side. We even concede that the action may well have been taken to prevent India from becoming a pivot to the US in the Asia-Pacific. China acts and we find explanations for their action.

The Chinese reputation for inscrutability, developed over centuries, is its greatest blessing. A bewildered world, including India, spends more time deciphering its motives and intentions rather than responding to them.

Published: May 9, 2013

Xi Jinping: Architect of China's Ascendancy

Since 2007, when the Communist leaders picked up Xi Jinping as a potential leader, not only for his pedigree and record of service but also for his lacklustre personality, his ascent has been meteoric.

Born into a family of red aristocracy, he could have remained in the corridors of power in Beijing, but he followed the dictum that the educated youth should get re-educated by the poor and he moved to a province as a young aide to a General Officer Commanding dealing with anti-corruption measures.

By 2012, he was President, and by 2017, during his second tenure as President, his 'Thought on Socialism with Chinese Characteristics for a New Era' got accepted as the manifesto of the Party, making him the next helmsman after Mao.

He was also designated as a Core Leader, taking charge of the Party, Government, civilian life, the military, and the academic world.

When the National People's Congress amended the constitution to remove the term limit for President, it was obvious that it was specifically for Xi, who had become the strongman of China.

He consolidated his position step by step, particularly by applying brakes on economic liberalisation of the country. He applied restraints on gigantic companies and the newly rich corporate heads with the slogan "Socialism and Common Prosperity for all."

Vision 2035

Although there were rumours of a coup immediately after his first visit abroad after the pandemic, he was the very picture of self-confidence when he inaugurated the 20th Party Congress on October 16, 2022.

He had no doubt that he would continue as head of all the top bodies in China for five years more, if not longer. Even before the Congress approved his third term, he laid out his decade-long vision for China. He recounted the challenges he faced nationally and internationally and how he dealt with them successfully.

As for the future, his vision for 2035 was "to significantly increase economic strength, scientific and technological capabilities, and comprehensive national strength."

China would join the most innovative countries with great self-reliance and strength in science and technology, strengthen national security and achieve basic modernisation of the armed forces.

Taiwan Policy

Xi spelt out his Taiwan policy because of recent events like the US House Speaker Nancy Pelosi's visit and China's stern actions in response.

He said that China would never promise to renounce the use of force, which was directed solely at interference by external forces, although Beijing would continue its efforts for peaceful reunification of Taiwan.

He said that resolving the Taiwan question and realising China's complete reunification is, for the Party, a historic mission and an unshakeable commitment.

The wheels of history are rolling on towards China's reunification and the rejuvenation of the Chinese nation, he said.

Neighbourhood Ties

On China's relations with neighbours, Xi said that he would seek enhanced friendly ties, mutual interest, and converging interests. "We will enhance the military strategic capabilities for defending Chinese sovereignty, security and development interests," he said.

Considering that China is being accused of expansionism in the neighbourhood, including India, Xi was cautious about dealing with the subject, but he made it clear that China would enhance the military strategic capabilities for defending itself against any aggression.

Gloomy Global Outlook

Xi's assessment of the global situation was more pessimistic than in 2017. He said that the world was in a flux and listed backlash against globalisation, unilateralism, and mounting protectionism as negative trends.

China would oppose the forming of blocs and exclusive groups that leave out particular countries. This was obviously a reference to the Quad, consisting of the US, Australia, Japan and India, but there was no mention of the Indo-Pacific, where China's penetration is sought to be countered by the Quad.

Unease in Sino-India Relations

India did not figure in Xi's speech, but his aggressive posture against India came to light when a video clipping of the conflict between China and India in the Galwan Valley was shown at the Congress.

A PLA Commander, Qui Fabao, was shown with his arms outstretched facing Indian soldiers in Galwan, where there were casualties on both sides. Moreover, Qui Bao himself was present at the Congress as a Chinese hero.

If China is sincere about friendly ties with its neighbours, such an episode should have been avoided. Even though disengagement has taken place in some sectors in Ladakh, tension prevails in Damchuk and Depsang.

The fact that no meeting took place between Xi and Modi at the Shanghai Cooperation Organization summit in Samarkand was a clear indication of the continuing tensions between India and China.

The question whether the emergence of Xi as the helmsman in China augurs well for India is not clear.

Though Xi and Modi spent considerable time among themselves in the informal summits in Wuhan and Mahabalipuram, the Chinese aggression in Ladakh showed that those conversations made no impact on Chinese policy towards India.

In fact, China violated all the principles of cooperation agreed between the two countries under Xi's watch and there is no desire on China's part to make amends. Xi's continuation for another decade is not a good omen for India.

Of course, much will depend on the outcome of the Russia-Ukraine war, the consequent geopolitical changes, and the Russia-China partnership.

A power struggle in China is still possible as Xi has manipulated his way to be the helmsman for life. His vision may be adopted by the Chinese Communist Party, but it is not at all clear that there will be no revolt against Xi in the coming years.

Published: October 23, 2022

Panchsheel Revisited:
India-China Agreements

In 1954, India and China signed an agreement in which the two sides emphasised that the Five Principles ("Panchsheel") of mutual respect for sovereignty and territorial integrity, mutual non-aggression, non-interference in each other's internal affairs, equality and mutual benefit, and peaceful co-existence would ensure peace and stability in Asia. But what followed was a period of conflict, war and tension on the border, which necessitated many agreements to deal with specific situations.

Now we have another "Panchsheel" signed in Moscow by External Affairs Minister S Jaishankar and Foreign Minister Wang Yi on 20 September 2020, but it is still not clear whether it will lead to dialogue, disengagement and distancing, considering the distrust between the two countries and the deep Chinese conspiracy which created the incendiary situation along the Line of Actual Control (LAC). But there is reason to believe that India's three-pronged strategy of dialogue, military preparation, and economic action has halted the Chinese adventurism for the time being.

The roaring of the Rafael jets, the Indian occupation of a few commanding heights on the southern bank of the Pangong Tso, setting up of the barbed wire "Lakshman Rekha", and the deployment of the Tibetan forces may well have prompted the Chinese to grasp "the last chance for a peaceful resolution," as they called the Moscow meeting.

Disengagement was promised before, but what followed was a period of casualties on both sides, escalating tensions, and some proactive movements of troops from India. The second "Panchsheel" is no guarantee of implementation, and it may have a shorter shelf life than the first one. A record of the "frank and constructive discussion" in Moscow with the apparent blessings of Russia and Iran has a chance of implementation, though the text has the potential to be interpreted in different ways.

Significantly, Wuhan and Mamallapuram made an appearance in Moscow at a time when it appeared that they were thrown to the winds by the Chinese when they planned the incursions. PM Modi and President Xi had appeared to be engrossed in each other and no one believed that those conversations would be in vain. PM Modi was accused of misreading Xi even after fifteen meetings with him.

We do not know the nature of the "consensus" reached between the leaders, but certainly the reset was not to have a bash at each other on the border. India gave some concessions to China in the wake of the Wuhan spirit, but there was no sign of reciprocity from the Chinese side.

To say that "the current situation in the border areas is not in the interest of either side" is to acknowledge the obvious. It is logical, therefore, to continue the dialogue, quickly disengage and maintain proper distance, as the pandemic has taught us, to avert danger.

The word "disengagement" is crucial as the Chinese believe that they have disengaged enough and it is India which has to disengage from the Chushul area. This determination is as hard as determining the border and the process may go on till the winter and beyond, leaving the situation favourable to the Chinese, who may not have intended to achieve more.

We have acquired a few bargaining chips by our action in Chushul, but the Chinese have many more of them along the LAC and that explains their reluctance to agree to restoration of the status quo.

The consensus to abide by all the agreements, including the agreement of 1993, to maintain peace and tranquillity is mandatory and logical, but China is a habitual violator of this obligation and the way it has been written this time is simply a reminder of the violations that have taken place. Agreements are meant to be followed and not to be flouted.

The agreement to continue the dialogue through the mechanism of the Special Representatives and the Working Mechanism for consultation and coordination is welcome, but without a commitment to move to a time-bound programme to conclude these consultations, such an agreement is redundant.

The Chinese seem to consider the negotiations on the border endless till they have sorted out the LAC to their complete satisfaction. Such a dual path is fraught with dangers as the process of sorting out of the LAC is pure banditry and lawlessness.

The Joint Statement ends with a call to conclude new and undefined Confidence Building Measures, making enhancement of peace and tranquillity in the "border areas", not LAC, conditional to the CBMs. This amounts to a rewriting of the agreement of 1993 and makes violations legitimate in the meantime.

It was feared that the Moscow meeting would end in a fiasco in which China would give an ultimatum to India to withdraw from Chushul and India would insist on restoration of the status quo as in April 2020, leading to a conflict situation. The Joint Statement has averted such a disaster for the time being.

When India is battling Covid-19 and the looming economic crisis, any respite is welcome, and China itself is facing serious international hostility for flexing its muscles in multiple areas. At best, the Moscow consensus is a breather for the two countries only to be tested in the process of implementation.

China has not given any explanation for its initial moves, though the changes in Jammu and Kashmir and Ladakh have been cited as a possible provocation. Such a reason, if raised, would be disastrous for India-China relations in the long run. The present consensus makes it possible to veer away from such a fundamental position and to stay close to the delineation of the border as the core issue.

Scepticism is the prevalent mood in the country and the Joint Statement has many elements in it to make anyone sceptical. But the effort made to define the larger picture by focusing on history and the wish not to turn differences into disputes and conflicts is welcome.

In the obtaining circumstances today, nothing more could have been possible. At least the vicious circle of Chinese incursion, discussion and partial withdrawal has been broken and attention has turned to long-term solutions rather than short-term gains.

Surprisingly, the defence minister referred to the Moscow agreement at a low key in the Lok Sabha on September 15. After stating that he had clearly told the Chinese side that any unilateral attempt to change the LAC would be strongly resisted, he said: "My colleague, Shri Jai Shankar, the External Affairs Minister, has thereafter met the Chinese Foreign Minister in Moscow on 10th September.

"The two have reached an agreement that, if implemented sincerely and faithfully by the Chinese side, could lead to complete disengagement and restoration of peace and tranquillity in the border areas." This obviously means that India does not consider the Moscow agreement a breakthrough, not even a temporary reprieve.

The million-dollar question is what China's next move would be. Would they be content with holding on to the Galwan Valley till the snow melts next year, leaving India to hold the heights it has taken? If not, what will save the face of President Xi? If he considers it a setback, heads will roll in CPC and PLA. Further, if he needs a personal victory, he could force further conflict in Ladakh.

In that conflict, the Chinese, Richard Fisher of the Virginia-based International Assessment and Strategy Center tells Gordon Chang of Newsweek, could roll out "joint mechanized warfare for which they have been preparing for 30 years."

But victory is not guaranteed after the smart moves of India this time. "Unfortunately, it looks like China's leader, who had looked invincible, now has something to prove. As a result, he appears absolutely determined to make his point by launching another attempt to break India apart," says Gordon Chang.

If the first Panchsheel did not prevent 1962, there is no guarantee that the second Panchsheel will prevent a repeat of 2020. As far as India is concerned, a return to the situation in April this year will be victory.

Published: September 16, 2020

China's Communist Resurgence: Lessons from Economic Reform

After 40 years of allowing market forces to drive prosperity and becoming the second biggest economy in the world, China is discovering the merits of "common prosperity" by demolishing mammoth enterprises and imposing state control over the vital sectors of the economy.

It is not very clear whether this change is prompted by the extraordinary economic problems China faces, like the slowdown of the rate of growth, falling property market and power failures, or by the pressures within the Chinese Communist Party on the eve of President Xi Jinping's unprecedented third term. The pandemic, measures in the Indo-Pacific against China and its adventurism in Ladakh, Hong Kong, and Taiwan also had an impact on China.

Story goes that President Xi was having a chat with some school students in June this year when the issue of the enormous cost of private tuition came up. Acknowledging the growing pressure on students and their parents to spend time and money on private tutoring, Xi promised to ease their burden.

"We must not have out-of-school tutors doing things in place of teachers," he said. "Now, the education departments are rectifying this." Soon, there was a crackdown on tutoring companies, showing the starkest illustration yet of the Chinese president's commitment to a sweeping new vision for China, where the interests of investors take a distant third place after social stability and national security.

China ordered tutoring companies to become non-profits, accelerating a sell-off that erased $1.5 trillion from Chinese stocks and dented the portfolios of some major companies. Deng Xiaoping had held that there was no harm in some people getting rich ahead of the others, but now China has set different goals: common prosperity and national security.

"Three Big Mountains"

The spotlight is now on what has been dubbed the "three big mountains": the crushing burden of payments for education, healthcare, and property. With its Communist mindset, China has no concern about discouraging flourishing companies or even about letting them leave. Tech companies have been targeted in the name of data security, as seen in the cases of Alibaba and some other technology giants.

In view of the unaffordable property prices for the middle class, China has begun to clamp down on huge building conglomerates like Evergrande, driving them to huge debt.

Three Priorities Now

China this year began a new development phase with three priorities—National security, which includes control of data and greater self-reliance in technology; common prosperity, which aims to curb inequalities; and stability aimed to reduce discontent among stretched workers, stressed parents, and small start-ups.

The regulatory pace intensified when a top economic planning meeting chaired by Xi vowed to rein in the "disorderly expansion of capital." China sees the economy as something that can thrive through state planning, even if that rides roughshod over the rights of entrepreneurs and their backers. China is not even averse to the idea that some companies and financiers should leave China. There are already efforts to increase self-reliance in some areas, which entail replacement of foreigners.

Climate Change Too Matters

China appears to have also realised that it should give attention to climate change even as it fights, like India, for climate justice, pointing out that net carbon zero targets are not achievable without external funding and technology.

Having agreed tentatively to 2050 as the target year for net zero carbon status, China is keen to begin decarbonising during the Beijing 2022 Winter Olympics to demonstrate its sincerity. China is also reducing domestic consumption of coal and gas and appears willing to accept a slower growth.

Will New Direction Alter Growth Trajectory?

Though the direction that China is giving to its economy is clear, its impact may eventually hurt the economy and a push back may become necessary. The cost of the changes may take some time to show. Even if China succeeds to deliver on growth, the focus on "common prosperity" may alter the growth trajectory, and investors will likely have to settle for smaller profits.

Just as the US strategy of decoupling is not working as Chinese exports to the US are growing, China may not be able to reduce its dependence on foreign markets and investments. Once Xi secures his next term and the post-Covid world stabilises, the lure of the market forces may attract China again. Tasting the blood of the market economy may turn addictive even to the Communists.

Lessons For India, Others

The world gets impacted regardless of whether the dragon grows big and breathes fire or gets weaker with the passing of time and looks for alternative strategies. The changes in China will be deeply studied by the world. Some of its actions may have a message for India also.

The trend in India of tutoring agencies replacing school education at much higher costs with foreign investment is something we should look at in the light of Chinese experience. Like China, India already has an "atmanirbhar" (self-reliance) agenda. Whatever system China may adopt, the world will remain watchful and on the alert.

Published: October 21, 2021

D. CUBA

DERAILED NORMALISATION
WITH THE US

Obama's Historic Visit to Cuba: Strengthening US-Cuba Ties

Fidel Castro was credited with a prediction 43 years ago that 'The US will come and talk with us when it has a black President and the world has a Latin American Pope.'

This might well have been apocryphal, but even if it was true, the conditions were fulfilled quite a while ago. Obama became the first black President more than seven years ago and the Latin American Pope is already contemplating resignation.

The normalisation of relations between the US and Cuba was, therefore, long overdue. After the end of the Cold War, there was no real reason for the two countries to remain alienated.

If history could be reversed in relations with China and Iran, there was no reason for the inordinate delay in the case of Cuba. By visiting Cuba recently, Barack Obama was merely accepting the dictates of history and removing an anachronism.

By delaying the normalisation of relations with Cuba, which is not yet complete, the US has only hurt itself. Apart from the denial of Cuban cigars and Havana Rum to aficionados, the situation led to the growth of disaffection against the US in several Latin American countries as Cuba continued to be the rallying point for anti-American sentiments without any political or economic benefits for the US or its allies. Europe and Canada had gone ahead and removed the embargo.

The UN General Assembly passed resolutions year after year, urging the US to remove this vestige of the Cold War. With Obama at the helm, the harbinger of change, at the forefront of affairs, the logic was for change, not the status quo.

Pope Francis' role in speeding up the process of normalisation was a decisive factor in a situation, which was ripe for change. His intervention resonated not only with the public in the United States but also Cuban exiles in the US who had opposed such moves in the past.

In fact, the Cuban exiles in the US, who are estimated to exceed one million, have been the main drivers of the US policy towards Cuba since 1959. They came in different waves, some as political asylum seekers soon after the Cuban revolution and others seeking economic benefits.

Many made use of the Cuban willingness to let them go and the American welcome accorded to them as part of the destabilisation strategy against Cuba. Several people, who left in desperate situations, perished on the high seas.

The emotional baggage of the Cuban exiles was a factor that successive American administrations had to contend with in the formulation of the Cuba policy. Some of them, who rose in the political hierarchy of the US, actively campaigned against any softening towards Castro.

Several political organisations sprang up in the areas where Cuban exiles were concentrated. Apart from protecting the interests of the migrants, these organisations were concerned that any normalisation with Cuba would result in the loss of the refugee status that the new arrivals enjoyed in the US. The instinct of self-preservation rather than ideology dictated their attitudes.

I recall an encounter I had with a US Congressman of Cuban origin, who was hostile to India because of our continuing goodwill for Cuba. He asked me why India was still friendly with Cuba, and I gave him an honest answer that it was rooted in historical and friendly ties in the past.

He took it as an affront and spread the word on the Hill that an Indian diplomat had defended Fidel Castro in his chamber! He had expected that I would please him by making derogatory remarks about Castro. Such was the mentality of even Cuban-American legislators.

It should go to Obama's credit that he was able to overcome the fears about the reaction of the Cuban community in an election year by making the trip. He went beyond the requirements of the occasion to characterise it as historic, when he said, "I have come here to bury the last remnant of the Cold War. I have come here to extend the hand of friendship to the Cuban People."

He devoted a considerable part of his speech to the travails of the Cuban exiles, who went to the US in search of freedom and democracy. He tried to allay their fears about the US compromising with dictatorship, even when conceding that every people should choose their path themselves. He has to contend with the sentiments of the Cuban exiles in his effort to lift the embargo, which is a prerogative of the United States Congress.

It is not unusual for US Presidents, particularly Obama, to be frank about what they consider undesirable in their host countries. Obama's last speech in Delhi was a prime example of this practice. He gained nothing in terms of bilateral relations by speaking his mind, but it was a requirement that something should be said about the prejudices in India.

In Cuba, it was even more important to set the record straight on human rights and authoritarianism, even as he praised Cuba's achievements in education and health. President Castro paid back in the same coin by speaking of the embargo and Guantanamo. While these point to the difficulties ahead, the leaders were aware that the change was clearly irreversible.

Nit-picking by the press is inevitable on such occasions as they microscopically search for clues for the trouble ahead. One such instance was the body language of the two Presidents.

Did Castro stop Obama from a patronising pat on his back by an awkward lifting of Obama's limp hand in a wrestler-like gesture? Why did Fidel Castro administer a snub by denying Obama a photo opportunity?

The first was obviously not choreographed and showed the remaining nervousness on the part of both, while the latter was a clear signal that Fidel Castro was not yet ready to forgive and forget. He may have been sick, but he could easily have held Obama's hand in a gesture of reconciliation.

Obama publicly expressed his willingness to call on the old man, but there was no explanation from the Cubans as to what had happened. There must have been discussions on the issue before and during the visit and it is significant that the Americans did not consider it a litmus test of Cuban sincerity.

Perhaps, Fidel Castro considered the visit as unfinished business as yet, because the fate of the embargo was not known. It is also possible that Obama was not willing to promise to remain silent about the internal situation in Cuba as a price for a photo opportunity with the legend.

The situation was ripe for a US-Cuba *rapprochement* long before it happened. The winds of globalisation had not left Cuba unaffected. The Cubans have always been more comfortable with the Americans than with the Russians at a personal level. Miami, and not Moscow, has been their promised land.

After the Cold War, the two had learnt to deal with each other without intermediaries. The lifestyle and language of Cuban diplomats were more in tune with American aristocracy rather than with their comrades in Russia. Many points of crisis were resolved between them.

The Americans were quite comfortable with the beaches and bars of Havana. This natural affinity, rather than the terms of settlement, will determine the future of the relations between the US and Cuba. The fragrance of Cuban cigars and rum will embellish their ties.

Published: March 25, 2016

Remembering Fidel Castro:
Personal Reflections

A popular story about President Fidel Castro is about the three-hour (or longer) speeches that he used to make. At one stage, he decided to cut the speech down to one hour to give his audience a reprieve.

He called his speech writer and asked for a one-hour speech. But when he read it, it was again three hours. He severely reprimanded the speech writer, who sheepishly told him: "Excellency, I wrote a shorter speech, but you read all the three copies!"

The story cannot be true as Castro always reads his speeches with conviction, as if he is speaking from his heart.

Even in private conversations, he is passionate, forceful and mesmerising. Moreover, he has begun, since the Rio environment summit in 1992, to read one-page speeches with great effect at international gatherings.

From 1979 to 1983, when Cuba was the chairman of the Non-Non-Aligned Movement, Havana was my second home and I had innumerable occasions to listen to Castro in public meetings and private conversations. Every encounter left me spellbound.

More than his ideology, his personal charisma must be responsible for his longevity long after the collapse of the Soviet Union and Communism as we knew it during the Cold War.

Castro's most astonishing performance I witnessed was at the Sixth Summit of the Non-Aligned Movement in Havana in 1979, which he chaired with aplomb. It was his finest hour as he had assumed the leadership of the developing world, despite his known links with the Soviet Bloc.

He was determined to establish his credentials as his own man, whose mission was only the unity of the Non-Aligned Movement. While his comrades tried in the conference rooms to declare Non-Aligned Movement the natural ally of the Soviet Union, Castro chaired meetings, large and small, with total impartiality, dedication and patience.

The biggest issue in Havana was the charge of betrayal made by the Arabs against Egypt soon after the Camp David Accords. A move to expel, or at least suspend, Egypt was gaining momentum and Chairman Yasser Arafat personally led the charge against Egypt.

But Castro and the rest of the movement were not inclined to take drastic action against a founding member. Castro allowed the Arab leaders to have their say, but together with India, Yugoslavia and Algeria (the 'gang of four', as they came to be known in Havana), Castro managed to save Egypt from severe embarrassment.

I saw how Castro handled an unexpected challenge by the leader of the Indian delegation (he is no more) to the Havana Summit. It was the third day of the conference and our minister was quite upset that his turn to address the plenary had not come.

Castro, who was obviously aware of the Indian minister's displeasure, walked up to him during a break in the plenary and enquired about his welfare. The minister thought that this was his best chance to register his protest at the highest level and made his feelings known.

After the initial shock, Castro patiently explained to him that, according to non-aligned tradition, heads of State and government had precedence to speak over foreign ministers.

The minister said it was understandable, but he felt that the chairman should be more firm in controlling the speakers. He even said the chairman was superfluous if he did not exercise his judgement as to how long the delegates should speak. The interpreter was visibly embarrassed to translate the Indian minister's angry words to his chief.

Castro, however, was unmoved and he simply walked away. By the evening, we received word that Castro would receive the minister in his office the next morning. Some of us accompanied the minister, but it turned out to be a one-to-one meeting and that conversation was totally lost to posterity.

During another visit with another Indian dignitary, I met Castro in his office. On his desk were several books on the Gurkhas and he asked us a number of questions about the Gurkhas.

He was obviously impressed by what the Gurkha soldiers of the British Army did in the Falklands to Argentine soldiers. They engaged the Argentines in duels and finished them one by one with their *khukris*.

He had read all the literature on the Gurkhas and learnt about their valour and courage. He knew that the Gurkhas have been fighting in the British Army for over two hundred years.

Castro told us: "Give me a thousand Gurkhas and I shall keep my neighbour under control!" We pretended that we did not know which neighbour he meant.

Castro came to the Indian ambassador's residence in Havana often, particularly when there were senior leaders, visiting from India. The usual decoy car and other paraphernalia were there, but once he settled down, he was quite relaxed and talked to each one of us.

He always talked through an interpreter, but his body language was transparent enough to convey the intensity of his convictions.

Castro was a star at the New Delhi NAM summit in 1983, where Afghanistan and Kampuchea were major issues. To his credit, he did not stand in the way of the mild criticism of the Soviet Union that the summit voiced. New Delhi had its moderating influence on the supporters as well as the critics of the Soviet Union.

The historic moment of handing over of the chairman's gavel by Castro to Prime Minister Indira Gandhi presented an interesting spectacle as Castro proceeded to give her a bear hug after giving her the gavel and she quickly slithered away. He seemed surprised for a moment, but quickly joined the loud applause around.

The name of Castro creates strong feelings in the United States to this day, even though there have been several instances of the United States doing business with Cuba. The celebrated episode of Elian Gonzalez is a case in point. I had trouble with a US Congressman for saying some good words about Castro.

He asked me why India maintained good relations with Cuba. Thinking that it was an honest question, I gave an honest answer. I traced a bit of the history of the Non-Aligned Movement and the role played by Cuba and India in it. Even though the world situation had changed, as two developing countries, we worked together on several issues.

Ideology had nothing to do with it, I said. But, for this particular Congressman, no good word about Castro was acceptable. I learnt the hard way that I should keep my admiration for Castro to myself during conversations with US Congressmen with Spanish names.

Published: November 26, 2016

E. JAPAN

NEW WARMTH IN BILATERAL RELATIONS

Netaji's Final Journey: Bringing His Ashes Home

A grateful nation has been trying to undo the many wrongs done to one of its bravest sons, Netaji Subhas Chandra Bose, in various ways on the occasion of his 125th birthday. Today, his hologram image adorns the canopy at the India Gate, to be remembered and saluted by everyone who traverses Rajpath.

Even the statues of Mahatma Gandhi and Jawaharlal Nehru do not have such pride of place in the national capital of India. Netaji's admirers around the world will be delighted that his role in the liberation of India has been recognised.

But far away from New Delhi, in the Japanese city of Tokyo, the ashes of Netaji await their return to their motherland to be immersed in the Ganga or scattered over the Himalayas.

The Renkoji temple in Tokyo has been reverentially keeping those ashes in the hope that they will be taken back to India to be merged with the water and earth of the country he loved most. It has not been possible to bring the ashes back to India. In the early 1950s, Prime Minister Nehru had sent the then acting consul general in Tokyo to the temple.

After determining and establishing through various investigations that the ashes were indeed those of Netaji, the Government of India offered the maintenance, upkeep, and preservation of the ashes. Since then, the Ministry of External Affairs (MEA) has been paying the temple to preserve the remains with the highest honour and respect.

The gross injustice by way of leaving Netaji's ashes is a blot on India and an irritant to the people of Japan, who have adored him for his bravery and patriotism. A generation of Japanese who worked with Netaji and loved him are disappearing. Some of them had sworn that they pulled out his body from a charred aircraft in Taipei airport. The aspersion we have cast on their integrity and honesty must be erased. Netaji's soul will not rest until his ashes come home.

Documents show that Netaji died in a plane crash on August 18th, 1945. After the crash in Taipei, he was taken to a Japanese military hospital, where he passed away six hours later. His remains were taken to Tokyo in September 1945.

The Japanese government was anxious to return Netaji's ashes to India, but it became impossible for India to bring them back because of the refusal of his friends and admirers to accept that he was no more. He was very young and dashing and it was hard to reconcile with his death. Moreover, there was a sense that he would be working incognito somewhere for India's Independence, which was his life's mission. It was rumoured that he was seen in various guises in India and abroad.

Various commissions investigated his disappearance, and all of them reported that he died in the Taihoku air crash, but since there were dissenting voices, it was not possible to convince everyone that his ashes should be brought back.

The British authorities naturally took an interest in the death of their arch-enemy. The report submitted by John Figges confirmed that Netaji was involved in an air crash near Taihoku airport; he died in a military hospital the same day. He was cremated in Taihoku and his ashes were sent to Tokyo.

The Government of India in 1956 appointed a three-man committee headed by Shah Nawaz Khan, who was a member of the Indian National Army. Netaji's elder brother Surendra Bose was also part of the commission. After interviewing 67 witnesses from Thailand, Vietnam, India and Japan, including Dr. Yoshimi who treated Netaji at the hospital in Tokyo and Habib-Ur-Rahman who accompanied Netaji on the flight, the commission found that Netaji had indeed perished. But

Surendra Bose filed a dissenting opinion due to alleged discrepancies in the witness testimonies, a charge denied by other members of the commission.

The Indian Government set up another inquiry commission, consisting of Justice GD Khosla, a retired judge of the Punjab High Court, in 1970. As a young diplomat in Japan, I had the privilege of travelling the length and breadth of the country with Justice Khosla to assist him. I witnessed several aged people who appeared before the commission despite ill health because they wanted to bring the question of Netaji to a closure. They pleaded with Justice Khosla to return Netaji's ashes to India. They were frustrated that even after several inquiries, the people of India did not trust them.

Justice Khosla brought his legal background to bear on the issue in a methodical fashion, not only concurring with the earlier reports of Figges and the Shah Nawaz Committee on the main facts of Netaji's death but also evaluating the alternative explanations of his disappearance and the motives of those promoting stories of Netaji sighting.

He showed remarkable patience in listening to a range of stories, some of which were far too emotional to be believed. But I could easily anticipate his findings as he considered most of the evidence given was genuine.

A lawyer representing a group which did not accept the air crash theory accompanied Justice Khosla and he was rude to the witnesses, telling them to their face that they were lying. They complained to the commission, but the lawyer could not be stopped. He went to the Renkoji temple and wrote in the visitors' book that the ashes kept there were not Netaji's!

Even after these inquiries, which convinced the Government about the truth of the matter, there was a contradiction between the position of the Government of India and what is being played out in West Bengal politics. There has been resistance to the remains coming back to India from a section of Netaji's extended family, and in some political parties. Prime Ministers Nehru and PV Narasimha Rao attempted to bring the remains back, but unfortunately they failed because of the stiff opposition.

The most recent commission, ordered by the Calcutta High Court in 1998 and headed by Justice MK Mukherjee, explored the possibility of a DNA test, but observed that "on account of the temple authority's reticence, the commission could not proceed further" with the test and concluded that the ashes were not of Netaji. Subsequently, a full version of a letter written by the priest at Renkoji revealed that the permission was indeed given, but the test was not found possible with cremated ashes.

Netaji's daughter had taken up the case of a DNA test with Prime Minister Narendra Modi in 2019 but stated that she shared the belief that her father had died in the air crash on August 18, 1945, unless there was proof to the contrary.

This opens the possibility of accepting the evidence available about Netaji's death in the air crash if a DNA test is not scientifically feasible. It is most unfortunate that even at this time, India cannot be united in the cause of doing the ultimate justice to Netaji by bringing his ashes to find their final resting place in India.

Published: February 11, 2022

Bullet Train Diplomacy:
India-Japan Relations

The penetration of China, Japan and South Korea into Asia, Africa and Latin America was referred to as "silver bullet diplomacy" or "cheque book diplomacy", as it was the economic push that enabled them to establish themselves in poor developing nations. China continues to use the silver bullet to expand economic and political influence in these countries, while Japan has moved on to a more sophisticated approach of developing mutually beneficial cooperation in trade and commerce, leading to political clout for itself.

The unprecedented warm welcome of Prime Minister Shinzo Abe by Prime Minister Narendra Modi in his home state of Gujarat, and the wide-ranging agreements reached there showed the extraordinary range and depth of India-Japan relations.

If the Buddha was the symbol of cordial relations between India and Japan in the past, today it is the bullet train, which has become the symbol of progress through technology that the two countries have agreed to foster.

PM Modi's "demonstrative diplomacy" broke all records in both language and body language when he used all the possible superlatives for his "best friend" and repeatedly embraced him. He put the sour and sweet visit to China, the pains of demonetisation and petrol prices and the general downturn of the economy behind him to roll out the red carpet and to stage a road-show to stress the importance of the visit. The bullet train for which the foundation stone was laid by him and

"Abe-San" was characterised as a reflection of the fast speed of India's economic development.

The Joint Statement issued by the two Prime Ministers was one of the most extensive and forward-looking documents signed recently by India, embracing all aspects of political, economic and cultural relations. Gone are the days of the bitter exchanges between India and Japan on nuclear non-proliferation issues and today, nuclear cooperation is an anchor of the new relationship. The whole exercise was to move toward a "free, open and prosperous Indo-Pacific", with a new partnership among India, Japan, the US and others, as seen in the "Malabar" exercise in the region, which has already caused flutters across the Himalayas.

The Statement celebrated the "Special Strategic and Global Partnership" between the two countries and the significant deepening of bilateral relations in the past three years and the growing convergence in the political, economic, and strategic interests, based on the firm foundation of common values and traditions, as well as on an emerging consensus on contemporary issues of peace, security, and development.

The Prime Ministers decided "to work together to elevate their partnership to the next level to advance common strategic objectives at a time when the global community is faced with new challenges." For Japan, which professes to be non-militaristic in its approach to security, the words used in the statement on security in the Asia-Pacific region broke new ground.

The statement pledged to reinforce their efforts to align Japan's Free and Open Indo-Pacific Strategy with India's Act East Policy, including through enhancing maritime security cooperation, improving connectivity in the wider Indo-Pacific region, strengthening cooperation with ASEAN, and promoting discussions between strategists and experts of the two countries and to enhance defence and security cooperation and dialogues. This includes the Malabar and other joint exercises, defence equipment, and technology cooperation in such areas as surveillance and unmanned system technologies, along with defence industry cooperation.

The economic cooperation sections of the statement are very detailed and specific in support of India's economic reforms and projects such as "Make in India", "Digital India", "Skill India", etc. indicating the readiness of Japan to invest heavily in the relevant areas. Even an area of contention relating to higher IP standards, undermining import of affordable generic medicines into Japan was sought to be dealt with by a reference to pharmaceuticals as an area of cooperation.

The entry into force of the Agreement between India and Japan for Cooperation in the Peaceful Uses of Nuclear Energy was welcomed as the Agreement reflecting a new level of mutual confidence and strategic partnership in the cause of clean energy, economic development and a peaceful, secure world.

Similarly, it was acknowledged that outer space is an ever-expanding frontier of human endeavour, and the deepening of cooperation between the space agencies of the two countries in the field of earth observation, satellite-based navigation, space sciences, and lunar exploration was welcomed.

Any direct criticism of China was carefully avoided, but the statement highlighted the importance of peaceful resolution of disputes, including through full respect for legal and diplomatic processes, without resorting to the threat or use of force, and in accordance with the universally recognised principles of international law, notably the United Nations Convention on the Law of the Sea (UNCLOS).

The two Prime Ministers also reiterated their desire and determination to work together to maintain and promote peace, stability, and development in the Indo-Pacific region, in a thinly veiled reference to Chinese expansionism in the region. But there was no restraint in the case of North Korea, which was condemned for its development of nuclear and missile technology and its threat of use of force.

India received the fullest endorsement of its concerns about terrorism when Japan joined India to condemn, in the strongest terms, the growing menace of terrorism and violent extremism. They shared the view that terrorism in all its forms and manifestations is a global scourge that must be forcefully combatted through concerted global action in the spirit of "zero tolerance".

They called for Pakistan to bring to justice the perpetrators of terrorist attacks including those of the 26 November, 2008, terrorist attacks in Mumbai, and the 2016 terrorist attack in Pathankot. They looked forward to the convening of the fifth India-Japan Consultation on Terrorism and to strengthening cooperation against terrorist threats from groups including Al-Qaida, ISIS, Jaish-e-Mohammad, Lashkar-e-Tayyiba, and their affiliates.

The strong partnership between India and Japan to seek permanent membership of the UN Security Council was restated and support was expressed for India's membership of the Nuclear Suppliers Group and APEC. Differences between India and Japan on climate change were papered over with a commitment to the Paris Agreement and related international agreements. A long list of people-to-people measures is the icing on the cake of a model relationship.

The new relationship between India and Japan, exemplified in the Abe visit, reflects Japan's own emergence out of the US security and foreign policy umbrella, which had inhibited development of relations with India, in spite of many cultural and historic links. The increasing threat from China has added the element of urgency for a security partnership, which is likely to flourish in the years to come.

Published: September 19, 2017

India-Japan Relations:
A Tapestry of History

A rare Festival of Japan including an exhibition featuring Japanese art and culture was staged in Thiruvananthapuram by the Alumni Society of Japanese technical training programmes. I was asked to speak at the inaugural function. Having learnt the Japanese language up to interpreters' level 40 years ago, I wanted to speak in Japanese, but I could manage to say only that "my Japanese has got rusted like an unused kitchen knife," quoting from my text book. I recalled how I could interpret not only for my ambassador, but also for the Indian Davis Cup team consisting of Ramanathan Krishnan and Jaydeep Mukherjee in 1970.

Tokyo was my first posting abroad in 1969 at a time the song 'Sayonara' was on everybody's lips because of the popular movie, *Love in Tokyo*. Japan was at the height of popularity, preparing for the Expo 70 at Osaka. My wife and I were very excited to go to Japan at that time and we thoroughly enjoyed our stay. Our first son was born in a Tokyo hospital though we had to struggle with a different system and culture.

Japan is a friendly country and the Japanese people go out of their way to be nice and kind to foreigners. But the culture shock was as intense at that time as it is today for first-time visitors.

I listed the discoveries we made in the first few days. We realised that we cannot expect black tea with milk and sugar at the famous tea ceremony to which we are invited on arrival, that wasabi paste is not mild like "pudina" chutney, but explosively hot, that raw fish they eat is not live fish, but cut and treated with condiments, that geishas are not women of ill repute, that men and women use different words for the same thoughts and things and so on.

The most priced fish in Japan is "Fugu", whose attraction is that unless it is properly cut by professionals, instant death is certain and the feeling of survival is ecstatic. In Kerala, if you ask someone for directions, we will be told casually to go straight, but in Japan, that person will assemble a crowd to consult and one of them will even accompany you to your destination. Husbands are privileged beings, who are not expected to come straight home from office, but after going to bars and moreover, they simply sit and watch television at home while the wives work hard. Japan never ceased to surprise me.

To guide us through the maze of Japanese culture, customs and manners, we luckily had two young engineers from Thiruvananthapuram, who were doing some technical training in Japan. Sasi and Babu came to the airport to receive us one midnight when we arrived. We offered to give them a lift back in the Embassy car, but the Japanese driver said that the car had to pick up the diplomatic bags also and there would be no space.

Our friends had to spend the night at the airport till the public transport system opened in the morning. They became our constant companions and guides till we ourselves found our way around Japan.

Another guide we had was our neighbour Mr. A.M Nair, also known as "Nair-san". He went to Tokyo as a medical student but was mesmerised by Netaji Subhas Chandra Bose and joined him as his valet and interpreter till Netaji passed away. He then settled down in Japan with his Japanese wife, whom he called Janaki Amma, and launched the popular Indira Curry Powder and the Nairsan Restaurant in the upmarket Tokyo locality of Ginza, bang opposite the world-famous Kabuki theatre.

He took us under his wings and made us feel at home in Japan. He kept away from the Indian Embassy because he felt that he was not recognised by Pandit Nehru after Netaji's death. But he went to the Embassy to salute the flag on the Independence and Republic days. Moreover, he and his family came to our home often.

He wanted his two sons, Vasudevan and Gopalan, to marry girls from Kerala and he threatened them with disinheritance if they did not. He sought my mother-in-law's help to find two girls for them from Kerala, but they chose their Japanese brides themselves. Nair-san is part of the Netaji folklore in Japan and the Indira Curry Powder, a mix of Indian and Japanese condiments that suit Japanese palates better. I believe Japanese tourists look for Indira Curry Powder in India and are disappointed that it is not available!

Netaji was one of the most famous Indians in Japan at that time after the Buddha and Gandhiji, together with Justice Radha Binod Pal, famed for the Tokyo Trials, and Rash Behari Bose, a revolutionary leader. One political issue that we have with Japan even today is that the ashes of Netaji is still in the Renkoji Temple in Tokyo as many people in India still believe that Netaji did not die in an air crash.

Many judicial commissions were appointed to find the truth and it was found several times that Netaji indeed died in an air crash and his body was brought to Japan and cremated. The Justice Khosla Commission came when we were still in Tokyo and I travelled with him to many cities where Netaji's surviving friends had lived at that time.

All of them swore to God they had seen and even carried his body to the funeral. The Khosla Commission strongly urged the Government of India to bring back the ashes with honour, but it was not acceptable to public opinion in West Bengal.

As for bilateral relations, they were friendly and diplomatic, but there was no substance in them because Japan had no independent foreign policy of its own then as it followed US policies world-wide. Moreover, India's nuclear policy was anathema to Japan since India refused to sign the Nuclear Non-Proliferation Treaty (NPT). The relations became even worse after our two nuclear tests in 1974 and 1998, but things improved significantly after the India-US nuclear deal, which gave India a special status.

After Shinzo Abe became the Prime Minister of Japan, the relations became stronger than ever before. Japan supplied military equipment to India and even signed a nuclear cooperation agreement. Together with the US, Japan, and Australia, India is part of the "Quad", a kind of partnership against China.

India and Japan are culturally different, but our common anxiety about China, our common aspiration for permanent membership of the UN Security Council, and the link of Buddhism have made us closer than what we were during my time in Japan. But even in those days, there was respect for each other and cordiality as I witnessed at the time of the visits of Indira Gandhi and Rajiv Gandhi. The present close political relations have a long history of contacts and cultural interaction.

Published: February 21, 2020

Shinzo Abe's Legacy: Championing Japan's Modernisation

Japan's influential and longest serving Prime Minister, Shinzo Abe, worked to modernise his country, revitalise its economy, and rebuild its image on the global stage. He fell to the bullets of an assassin, probably belonging to a fringe element in Japan, which felt uneasy about his reform as undermining the traditional values of the country.

Although free of violence and political assassinations, there have been instances in Japan of suicides and killings by people who suspect fundamental changes in the politics and economics of the country.

While Abe's reforms had the support of the ruling party, there are at least some people who believe that the various problems that Japan now has, were brought about by his administration.

Bloodshed has been absent from Japanese politics for more than six decades since the Liberal Democratic Party, to which Abe belonged, had gained support. In the early 1960s, violent clashes took place between the political left and right over Japan's security treaty with the United States and a socialist party leader was killed.

A consensus later emerged among politicians to keep political battles out of the public view, behind a harmonious facade. By and large, politics in Japan have been based on the principle of non-violence. Japan has tight gun-control laws, which prevent mass shootings, unlike the United States.

Radical Reforms Upset A Few

Abe's reforms, ranging from having an independent foreign policy, removing the constraints on developing Japan's military strength, increasing the use of nuclear power for peaceful purposes, even after the catastrophe in Fukushima, developing defence cooperation with democracies in the Indo-Pacific, setting up of the Quad with the US, India and Australia have enhanced Japan's place on the world stage, and benefitted the country economically and politically.

But the conservative minority in Japan may have found these changes too radical for their comfort and may have spurred negativity, which may have led to Abe's assassination.

Controversial Military Overhaul

Abe's most controversial move was to revamp the military on the ground that Japan was given an unfair verdict for its past. He resented Japan having to apologise for World War II. No policy of his was more divisive than his cherished dream to revise Japan's war-renouncing constitution. His ultra- nationalism also angered both sides of the Korean peninsula and China, all three of whom were once the wartime victims of Imperial Japan.

For him, the 1947 charter was symbolic of the unfair legacy of Japan's war defeat and the imposition of the victors' world order and western values. On his re-election as PM, one of his first acts was to visit the Yasukuni Shrine, a monument to the dead soldiers, which includes some, who were convicted of war crimes.

He actively pursued a revision of the constitution and got bills passed in the Parliament, but the opposition to the measures persisted and eventually the amendment to the constitution was postponed. He tried, however, even within the framework of the constitution, to strengthen the Japan Self-Defence Force, which works closely with the United States military.

What Upset Peaceniks

Abe's nuclear policy also was of concern to the peaceniks in Japan, which has been a victim of two nuclear attacks. The civilian reactors in Japan were believed to be a turn of the screw driver away from turning them into weapon making, but it was extremely critical of India for not signing the NPT. But after the signing of the India-US Agreement on Civil Nuclear Cooperation, Japan not only acknowledged India's new status as a nuclear power, but also signed a nuclear cooperation agreement with India.

Mixed Results of Economic Policy

Abe's economic policy, nicknamed "Abenomics" during his second term seemed to work initially, with the country recording a strong growth in 2013, but later there was a dramatic drop in Japan's economy, followed by a recession. In the election that followed, Abe retained his position as PM, but his popularity plummeted.

Indo-Pacific Forays

Abe's suspicion of China was evident in his efforts to work with the democracies in the Indo-Pacific and his proposal for the Quad. Even before the Quad became a reality, Japan launched military exercises in the region with the US, India, and Australia. The Quad remains a lasting legacy even after Abe left office on account of ill health in September 2020.

Warm Ties to India

Abe's grandfather, who was Prime Minister and his father, who became Foreign Minister, had good relations with India, but Abe was the architect of the current cordial relations between India and Japan.

He had a special rapport with PM Modi, who had visited Abe even when Modi was the Chief Minister of Gujarat. Abe's visits to India were marked by cordiality and concrete cooperation in many fields. No wonder Modi expressed deep condolences on the demise of a special friend and also declared national mourning for a day in India.

Lax Security Helped Assassin

Abe's nationalistic ideology and attempts at modernisation of Japan were widely accepted by his party and the public in general. But there are several individuals in Japan, including some in the armed forces, who felt uncomfortable with the speed with which he brought in the changes.

Since he wielded considerable influence in the party and his successors, some of them may have conspired to assassinate him. The fact that the security was comparatively lax because he was no more in office, may have also been a factor which led to the tragedy. But there is no question that he will be remembered as a revered martyr to the modernisation of Japan.

Published: July 11, 2022

F. SOUTH ASIA

POOR RESPONSE TO NEIGHBOURS FIRST POLICY

Afghan Chronicles:
Reflections on Conflict

In diplomatic life, we often tend to tumble upon historic moments without even realising their importance at the time. An odd picture or some notes taken on the occasion remind us of how we had witnessed the making of history. Such memories occasionally lead to the discovery of some mysteries which are either yet to be explored, or have been lost to time.

They may very well reveal some jigsaw puzzles that may have changed the course of history. Such footnotes of a mysterious past are left unrecorded and lost even for researchers. The diplomats remain note-takers at every stage of their career.

I have not stepped on the soil of Afghanistan. Nor has that country been in focus in my work at any time. All that I know about that country is through books or looking at the picturesque scenery of that land through pictures or video clips. Some names remain in memory, but they are not embedded enough to provide a comprehensive picture.

The rugged mountains and armed civilians and soldiers and glimpses of poverty and disorder present a stereotype of a chaotic country. It really looks like a graveyard of empires with no clear sense of direction. These superficial impressions may be misleading, but the sad part is that the tendency is to repeat history without learning.

Jogging my memory on the eve of another change in Afghanistan, I recalled two encounters I had with the reality of Afghanistan, which changed its history. Both of them influenced the turn of events at that time and still continue to have a bearing on the current events, which are shaping the future of Afghanistan.

First, it was the night in December 1979 when the Soviet forces entered Afghanistan at the invitation of a president who was killed in the first hours of the occupation. I was present at the meeting of the Soviet ambassador with the Indian Foreign Secretary. The ambassador read out a statement from a note from the Soviet leadership stating that a limited contingent of Soviet troops had entered Afghanistan at the invitation of the Afghan government to counter a threat to international peace. He added that the Soviet forces would withdraw from Afghanistan as soon as possible.

Since the Foreign Secretary had heard the *BBC* before the ambassador arrived, he was prepared for the news. After promising the ambassador that the message would be conveyed to the Prime Minister, the Foreign Secretary expressed concern that foreign forces had entered an independent country and expressed the hope that the situation would be reversed. The ambassador was visibly embarrassed, but said that the Soviet forces would remain in Afghanistan only for the shortest time necessary.

The Foreign Secretary met Prime Minister Charan Singh early next morning and briefed him on his meeting with the Soviet ambassador. The Prime Minister decided to receive the Soviet ambassador immediately and told him in no uncertain terms that India would not support foreign intervention in Afghanistan.

The Soviet ambassador responded rather calmly, but added rather triumphantly that he had just met the Prime Minister-designate Indira Gandhi, who showed some understanding of the Soviet compulsion for taking action in Afghanistan. The conversation ended abruptly.

The next few days were hectic as the Afghanistan issue virtually exploded at the United Nations. The entire non-aligned world opposed the Soviet intervention when the resolution demanding the withdrawal of Soviet troops was vetoed by the Soviet Union in the Security Council and the vote moved to the General Assembly.

India abstained on the resolution, but the speech given to our permanent representative, drafted in Indira Gandhi's residence, was supportive of the Soviet Union. From then onwards, India was accused by the West and many other countries of giving up a fundamental position of the UN Charter. India's position was a great relief to the Soviet Union, though India-US relations deteriorated.

Today, the Taliban is strongly anti-India because of the support we extended to the Soviet Union when the Mujahideen were fighting foreign occupation with the support of the US. When the Soviets left and the Taliban came to power, Pakistan used the Taliban government to increase terrorist activities in Jammu and Kashmir and, generally, in the region. It was only when the terrorists hit the heart of New York that the US realised the folly of supporting jihadis in Pakistan and Afghanistan.

Perhaps, the history of Afghanistan would have been different if India had not supported the Soviet Union. The Taliban would have been more amenable to India if it was not associated with the Soviet occupation. India had its own reasons to maintain stability in the region through the restraining influence of the Soviet presence. India was also supportive of the American War on Terror because of the same reason.

I witnessed another crucial moment in the Afghan saga when the UN Secretary General Boutros Boutros-Ghali paid an unscheduled visit to New Delhi on April 22nd, 1992 and met Prime Minister Narasimha Rao. Boutros-Ghali's aim was to persuade India to give former President Najibullah asylum in India. It was a bizarre conversation in which the lives of Najibullah and the UN envoy, Benon Sevan, were involved. The atmosphere in the meeting was tense as India and the UN were afraid that the blood of two lives would be on their hands.

After six days of deliberation on Boutros-Ghali's request, India indicated that it would be willing to shelter Najibullah if he managed to escape. But later, when the Mujahideen formed a government, India calculated that giving asylum to Najibullah might turn out to be prohibitively costly in political terms. Even though Najibullah was not saved, it was clear to the Mujahideen that India's sympathy was with the pro-Soviet Najibullah than with the new government. Benon Sevan, as UN envoy, was saved, even though he had taken a very proactive position to save Najibullah.

It is against the backdrop of these events we need to see the relationship with the Taliban, which became adversarial. The hijacking of an Indian aircraft, which led to the release of terrorists from an Indian prison, was another dramatic demonstration of the bitterness of the relationship between India and the Taliban. A Taliban-dominated government with the support of Pakistan and China will be hostile to India as the past cannot be erased. Much depends on whether the Americans are able to cobble up a coalition before the Taliban overtakes Afghanistan. Speculating on that possibility is like wondering whether the world would have been different if Cleopatra's nose was shorter.

Published: July 22, 2021

Afghanistan's Future: Assessing Post-Withdrawal Scenarios

The future of Afghanistan is yet to be determined, but the debate has abruptly shifted to the future of the United States after its withdrawal from Afghanistan. This may be the first time in history that a ruler is sought to be punished for ending a two-decade-long war. "Pax Americana died in Kabul," a strategic thinker declared. According to him, this is a watershed moment that will bring down the curtain on the West's long ascendancy. Others say that the damage can be limited if U.S. President Joe Biden resigns.

Some U.S. Congressmen have submitted a questionnaire to Mr. Biden raising such issues as the Taliban acquiring nuclear weapons. Mercifully, there is no significant opinion that the U.S. should not have withdrawn its troops or that the U.S. should re-occupy Afghanistan. "The U.S. has done the right thing in the wrong way," says another learned commentator.

Defining Event

To understand the present plight of the U.S., we need to go back to the terrorist bombing of 9/11, which was a game-changing global experience. It transformed the geopolitics of the world, which was determined by the size of the nuclear arsenals of the nuclear weapon states. The most powerful country in the world, which had the capacity to destroy the world many times over, became powerless before a few terrorists, who had only knives and forks as weapons.

In one clean swoop, the theories of the balance of power, mutually assured destruction, and nuclear weapons superiority went up in smoke with the Twin Towers of New York. Once the responsibility of the attack was traced to Osama Bin Laden and the terrorists in Afghanistan, it was imperative for the U.S. to retaliate by overthrowing the Taliban regime and hunting out and killing Bin Laden.

Benefits of the U.S. Presence

The U.S. accomplished its mission within a short period but it was not able to withdraw because the Afghanistan government was unable to withstand the onslaught of the Taliban and other terrorist groups. Even neighbouring countries, including India, were strongly in favour of continuing the American presence. Pakistan played a double game—of being a partner on the one hand and an adversary on the other.

It was not a matter of the Americans imposing themselves, but being invited to provide a certain stability for Afghanistan. The result of their presence was the prevalence of relative peace in the region except that Pakistan fattened the Taliban with American largesse. In the process, the troops in Afghanistan protected their homeland and the Americans, because the Taliban and other groups were kept engaged in Afghanistan territory.

At this moment, when American failures at the time of withdrawal dominate the news, it is worth recalling that the U.S. presence in Afghanistan had succeeded in containing the dangers of terrorism for two decades. Considering that terrorism has endured in the broader West Asia/Middle East, and the attacks and victims worldwide are three to five times higher annually than in 2001 (9/11), the benefits of the American presence should not be underestimated, even though the cost was high in terms of American money and lives.

We should also remember that the clear mandate given to Mr. Biden was to clean up the Augean stables left behind by his predecessor, President Donald Trump, and how the world as a whole and a majority of the U.S. citizens heaved a sigh of relief that the U.S. finally had a predictable, steady, and experienced leader to combat the novel corona virus pandemic and racism in the country, as well as recover its position in the centre of the world that the Chinese were hoping to grab.

Mr. Biden moved in earnest to return to the Paris Agreement (climate), resume the dialogue on the Iran nuclear deal and to reassure America's traditional allies that the U.S. would stand by them. He gave a clear signal to China and Russia that no confrontation would be tolerated, but cooperation, wherever possible, will be pursued.

The Afghan Exit

Withdrawal of troops from Afghanistan was yet another unfinished agenda he had inherited and what he did was merely to follow up the agreement reached with the Taliban and announce a deadline, in the expectation that the Afghan forces trained and equipped by the Americans and the Kabul government would step into the vacuum. As Mr. Biden pointed out, the decision about Afghanistan was not just about Afghanistan. It was about "ending an era of major military operations to remake other countries". But the series of events that happened till the end of August 2021 completely wiped out what should have been the good ending of a partly successful war on terror.

Even if the exit became a disaster because of the wrong calculations on the part of the military advisers—who stand condemned by the retired flag officers for the tragic and avoidable debacle—to declare it as the end of the road for Mr. Biden and the United States is unfair and graceless. History is replete with events of extreme folly by rulers who survived because of the many other mitigating factors in their favour. By those standards, the Biden presidency has every reason to survive.

The decisiveness with which he has handled the debris of the exit should receive approbation. As a true Commander-in-Chief, he stood by his Generals and took the blame. He has not even been provoked to attack the Taliban or to criticise the Afghan forces for their betrayal of their patrons. In fact, he went out of his way to announce that the Taliban were helpful in facilitating the evacuation, which was completed before the deadline. Interestingly, it was Mr. Biden who set the August 31 deadline, which was turned into an ultimatum by the Taliban.

Many commentators have argued that the Kabul fiasco was worse than Vietnam, Tehran, 9/11, Iraq, and Covid-19 because the details of the other disastrous developments had lost their sharpness with the passage of time. Whatever may have been the horrors of those events, no President was held accountable for them and removed.

In the case of U.S. President Gerald Ford, 59% of the people said that he deserved none of the blame at all. Only 2% held him responsible, though he lost the elections in 1976. President Ronald Reagan's misadventure in Lebanon was criticised by 60% Americans in 1984, but he won the election later that year. There were reasons for these Presidents to continue to serve the nation, taking the reverses in certain areas in their stride.

As of now, there is no alternative to President Biden to lead the country, after his having learnt a bitter lesson from the Afghan experience. A CNN commentator remarked that the withdrawal may hurt him in the midterm in 2022 and presidential election in 2024. "They could just as easily have no impact at all."

No Setting Sun

Even more unfortunate is the conclusion that the U.S. itself lost its place in the world on account of its failure to have a sagacious leader or a competent Commander-in -Chief. A superpower does not sink or rise on account of a single leader. It is still the most powerful economic and military power around which the whole constellation of the world rotates. In fact, the world has a stake in ensuring that a democratic nation leads the world rather than an expansionist dictatorship which has no public opinion to restrain it.

The free world has a responsibility to maintain the American leadership of the world till a wiser and more benign alternative is found. Much has been written about a post-American world for some years now. But it looks that the demise of America, as Mark Twain said about the reports of his own death, is greatly exaggerated.

Published: September 4, 2021

Chanakya Revisited: Lessons for Modern Diplomacy

Chanakya's 'Arthasastra' has been on my mind for a couple of weeks since I was invited to inaugurate a National Seminar on the subject at the Indian Institute of Advanced Study (IIAS) in Shimla this week.

I did not make it to Shimla, though the IIAS was most considerate, but I thought that I should share my thoughts in this column.

Apart from reflecting over the vast amount of literature already available, I came across a few volumes on Chanakya by Radhakrishnan Pillay, published in 2014 and after, which brought the ancient legend to the contemporary world through not only research but also the author's personal experience of people, who have adopted the precepts of Chanakya to make models of leadership to meet the challenges of today.

Pillay established that the treatise on politics, economics, military strategy, statecraft, and social organisation, written for kings in the fourth century BC and followed by leaders of yore, is relevant today, even in the management of a police establishment.

In popular imagination, Chanakya is often portrayed as a ruthless strategist, or a king maker, who acts in his own self-interest, with little regard for others.

But his 'Arthasastra' is the most comprehensive treatise on statecraft that has shaped and influenced Indian politics and diplomacy for nearly two thousand years. It is a civilisational gift from India to the world, which came long before Machiavelli's 'The Prince'.

As for its global influence and relevance, there is no greater testimony than the one given by the modern Chanakya, Henry Kissinger. He characterised 'Arthasastra' as a work that lays out the requirements of power, which is the "dominant reality" in politics.

He deemed it a combination of Machiavelli and Clausewitz. Machiavelli became synonymous with cold calculation and ruthlessness in politics. But the German sociologist Max Weber once called it "truly radical 'Machiavellianism'... compared to it, Machiavelli's 'The Prince' is harmless."

In essence, 'Arthasastra' is a study of leadership in all areas of human activity, covering rulers, managers, customers and others. It lays down certain principles and strategies that should guide leaders at different levels. It deals comprehensively with the way to enhance the efficacy of leaders, including techniques to vanquish enemies and to expand territories.

Chanakya's analysis of statecraft is devoid of morality, it is cold, pragmatic, efficient, and unsentimental. But it was still rooted in principles and neither was it fully devoid of morality, as he expected leaders to carry out their duties according to the law, even while conquering the Earth. He did not endorse the Indian virtue of believing in fate and waiting for the auspicious confluence of stars and planets.

As for strategy, Chanakya considered it essential to analyse every situation deeply, including the strength of the enemy and the relative strength of the leader himself.

He made his prescriptions of eternal value by picking and choosing measures that have worked out in specific situations in running a state and conducting international relations. He provided a menu of options, a virtual textbook for kings, ministers, public servants, and most importantly, diplomats.

Of all the theories of the international system propounded by Chanakya, the most significant for India is called the "circle of states", or "raja mandala".

According to this theory, hostile states are those that border the ruler's state, forming a circle around it. In turn, states that surround this set of hostile states form another circle around the circle of hostile states.

This second circle of states can be considered the natural allies of the ruler's state against the hostile states that lie between them. The idea of the raja mandala also holds that relations between two contingent states will generally be tense, a fact that is definitely true of many regions.

An odd country may be friendly to a dominating and big neighbour, but its status will be of a vassal. Nothing describes the eternal dilemma in South Asia, which has plagued India's foreign policy.

The 'Arthasastra' speaks at significant length on the policies necessary to secure the goals of the state. There are several guiding principles that govern Chanakya's views on foreign policy.

These include: a ruler ought to develop his state by augmenting and exploiting its resources and power; the state ought to try and eliminate enemy states; those who help in this objective are friends; a state ought to stick to a prudent course; a ruler's behaviour must appear just; and peace is preferable to war in attaining a goal.

Looking for streaks of Chanakya in makers of foreign policy in India is like looking for the influence of Vedanta and Mahatma Gandhi in the leaders of modern India. We know it is there as a pervasive spirit, but it is difficult to pinpoint it in specific situations.

No Prime Minister has claimed that Chanakya is their role model, probably because of the stigma of extreme nationalism and ruthlessness attached to his prescriptions. But every Prime Minister has employed the Chanakya precepts in situations that demanded decisiveness, finesse and shrewdness.

Jawaharlal Nehru saw himself as a pacifist and internationalist, who projected India's dreams as those of the world. But the ideas of decolonisation, disarmament, equitable distribution of wealth, and human rights were fundamental to Indian interests at the time.

Similarly, Nehru's neighbourhood policy reflected Chanakya's advice to conquer the hearts of neighbours with assurances of friendship and security and be tough, if necessary, when India's territorial integrity was breached. But the Chanakya of the time was Sardar Patel, the mastermind that united India and advised Nehru to be unsentimental to China.

Indira Gandhi came closest to Chanakya in her leadership in national and international politics. The way she managed the liberation of Bangladesh was strictly according to Chanakya's prescription of "sama, dana, bheda and danda" in dealing with adversaries. She cared for public opinion to a certain extent, but was ruthless in decision making. The Bangladesh War, the nuclear explosion, the Emergency, and the attack on Bhindranwale were actions that Chanakya would have approved of.

For scheming and posturing, PV Narasimha Rao could teach something to Chanakya. His seeming indecision and bewilderment over global and domestic events camouflaged his steely determination, capacity for manipulation, and stern action when necessary.

Nobody else could have handled the transformation of India in the post-Cold War world as effectively as he did. He even defended the tactics of saving his government as the duty of a leader to preserve his leadership by any means, going ahead of Chanakya in defining the role of the leader.

Atal Bihari Vajpayee had his own Chanakya in the person of Brajesh Mishra, once my boss in New York. Some of the actions of Vajpayee like the nuclear tests of 1998 were attributed to Mishra.

Nobody seems to have characterised Narendra Modi as Chanakya, as that appellation has gone to one of his most trusted advisers. But his journey from being a "chaiwala" to Prime Minister could not have been accomplished without a Chanakyan mind.

Nor could Modi have won an overwhelming victory in the recent elections without cold calculations, correct self-assessment, and thorough knowledge of the adversaries, which Chanakya advocated for leaders. No further evidence is required to prove that Chanakya is very much alive and well in twenty-first century India.

Published: July 10, 2019

Indo-Pak Peace Talks:
Cynicism and Distrust

A dialogue that began between India and Pakistan with the purpose of removing the trust deficit between them has ended up sowing greater distrust. Mystery remains as to why the two sides went ahead with talks last week when the preparatory meetings had not shown any sign of success. The theory that any dialogue will bring some incremental benefits has been proven wrong.

Sparks flew right, left and centre when Foreign Ministers S.M. Krishna and Shah Mahmood Qureshi of India and Pakistan, respectively, gave an account of the "cordial and positive" talks they held in Islamabad on July 15. On every issue that came up in the final press conference, the positions of the two countries remained far apart. No advance was made on investigations into the November 2008 Mumbai terrorist attack; no respite was indicated on infiltrations or ceasefire violations across the Line of Control separating Indian- and Pakistani-controlled areas of Kashmir; and Pakistan continues to allege that India is stirring up trouble in Baluchistan. If there was any good news on other issues, nothing was heard about it.

The timing was a big part of the problem. India had just received evidence from its questioning of the architect of the Mumbai terrorist attack, David Headley, suggesting that Pakistan's intelligence agency was involved in the attack, a charge Pakistan denies. That was good enough reason for the talks to be suspended until the cobwebs in the case were cleared.

Instead, Pakistan rebuffed the allegation from Indian Home Secretary G.K. Pillai, repeated on the eve of the summit. Pakistan's foreign minister equated Mr. Pillai's comment to remarks made by one of the prime suspects in the attacks, Hafeez Sayeed, by saying that both were equally unhelpful. This cast further doubt on Pakistan's commitment to bringing the perpetrators to book. Without that determination, no progress was possible on other issues as far as India was concerned.

Meanwhile, even as Pakistan's army was firing a salute for the Indian foreign minister, guns were booming across the line of control in Kashmir. On July 13, a major of the Indian army was killed and a colonel wounded by the firing from across the line. Mr. Krishna also told Mr. Qureshi that there was a 40% increase in the infiltration of Pakistan terrorists into Jammu and Kashmir. The sound of guns on the border cannot provide background music to talks on peace.

Complicating matters, Pakistani President Asif Ali Zardari had just returned from his fifth visit to China since he became president. The president brought back with him not just the two nuclear reactors China had agreed to build in defiance of world opinion and Nuclear Suppliers Group guidelines, but also additional infrastructure to be built on what India considers its own territory in Jammu and Kashmir. The message was one of eternal friendship between Pakistan and China, clearly aimed at keeping India in check. Pakistan believes it can afford a bit of distrust with India if it has a surfeit of trust with China.

India may have calculated that some progress with Pakistan would help bolster India's own reputation in the forthcoming international conference on Afghanistan, which both India and Pakistan are scheduled to attend. Pakistan, already concerned about the U.S. position that India has a legitimate role in Afghanistan, may not have wanted any change in the equations in Afghanistan at this stage. Letting this round of dialogue go without results may have been part of Pakistan's calculation.

In a similar vein, U.S. National Security Adviser Jim Jones arrived in India a day before the Islamabad parleys to prepare for President Barack Obama's scheduled November visit. His outright condemnation of terrorism and the blunt message he conveyed to Pakistan about harbouring terrorists within its own territory may have made alarm bells ring in Islamabad. Any admission of Mumbai guilt at this time could have undermined Pakistan's credibility with the United States.

Such a configuration of events and trends provided a sure recipe for disaster at the Islamabad talks. Perhaps the two countries felt they had gone too far along in the preparations to postpone the summit without losing face. But it's far worse for peace talks to end in a war of words. Mr. Qureshi rubbed salt in the wound by criticizing Mr. Krishna personally when he was still on Pakistan soil.

Hope remains alive. The two sides will reconvene in November, and when they do, they could usefully remember the experience of this round: Talking for talking's sake, without a clear path toward results, risks adding a war of recriminations in addition to all the countries' other troubles.

Published: July 19, 2010

Kargil Conflict: Clinton's Intervention

As we celebrate the 20th anniversary of the Kargil Victory Day this week, we should recall the role played in ending the conflict by President Bill Clinton and the United States. No doubt, India put up a strong fight in the difficult terrain of Kargil and thwarted Pakistan's plans to occupy positions on our side of the Line of Control (LoC) and to use it as a bargaining point to negotiate a Kashmir settlement.

As the first war between the two countries after both had become nuclear weapon states, the situation had caused international concern and Clinton decided to step in to prevent an escalation of the conflict. The "Kargil Spring" came in India-US relations after the "Nuclear Winter" that had set in after India's nuclear tests in May 1998.

For the first time in history, the US stood by India against Pakistan as there was clear evidence that the latter had initiated the war by sending its soldiers to infiltrate into Kargil. India, even in the face of grave provocation and with more than enough capability to cross the LoC, refrained from doing so and thus won the support of the US and the international community.

I recall the historic meeting Prime Minister Nawaz Sharif had with President Bill Clinton on July 4, 1999, at the Blair House in Washington, which marked a turning point in the conflict that lasted 60 days. The details of the Clinton-Sharif meeting have been revealed in the writings of Strobe Talbott, Bruce Reidel, and Bill Clinton himself.

My own book, *Words, Words, Words* has a chapter titled, 'Nuclear Winter, Kargil Spring', which contains the information given to me as the designated representative of the Embassy throughout the day of the meeting by Assistant Secretary for South Asia, Rick Inderfurth.

It is clear that Sharif went to Washington in desperation to end the conflict, but made a heroic effort to drag Clinton to undertake a mediation mission like he had done in the case of the Israel-Palestine situation. "Sharif was concerned that the situation that Pakistan had created was getting out of control, and he hoped to use my good offices not only to resolve the crisis, but also to help mediate with the Indians on the question of Kashmir itself," Clinton wrote in his autobiography, *My Life*.

Clinton's attention was drawn to the Kargil conflict on account of the intelligence he had received that Pakistan was contemplating to use nuclear weapons in case it was defeated in the Kargil conflict. He wrote letters to the two Prime Ministers to seek a resolution, abandoning the traditional hyphenation between India and Pakistan by saying clearly that the solution was for Pakistan to withdraw to the LoC and for India to refrain from crossing the LoC in retaliation.

Clinton was impressed that even after Pakistan crossed the Line of Control and captured Kargil, India refrained from crossing the LoC to repel the aggressor. Moreover, the United States condemned Pakistan's "infiltration of armed intruders" and went public with information that most of the 700 men who had crossed the Line of Control were attached to the 10th Corps of the Pakistani Army. This completely debunked the Pakistani claim that the intruders were freedom fighters of Kashmir.

The initiative to seek the good offices of Clinton to resolve the issue came from Sharif as he felt that Pakistan would not get the support from the US to continue the conflict. But Clinton made it clear to Sharif that he should come only if he was willing to agree to withdraw the Pakistani forces. But in a special gesture, the President agreed to spend the US National Day to discuss the issue with Sharif.

He informed Vajpayee about the visit and invited him also to join. But Vajpayee declined because of India's position against any third country intervention in India-Pakistan issues. Clinton informed Vajpayee that he would convey the gist of the discussion to him as the talks proceeded.

Although Clinton had made it clear that unconditional withdrawal was the only option for Pakistan, Sharif's opening proposal was a ceasefire to be followed by negotiations under American auspices.

His fallback was to make Pakistani withdrawal conditional on Indian agreement to direct negotiations sponsored and probably mediated by the United States. After a day of gruelling negotiations, during which Clinton threatened to declare failure of the talks, Sharif agreed to "take concrete and immediate steps for the restoration of the LoC."

In return, Sharif got an assurance from Clinton that he would take "personal interest to encourage an expeditious resumption and intensification of the bilateral efforts once the sanctity of the LoC had been fully restored."

The decision on withdrawal was firm and explicit, while the face saving given to Sharif was virtually meaningless. Instead of Clinton mediating, the assurance was only to encourage an expeditious resumption of the bilateral efforts, which was not against the basic Indian position. Still, I made a reservation on that formulation when Rick Inderfurth read it out to me after the meeting.

According to US sources, Clinton telephoned Vajpayee twice during the day to seek his views, but Vajpayee was totally noncommittal. Even when the news of the agreement was conveyed to him, Vajpayee's reaction was only—"What do you expect me to say, Mr President?" In other words, he kept his distance from Clinton's efforts even though he may have been grateful about the outcome.

Interestingly, Sharif had gone to Washington with his family, hinting that he might not be able to return to Pakistan if he did not secure US support for Pakistan's position. But apparently, Clinton leaned heavily on him to agree to withdraw.

Sharif refuted the suggestion that Kargil was similar to the Israel-Palestine situation and that it was the duty of Clinton to mediate. Clinton clarified that in the Israel-Palestine situation, he had requests from both sides to intervene, while India was clearly against his mediation.

Clinton compared the Kargil situation to the Cuban crisis, which had brought the world to the brink of a nuclear war. When Clinton told

Sharif that he had information that the Pakistan Army was ready to use nuclear weapons, Sharif expressed total surprise.

The discussion took the whole day essentially because Clinton was careful not to give Sharif a sense of defeat, leading to Sharif staying on in the US as a political refugee. It was important to keep his credibility with the army intact so that he could return to Pakistan with a face-saving device to order the army to restore the sanctity of the LoC.

Clinton proved to be a master negotiator in this particular case as he was convinced that the military adventurism by the Pakistan Army should be sternly rebuffed.

According to Talbott, at one point, "Clinton had worked himself back into real anger—his face flushed, eyes narrowed, lips pursed, cheek muscles pulsing, fists clenched. He said it was crazy enough for Sharif to have let his military violate the Line of Control, start a border war with India, and now prepare nuclear forces for action.

"On top of that, he had put Clinton in the middle of the mess and set him up for a diplomatic failure. Sharif seemed beaten, physically and emotionally. He denied he had given any orders with regard to nuclear weaponry and said he was worried for his life."

India-US relations have a long history of ups and downs and many of the downs have been on account of the US support for Pakistan.

But Kargil was the one case in which spring broke out in India-US relations after they were frozen in the wake of the Indian nuclear tests. The Kargil victory belonged to India, but the decisive step taken by Clinton and the role of Nawaz Sharif in it may well have prevented a catastrophe. The conflict would have continued and many more lives would have been lost.

It was Clinton's firm support to India on Kargil, which led to his own visit to India and Vajpayee's visit to the US in 2000 and marked a major improvement in bilateral relations.

Published: July 16, 2019

6

Lakshadweep's Significance: Strategic Island Challenges

The present political debate in the country on Lakshadweep, particularly in Kerala, is part of the environment versus development discussions, and the stress is on preserving and promoting the cultural integrity and religious freedom of the islands.

No doubt, any regulations for the development of the islands that impinge on the islanders should have the acceptance of the local population and the democratic bodies should be fully consulted. Similarly, there should be a balance between protection of the ecology and development.

The genius of the local population depends on their food habits, language, their way of life and how it should be preserved even when they are given new facilities for a higher standard of living along with the use of new technologies in keeping with the aspirations of the people.

For centuries, Lakshadweep has been a beauty spot in the vast expanse of the Indian Ocean, and India inherited it from the British as an integral part of its territory. The islands should be treated as an extension of the country into the sea and it should have the same level of development as the rest of the country.

In fact, the islands should have priority in development because they have been greatly neglected in the past. The population is small enough to benefit from modest investments. Only 10 of the 36 islands are inhabited and the total population is 65,000, smaller than an average district capital. It also has a low population growth of 6% as against the national average of 17%. But the islands give India 20,000 km of territorial waters and 4,00,000 km of Exclusive Economic Zone (EEZ).

Lakshadweep has assumed strategic importance in recent years with the rise of China and its efforts to dominate the Indo-Pacific. Lakshadweep and the Andaman and Nicobar Islands are two natural sentinels for India on the east and the west. They are two virtual aircraft carriers and candidates for developing naval facilities there. Lakshadweep has only a small naval facility in Kavaratti, which needs to be expanded to meet the new requirements of security.

The setting up of the Quad will mean joint exercises with the other three members of the security dialogue—the US, Japan, and Australia. Lakshadweep should be a gateway or chokepoint for friends and foes. The efficacy of Quad will depend on the deployment of the naval assets of the participants in an integrated manner.

The 200-km wide funnel referred to as Nine Degree Channel (named after the latitude) near the island is an important sea lane of communication, linking the Persian Gulf with East Asia. The South Western Naval Command, based in Kochi, keeps an eye on the cargo passing through this area against illegal activities including piracy.

The significance of Lakshadweep and Andamans has increased greatly in recent times, and has been given special attention on account of different factors. The US Navy conducted a Freedom of Navigation Operation (FONOP) in India's EEZ recently.

The US 7th Fleet's USS John Paul Jones "asserted navigational rights and freedoms approximately 130 nautical miles west of the Lakshadweep Islands, inside India's exclusive economic zone, without requesting India's prior consent, consistent with international law," as stated by the US authorities.

The statement even asserted that India's policy of requiring prior notification to be "inconsistent with international law." India's Ministry of External Affairs conveyed its concerns regarding this passage through our EEZ to the Government of USA through diplomatic channels.

It is not clear even now why the US chose to conduct the operation in India's EEZ. If it was to give China, which has a similar position as India, a message, targeting India was particularly objectionable. The Biden Administration has made it clear that it will fly, sail and operate whenever international law allows. Ironically, the US is not a signatory to the Law of the Sea, which it quotes. But the choice of the vicinity of Lakshadweep may indicate the importance of the islands.

The Chinese strategy to enforce its claims in the South China Sea is to create as many artificial islands as possible to measure China's territorial waters from these islands rather than from the mainland. India has a case to create islands in the vicinity of Lakshadweep, so as to expand our territorial sea and EEZ. At the minimum, Lakshadweep should be developed as a naval facility.

This will also benefit the inhabitants by way of jobs and excellent infrastructure. Some small island states in the Caribbean and the South Pacific prefer to be administered by their former colonial masters as they are not viable as independent states.

In the context of climate change, the developed countries advise us not to do what they did, but what they prescribe. They say that developing countries should protect their natural environment so that trees and water bodies serve as sinks to their emissions of greenhouse gases. That is the only way the rich countries can continue to enjoy their style of living based on conspicuous consumption.

I remember the King of Bhutan saying to a Western expert: "Your advice will amount to building a fence around us to keep us like animals in a zoo for you to view." In fact, Bhutan has become a model of eco-friendly development by embarking on a campaign for sustainable growth, which has made this Himalayan Kingdom the only country which is carbon free.

We should adopt a similar strategy for Lakshadweep, bearing in mind the interests of its people and the importance of the island for our security. Instead of treating it as a distant island, we should integrate it into India's development and security architecture with the concurrence of the local people, as stressed by the Kerala High Court.

Published: June 2, 2021

Lessons from Lanka:
Sri Lanka's Debt Crisis

"Neither a borrower nor a lender be; for loan oft loses both itself and friend," warned Shakespeare many years ago, but nations make it a habit of borrowing and often living beyond their means. Sri Lanka, a fairly prosperous and successful nation, developed the art of borrowing from Peter to pay Paul for years and appeared to be doing well.

Colombo was the paradise for Indian shoppers for purchasing foreign goods long before India liberalised its own economy. It became a consumer state which paid for its ship-to-mouth existence from tourism and tea. Even the long conflict and war did not break the back of the island country as Chinese largesse poured in to build infrastructure much beyond their needs. Each succeeding government borrowed more and more in the expectation that it will be for their successors to repay the debt.

The debt spiral has finally caught up with the Gotabaya Rajapaksa government, driving the population to desperation on account of the debt service burden which was 96 per cent of the total GDP in 2019, and over 119 percent in 2021. The projection is that the public debt will remain 64.2 per cent of the GDP till the year 2026.

Prices of essential imported commodities have risen to unprecedented levels and there is a trickling of economic refugees to India. Sri Lanka has no choice except to reduce imports, adopt a tighter monetary policy, and build foreign exchange reserves. But instead of counting dollars in his hands, President Gotabaya is counting days for a possible dissolution of Parliament, now that the deadline of March 20 for dissolution is over. The election is expected to provide a commercial break like in a TV show to distract the public.

Normally, countries in such dire straits resort to loans from international financial institutions like the IMF and World Bank. But with Sri Lanka's record of dynastic rule, poor governance, and high corruption, President Gotabaya was not very keen to go to these institutions, which have tough conditionalities. The choice, therefore, for him was to go to friendly countries like China and India, which have chipped in. But since the country is in a deep financial crisis, he went to the IMF also for consultations.

In its report on the consultations issued on February 25, the IMF identified the possible reasons for the present situation—the severe pandemic that hit the island, vulnerability to external shocks and high risks to public debt sustainability, the Easter Sunday terrorist attacks in 2019, policy changes including tax cuts in 2019, contraction of the GDP by 36 per cent due to loss of tourism, loss of access to international sovereign bonds market, and the alarming deficits amounting to 10 per cent of GDP.

It did not mention the long civil war, which resulted not only in great financial loss but also in the loss of significant Tamil intellectuals and civil servants. The IMF recommended a tighter monetary policy, the building of international reserves, and prudent management of infrastructure facilities like the Colombo Port. Since none of these is easy to accomplish, no amount of possible assistance is going to rescue Sri Lanka from its tight spot.

To restore macroeconomic stability and debt sustainability, the IMF has recommended the implementation of a credible and coherent strategy covering both the near- and medium-term, a comprehensive set of policies with specific measures such as substantial revenue-based fiscal consolidation, fuel pricing policy, controlling inflation, restoring a market-oriented and flexible exchange rate, development of social safety mechanisms, and other tough measures. While the IMF has complimented Sri Lanka on measures taken during the pandemic, it has predicted a bleak economic outlook in the short- and medium-term.

China is reportedly considering a Sri Lankan request for a $2.5 billion credit to overcome the present crisis. The Chinese ambassador to Sri Lanka confirmed that China is considering a $1 billion loan and a $1.5 billion credit line to purchase goods from China, both of which would be new lines of financing. He provided no details on when an agreement would be finalised, and in what form. China's Belt and Road Initiative (BRI) has already got Sri Lanka ensnared in a debt trap, leading to the Hambantota Port being leased out to China for a period of 99 years against $1.2 billion. In the absence of any assurance from China, Sri Lanka seems to be re-assessing the extent to which it can bank on China. It is no secret that China's agenda is to subjugate Sri Lanka economically.

India, on the other hand, has extended a $1 billion credit facility to Sri Lanka to assist the island nation to enable it to procure food, medicines, and other essential items. "Neighbourhood first. India stands with Sri Lanka. US$1 billion credit line signed for the supply of essential commodities. A key element of the package of support extended by India," tweeted the External Affairs Minister.

So far, India has extended $1.4 billion support to Sri Lanka, through a $400 million RBI currency swap, deferral of a $0.5 billion loan, and another half-a-billion dollar as a line of credit for the country to sustain its essential fuel imports. A leading expert on Sri Lanka in India of the Observer Research Foundation (ORF) believes that Sri Lanka now has become more confident about India than China.

The successive Sri Lankan governments have been generally socialist in their approaches, and their projects are aimed at pleasing the public. However, these governments have a tendency to undertake populist measures with borrowed money, which do not produce sufficient income even to repay the loans. While funds may be available in plenty, unless they are invested in viable projects with adequate returns for paying the interest as well as the principal, the consequences could be disastrous.

The present controversy in Kerala on the government's pet project of building a superfast rail service revolves around this obsession. There has been resistance to the project not only from the opposition but also from the public on considerations of losing land and environmental degradation.

The resistance movement has only hardened the position of the government, but unlike Sri Lanka, Kerala has supervisory authority in the Union government, which keeps an eye on the debt burden of the state. But the Sri Lankan experience of spending borrowed money on unproductive projects beyond its means and running the risk of endangering people's lives should be a lesson to learn from Lanka.

Published: March 28, 2023

Bangladesh Impressions: Reflections on a Visit to Dhaka

As we celebrate the 50th anniversary of Bangladesh and the centenary of 'Bangabandhu' (Friend of Bengal) Sheikh Mujibur Rahman, I recall three "Bangladesh Moments" in my life, which remain indelible in my memory. I had joined our mission in Bhutan just before the beginning of the war. Travelling through Siliguri and Phuentsholing before entering Bhutan, there was a palpable sense of the impending war.

We naturally followed the war from Bhutan, primarily through the military officers of the Indian Military Training Team (IMTRAT) in Bhutan and we were also glued to the All India Radio for the news broadcasts. We had no television in Bhutan those days.

Three days after the war started, India formally recognised Bangladesh as an independent nation on 6 December, a day which has been designated "Maitri Divas" by the two countries a few days ago. The news had come late in the evening and we were calling it a day when I received a call from the Foreign Minister of Bhutan, Lyonpo Dawa Tsering, a friendly and sophisticated person I could count as a personal friend. But what surprised me was that he wanted to see me in his office immediately. As I got ready to leave, I recalled stories of diplomats being summoned by Foreign Offices at night to convey unfriendly news or to indicate diplomatic displeasure.

Tsering received me warmly, prefacing that he had some good news to convey to me in the absence of Ambassador Ashok Gokhale, who was in Delhi. Then he read out a formal note conveying that His Majesty's

Government had decided to extend recognition to Bangladesh. I was overjoyed and said that Bhutan would be the second country in the world to recognise Bangladesh.

Tsering said that it was the intention to express solidarity with India and Bangladesh. I could not wait to convey the message to Delhi and so I rushed back home, called up our wireless operator and sent a crash message to the Ministry. I slept only after hearing the main headline of the 9 pm news about this historic development. I felt fortunate to have received the news from the Bhutanese Foreign Minister.

The second moment was a totally unexpected turn of events by which I became one of the first Indian diplomats to be received by Gen. Hussein Muhammad Ershad, who staged a coup on 24 March 1982 and later became President. On the day of his coup, I happened to be in Colombo as part of a UN Council for Namibia on a mission to promote the cause of the independence of Namibia.

Those were the days when the UN was flush with funds to promote decolonisation and we used to travel around several countries, whether they were supportive of Namibia or not. The delegation was led by the ambassador of Cyprus and I was designated as his Deputy.

We were scheduled to fly to Dhaka the next morning, but when we heard about the coup, we sought permission to skip Dhaka and go directly to New Delhi, which was our next destination. We informed all concerned about our change in schedule before we went to sleep.

The first person who met us in the morning was the Bangladesh High Commissioner to Sri Lanka. He had come with a message from his government to say that we should stick to our schedule to visit Dhaka and that General Ershad would be happy to meet us and convey his support for Namibia. He was very persuasive and asked us to change our plans again.

We realised that Bangladesh felt that the cancellation of the visit of a UN delegation would be seen as indicative of instability in the country, following the coup. We were not too happy to land in Dhaka and that too just a day after the coup, particularly since we had two lady diplomats also with us. But Bangladesh had already approached our governments and the clearance for our visit to Dhaka came even before we asked.

The reception we received in Dhaka was much beyond the normal protocol requirements of a UN delegation and we were whisked away from the airport to the State Guest House reserved for Heads of States and Governments and we were given the best suites. Within hours, General Ershad received us warmly and also served us a fabulous lunch. He was particularly warm to me and asked me to convey his warmest greetings to Prime Minister Indira Gandhi and others.

We confined ourselves to matters relating to Namibia, but before we left, General Ershad took me aside and said that the relations with India would be strengthened under his watch. I was able to convey this message not only to our High Commissioner in Dhaka but also to Indira Gandhi herself when she received our delegation.

My third Bangladesh moment was the most memorable of all. As the Chief Adviser of Dr. Kalam Smriti Advisory Council in Thiruvananthapuram, I was asked to address a letter to the Bangladesh High Commissioner in New Delhi, inviting Prime Minister Sheikh Hasina to come to Thiruvananthapuram to receive the Dr. Kalam Smriti International Excellence Award.

The award was given every year to honour statesmen or leaders who have shown excellence in their fields to achieve the best for their countries. Earlier, the Presidents of the Maldives, Ghana and Mauritius received the prestigious award since its introduction in 2015.

The Bangladesh High Commissioner happened to be Muazzem Ali, who was my colleague in New York. He made a sincere effort to persuade the Prime Minister to include a visit to Kerala during her next visit to India, but it did not work out. Instead, the High Commissioner was asked to receive the award on her behalf.

But he asked me whether I could travel to Dhaka to present the award to Sheikh Hasina, an offer we could not resist. A date was fixed and five of us from the Kalam Smriti International were invited to visit Dhaka.

We received an extremely warm welcome, and a special function was held at the official residence of the Prime Minister. We were given very high protocol courtesies, though none of us were representing the government. Not only that, Sheikh Hasina also spent an hour with me before the ceremony and another hour with the whole delegation at dinner afterwards. She was very cordial and friendly, and spoke highly of her association with former Indian President Abdul Kalam.

"For an award for world leaders, in the name of such a person, we could not have thought of anyone better than Her Excellency Sheikh Hasina, a visionary, thinker and an inspiration for millions. The longest serving Prime Minister of Bangladesh is well on her way to build the 'Sonar Bangla' (Golden Bengal) that her father, 'Bangabandhu' Sheikh Mujibur Rahman, dreamt of and died for," I said.

Sheikh Hasina reminisced about Dr. Kalam most affectionately, saying that her husband also was a nuclear scientist and that his transformation from a scientist to a statesman was amazingly smooth. It was obvious that she accepted the invitation readily because the award was in the name of Dr. Kalam.

"This award will inspire me and my government to strive for the achievement of greater inclusive development."

The event was widely publicised and we were also invited to visit the Sheikh Mujibur Rahman Museum, his home, where he and his entire family were shot dead. Sheikh Hasina and her sister survived as they were abroad.

As a special gesture, Sheikh Hasina invited two of us to visit her in Delhi when she came a few weeks later on a state visit. She gave us an audience at the High Commissioner's residence in Delhi, and profusely thanked us for the award. Sadly, Muazzem Ali, the Bangladesh High Commissioner, who was most helpful to us, returned to Bangladesh a few days later and passed away soon after.

My Bangladesh moments were providential and unexpected. But there was some poetic justice in my being touched by the warmth in India-Bangladesh relations, which have now reached a new high point after the visit of Prime Minister Narendra Modi.

Published: April 3, 2021

Pakistan's Development Dilemma:
A Comparative Analysis

Getting ensconced in the Marriott Hotel in Islamabad for three days to attend a conference is not the way to feel the pulse of Pakistan, but rather it was a physical glimpse of the country's national capital for the first time. After having professionally followed the events there for decades, an actual look at the country helped me to confirm some of my impressions and to explode some others.

As expected, the country is paranoid with India and is desperately fighting against heavy odds to maintain its rival status in the eyes of the world. The current freeze in relations with India, except for the thrust and parry on the Line of Control, the tough US position on terrorism, and Afghanistan having become an 'extension of India' seem to greatly bother Pakistan's intelligentsia.

At the drop of a hat, they would lambast India for having annexed Jammu and Kashmir, using the excuse of a tribal rebellion for sending Indian forces before the accession was completed, and for having forged an Instrument of Accession, which itself has been lost, and for not holding a plebiscite. The Indian demands, they would say, would not be acceptable to any self-respecting nation. They have no vision of peace and mutually beneficial relationship with India in the near future. Their expectation is that China and Russia would come to their rescue, now that the US was discarding them. They are optimistic that a Taliban-dominated dispensation will wean Afghanistan away from India and bring it to their camp.

More of geopolitical involvements, balance of power, friends and masters and overarching presence of nuclear weapons are in the horizon, not peace, cooperation, and mutually beneficial balanced trade.

Pakistanis attribute their economic ills to the military control of the civilian government and growth of religious extremism.

On the day of my departure from Pakistan, *Dawn,* the country's biggest English newspaper, published an op-ed by senior retired Pakistani diplomat Ashraf Jehangir Qazi, titled 'Why should India try to destroy Pakistan when the country's rulers are doing it themselves?'

A former ambassador to the United States, Qazi argued that Pakistan, despite its poverty and inequalities, does not have a single significant pro-poor or progressive political party. There are only religious, nationalist, and populist leaders, who are all right wing, conservative and pro-establishment.

He virtually called for "a historic struggle to rid Pakistan of rulers without a cause, other than to escape accountability." In his publication, he saw the signs of a failing state in every walk of life. The myth that exploded on stepping on the soil of Pakistan was that Pakistan was in some ways comparable to India.

Most countries equate India and Pakistan as though there is some parity between them and they are of the same strength and size, because they believe that the two countries are equally responsible for the debacle in Kashmir.

The hyphenation that many countries have developed between India and Pakistan is the priceless legacy that Pakistan has acquired because of the internationalisation of the Kashmir issue and other differences.

Such a comparison is an existential need for Pakistan as if all disputes were to disappear, the question will arise as to what the justification for Pakistan was.

There is no comparison between the two in any area, particularly after the liberation of Bangladesh. Islamabad is only as big as a Delhi suburb with a two million population and broad roads with modest traffic.

How can a city with just two five-star hotels and only one departure gate at their international airport, named after Benazir Bhutto, be compared to Delhi with its sprawling airport, named after Indira Gandhi?

Like the 'parity' between the US and the USSR during the final days of the Cold War, the best kept secret is that there is nothing to equate Pakistan and India except the nuclear capability, which eliminated the military imbalance.

Pakistan is many years behind us in virtually everything. The style and sophistication of the Pakistani diplomats abroad had led me to expect a better style of living in Pakistan.

The fond hope that the China-Pakistan Economic Corridor (CPEC), and Chinese investment in the country will pull the country out of the the morass is universal in Pakistan. The country's political parties and regions, however, have been deeply divided on the subject of equitable distribution of and control over CPEC projects.

The expectation is that the CPEC will begin to address Pakistan's energy and infrastructure needs in the near term. They expect that the CPEC could prove an opportunity to decisively overcome the Baluchistan insurgency.

A broader CPEC authority is necessary to ensure that the project moves forward on a consensus basis. Neither the Pakistani military nor the civilian bureaucracy has the economic and political aptitude to steward the project to success.

It may well be that the strategic content of the CPEC is being exaggerated. Pakistan's primary goal should be to put itself on a trajectory of rapid, equitable, and sustained macroeconomic growth.

The ultimate evidence of the success of CPEC will be whether it boosts industrial productivity, exports, and job creation in Pakistan, putting the country on a path toward sustained, high levels of equitable economic growth.

Russia is expected to provide political and moral support to fill the gap being left behind by the United States, when it leaves Afghanistan.

The present policy of India to leave Pakistan alone to deal with its problems without chasing a dialogue process and merely dealing with the military situation on the border and terrorism in Jammu and Kashmir appears well-advised.

Prime Minister Narendra Modi appears to have exhausted all his weapons of a peace offensive with Pakistan. Nobody will lament the dormant state of SAARC, as long as modest bilateral cooperation and trade is maintained with our other neighbours in South Asia.

In the meantime, what remains is Track II sherpas and other peace merchants who jet themselves to Bangkok and Macao in search of elusive peace.

India has more options with regard to Pakistan than Pakistan has with India, because our economic development and position in the world are not determined by our relations with Pakistan, which is now little more than a side-show.

But for Pakistan, respectability is contingent upon good relations with India. The United States had wanted India and Pakistan to maintain a dialogue essentially to prevent a nuclear confrontation between them.

Pakistan's conditions and terrorist attacks have finally frozen the dialogue and there is no pressure on either country to resume the dialogue. For India, the frustration is on account of Pakistan's refusal to take any action on terrorist leaders, even after clear evidence has been produced about their complicity. The recent decision to allow consular access to Kulbhushan Jadhav is indeed a welcome development, which may help reduce tensions.

The Indian High Commission in Islamabad is about to have a leadership change when Ambassador Ajay Bisaria shifts from cold Warsaw to hot Islamabad. These two developments may augur well for the future.

But peace cannot come unless Pakistan realises that maintaining good relations with India will be more important than the illusory parity they perceive in keeping the Kashmir pot boiling.

Published: December 11, 2017

Pervez Musharraf's Legacy:
Evaluating Leadership

The perennial love-hate relationship Indians have with the leaders of Pakistan is proverbial.

Pakistani leaders are the cynosure of all eyes when they visit India during multilateral conferences, not to speak of the way they are feted on bilateral visits. The adversarial relationship makes both sides particularly careful in dealing with each other so as to maintain the delicate balancing act, regardless of the ups and downs in the relationship.

Leaders of Pakistan, particularly of the military variety, are Westernised and generally sophisticated and inspire some awe in their counterparts.

The diplomats of India and Pakistan are fairly cordial socially and find more in common with each other than with those from other regions, who may be closer to them for political reasons. This particular chemistry often results in Indians looking for positive points in Pakistani leaders and diplomats.

Perhaps, Indians find their courtesy and courtly manners quite charming even when the hatred is palpable and Pakistani leaders stick to their positions on core issues.

The Bhuttos had their fans in India and there are many, who claim kinship with Pakistani leaders. Prime Ministers I K Gujral and Nawaz Sharif got along well in Punjabi. They agreed that India could not give Kashmir to Pakistan, nor could Pakistan take it.

Imran Khan likewise had many friends in India, but did not lift a finger to improve relations with India.

Our journalists and others who visit Pakistan are generally treated well and they write nice things about the courtesy and hospitality of even leaders like Zia-ul Haq. They even remark that it is our failure that India and Pakistan are at loggerheads even when there are those in Pakistan who mean well for India.

The peaceniks in India engage in track II diplomacy with and without the knowledge of the Government of India, and find possibilities in fake proposals like 'No War Pact' and South Asia as a Nuclear-Weapon Free Zone.

The peace industry was very much alive and well till Prime Minister Modi learnt the hard way that personal gestures like gifts and attending weddings were of no value in building peace with Pakistan.

Those who shed tears over the demise of former President, General Pervez Musharraf are victims of the peace syndrome who have not realised that behind every peace proposal put forward by succeeding Pakistani leaders, is a trap to undermine the fact that Jammu and Kashmir is an integral part of India.

Musharraf's four-point proposal for Kashmir, for instance, appeared to move away from the UN resolutions. By suggesting that identified regions in Kashmir should be demilitarised, self-rule should be introduced, and a joint management mechanism involving Pakistanis, Indians and Kashmiris should be established, Musharraf not only questioned India's position but also its intelligence. To consider such a person a real force for peace is an absurdity. He cannot claim to be a martyr of peace through such pretenses.

Musharraf was certainly a bundle of contradictions. A dictator, who encouraged press freedoms, a soldier who enjoyed his Scotch in secret, engineered Kargil but wanted to change India-Pakistan relations in Agra, condemned to death but wanted to stage a comeback, the list is endless.

As for Kargil, there was never any doubt that Musharraf had masterminded it and executed it, but left it to Nawaz Sharif to face the music when President Clinton gave him an ultimatum to withdraw.

Musharraf states in his book that "One myth is that the operation was launched without taking the political leadership into confidence," without elaborating further.

But he takes the full credit for Kargil by asserting that "I would like to state emphatically that whatever movement that has taken place so far in the direction of finding a solution to Kashmir is due considerably to the Kargil conflict."

Musharraf's accounts of his meeting with Prime Minister Vajpayee and subsequent meetings with Prime Minister Manmohan Singh read like an elaborate plot he had hatched to change the Kashmir story. He was disappointed that the draft Agra Declaration was rejected by India at the last minute, but it was obvious that the Declaration would have opened up a new set of problems. Musharraf's record with India was such that India decided not to trust him.

Though he promised that Pakistan territory would not be used for terrorism against India, he would have resorted to terrorism had he not faced assassination attempts and problems with the judiciary and politicians in Pakistan.

The train bombings in Mumbai 2006 ended the act that he put on to change the Kashmir story by various devious proposals.

Musharraf's efforts at peacemaking gave the impression that he was a changed man. But his moves were aimed not at seeking peace, but to secure a place in history as a peace maker without relenting on Pakistan's position that the final settlement of Kashmir will not be the acceptance of the Line of Control, as anticipated in the Shimla Agreement.

An illusion of peace, generated by an Agra declaration that Musharraf tried to promote, failed because it was patently insincere and opportunistic. His subsequent actions only proved the point. The leopard had not changed its spots.

Published: February 10, 2023

Article 370 Revocation:
Implications and Reactions

The Article 370 bomb that burst in the Rajya Sabha on August 5, 2019 was very much like the then Prime Minister Atal Bihari Vajpayee's Pokhran II of May 11, 1998. Both were essential for the security of India, both should have been done much earlier, and while many Indian leaders had thoughts of doing both earlier, nobody had the courage to do them for fear of internal and external repercussions. Both were carried out in utmost secrecy, with only a handful of people being privy to the decisions and the elaborate preparations which preceded them.

Pokhran II had the near unanimous support of most people in India (80% according to US estimates), but it was very unpopular abroad as it was considered a violation of international norms. However, the reaction on the latest abrupt move on Kashmir, which could be deemed as a 'Pokhran III', will be the exact opposite. Most countries will look at it from the point of view of the UN Charter, which prohibits interference in the internal affairs of states.

While many people in Kashmir and the rest of India will see it as the delivering of the BJP's long-standing agenda and oppose it for political reasons, like Pokhran II, the current Kashmir action will also be eventually accepted by the whole of India and the international community.

No one is happy with the situation in Kashmir today despite the best efforts to alter the course of violence and destruction. The expectation was that Article 370 will serve as an incentive for the people of Kashmir to gradually integrate with India as they will be able to preserve their "Kashmiriyat" under that provision of the Constitution.

Most people in India accepted it as a positive measure, but the so-called moderates began to see Article 370 more as a bargaining point to gain more concessions rather than to give their loyalty and to discourage separatism. For this reason, the value of the Article diminished and the time came to remove it. But the concern was the negative message this would give to the Kashmiris. Moreover, the climate in the Parliament was not conducive to take such a drastic measure. The Modi Government gathered the courage and determination to take a calculated risk. The disruptive action taken by it may well lead to a solution, even if a period of uncertainty and chaos will prevail for some time.

The methodology used was constitutional and democratic. Consultation and consensus building was preferable, but 70 years were not enough to unfreeze the situation without a disruptive action. Any operation is painful, but the final outcome may benefit the new Union Territory of Jammu and Kashmir, Ladakh, and the rest of India.

The deployment of security forces became necessary to prevent bloodshed, given the explosive nature of the change and the Pakistani tactics to incite the people of Kashmir.

The negative reaction from abroad has come so far only from Pakistan and China. Pakistan took extreme measures like threatening to close down its diplomatic mission in New Delhi and pledged to oppose the Indian action tooth and nail.

China said that it opposed India's decision to revoke Kashmir's special status and that New Delhi needed to be cautious on border issues. "India's action is unacceptable and would not have any legal effect," Foreign Ministry spokeswoman Hua Chunying said in a statement, drawing an immediate rebuke from Delhi that Kashmir was an internal affair.

China urged India to strictly abide by the agreements reached by both countries in order to avoid any actions that would further complicate boundary issues, Hua said. India and China have a longstanding dispute over the border including in Ladakh, the high-altitude area.

Indian foreign ministry spokesman Raveesh Kumar said splitting Jammu and Kashmir into federal territories was a domestic issue. "India does not comment on the internal affairs of other countries and similarly expects other countries to do likewise."

Both Pakistan and China have a stake in the issue, as they hold parts of the Kashmir region, Pakistan in the west and China a thinly populated high-altitude area in the north. This gives Pakistan and China some locus standi, but the legitimacy of their occupation itself is in question.

The United States, whose President recently expressed an interest in mediating between India and Pakistan, has merely stated that it was following the events closely. The UN Secretary-General issued the customary appeal for restraint by India and Pakistan for the sake of peace and international security.

Technically, the UN still has a role in Jammu and Kashmir as the "dispute" over Kashmir was taken to the UN Security Council by India and it remains on the agenda of the Council. But the issue has not been raised in the Council, except by Pakistan in an all-out effort to agitate the issue in every UN forum and internationalise it soon after the end of the Cold War.

Pakistan failed as none of the permanent members had any interest in raking up the issue. The general consensus in the international community is that the matter should be settled through bilateral discussions between India and Pakistan.

Pakistan is likely to argue that Jammu and Kashmir have been recognised as a disputed territory, and marked as such on the UN maps, with the notation that the final status of the territory is yet to be determined. Moreover, Pakistan will argue that the relevant Security Council resolutions have not been implemented, by playing down the stipulation that the first step in implementing the resolution is the withdrawal of Pakistan from Pakistan-Occupied Kashmir (POK).

When India and Pakistan converted the ceasefire line into the Line of Control (LoC), India had suggested that the UN Peace Keeping Operation (POK) inducted at the time of the ceasefire was no more relevant and it should be withdrawn. But since both the parties have to agree to such a withdrawal, the UN Military Observer Group for India and Pakistan(UNMOGIP) continues on the Pakistan side of the LoC. India does not recognise UNMOGIP but extends the courtesy of hosting an office in New Delhi, albeit with limited contact.

In the last several years, a report on the situation in Kashmir has made its way to the UN Secretary General's Annual Report, much against India's wish. It is easy to take an issue to the UN but hard to withdraw it! Many vestiges of old disputes linger in the UN even years after the concerned parties have moved on.

Another UN body which is likely to be involved at Pakistan's behest, if the law-and-order situation in Jammu and Kashmir deteriorates, is the Human Rights Council (HRC). But no resolution is likely to be adopted even if a draft is floated by Pakistan as it will be seen as a political move.

The Organisation of Islamic Cooperation (OIC) has traditionally taken a strident position on Kashmir and Pakistan has already decided to raise the matter in the OIC. But it has no great credibility in the matter, particularly after the then Indian External Affairs Minister Sushma Swaraj (RIP) was invited to speak at a meeting of the OIC in the UAE.

The Foreign Secretary has already briefed the Heads of Mission in Delhi about the steps taken by India and the expectation is that the external ramifications of the Kashmir move can be contained. But the situation in Jammu and Kashmir itself has to be carefully watched to prevent bloodshed inside or on the border.

Published: August 11, 2019

Bangladesh's Evolution: Changing Relations with India

I was never posted in Bangladesh as we have a large number of competent diplomats who speak Bengali, but I had witnessed the birth pangs of Bangladesh when I was in Thimphu during the 1971 war, and in Moscow in the aftermath of it.

I had the unique privilege of accepting a letter from the King of Bhutan addressed to the Rashtrapati, conveying the recognition of the People's Republic of Bangladesh by Bhutan, the first country in the world to do so after India.

In Moscow, I was involved in assisting new Bangladesh diplomats to settle down to business. I visited Bangladesh for the first time in strange circumstances in 1982, when I was at the permanent mission of India to the United Nations in New York.

As a delegation to promote Namibian independence, six diplomats from various countries reached Colombo on our way to Dhaka and Delhi when the news broke out that General Mohammed Ershad had taken over the government in a coup.

We promptly cancelled our trip to Dhaka. But within minutes, the Bangladesh High Commissioner to Sri Lanka came to our hotel and said that General Ershad was ready to meet us and that we should not cancel the visit.

Apparently, he felt that it would generate negative publicity if a UN delegation cancelled its visit. Our respective governments were not happy, but left it to us to travel at our own risk. General Ershad was so happy about our arrival in Dhaka a day after the coup that he ordered the highest protocol treatment for us.

We were put up at the Padma guest house, normally reserved for heads of state and government, and treated like them. We were the first diplomats to call on him and a story was put out that we were convinced that the situation was normal.

General Ershad received us warmly and said he had just saved his country by stepping in, something which all dictators say after coups.

He separately spoke to me about India and asked me to assure the Indian government that he would be friendly to India. He said the Indian High Commissioner would be meeting him the same day.

I thus became the first Indian official to meet him after the coup. Back in India, I was asked questions about him at different levels and I said that he appeared positive. They appeared a bit sceptical. As it turned out, India-Bangladesh relations were not particularly smooth during his time.

Another set of circumstances took me to Dhaka this week. When Sheikh Hasina was invited to the village of Punalal near Vellanad to receive the Dr. Kalam Smriti International Award of Excellence, instituted by the Dale View educational institutions, she suggested that some of us should visit Dhaka to present it; I led a delegation to visit Dhaka.

I thought that we would get only a few seconds to present the award in an assembly chain format. Seven of us travelled from Thiruvananthapuram to Dhaka without any great expectations, except that we would be able to reach the award, a sculpture by Kanayi Kunhiraman to Sheikh Hasina's hands.

But the importance that she gave to the event was most exceptional, essentially because of the 'Kalam magic' and her respect for India.

The protocol designed the event for half an hour, but she spent more than two hours with us, including two meetings with me—one before and another after the ceremony.

Every word she spoke about India and Dr A P J Abdul Kalam was positive and respectful. I presented the award while a citation, a plaque, a saree and a *ponnada* were presented by the trustees of the Kalam Smriti International.

After we had a pleasant conversation about cabbages and kings, she asked me "in confidence" as to how she was selected for the award.

When I said that she was the only and natural choice for the award, because of her being the architect of excellent India-Bangladesh relations, she appeared satisfied that the award was truly a people's choice.

Bearing this in mind, I said in my speech: "For an award for world leaders, in the name of such a person, we could not have thought of anyone better than Her Excellency Sheikh Hasina, a visionary, thinker and an inspiration for millions. The longest serving Prime Minister of Bangladesh is well on her way to build the 'Sonar Bangla' her father, Bangabandhu Sheikh Mujibur Rahman dreamt of and died for."

Sheikh Hasina reminisced about Dr. Kalam most affectionately, saying that her husband also was a nuclear scientist and that his transformation from a scientist to a statesman was amazingly smooth.

It was obvious that she accepted the invitation readily because the award was in the name of Dr. Kalam. "This award will inspire me and my government to strive for the achievement of greater inclusive development."

In a final gesture of goodwill, she said that the Bangabandhu Museum would close at 5 pm, but we should not go away without visiting it and she volunteered to open it for us.

The traffic was tough and we reached at 7 pm, but the whole staff of the museum was waiting for us. They patiently took us around the museum and explained all its features.

The museum is the house in which Sheikh Mujib lived for many years, before and after he became the Prime Minister. He and his eight relatives, including children, were murdered in cold blood by a group of soldiers to avenge the division of Pakistan.

The building is replete with bullet and blood marks, showing signs of a struggle. The building has been preserved as it was except for some ramps which were built to facilitate access for the visitors.

The Bangabandhu Museum is certainly a monument to the Father of the Nation, his life and his martyrdom, but it is also a memorial to the depravity and cruelty of human beings, which make them worse than animals.

How could those criminals be so heartless as to murder the one man who had dedicated his life to his motherland?

Sheikh Hasina had explained to us how, as PM, she had brought them to book. She had tears in her eyes when she recalled how she and another sister had escaped because they were abroad at the time.

She is totally indebted to India for taking care of her during those days of extreme danger and anxiety. Without India and Indira Gandhi, we too would have become martyrs, she said, choked by emotion.

Sheikh Hasina expressed full confidence in India and said sky was the limit for bilateral cooperation. She said India was the first priority for her and India was welcome to invest in Bangladesh on a partnership basis.

She expressed appreciation for Prime Minister Narendra Modi's 'Neighbours First' policy. Even when she spoke of the future of the country, she laid great stress on India's generosity and friendship.

"Over the last decade, Bangladesh-India relations have reached a new high, marked by mutual trust, confidence, and goodwill. We have witnessed remarkable progress in cooperation between our two countries in different conventional and unconventional areas."

"I believe that this trend of cooperation will continue and, coupled with the achievement of the SDGs, these will help build a prosperous Bangladesh by 2041... Long live Bangladesh-India friendship."

The contrasting two faces of Bangladesh struck me as characteristic of South Asia. Our relations fluctuate when leaders change in these countries.

But, with Sheikh Hasina in Dhaka, all is well with the world of India-Bangladesh relations.

Published: September 20, 2019

Bhutan's Recognition of Bangladesh

Thimphu, the capital of Bhutan, had very few comforts in 1971. For us, who went to Bhutan from Tokyo, with a nine-month-old baby 42 years ago, the feeling was that we had walked backwards in time by about half a century.

The first motorable road was opened only in 1968 and there were no commercial flights into Bhutan. The drive from the border town of Phuntesholing in India to Thimphu took the whole day, with a lunch break at Chukha, a small rivulet at that time, but a gigantic hydro-electric project now. Electricity was a rarity and we had to huddle around a *bukhari*, which burns wood to provide a level of comfort in the bitter cold.

Life did not, however, stand still in Thimphu. 1971 was an exciting year in Bhutan and as the only diplomatic mission in the country, India was very much a partner in the changes that took place. Even at a time when tension was high on the India-East Pakistan border, Bhutan and we were celebrating Bhutan's admission to the United Nations in September 1971. Celebrations went on for days together as the UN admission marked a turning point in Bhutan's history.

King Jigme Dorji Wangchuk personally participated in the festivities. India took time to take this decision and Bhutan was quite excited when India, in a grand gesture, sponsored Bhutan for admission to the world body.

According to the 1949 treaty between India and Bhutan, Bhutan had agreed 'to be advised by the Government of India in regard to its external relations,' and therefore, India's support was necessary for Bhutan to make any initiatives in foreign policy.

The Indian gesture was of immense value to Bhutan and there was a new high in India-Bhutan relations. At a moment when India was seeking support from the international community, the emergence of a close friend in the UN was very welcome for India.

The tensions between India and Pakistan rose sharply by the end of November and it was clear that a war was imminent. We had nothing but the All India Radio for news. Not being far from the war zone, Bhutan had a sense of foreboding. The Indian Military Training Team and the Border Roads Organisation were on full alert. Pakistani strikes in the western sector were the spark that lit the fire in the east.

As we were eagerly following news of the war, the announcement came on December 9 that India had recognised the independent state of Bangladesh. Ambassador Ashok Gokhale, the representative of India, as he was designated, was in India for consultations, and I was acting in his place with less than four years' experience in diplomacy. I felt very important representing India in Bhutan at a critical time.

A few hours after we heard the news of the recognition of Bangladesh by India, I received a call from Lyonpo Dawa Tsering, the then Foreign Minister, one of the most intelligent and suave Bhutanese diplomats I have ever met, asking me to meet him immediately in his office.

I thought that it was to seek information on the war and to express solidarity. But he promptly handed me a note conveying the news that Bhutan had decided to recognise Bangladesh.

I was overjoyed to receive the news and I rushed back to the mission to break the news to Delhi. AIR had the first headline that evening that, following India's recognition, Bhutan had also decided to recognise Bangladesh. Ambassador Gokhale told me on the phone that he was going to return to Thimphu the next day with a letter advising Bhutan to recognise Bangladesh.

Bhutan had clearly anticipated it and decided to act on its own and the King knew that it would please India immensely.

It appears that a controversy has been raging in the press in Bangladesh as to whether Bhutan recognised Bangladesh first. The Bangladesh government has apparently clarified that the Bhutanese recognition came hours before Indian recognition. I do not know whether Bhutan had directly informed Bangladesh of its recognition of the new state before the Indian announcement, but my clear recollection is that the news was given to us some hours after the Indian announcement.

It is quite possible that the King acted with alacrity and conveyed the news even before India recognised Bangladesh. If he actually did that, he was carrying out two diplomatic coups, as against the one we had sensed earlier.

According to the 1949 treaty, Bhutan should be guided by India in foreign policy and, strictly speaking, the announcement was a violation of the letter of the treaty, though not the spirit of it. The King was absolutely certain that India would be delighted and that no procedural objection would be raised.

Even the thought of questioning Bhutan on this matter did not cross the minds of the Indian leaders. But if he did recognise Bangladesh before India did, he was taking a calculated risk.

If India's intention was not to recognise Bangladesh immediately and to hold Pakistani territory for tactical reasons, Bhutan would have ruined it and incurred the wrath of India. The King was too shrewd to make such a mistake and must have taken the actual decision and announced it only after the Indian recognition.

But we have no reason to doubt the Bangladeshi government that it was informed about Bhutan recognition even before the Indian move. This will remain a mystery unless Bhutan itself reveals the sequence.

The mystery is inconsequential at this time, but it may be of historic importance to know when Bhutan decided to take an independent path in foreign policy. Within months after its entry into the UN, Bhutan showed signs of taking an independent line at the UN on issues, which were not crucial for Indian interests.

It became active in the group of land-locked countries and the group of least developed countries, which had a perspective different from that of India. The treaty itself was amended several years later to accommodate the aspirations of Bhutan.

Bhutan's recognition of Bangladesh without waiting for Indian advice was a clever move, but if it did it even before India did, it was a calculated gamble to assert its independence.

Published: December 15, 2014

G. UKRAINE

A TIGHTROPE WALK
FOR INDIA

India's Ukraine Challenge: Navigating Geopolitical Turmoil

Russian President Vladimir Putin's journey from a scheming villain to a victor is perhaps the shortest in history. But it will be a pyrrhic victory.

Having harped on the vulnerabilities of Russia in the face of a menacing NATO and the US, he moved on to challenge his legendary predecessors like Lenin, Stalin, Khrushchev and Gorbachev and put on the mantle of a saviour of the old Soviet Union and pledged to do his duty.

The US and NATO played right into his hands by saying and later demonstrating that they will do nothing against him except imposing sanctions, which will hurt some others even more.

When he tested the waters by entering the "free" provinces of Ukraine, Donetsk, and Luhansk, Putin faced nothing but pious declarations and tame sanctions. He is clearly a victor in the first leg of his journey to rebuilding the great Soviet Union of old, but the road ahead is hazardous and difficult even for a man of his mettle to complete in one lifetime. He will go down in the annals of Russian history as the first martyr for the cause of what can be dubbed the 'Soviet Renaissance'.

The personality of President Putin, who has prioritised the correction of various historical injustices and restoring his nation's place at the forefront of the world once again, regardless the cost, lies at the heart of the present crisis. The reluctance of the US and Europe to intervene militarily in Ukraine encouraged him to embark on an adventure with grave implications for the globe.

Max Hastings, who has done a major study on the Cuban missile crisis of 1962, has stated, "He (Putin) is not Hitler, not Stalin, not Mao. Instead, he is something much smaller, the capo of a nuclear armed gangster clique. But he has shown willingness to use terrible force to promote his own grandeur in a fashion that, unlike the Cuban missile crisis, may yet need to be met with Western arms." In other words, the birth pangs of a post-Covid-19 world have just begun. The unscripted story of the future is yet to be played out.

Early Signs of Aggression

The massive deployment of Russian forces on its border with Ukraine in November 2021 was the first sign of the present disaster, though it can be traced back to 2014, when Russia annexed Crimea on the ground that it was a Russian gift to Ukraine in the first place.

Putin insisted that he had no intention to invade Ukraine, stating that the redline for any action would come only if Ukraine joined NATO. Except President Biden, most people believed that an attack was an empty threat and the US and NATO even indicated that no military action would be taken even if an attack took place.

The threat of sanctions did not deter Putin from launching an attack, first by recognising the independent states of Donetsk and Luhansk and entering the region on a peace-keeping mission and then, after his historic declaration of his larger intentions, launching "special military operations" with the objective of fully demilitarising Ukraine, but not occupying it.

Putin's credibility was completely lost and he is currently entangled in a major unequal war with tiny Ukraine, without any sign of an immediate victory because of the staunch resistance of President Volodymyr Zelenskyy, although it is only a matter of time before Ukraine is subdued and brought under a Russian puppet regime. But judging from the resistance so far, a long guerrilla war appears to be in the offing.

India, China on Same Page

The international reaction to the events is one of shock, surprise, and condemnation, but, as expected, a strong draft resolution of the Security Council was vetoed by Russia, with 11 positive votes and abstentions by China, India and the UAE. Ironically, China and India appeared to be on the same side, despite vast differences between them on their worldviews. For India, it was a matter of balancing two friends, while for China, it was a gesture of solidarity with its new ally. But though the Indian vote was "neutral", its explanation was explicit in its criticism of the Russian actions. India took back with the left hand what it had given with the right.

Though India did not mention Russia, it stated that India is deeply disturbed by the recent turn of developments in Ukraine. It reiterated its appeal for cessation of violence. "No solution can be arrived at the cost of human lives," said Ambassador T S Tirumurti. He also flagged India's core concern about the safety of about 16,000 Indian nationals stranded in Ukraine. India also touched upon the fundamental principle of respect for territorial integrity enshrined in the UN Charter.

Most significantly, India regretted that the path of diplomacy was given up, a clear indication of India's displeasure over the Russian action when the Indian Minister of External Affairs was in Paris to help the diplomatic process. "It is a matter of regret that the path of diplomacy was given up. We must return to it," said India, citing it as an important reason for its abstention.

The history of the Indian vote on Afghanistan in 1979 appeared to repeat itself, in spite of the many changes that had taken place in the world and in India's own relationships, including the formation of the Quad. But now, as before, India's vote was dictated by paramount national interests. Interestingly, the US, Russia, and Ukraine appeared to grudgingly accept the Indian vote.

The emergence of a China-Russia-Iran-Pakistan axis is the gravest challenge that India is likely to face as a result of the Russian actions. As was demonstrated in Melbourne, Russia joining the Chinese battle against an "Asian NATO" has altered the status and mandate of the Quad as a bulwark against Chinese expansionism and directed it towards cooperation among the four countries for fighting the pandemic, combating climate change, promoting technologies, and establishing new supply chains.

India has become more vulnerable to terrorism and tensions on its borders with China and Pakistan. Deft diplomacy, military preparedness and self-reliant economic development have become more important than ever before.

Published: February 27, 2022

Ukraine: Worries over Possible Use of Nuclear Weapons

A shudder went down the spine of the world when the N-word was heard across news channels on the third day of the Russian attack on Ukraine. It sounded as though President Putin had ordered his nuclear force to be in full preparedness to act, but it was soon clarified that it was only an order to the nuclear force to be ready to defend the country in the event of an attack. That brought the temperature down and the world heaved a collective sigh of relief.

But it was ominous that Putin made the world aware of his nuclear capability at a time when he confronted unexpectedly stiff resistance from Ukraine and tough sanctions from the US and the European Union. The nuclear button is susceptible to accidental use by sick, mad, or frustrated rulers. Mercifully, the button in their hands will pass through several levels of scrutiny in seconds before the weapons are launched.

Many years ago, I was at a summit meeting between Prime Minister Morarji Desai and President Leonid Brezhnev in the Kremlin. While a visibly unstable and forgetful Brezhnev was reading his address, I was suddenly gripped by the fear of an accidental click of the nuclear button by the Soviet leader. I shared my anxiety with the then Foreign Secretary by passing a slip to him. He quickly replied saying, "Don't worry, at this stage, it must be a fake button on his table!" Putin is too young and too smart to be deceived with fake buttons, but his state of mind and determination may lead to a catastrophe.

It was not long ago that Putin had played a video of the trajectories of Russian missiles raining havoc on major US cities to an audience to demonstrate that his nuclear arsenal was sophisticated, its range was long, and its lethality was absolute. Russia keeps several of its missiles targeted and ready to launch against its enemies.

Moreover, Putin had stated more than once that he would not hesitate to use nuclear weapons if anyone posed a threat to his country. He does not subscribe to the theory of non-first use of nuclear weapons like India and China. Russia is more like Pakistan which claims that it has tactical nuclear weapons, which can be used for the multiplication of forces at its command. Countries that have a sense of inferiority about their conventional capabilities are the ones that threaten to use nuclear weapons. A threat assessment is crucial, but it may happen also because of fear, ambition, or sheer madness.

Countries like North Korea and Pakistan have developed nuclear weapons to rectify the imbalance in their conventional capabilities compared to powerful nations. Israel maintains a nuclear option to meet the threat of chemical weapons. Since the weapons are made abroad without any fundamental research in their own countries, their safety standards are a matter of concern for the world. Russian weapons are not known for accuracy or foolproof targeting. Concerns of safety and accidental use exist about the Russian nuclear system also.

I recall that the US was gravely concerned about the command-and-control systems of India when we declared ourselves a nuclear weapon state in 1998. After the initial anger and imposition of sanctions, the US gave us a series of briefings on command-and-control systems. That was the first time that some of us entered the Pentagon. But our scientists and strategists found the briefings elementary. They assured us that our systems were far ahead in the matter of safety and inadvertent use.

Needless to say, the Russian announcement of nuclear alert, whether for offensive or defensive purposes, will have its adversaries take counter-measures as they consider necessary. They may have serviced them thoroughly, made them even more lethal, and targeted them more accurately. In other words, the stage is set for a nuclear war, even if it does not take place.

The personality of President Putin is a matter of concern for the world. Even his allies hold him in awe as a former KGB agent and a confirmed Russian nationalist. His recent statement suggest that he sees himself as the saviour of Russia. He is known to be ruthless in pursuit of his goals and uncompromising. With all of these factors taken in, his mood today will only have soured and likely reflects a mix of calculated planning and strategising, alongside feelings of frustration and even despair.

Foreign Minister Sergei Lavrov is a seasoned strategist and diplomat, but he is known to be more his master's voice rather than his conscience-keeper. No global leader appears to be available for Putin to get the right advice at the right moment. Nuclear weapons in his hands may well be doubly dangerous.

The nuclear weapons issue came into the present discourse in another bizarre manner. As part of the Soviet Union, Ukraine and Belarus had held Soviet nuclear weapons. Now, there is considerable speculation that things would have been different if they had kept the weapons for themselves and not returned them to Russia.

The obvious answer to that is Russia, as the successor state of the USSR, became a nuclear weapons state, but the other former Soviet republics became non-nuclear weapons states. The NPT regime ordained that they should sign the NPT as non-nuclear weapons states and transfer all nuclear materials to Russia or to the International Atomic Energy Agency (IAEA). There was no way in which they could hold on to the Soviet nuclear weapons.

Even more bizarre is the decision taken by Belarus to declare itself a nuclear weapons state after a national referendum. Do they expect to get back the weapons they gave to Russia? Or do they have the capacity to make their own weapons? But the Belarus president is known for unconventional thoughts and actions.

The talk of nuclear weapons at this crucial time is extremely dangerous and may lead to unforeseen consequences. It has already moved the hands of the Doomsday Clock closer to the moment of a global nuclear catastrophe.

Published: March 1, 2023

Ukraine's Shadow: Impact on Indo-US Relations

The unprecedented attention that India received on account of the Russia-Ukraine war was flattering to India as it appeared that its neutrality had become a case study for other countries in balancing the US and Russia. But it emerges that the idea of many of the visits and conversations by Western leaders was also to push India in one direction or another because we seemed flexible.

India's consistent position of abstention beginning with the first UN Security Council resolution to the General Assembly resolution to suspend Russia was seen by many as a balancing act, which could topple one way or another.

The US, which had expected India to abstain in the Security Council, considered the Indian position "shaky", but when it found out about certain Indian actions like the purchase of Russian oil and development of innovative financial arrangements for trade, the US decided to pursue a carrot and stick policy to wean India away from its tilt towards Russia. Some of the US statements in this connection were counter-productive, particularly when an official pointed to the possibility of sanctions against India and another suggested that India should move away from its "NAM and G77" relationship with Russia.

The opportunity of the 2+2 meeting in Washington was taken by the US not only to raise these issues, but also to seek a virtual meeting between President Joe Biden and Prime Minister Narendra Modi to review India-US relations in the light of these developments even while the war was still raging.

The White House stated that President Biden held a "constructive, direct conversation" with the Indian Prime Minister, as the US is seeking more help from India to apply economic pressure on Russia over the war in Ukraine. It also said that President Biden told Prime Minister Modi that his administration could help India diversify its oil imports, but that it was not in New Delhi's interests to increase energy imports from Moscow.

The US did not want to see a significant increase in Russian energy imports by India. "The President conveyed that we are here to help them diversify their means of importing oil. The imports from the United States are already significant, much bigger than the imports that they get from Russia. The President conveyed very clearly that it is not in their interests to increase that."

India's Response

The US virtually laid out some benchmarks relating to Russia to enable India to have a productive relationship with the US. The new dimension introduced by the US was not acceptable to India as it was something that had not happened even during the Cold War.

At the virtual summit as well as during the 2+2 talks, India focused more on the concerns over the continuing Russia-Ukraine war and the need to resolve issues through peaceful negotiations and stressed that Prime Minister Modi had spoken to both Russian President Vladimir Putin and Ukrainian President Volodymyr Zelensky several times and urged them to return to the negotiating table.

As for import of Russian oil, which was important for India's energy security, it was pointed out that Western Europe had imported more Russian oil "one afternoon" than what India imported in a whole month since the beginning of the war. India believed that it had a stabilising role in the global economy and this applied to both fuel and food.

PM Modi recalled that India had condemned the killings in the Ukrainian city of Bucha, where the discovery of hundreds of civilian bodies following a Russian withdrawal from the town sparked international outrage, and called for an independent investigation.

Biden Stresses on Defence Partnership

President Biden emphasised the defence partnership between the two countries and said that the US and India are going to "continue our close consultation on how to manage the destabilising effects of this Russian war". "The root of our partnership is a deep connection between our people, ties of family, of friendship and of shared values," he said, hinting that the Ukraine war had become a source of tension in recent weeks.

The fact that the other members of the Quad, which was a bulwark against China, had not only supported the US but also imposed sanctions against Russia was a factor he had in mind when he spoke of defence cooperation. The hint was clear that the Quad had imposed a certain obligation on the member countries to work together in defence matters.

Although defence cooperation between India and Russia is a matter of legacy, which was recognised by the US, it may also emerge as another benchmark for establishing a stable defence partnership between the US and India. The threat of CATSAA over the supply of S-400 missiles is still in the distant horizon. (CATSAA or Countering America's Adversaries Through Sanctions Act is a US federal law.)

No "Red Line" For India

The US Deputy National Security Adviser for International Economics Daleep Singh, who visited India recently, had said the US will not set any "red line" for India on its energy imports from Russia but does not want to see a "rapid acceleration" in purchases.

Though it was clarified that this was not a threat of sanctions, only a wish expressed that India should be on the right side of history. "But this was a constructive call, it was a productive call. It's a relationship that is vitally important to the United States and to the President. I would not see it as an adversarial call," the spokesperson said.

The summit discussions and the 2+2 dialogue were in the spirit of greater cooperation between India and the United States as members of the Quad, which should not be disturbed by the Indian position on the war. The pressure on India to take a hostile attitude towards Russia and China was guarded, but the message was clear. Those who are familiar with the roller-coaster ride nature of India-US relations will not miss the danger lurking in the present situation. Secretary of State Antony Blinken said rather bluntly that the US was monitoring human rights abuses in India by the Government and some officials, revealing a traditional weapon in the US armoury. India has successfully withstood the pressure tactics employed on it by the US and the West so far, but it is obvious that both sides have to work together to avoid deepening the differences.

Published: April 23, 2022

H. NUCLEAR DISARMAMENT

RECEDING GLOBAL ZERO

Nuclear Deals: Comparing Iran and Indo-US Agreements

The finalisation of the P-5+1-Iran nuclear deal coincided with the 10th anniversary of the India-U.S. nuclear deal by sheer chance. But the two deals, which came ten years apart, reveal a part of the American strategy to deal with nuclear proliferation in two distinct situations and two different times. The U.S. appeared to make concessions in both cases, but the deals served their immediate strategic interests.

The objective was to put the nuclear genie back in the bottle in both cases, though it looked positive in the case of India and negative in the case of Iran. The U.S. was alarmed by the weapon tests of India in 1998 even more than the revelation in 2002 of Iran's nuclear activities. Imposition of sanctions against India and Iran were swift and severe, but it became clear that India would not sign the Comprehensive Test Ban Treaty (CTBT) and Iran would not abandon uranium enrichment.

Crippling Sanctions

The position of strength the U.S. had in both cases derived from the crippling sanctions that India and Iran feared, though in the case of India, the sanctions had disappeared for extraneous reasons even before the negotiations on the deal began. The sanctions were, however, hanging over the head of Jaswant Singh when he negotiated with Strobe Talbott for two years, which actually led to the India-U.S. nuclear deal.

Of course, Jaswant Singh pretended that sanctions were not an issue, but Talbott was very specific about the benchmarks to be reached for sanctions to be lifted. Had 26/11 not intervened, sanctions would have been the central issue of the India-U.S. nuclear deal also.

Sitting next to the Iranian Ambassador in the Board of Governors in the early stages of the Iran issue at the IAEA from 2002 to 2004, this writer was aware that Iran's aspiration was to acquire the status of pre-1998 India. That was the time when India had an ambivalent position on its nuclear capability, with the option of weaponisation.

Iran was aware that the major difference between the two countries was that India was not a signatory to the NPT, but expected that it could make up for it by hide-and-seek. Iran expressed readiness to allow inspection of their facilities, but each time the inspectors came back with more questions than answers. The IAEA concluded that there was "something rotten in the state of Denmark" but could not locate the source of the stench.

Iran realised that the game was up when the matter went to the UN Security Council, with the support of India, which was in the middle of the negotiations for its own deal with the United States. Though the Indian vote was in keeping with the position that India had taken since 2002, it was believed that the Indian vote was cast at the instance of the United States.

The subsequent massive sanctions and the dire situation of the Iranian economy forced Iran to take the bitter medicine of curtailing its nuclear activities to revitalise its economy.

In the case of India, the negotiations were between two countries which had a long history of engagement, though did occasionally tend to get estranged. The George W. Bush Administration was merely taking the "next steps" in a strategic partnership established by the Clinton Administration.

In the case of Iran, it was a matter of breaking the ice and proceeding to negotiate a deal, which was hard for a proud nation to swallow. The trust deficit was so great that every detail had to be worked out with sufficient safeguards.

In the case of India, the U.S. was confident enough to accept the reality of its nuclear capability and seek limitations only in the future development of nuclear weapons. But when it came to the Iranian front, the American effort was to halt and roll back the capability that Iran could acquire.

Liberated

Ten years down the line, the India-U.S. nuclear deal looks like a major concession to India, without any concomitant benefits to the U.S. But at the time of the negotiations, there were multiple levels of political dialogue at the levels of Governments, the U.S. Congress and the members of the Nuclear Suppliers Group, all aimed at tying India in knots.

The Hyde Act appeared to circumscribe not only India's nuclear ambitions, but also its foreign policy itself. But today, India remains unaffected by the political restraints imposed on it. Even after problems arose in nuclear trade between the U.S. and India, there is little acrimony between them on the provisions of the deal. The deal liberated India from the shackles of being a non-signatory of the NPT.

In a sense, the deal has proven beneficial to Iran as well as it has liberated it from the threats of war and crippling sanctions, without having to abandon its nuclear programme altogether. It is more transformational to the region and the world than the India deal.

Iran's new economic freedom and consequential prosperity will propel it to the forefront of the region, posing a challenge to Saudi Arabia and others. It may even become a partner of the United States and others in their battle against the Islamic State. The Iran deal marked a new beginning in Iran-U.S. relations, while the India deal was a culmination of a process of reproachment.

The nuclear opening that India gained by the U.S.-India deal fell short of expectations because of the Civil Nuclear Liability Law and the Fukushima disaster, but it played a role in the emergence of India as an economic power. In the case of Iran, the deal will be more transformational for the country and game changing for the world.

Published: August 30, 2016

India's Nuclear Journey:
From Dream to Reality

Global zero, or a world without nuclear weapons, is not just a desirable goal; it is an imperative for the survival of mankind. A nuclear war between nations is unlikely, but not impossible. Most strategists and nations rule out the use of nuclear weapons as an instrument of war. But the alarming picture of a terrorist group holding a particular country or region, or even the whole world, to ransom by threatening to use a nuclear weapon looms large on the horizon. Instability in countries that possess nuclear weapons is a cause of particular concern.

Even the most elaborate command and control systems are not immune to viruses or hackers. Today's civilisation can be protected and preserved only if nuclear weapons and other lethal materials are eradicated. Nuclear technology itself must be defanged sooner rather than later to make it benign enough to serve mankind. In other words, Global Zero must have no caveats.

Advocates envisage a phased plan for the verified elimination of nuclear weapons, starting with deep reductions in the Russian and U.S. arsenals, to be followed by multilateral negotiations among all nuclear powers for an agreement to eliminate all nuclear weapons. The commitment of the presidents of Russia and the United States to be at the forefront of a nuclear-weapon-free world represents a historic opportunity. This opportunity, however, is not just limited to the superpowers of the Cold War but is also available to rising powers such as India.

The world has a stake in the success of the initiative, and it is essential that New Delhi play a role in finding an effective and efficient path to reach that goal. Although experts and analysts question the very feasibility of such a goal, India not only believes that "getting to zero" is possible, but it is the only country that has actually put forth a potential disarmament framework.

Even after declaring itself a nuclear-weapon state in 1998, India has pursued its disarmament agenda aimed at the elimination of nuclear weapons. India saw its nuclear arsenal only as a necessary evil in a world in which every major country had nuclear weapons or a nuclear guarantee for its security. The general reduction of tensions in the world and the U.S.-Indian nuclear deal, which has made India a partner rather than a target in non-proliferation and disarmament efforts, augur well for the Indian dream.

The concept of a nuclear-weapon-free world is attributable to India, where it was articulated with different names by Indian leaders since 1947. The idea of general and complete disarmament goes beyond a nuclear-weapon-free world; it also seeks a nonviolent world envisaged by the likes of the Buddha, Mahavira, Thiruvalluvar, Sri Aurobindo, and embraced by Mahatma Gandhi, who said:

"The only moral which can be legitimately drawn from the supreme tragedy of the bomb is that it shall not be destroyed by counter-bombs. Violence cannot be destroyed by counter-violence. Mankind will only emerge out of violence through non-violence."

India brought the concept to the international political level in 1988 when Prime Minister Rajiv Gandhi presented his action plan for a "world order free of nuclear weapons and rooted in nonviolence" to the UN General Assembly.

There were four essential features of the plan:

1. A binding commitment by all nations to eliminate nuclear weapons in intervals by the year 2010 at the latest.
2. Participation of all states in the process of nuclear disarmament, whether or not they have nuclear capabilities.
3. Demonstration of good faith by all states by making tangible progress at each stage toward the common goal.

4. An ideological change in policies and institutions to sustain a world free of nuclear weapons by undertaking negotiations to establish a comprehensive global security system under the aegis of the UN.

The plan also suggested specific negotiations and treaties at different stages until the world could not only reach global zero, but also sustain it without apprehensions. Unfortunately, 2010 is already here, and the goal that India had envisioned to be reached by now is not even close.

But there is hope. In April 2009 in Prague, President Barack Obama declared, "So today, I state clearly and with conviction America's commitment to seek the peace and security of a world without nuclear weapons." Even though he acknowledged that the goal would not be reached quickly and perhaps not even in his lifetime, his words raised new hopes around the world. The trajectory Obama suggested, however, was not new or unfamiliar.

He advocated reducing the role that nuclear weapons play in national security strategies, renegotiating the Strategic Arms Reduction Treaty (START) with Russia, ratifying the Comprehensive Test Ban Treaty (CTBT), seeking a new fissile material cut-off treaty (FMCT), strengthening the Nuclear Non-Proliferation Treaty (NPT), and preventing terrorists from acquiring nuclear weapons.

To strengthen the basic bargain of the NPT, Obama stressed that countries with nuclear weapons should move toward disarmament and countries without nuclear weapons should not try to acquire them, while all should have access to peaceful nuclear power.

The Mistake: Revitalising the NPT Bargain

The major disappointment of the Prague speech was that although the ultimate objective was laudable, the path suggested was the same old NPT track, which is considered discriminatory by non-nuclear-weapon states. Although discrimination would end with the attainment of the goal, the world in the long interim period would remain divided, with the haves accumulating more weapons and the have-nots feeling a sense of diminishing security.

The NPT, ratified in 1970, originally only had a shelf life of 25 years, and the review mechanism left open the possibility of it evolving with the times. No treaty, particularly one that bases itself on scientific knowledge and developments, can be made effective without making the appropriate changes over time. Extending the treaty indefinitely in 1995, turning it into a perpetual treaty with no possibility of review, was a sure way of making it a historic relic rather than a dynamic instrument to determine international behaviour.

The ultimate irony is that indefinite extension of the NPT prompted the Indian and Pakistani nuclear tests of 1998, adding two more nations to the list of nuclear-weapon states. The perpetuation of the NPT, and that too as an unchangeable document for all time to come, removed the last hope that India had of shaping a new non-discriminatory regime by consensus.

With the possibility of disarmament by the nuclear-weapon states receding further, it had to blast its way into the nuclear club to secure a seat for itself among the club members, with Pakistan and later North Korea following suit.

The NPT has become an anachronism today as it unfortunately no longer has any possibility for change. The only alternative is to let it lie and pursue an alternative system that ensures universal participation and adherence. This is a great opportunity for India, as U.S. Secretary of State Hillary Rodham Clinton herself declared in October 2009: "India we see as a full partner in this effort and we look forward to working with them as we try to come up with the 21st century version of the NPT."

Unfortunately, there is no real evidence of such an effort in any of the road maps in Washington. "The 21st century version of the NPT" must necessarily move away from the presumptions of the 1960s and take into account the dictates of the present day, including the energy crisis, the advent of non-state actors, and technological advancement.

The energy crisis and the threat of climate change would inevitably demand greater use of nuclear energy for peaceful purposes. The International Atomic Energy Agency (IAEA) was originally conceived as a promotional body, but as the implementing agency of the NPT, the IAEA became a watchdog against non-proliferation rather than an engine for energy growth. A new arrangement with international facilities for enrichment and a fuel bank will support the energy development of developing countries.

Programs for the development of economical and proliferation-resistant reactors do exist in the agenda of the IAEA, but they receive little attention. The new system should lead to increases in the IAEA budget for new technology and technical cooperation. Non-state actors will never be amenable to treaties, but there should be greater accountability on the part of states to safeguard nuclear material.

The present system has no provision to deal with either the nuclear "Wal-Mart" of Abdul Qadeer Khan or the leakage of nuclear material from state sources. The IAEA suggests that all nuclear material reported lost has not been recovered and that some of the recovered material was never reported lost. The new non-proliferation system must address these three key considerations.

The grand bargain of the NPT has not led the world to security, essentially because it seeks to perpetuate, rather than eliminate, nuclear-weapon in a discriminatory manner. By condoning vertical proliferation, it permits the further sophistication of nuclear weapons by the nuclear-weapon states.

The NPT does not impose any restrictions on the designated nuclear-weapon states to control their arsenals. It addresses horizontal proliferation by asking the non-nuclear-weapon states not to cross the nuclear Rubicon, without any restraint complete disarmament has not materialised as well. Even the CTBT permits laboratory tests, which only the technologically advanced states can perform.

No less alarming is the fact that the nuclear powers have deliberately violated the NPT provisions not to transfer weapons technology to non-nuclear-weapon states. The most celebrated case of such violation is by China, which shared technology with Pakistan and North Korea. Pakistan and North Korea have, in turn, helped others such as Iran and Libya with equipment and technology.

The solemn commitment of the nuclear-weapon states, in adherence to Article VI of the NPT, to pursue negotiations in good faith for general and complete disarmament has not materialised as well. The projection of the NPT, therefore, as an end in itself rather than as the first step in a long journey toward international peace and security has transformed the context and rationale of the grand bargain.

Relying on the NPT bargain as the path for the future undermines the credibility of the goal of a truly nuclear-free world. A fundamental change from mutual assured destruction to a collective security structure, which encompasses nuclear and non-nuclear states, must take place right now.

Similarly, the CTBT and the projected FMCT will only be partial measures, even if they come into force in the near future. The U.S. Congress is not yet ready to ratify the CTBT. Even if it does, the caveat enshrined in the treaty that a number of designated countries should ratify it before it comes into force will delay its implementation. There is also criticism that it is neither comprehensive nor is it a ban on testing, as those with the capacity to do simulation tests can merrily test in laboratories and refine their weapons many times over.

An FMCT is still in its infancy in Geneva, and its growth and maturity are not guaranteed. The demand that an FMCT should cover eliminating existing stockpiles may sound its death knell before it even develops. Both these treaties should be linked to disarmament rather than remain the pillars of the NPT edifice, which has begun to crumble.

The first requirement of moving toward a nuclear-free world is for its proponents to recognise the antiquated nature of the NPT. A paradigm shift from relying on the treaty is a fundamental requirement for the idea of the elimination of nuclear weapons to be universally accepted. The May 2010 NPT Review Conference will show that no amount of declarations on the part of the nuclear-weapon states will satisfy the non-nuclear-weapon states, nor will it deter those states from pursuing security by any means necessary, as their sense of insecurity increases and their disappointment over inadequate resources and technology to develop peaceful uses of nuclear energy deepens.

The IAEA spends a disproportionately huge sum for its watchdog role, while paying only lip service to its responsibility to promote nuclear energy. Faced as they are with the threat of global warming, many countries are knocking at the IAEA's door to seek technology for using nuclear power in various crucial sectors as power generation, academic research, medicine, and water. Unless the IAEA has sufficient resources to meet these increasing needs, it cannot play its non-proliferation role effectively.

The vision of a nuclear-weapon-free world is shared by most countries, but the way forward is far from clear. It is highly desirable to reach that goal, but its feasibility is in question because of differing perspectives and priorities. Mutual suspicion about motives and methods make achieving a nuclear-free world a distant dream.

Mutually reducing nuclear warheads is the only way to go for nuclear states. The START process, delayed though it has been, is reassuring, but it should bring in the other nuclear-weapon states as part of the move toward global zero. Freezing the production of weapons and related materials should add credibility to reduction proposals.

Finally, concerns over evolving requirements for what countries believe is necessary for minimum deterrence will have to be tackled as countries' nuclear arsenals decline. The number of weapons that each country will insist on keeping until they are certain about their security will change as their perceptions of the external threat evolves. Altogether, these obstacles to achieving a world without nuclear weapons are enormous, but not insurmountable if a step-by-step approach with measures for verification can be devised that does not rely on using the outdated NPT framework.

How to Use the U.S.-Indian Partnership to Get to Zero

India, as stated earlier, had believed in and championed general and complete disarmament, particularly nuclear disarmament. Even with a robust nuclear program at its disposal, India refrained from developing explosive capability until 1974 and declared itself a nuclear-weapon state only in 1998.

The indefinite extension of the NPT in 1995 and the threat of sanctions against the non-signatories to the CTBT contributed to India's decision to go for nuclear weapons as a minimum deterrent in the

1990s. The CTBT had held out a threat that appropriate action would be taken at the end of 1999 with regard to those who did not join the treaty by then.

India's nuclear doctrine, to the extent it is known to the world, is based on a minimum deterrent. The development of nuclear weapons by China, which had invaded India in 1962 "to teach India a lesson" and still had a border dispute, was a compelling factor in India's decision to test. It was also well known that Pakistan had developed a clandestine nuclear capability long before the Indian tests of 1998.

India had to equip itself for its tough neighbourhood. India's no-first-use doctrine, its declaration of a moratorium on testing, and its readiness to engage in negotiations on an FMCT reassured the international community that India was not embarking on a nuclear arms race. Moreover, India has not abandoned its various initiatives for nuclear disarmament at the UN, even after it acquired nuclear weapons, and is committed to eliminating nuclear weapons together with the other nuclear-weapon states.

The U.S.-Indian nuclear deal, whose framework was presented in a joint statement on July 18, 2005 by President George W. Bush and Prime Minister Manmohan Singh, was testimony to the good faith with which India has sought to allay the fears of the international community about Indian nuclear weapons.

Due to the deal, India assumed the responsibilities of a signatory of the NPT without actually signing the treaty by agreeing to:

1. Subject its non-military facilities to IAEA inspections, which included 14 out of its 22 power reactors.
2. Sign the Additional Protocol, which will allow for more detailed inspections by the IAEA.
3. Commit to halting further nuclear testing.
4. Work to strengthen the security of its nuclear arsenals.
5. Pledge to negotiate an FMCT with the United States in good faith and to sign it when ready.
6. Ensure that all equipment for nuclear reactors and fuel imported by other states, including the United States, will be for peaceful uses only.

In other words, an India-specific dispensation was made in light of the new confidence in U.S.-Indian relations during the Bush administration. Yet, the Obama administration has begun to hark back to the NPT, the CTBT, and an FMCT, essentially setting the clock back. India and the United States, however, can work together if they pursue their shared vision of a nuclear-free world.

Once the commitment of the nuclear-weapon states to complete disarmament is established, with concomitant changes insecurity strategies and related global postures, the others, such as India, will feel confident about the intentions of those with abundant nuclear arsenals.

On the other hand, as long as the nuclear powers continue to believe that nuclear weapons constitute the most critical element of their security strategy, the goal of eliminating nuclear weapons will be elusive. The international situation is still characterised by lack of trust and political will, as demonstrated by the total absence of any reference to non-proliferation and disarmament in the 2005 UN World Summit outcome.

The first step, therefore, is to seek international consensus in the UN General Assembly through its only multilateral negotiating body, the Conference on Disarmament, which was established in 1979 as the only multilateral disarmament negotiating forum. Unilateral declarations, however sincere, and UN Security Council resolutions, no matter how well intentioned, will be no substitute for such a global consensus. India will be able to join the United States in the quest for an alternative non-proliferation system once there is a global consensus on complete disarmament.

The action plan presented by Gandhi on behalf of India, along with 27 other states, to the Conference on Disarmament in 1988 still remains the most comprehensive initiative on nuclear disarmament, covering issues from nuclear testing and fissile materials trade to a time-bound elimination of stockpiles and eventually of nuclear weapons.

Currently, India has five basic priorities in the global dialogue regarding disarmament and non-proliferation:

1. To have all nuclear powers reaffirm to completely eliminate their nuclear weapons, either through a global convention that completely prohibits their use, or threat of use, or an agreement on their non-discriminatory and verifiable elimination, with a specified framework of time.

2. To issue a promise from these states to reduce the salience of nuclear weapons in their national security doctrines.

3. To reduce nuclear danger, including the risk of accidental nuclear war, particularly by de-alerting nuclear weapons to prevent unintentional and accidental use of nuclear weapons.

4. To negotiate a global agreement among nuclear-weapon states on no-first-use against other nuclear powers and the non-use of nuclear weapons against non-nuclear-weapon states.

5. To enable multilateral disarmament bodies such as the UN's Disarmament Commission and the Conference on Disarmament to make effective contributions to the goal of nuclear disarmament and the elimination of nuclear weapons worldwide.

Broadly speaking, the two political aims pursued by India are nuclear disarmament through a process of de-legitimisation of nuclear weapons and reducing immediate nuclear danger, including lowering the possibility of terrorist access to nuclear devices.

New Delhi has supported negotiations on a universal, non-discriminatory, and verifiable FMCT. India has also shown interest in the Proliferation Security Initiative as well as in regional fuel banks under appropriate safeguards. India would like to have international agreements to ban anti-satellite weapons as well as the deployment of weapons in outer space.

As for the CTBT, however, India is unenthusiastic on account of the history of its negotiations, which gave the impression that it discriminatory, biased in its assessment, and was targeting India. There are indications that this could change with time if the United States and others move toward the elimination of nuclear weapons.

A window of opportunity has presented itself for India and the United States to shape a common strategy to attain their objectives because of the advent of the bilateral nuclear deal, which sought to give India the same rights and obligations as other states possessing advanced nuclear technology, and the emergence of the idea of de-legitimisation of nuclear weapons in the United States itself.

The so-called 'Four Horsemen's proposal' issued by Henry Kissinger, Sam Nunn, William Perry, and George Schultz in 2008 advocated "a series of steps that will pull us back from the nuclear precipice." The first of these steps is changing the Cold War posture of deployed weapons to increase warning time and reduce the danger of accidental or unauthorised use of nuclear weapons.

Obama's declarations have transformed the scene, not only with his vision of a nuclear-weapon-free world declared at Prague but also with his emphasis on the need for the United States to take the lead in reducing the strategic significance of nuclear weapons.

Less Words, More Action

Any initiative to move toward a nuclear-weapon-free world should address the threat or use of nuclear weapons by any state or non-state actor. This would entail a combination of non-proliferation and disarmament because horizontal and vertical proliferation pose grave challenges to humanity. Simultaneously, it should promote peaceful uses of nuclear energy without fear of safety or proliferation.

Particular attention should be given to prevent nuclear terrorism, which has become a high priority. Universality of participation is essential for decision-making, so the existing UN mechanisms should be strengthened.

In this context, the IAEA presents a ready and available forum to assist the UN General Assembly to shape a consensus. The IAEA needs to restore balance in its activities with regard to promoting nuclear energy, safety, and safeguards. Its safeguards inspection mechanism should be streamlined to avoid wasteful inspections, and its resources should be increased to strengthen technical cooperation as the demand for nuclear energy increases, particularly in the context of global warming.

The UN has been engaged in a quest for a nuclear-weapon-free world from its very inception. The very first resolution of the UN General Assembly, adopted on January 24, 1946, sought the elimination of nuclear weapons and other weapons of mass destruction.

Three special sessions on disarmament made significant contributions to that goal, but a lack of a consensus has prevented the General Assembly from holding another such session. The extreme urgency for the world to respond to the new global situation was underlined by Obama in his Prague speech:

"In a strange turn of history, the threat of global nuclear war has gone down, but the threat of a nuclear attack has gone up. More nations have acquired these weapons. Testing has continued. Black market trade in nuclear secrets and nuclear materials abound.

"The technology to build a bomb has spread. Terrorists are determined to buy, build, or steal one. Our efforts to contain these dangers are centered on a global non-proliferation regime, but as more people and nations break the rules, we could reach the point where the center cannot hold."

Although the diagnosis is perfect, the treatment envisaged is far too inadequate to address the emergency. A fundamental change in perspective, amounting to the de-legitimisation of nuclear weapons and the abandonment of the outdated NPT, is required to change the strategic mind-set of the nuclear powers.

The proposed Global Nuclear Security Summit in April 2010 presents an opportunity for a fundamental change in security doctrines, which currently legitimise nuclear weapons. The United States and Russia have the primary responsibility to take the lead. The ominous developments in their relationship, with Russia hinting at an aggressive nuclear-weapon doctrine, do not augur well for the quest for a nuclear-weapon-free world. Apart from doctrinal changes, these countries could support a fourth UN-sponsored special session on disarmament, propose negotiations on a nuclear weapons convention, and promote abroad security guarantee against the use or threat of use of nuclear weapons against any state.

A nuclear-weapon-free world is far in the distance, but the time has come to move from pious declarations to concrete action. As a reluctant nuclear-weapon power with a minimum deterrent and an active disarmament agenda, India will be in the forefront of the movement for a nuclear-weapon-free world.

It is already ahead of some of the nuclear weapon's states by advocating de-legitimisation of nuclear weapons and negotiations on a nuclear-weapon convention. The world can count on India as a partner in non-proliferation and disarmament, particularly if there is a universal commitment to move toward a verifiable nuclear-weapon-free world.

Published: March 25, 2010

Nuclear Energy Outlook: Assessing India's Future

The development of nuclear power in India is driven as much by fantasy and romance as by scientific and strategic calculations. Like its foreign policy, planning and scientific temperament, Pandit Nehru bequeathed nuclear policy to India, on which there has always been a national consensus. Homi Bhabha is a national hero and his tragic death in an air crash is considered part of a conspiracy against India. Extreme secrecy surrounds nuclear policy and programs in a country, which is brutally open about other matters of national importance.

Even when prophecies and projections are proved wrong and official actions become inexplicable, no system exists to explain the unforeseen developments, which may have altered the course. Sanctity is attributed to policies formulated and projects launched many years ago and course correction, even when it is made, is projected as business as usual. Much has happened in the nuclear arena, but India is by and large committed to its nuclear future.

A quick and direct answer to the question that we ask ourselves today is, therefore, yes, India will have nuclear power for the foreseeable future. It will certainly grow despite dire predictions to the contrary and the fact that public opposition is growing both on account of safety considerations and new scientific information, which calls into question the feasibility, the cost effectiveness and the wisdom of long-term reliance on nuclear power.

The way India has dealt with the issues arising out of the India-US nuclear deal, Kudankulam and Fukushima confirms that its faith in nuclear power still abides. The three-stage nuclear power development program adopted more than half a century ago is alive and well, though the pace of progress from the second to the third stage has been slow and the envisaged use of thorium has not become viable as yet.

Many of us in this room have been champions of the India-US nuclear deal and some, like our moderator today, Ashley Tellis, are its architects. The bewildering twists and turns in the negotiations and the political storm it created in both countries are evidence of its complexity. The steadfast pursuit of the deal on the part of President Bush and Prime Minister was admirable.

For diplomats like me, who worked at the IAEA, with just Pakistan and partly Israel for company, it was a dream come true. India emerged out of its isolation in the nuclear community and it became possible for India to import nuclear fuel and other materials for its nuclear power industry. We paid a heavy price for it, but it was considered small to usher in a brave new world of international nuclear cooperation.

But as of today, no new imported reactor has been commissioned, no dramatic increase has been achieved in power generation, and our non-signatory status in NPT and CTBT regimes is still an impediment when it comes to bilateral agreements or membership of bodies like the NSG. Some frontiers of nuclear science are still closed to us. No nuclear trade has started with the US, the prime mover and an intended beneficiary of nuclear trade with India.

Indeed, everyone knows that the villain is the Indian liability law, which makes the supplier liable to damages in the event of an accident in contravention of the existing international practice. In reality, the opponents of the nuclear deal, particularly its provisions for trade with the US, achieved with the liability law what they failed to achieve by opposing the deal. They created an aura of sentiment around the issue by invoking the plight of the Bhopal victims and got the law passed. It is arguable that the existing laws were quite sufficient to deal with the liability issue, if it ever arose.

I suspect there may be other reasons for the nuclear deal not being able to deliver the deliverables. In August 2009, after a visit to Washington, I wrote an essay for Rediff.com with the title, The US may not have nuclear trade with India'. I quoted unnamed sources, which told me then that the US had no intention to export nuclear reactors and technology to India.

The US had not developed a reactor for more than thirty years and India had nothing to gain by such trade. The US would be quite happy to see India securing energy security, but it would not want to be party to India developing technology that might directly or indirectly support its nuclear arsenal. I was told that President Obama was not willing to dilute his commitment to non-proliferation for the sake of commercial benefits.

The quid pro quo that the US expected for the deal was purchase of defence equipment, not nuclear trade, I said. Except for some bewildered enquiries from some US companies, I saw no attention being given to such straws in the wind. Today, neither side has disavowed nuclear trade, but no way has been found to get around the Liability Law and other issues.

The story of Kudankulam has demonstrated the perils of setting up an imported nuclear power plant. The signing of the Kudankulam agreement with the Soviet Union barely two years after Chernobyl had raised eyebrows and finding a location for it was not easy. Subsequent developments, particularly Fukushima, have added fuel to the fire.

Today, after years of planning and huge expenditure, Kudankulam stands uncommissioned even after the Supreme Court decreed that the project should go ahead. Dismissing a petition challenging the Madras High Court's earlier order in favour of the plant, the Supreme Court termed the operationalisation of Kudankulam nuclear power plant as necessary for the country's growth.

The court stressed that development of nuclear energy is important for India and said, "While setting up a project of this nature, we have to have an overall view of larger public interest rather than smaller violation of right to life guaranteed under Article 21 of the Constitution."

The court dismissed the risk element by stating that we have to balance economic and scientific benefits with that of minor radiological detriments on the touchstone of our national nuclear policy. "Public money running into crores and crores of rupees has already been spent for the development, control, and use of atomic energy for the welfare of the people and hence, we have to put up with such minor inconveniences, minor radiological detriments and minor environmental detriments," the court said.

The delays, allegations of corruption in Russia and the local protests have combined to make the future of the Kudankulam plant uncertain. But the Government is committed to commission the plant and expand it further as soon as the technical hitches are removed. It is imperative at this point of time that the trust deficit is tackled in some way or the other.

Apart from an international inspection of the safety features of the plant, adequate provision should be made for medical facilities, evacuation areas and disaster management. The situation will be replicated in other locations of new nuclear power plants and delays will be inevitable in the nuclear program.

The crippling effect of the Fukushima disaster on the future of nuclear power has not been fully comprehended in India. Fukushima has dealt a severe blow to the nuclear renaissance envisaged in the IAEA 2020 report. The responses have ranged from outright rejection of nuclear power, to uneasiness and delays. Reduction of reliance on nuclear power has been felt globally and even countries which swear by nuclear power would not remain unaffected. India will be no exception to this. The initial official reaction in India that Fukushima would be forgotten like Chernobyl, where there were many more deaths and greater devastation, is giving way to anxiety and efforts to find alternatives.

According to the *Nuclear Intelligence Weekly* of May 31, 2013, the renewables program is rapidly overtaking nuclear power generation in India, with renewables generating 72% more electricity than nuclear plants. *The Weekly* avers that India is unlikely to attain the goals set out in 2005.

Nuclear power still accounts for just 2% of India's total installed power generation capacity. The latest data covering April-August 2012 shows nuclear power at 13.72 billion Kilowatt-hours, compared to 23.6 billion Kilowatt-hours for renewables. The slow growth in nuclear power is attributed to the Liability Law, the protests and administrative delays.

It also makes a big difference, as nuclear power is in the hands of the Government, while renewables attract a high level of private investment, lured by tax holidays and other incentives. But renewable energy is still priced higher than nuclear energy in India as the investments in nuclear energy is not fully taken into account, while calculating costs.

M V Ramana argues in his significant, but combative book, 'The Power of Promise', "projecting nuclear capacity has always been easy. Translating those forecasts into reality, however proved impossible, and the installed capacity in 2000 was only 2720 MW. Understanding the reasons for this enormous gap between achievements and projections is crucial for judging whether the setting up of hundreds of GW of nuclear power capacity by mid-century is feasible."

India cannot but be affected by the gloomy nuclear energy scenario around the globe. It is becoming increasingly clear that targets cannot be achieved, the anti-nuclear lobby is gaining strength and the cost of nuclear energy will be higher if all the hidden costs are taken into account. The costs of waste disposal and the clean-up costs in the event of an accident are enormous.

Indian public opinion is divided between a majority that has abiding faith in nuclear power and a minority, which opposes it. In my view, which does not seem to have any takers now, is that we should gradually alter our energy mix to reduce our dependence on nuclear power for generation of electricity with the long-term intention of eliminating it.

As of now, India cannot abandon nuclear power as a means of production of electricity as the policy followed so far cannot be reversed. But if greater attention is given to research and development of alternate sources, it should be possible for us to make a transition within a time frame. This will mean freezing the use of nuclear power at the present level and reducing it gradually, as we develop alternatives.

For the small component of nuclear power that we envisage in our energy mix, we should find viable alternatives which are already available. More than anything else, such a step will remove the fear, that for generations to come, India will face the danger of nuclear accidents, a fear that fuels the agitation against nuclear plants in India.

Indeed, the policies of every government that has come to power in India and the popular sentiment in India have coincided in favour of nuclear power being an important part of the energy mix for the foreseeable future.

In fact, the global trend against nuclear power has presented opportunities for India in terms of prices and availability of nuclear plant and material. But the nuclear power scene in India cannot but be influenced by new scientific research on nuclear power, including its costs and dangers, as well as on availability of safe and efficient alternatives.

Published: June 13, 2013

IAEA's Role Beyond Inspections: Promoting Clean Energy

Events in Iran, North Korea, and Syria have once again brought the International Atomic Energy Agency's "nuclear watchdog" role to the forefront. But while that is an important part of the IAEA's mandate, it is not the agency's only function. Indeed, the focus on IAEA's non-proliferation enforcement work is proving detrimental to what could be an even more important job: its role as a safe disseminator of green civilian energy technologies.

Unique in the United Nations system, the IAEA has strategic scientific capability which can benefit mankind in diverse ways. Apart from promoting nuclear energy, the IAEA can contribute significantly to other technologies on account of its extensive knowledge in areas such as thermal engineering, materials and computational fluid dynamics.

Enforcing non-proliferation is certainly one of its important responsibilities. The IAEA's effective imprimatur recently on Western claims that Iran is building a nuclear program has convinced Tehran that it cannot play hide and seek with the agency—perhaps an important step toward forcing it to comply with international non-proliferation standards.

But to focus only on those activities is to miss the agency's equally significant "civilian" role. True to its original mandate to promote atoms for peace, the agency has been engaged in enhancing the use of nuclear power for radiation treatment, hydrology, food preservation, and desalination of sea water. Sterile insect technique, which eliminates pests by sterilising them, is one of its success stories in Africa and Latin America.

And the agency works to ensure the safety of civilian nuclear reactors such as power plants, springing into action whenever minor or major nuclear accidents take place and constantly refining safety standards to prevent such accidents. Within days of 9/11, the General Conference of the IAEA kicked into high gear, devising plans to prevent nuclear weapons or other materials from falling into the hands of terrorists.

The IAEA's non-proliferation role isn't divorced from its civilian function; in fact, the two are intertwined. Technical assistance for peaceful uses is a part of the nuclear non-proliferation treaty's grand bargain, under which a large number of countries forswore nuclear weapons in exchange for nuclear technology for peaceful purposes.

Many developing countries are concerned that the IAEA has not yet struck the balance envisaged between its twin roles as a nuclear watchdog and management of civilian-technology . Safeguards, security and safety work of the agency far outweigh the development dimension in terms of the money spent. The IAEA's technical cooperation fund is not even a part of the agency's regular budget. It is funded by voluntary contributions, which do not grow at the same pace as the regular budget—this is especially true of the safeguards budget.

For example, while the regular budget is adjusted for inflation, the technical cooperation fund isn't. This disparity is also reflected in terms of the attention the IAEA's functions receive from the public. Many believe that the development agenda of the IAEA is less important than its non-proliferation role.

The danger is that, divested of its scientific role, the IAEA will become another U.N. monitoring mechanism without a soul. That would represent a serious missed opportunity. As the price of fossil fuels skyrockets and climate change stares us in the face, nuclear power is a logical alternative that should be actively promoted. The IAEA is uniquely situated to guide countries in the responsible adoption of this technology.

Indeed, over the past five years, nearly 40 countries have approached the agency for the first time, seeking advice on the use of nuclear power as an alternative source of energy. This is in addition to India, China, Russia and South Africa, which have significant nuclear-power expansion plans of their own. The IAEA has the mandate to encourage all these countries to pursue their energy strategy with the necessary safeguards for safety and security concerns, and against proliferation.

Unfortunately, the agency is currently hobbled in its efforts to promote these technologies, both due to inadequate funding for these efforts and because of political differences among the agency's most prominent member-states. As a 2008 report of a group of eminent persons appointed by the director general of the IAEA shows, there is no consensus on the desirability of promoting nuclear energy.

Some countries—chiefly in Europe; namely, Austria—are sceptical about the prospects of nuclear energy because of safety and security concerns. Others feel that such risks have been exaggerated, and that these issues have been adequately addressed and improvements continually made. This controversy has stood in the way of the agency's ability to acquire adequate resources to assist "newcomer states" to develop and sustain the necessary nuclear power infrastructure and to build expertise in managing nuclear facilities.

That is both a short-sighted and an unscientific approach. A nuclear renaissance is in the offing. It need not be a dangerous one, either in terms of weapons proliferation or unsafe civilian reactors. Properly managing this renaissance should be the IAEA's future role. The IAEA has the structure, the scientific base, the reputation and the expertise to be the anchor of the emerging nuclear scene. Non-proliferation concerns do exist today. But instead of spending on inspections in the countries which have already crossed the nuclear Rubicon, the IAEA must focus on security and safety in countries that want to obtain technologies for strictly civilian uses.

Published: June 24, 2008

India's Nuclear Tests:
Reflections 20 Years Later

India crashed into the nuclear club on May 11, 1998 as the result of a bold decision by the political and scientific establishment after a long period of debate, anxiety, hesitation, speculation and a technology demonstration in 1974.

The reaction of the international community to India's defiance of the NPT (Nuclear Non-proliferation Treaty) regime was stronger than expected and its ripples are still palpable even after 20 years, like the resistance to India entering the Nuclear Suppliers' Group (NSG). In fact, India's political, diplomatic and scientific capabilities were put to the severest test during this period.

After 20 years, India has reason to be satisfied over having accomplished many of the objectives of Pokhran II. Indian diplomacy triumphed in turning the crisis into an opportunity by securing legitimacy for its nuclear arsenal and removing obstacles in generating nuclear power.

However, the hasty enactment of a liability law, which inhibited nuclear trade and the setback globally to nuclear power on account of the Fukushima disaster in Japan, stood in the way of India benefiting fully from Pokhran II and the subsequent agreements reached.

But the fact remains that the tests of 1998 and the subsequent nuclear deal have brought India to the nuclear mainstream and opened up the global nuclear market for development of nuclear power without signing the NPT or the Comprehensive Test Ban Treaty (CTBT).

India's declaration as a nuclear-weapon state took a long way in coming. Its nuclear policy had not ruled out the bomb, but the issue became acute after the NPT turned out to be discriminatory and India retained its nuclear option.

After what was called the Peaceful Nuclear Explosion (PNE) of 1974, nobody was in doubt that India would test again and claim to be a nuclear-weapon state. Successive Prime Ministers kept the powder dry for a test, but hesitated on account of the economic pressure that would follow.

At one stage, the US Ambassador confronted Prime Minister P V Narasimha Rao with photographic evidence that Pokhran was getting ready for an explosion and President Bill Clinton sternly warned Rao of grave consequences. During his visit to Washington in 1993, Rao apparently gave an assurance that he would not test as long as the US joined efforts for total nuclear disarmament. But the US was not willing to acknowledge that bilateral understanding multilaterally.

While South Block (Ministry of External Affairs and Ministry of Defence) was ready to go for tests, North Block (Ministry of Finance) opposed it for fear of severe economic problems. Many studies were prepared on the possible impact of economic sanctions and all of them predicted dire straits for the economy.

Prime Minister Atal Bihari Vajpayee came to power in May 1998 with the promise that nuclear weapons would be inducted after a defence review. The tests shocked the US, particularly because it was done in utmost secrecy and the India-US rollercoaster hit rock bottom. For nearly two months, the US refused to have any dialogue with India and it was in a punishment mode, having to implement the Glenn Amendment for the first time. Newer and newer sanctions were imposed and, at one point, it looked that the relations would never recover.

The Strobe Talbott–Jaswant Singh talks over the next two years were the most comprehensive dialogue India had with the US on nuclear policy, including its threat perception and future plans for security. India was anxious to have the sanctions lifted, but Jaswant Singh, who was then the Foreign Minister, sought to delink sanctions from the security dialogue, not to be pressurised to take quick decisions.

Talbott began by insisting that the objective was to get India to sign the NPT, "a crucial and immutable guidance" of US policy. Then he listed five benchmarks as non-proliferation goals to normalise relations: (1) signing of CTBT, (2) halting of production of fissile material, (3) strategic restraint, (4) strengthening of export control regimes and (5) normalisation of relations with Pakistan. These were strongly rejected by India, but the talks proceeded on the assumption that India's security concerns should be fully understood and that India would take certain measures to suit its new status.

But, in effect, India met the US demands more than half way, leading to an understanding, which led to President Clinton's visit to India and Vajpayee's visit to the US in 2000.

India refused to sign the CTBT, but declared a moratorium on testing, agreed to join the Fissile Material Cut-off Treaty (FMCT) negotiations without halting fissile material production, reaffirmed minimum deterrent without giving any number of warheads, and agreed to strengthen export controls. Additionally, India declared no-first-use and a commitment to disarmament.

Though no deal could be struck, the foundation was laid for what became the nuclear deal in 2008. The BJP government would have been ready to sign a similar deal, but Clinton's reluctance to dilute the NPT and lack of time were responsible for the delay till President George Bush and Prime Minister Manmohan Singh decided to take the final plunge for a nuclear deal.

It took three long years to resolve a large number of issues that arose after signing of a framework agreement in 2005. Apart from political hesitations from both sides, there were a large number of technical issues to be resolved, but the diplomats from both sides managed to deal with them imaginatively because of the commitment of the leadership on both sides.

It was not without a number of pitched battles in Delhi, Washington and Vienna, but eventually, India gained much more than nuclear legitimacy and access to global nuclear trade. Though India placed its civilian nuclear facilities under perpetual safeguards, its nuclear assets remained fully insulated against external scrutiny and interference.

India secured rights to receive uninterrupted nuclear fuel supplies as a trade-off against safeguards. India kept open its right to acquire advanced enrichment and reprocessing technologies, although it would require bilateral negotiations with the US and others.

India's sovereign right to test a nuclear device in the future has remained intact, although the deal would be in jeopardy in such an eventuality. Bush and Manmohan Singh remained committed to the deal throughout the negotiations and made decisive interventions at crucial moments.

Apart from the specific gains in the nuclear area, the new India-US partnership, which promised investment and high technology, was a turning point in Indian foreign policy. On the negative side, the deal generated mistrust in Russia and China, which had to be dealt with in future years.

The ten years after the signing of the deal, its gains and losses proved much less game changing than it appeared in 2008. Though not a champion of the deal as a Senator, President Barack Obama committed himself to the implementation of the deal as part of his strategy to build good relations with India.

But his personal affinity to the NPT and non-proliferation made him reluctant to interpret the 123 Agreement liberally. The expectation was that the prospect of nuclear trade with India was a great attraction but in 2009, Obama gave some indication that he would not sacrifice his non-proliferation agenda for commercial reasons.

"President Obama does not want to stand in the way of the implementation of the 123 Agreement, but he is sensitive to the criticism that he is willing to dilute his commitment to non-proliferation for the sake of commercial advantages," I wrote in August 2009.

Much has happened since then, but the fact remains that there has been no nuclear trade till today. India's nuclear liability law, forced on the government by the enemies of the deal, became a smokescreen for the US not to supply nuclear material to India.

The repeated declarations about a way out of the liability law and planning for setting up US reactors in India after Prime Minister Narendra Modi assumed office have not changed the lack of enthusiasm of the US in nuclear trade with India. They are banking on defence supplies and cooperation after India became a close defence partner of the US.

The situation has become more volatile after the advent of President Donald Trump. With his assertion of nuclear weapons as fundamental to US security, a new dialogue may be necessary with him sooner or later to update the nuclear deal and to make it meaningful.

Another major event that has shaken our confidence in the value of nuclear power in our energy mix arising out of the nuclear deal was the Fukushima disaster. It has changed the global nuclear power scenario beyond recognition, though India has maintained that it is "business as usual" for India.

The recent decision of the government to build more indigenous reactors points to the fact that the dream of imported nuclear reactors dotting the country has disappeared. Except for Kudankulam, which predates 1998, there is no single foreign reactor operating in India. As such, India's focus has rightly shifted to solar and other new sources of energy.

The nuclear tests of 1998 constituted a major disruptive strategy to unfreeze an unsatisfactory status quo of nuclear apartheid, which was impeding India's security and development in various ways. The shock waves created by the tests were successfully contained by astute diplomacy and strong political will.

But a combination of the unwise enactment of the liability law, the Fukushima tragedy, and the advent of an unpredictable and unreliable US administration have cast a shadow on the nuclear scene in recent years. The time has come for a realistic appraisal of India's nuclear future and to adopt a realistic policy, taking the global situation into account.

Published: March 25, 2023

NSG Membership: Historical Hurdles and Future Prospects

Brexit, which was a seismic moment in Europe, came as a blessing in disguise for India as it came on the same day as the setback in Seoul, India's miscalculation on the Nuclear Suppliers Group (NSG) bid paled into insignificance compared to the British Prime Minister's misadventure in holding a referendum on the U.K.'s membership of the European Union. Otherwise, there would have been greater criticism of the foreign policy fiasco, which not only resulted in a rebuff to India but also gave a veto to China on India's nuclear credentials and hyphenated India and Pakistan.

Moreover, we have elevated NSG membership to such heights that it appears more important and urgent than other items on our wish list such as permanent membership of the UN Security Council, signing of the Nuclear Non-Proliferation Treaty (NPT) as a nuclear-weapon state, and membership of Asia-Pacific Economic Cooperation (APEC).

Keeping Credibility Intact

The Seoul experience should be a lesson in multilateral diplomacy for India. First and foremost, credibility is the hallmark of success in the international community. Policy changes should appear slow, deliberate, calculated and logical as sudden shifts and turns are viewed with suspicion. India had a fundamental position that our objective is disarmament and not merely non-proliferation.

Not signing the NPT and Comprehensive Nuclear-Test-Ban Treaty arose from the conviction that arms control is not a substitute to disarmament. Distancing ourselves from NPT-centred entities was also part of that philosophy. Rejection of discriminatory regimes and selective controls appeared logical and just. Even after declaring ourselves as a nuclear-weapon state, our readiness for nuclear disarmament maintained our credibility.

Our sudden anxiety to join the NSG and other non-proliferation groupings is a departure from the traditional Indian position, particularly since we have not fully utilised the waiver given to us by the NSG. An invitation by the U.S. was not enough to justify our enthusiasm for membership, and canvassing at the highest level in selected countries made matters worse. Having applied for membership only in May this year, we did not allow ourselves time to explain the rationale of our policy change, not only to the NSG members but also the other adherents to the NPT. This explains the hesitation of many friendly countries to support us. Any indication of change in the non-proliferation architecture makes them nervous.

The fact that many Indian initiatives have been successful in the multilateral arena should not lead us into assuming automatic support for our suggestions and requests. Many of our initiatives in the UN in the initial years, such as decolonisation, disarmament, development, human rights and apartheid, were more for the common good rather than for our own sake.

Problems arise when we seek advantages and concessions to ourselves, like in the case of Jammu and Kashmir, non-proliferation and Bangladesh or when our positions are perceived as siding with another major power, as in Afghanistan and Cambodia.

Our positions on self-determination and terrorism are not fully appreciated in the international community as yet. It was with patience, persistence, and extraordinary diplomatic skills that India had managed to steer clear of embarrassment or rebuff. Approaching multilateralism with an illusion of grandeur or presumption of justice, fair play and reasonableness may be hazardous.

Spreading Itself Thin

Having a powerful nation to pilot matters of importance to us is helpful, but even the U.S. does not always get its way in the multilateral bodies which require a majority vote or consensus. It loses votes in the UN General Assembly not only on substantive issues but also in elections. Since the real power is in the Security Council, the permanent five manage to wield power there, but wherever votes are of equal value, there is no guarantee that they can get support automatically.

The votaries of non-proliferation tend to be more loyal than the king and they are aghast that the U.S. appears to be undermining the regime that it had built. In 2008, they went along when the U.S. moved heaven and earth to get India a waiver to secure the nuclear deal, but this time they felt India was overreaching itself.

They were not supporting China when they opposed India's admission but merely proclaiming their faith. Brazil, South Africa, Austria, and Switzerland are serious nations with extraordinary commitment to the NPT, which they consider to be the cornerstone of international security.

Another lesson India should have known is the undesirability of pursuing too many objectives at the same time. India's claim for a permanent seat on the Security Council as part of the exercise to reflect the realities of global power is well understood, though a global compact to accomplish it is still elusive. Our pressing the point in the appropriate forums is considered legitimate, but any effort to press it to a vote to embarrass and pressurise anyone is bound to fail.

At one time, India made an attempt to have a vote in the General Assembly to secure a two-thirds majority just to embarrass the permanent members. But the effort failed when the opposition came not from the permanent members, but from the African Group. The art of persuasion works only when the ground is prepared and there is a degree of satisfaction for all parties involved. Our NSG push in the last two months violated this sacred principle.

In bilateral relations, the reality of power is what matters and deals can be struck on the basis of give and take. But the dynamics of multilateral diplomacy depend on equations that go beyond the actual size and power of individual countries. Often, clever use of the rules of procedure alone can bestow extraordinary powers on nations. India has no shortage of experts in multilateral diplomacy to handle such matters, but it appears that they have no say in decision-making. They end up getting impossible briefs and misinformation regarding assurances received from the capitals and operate in a vacuum.

India could have pursued membership of the NSG quietly, without making any claims of support from anyone. It appears that there is a feeling in the U.S. circles of getting India entangled in the non-proliferation net instead of leaving it alone to work on the basis of the nuclear deal and the NSG waiver. We should have handled the issue with dignified detachment and waited for a consensus to emerge among the interested countries. If only we had played by the rules of the multilateral game, the Seoul fiasco could have been turned into a victory.

Published: June 29, 2016

7

NSG's Hypocrisy: Addressing Nuclear Supply Concerns

Non-nuclear New Zealand was an unusual chairman to guide the 46 nuclear big wigs at the contentious meeting of the Nuclear Suppliers Groups this weekend in Christchurch. An army of non-proliferation enthusiasts descended on the event to press for nuclear-trade guidelines to be observed by all concerned. Yet China's blatant violation in the form of supplying two new nuclear reactors to Pakistan, was on everyone's mind, but on nobody's lips.

China didn't elaborate publicly on its plans to provide new reactors to Pakistan, having announced its intention to have a nuclear deal by proxy with Islamabad earlier this month. Two state-owned firms agreed to build two more reactors at the Chashma atomic complex in Punjab. Beijing justified the deal on historical grounds, citing its grandfatherly obligations to Pakistan, and also on the logic of restoring nuclear balance in South Asia. The only assurance the Chinese gave was that its nuclear commerce with Pakistan would be in accordance with China's international obligations.

Meanwhile, the United States was nowhere to be found. "India imitates China, Pakistan imitates India. What can we do to stop their nuclear activities?" a senior White House official lamented to a group of non-proliferation experts earlier this month, as though he was speaking for a weak state, not a superpower. He added the U.S. did not want to displease China or Pakistan at this juncture.

American priorities today are the economy and the war on terror; two more peaceful reactors will not make much of a difference to the world. And how could the U.S. object, having agreed to supply reactors to India? Neither did India protest, even though Chinese nuclear sales to Pakistan are a fundamental non-proliferation issue of concern to Delhi and to the NSG, more broadly. In fact, the Indian government has hardly uttered a word in public since the deal was announced.

The NSG already has guidelines for nuclear trade by its members and should decide whether the Chinese move violates those rules or not. China obviously wants to present a fait accompli rather than invite the group to impose conditions on the supply of the reactors to Pakistan. Beijing argues that the twin reactor deal was agreed before Beijing formally joined the NSG, and thus, isn't subject to current NSG rules. Beijing also points to the exception made for India in its 2008 civil-nuclear deal with the U.S.

To draw a parallel between a specific exemption given to India and the unilateral action by China is to ignore the three years of agonising negotiations based on India's record of responsible behaviour and its pressing energy needs.

India separated its military reactors from civilian stations, agreed to International Atomic Energy Agency-led safeguard inspections of the latter, applied for a waiver of NSG guidelines, and gave various assurances to the international community.

Pakistan, which sold nuclear-weapon technology to clients in North Korea, Libya, and Iran, can hardly be equated with India. Islamabad is compiling a nuclear arsenal far in excess of the minimum deterrent that the country is supposed to possess. Pakistan is also blocking negotiations on the Fissile Material Cut-off Treaty in Geneva precisely to gain time to accumulate more fissionable material. This is hardly an opportune time to signal acceptance of the peaceful nature of Pakistan's nuclear program.

China's own credibility as a disciplined member of the NSG has often been called into question. Even while China has been using Pakistan as a conduit for supply of nuclear technology, it has directly assisted Iran in developing missile technology and supplied missiles to Saudi

Arabia. Its nuclear activities reveal a clear strategy to use their nuclear assets to secure economic and political concessions in South Asia and the Middle East.

Placing additional nuclear capability in the hands of Pakistan, even peaceful nuclear reactors, will fly in the face of NSG guidelines. China's silence is no indication of its willingness to change its behaviour. In fact, if past experience is any guide, neither China nor Pakistan can be expected to further the cause of non-proliferation. If the NSG doesn't speak out now, its very credibility will be undermined. And what will happen then?

Published: June 28, 2010

Pokhran II Revisited: Two Decades Later

Twenty years ago, on May 11, 1998, India took a leap into the unknown world of nuclear-weapon powers with the tests at Pokhran. Though the decision was taken after great deliberation and with preparation, how the reaction of the world would affect the future of India was unknown. But today, it is certain that the action was timely and inevitable.

Obstacles Removed

India has enough reasons to be satisfied over having accomplished many of the objectives of Pokhran II. Indian diplomacy triumphed in turning a grave crisis into an opportunity by securing legitimacy for its nuclear arsenal and removing obstacles in generating nuclear power. But the hasty enactment of a liability law, which inhibited nuclear trade, and the setback globally to nuclear power on account of the Fukushima disaster stood in the way of India benefitting fully from Pokhran II and the subsequent agreements reached.

The fact, however, remains that the 1998 tests and the subsequent nuclear deal have brought India to the nuclear mainstream and opened up the global nuclear market for development of nuclear power without signing the Treaty on the Non-Proliferation of Nuclear Weapons (NPT) or the Comprehensive Nuclear-Test Ban Treaty (CTBT).

The tests shocked the world, particularly because they were done with utmost secrecy and the India-U.S. ties hit rock bottom. For nearly two months, the U.S. refused to have any dialogue with India and implemented the Glenn Amendment for the first time. Newer sanctions were imposed, and at one point it looked that relations would never recover.

The talks between U.S. Deputy Secretary of State Strobe Talbott and Foreign Minister Jaswant Singh over the next two years were the most comprehensive dialogues India had with the U.S. on its nuclear policy, including the threat perception and future plans for security. India was anxious to have the sanctions lifted, but Mr. Singh sought to delink sanctions from the security dialogue, not to be pressurised to take quick decisions. Mr. Talbott began by insisting that the objective was to get India to sign the NPT.

Then he listed five benchmarks as non-proliferation goals to normalise relations: signing the CTBT, halting production of fissile material, strategic restraint, strengthening export control regimes, and normalisation of relations with Pakistan. These were strongly rejected by India, but the talks proceeded on the assumption that India's security concerns should be fully understood and that India would take certain measures to suit its new status.

But, in effect, India met the U.S. demands more than half way, leading to an understanding, which led to President Bill Clinton's visit to India and Prime Minister Atal Bihari Vajpayee's visit to the U.S. in 2000. India refused to sign the CTBT, but declared a moratorium on testing; agreed to join the Fissile Material Cut-off Treaty negotiations without halting fissile material production; reaffirmed minimum deterrent without giving any number of warheads; and agreed to strengthen export controls. Additionally, India declared no-first-use and commitment to disarmament. Though no deal could be struck, the foundation was laid for what became the nuclear deal in 2008.

Though India placed its civilian nuclear facilities under perpetual safeguards, its nuclear assets remained fully insulated against external scrutiny and interference. India secured rights to receive uninterrupted nuclear fuel supplies as a trade-off against safeguards. It kept open its right to acquire advanced enrichment and reprocessing technologies, although it would require bilateral negotiations with the U.S. and others. India's sovereign right to test a nuclear device in the future has remained intact, although the deal would be in jeopardy in such an eventuality.

President George W. Bush and Prime Minister Manmohan Singh remained committed to the deal throughout the negotiations and made decisive interventions at crucial moments. Apart from the specific gains in the nuclear area, the new India-U.S. partnership, which promised investment and high technology, was a turning point in Indian foreign policy. On the negative side, the deal generated mistrust in Russia and China, which had to be dealt with in future years.

Reality Check

A decade after signing the deal, its gains and losses have proved much less game-changing than it was hoped in 2008. Though not a champion of the deal as a Senator, President Barack Obama committed himself to the implementation of the deal as part of his strategy to build good relations with India. But his personal affinity to the NPT and non-proliferation made him reluctant to interpret the 123 Agreement liberally. The expectation was that the prospect of nuclear trade with India would be a great attraction, but in 2009 Mr. Obama gave clear indication to his advisers that he would not sacrifice his non-proliferation agenda for commercial reasons.

Much has happened since then, but the fact remains that there has been no nuclear trade till today. India's nuclear liability law, forced on the government by critics of the deal, became a smokescreen for the U.S. to not supply nuclear material to India. The repeated declarations about a way out of the liability law and plans to set up American reactors in India after Narendra Modi became Prime Minister have not changed the lack of enthusiasm in the U.S. on nuclear trade with India. In any case, the situation has become more volatile after Donald Trump became U.S. President.

Another major event that has shaken confidence in the value of nuclear power in India's energy mix was the Fukushima disaster. It has changed the global nuclear power scenario beyond recognition, though India has maintained that it is "business as usual". The government's recent decision to build more indigenous reactors points to the fact that the dream of imported nuclear reactors dotting India has disappeared. India's focus has rightly shifted to solar and other new sources of energy.

Published: May 10, 2018

Pursuing NSG Membership:
India's Quest Continues

India's 30-year-old effort to secure a permanent seat on the UN Security Council has been characterised as the pursuit of a diplomatic holy grail. The chance of success in that pursuit has been receding like a mirage, though there have been tantalising signs of progress. A similar, but less intense effort is on to seek admission to the Asia-Pacific Economic Cooperation (APEC), a body which should have included India in the first place.

Here again, there is no sign of India being invited, even as the 10-year moratorium on new membership has expired. India has now embarked on another quest, this time to seek membership of the Nuclear Suppliers Group (NSG). The Prime Minister himself has travelled to Switzerland to seek support and he will also go to Mexico for the same purpose. It is surprising that India is investing so much diplomatic effort on this issue when there is little chance of India being invited to the group.

An American Initiative

India seeking membership of the NSG is like Russia seeking membership of North Atlantic Treaty Organisation: the NSG was invented to prevent Indian advance towards possession of nuclear weapons after the technology demonstration test of 1974. If India joins it, the very nature of the NSG will change and dilute its fundamental position that all members should be signatories to the Non-Proliferation Treaty (NPT). Though the U.S. has stated repeatedly that it would like to see India in the NSG, it cannot be expected to be a party to the fundamental alteration of the NPT regime.

Interestingly, it was a U.S. think tank which brought up the topic in a Track II discussion with some of us in 2007. The suggestion was not that India should be given membership of the NSG, but that India should join all multilateral export control regimes like the NSG, Missile Technology Control Regime (which it is set to join later this year), the Wassenaar Arrangement for control of conventional weapons, and the Australia Group for control of chemicals that could contribute to chemical and biological weapons.

It appeared then that the whole proposal was to drag us into Wassenaar Arrangement and the Australia Group by presenting them as a package. We had refrained from joining both, though they were open for us from the beginning, for our own reasons. Our response to the U.S. proposal was guarded as we did not want a bargain on all the groups together. We did, however, emphasise that India's membership of the NSG would be helpful as it had received an exemption from the NSG guidelines. As a member of the group, we could contribute to the discussion if it sought to amend the guidelines in any manner. In other words, it was not an Indian initiative to press for admission to the NSG.

U.S. President Barack Obama formalised the proposal in 2010, as though it was a concession to India, in his bid to win various contracts, including nuclear supplies. Perhaps, he was aware that a decision on the NSG was not in his hands, but promised to take up the matter with the others just to win some goodwill in the process. As was expected, the fundamental requirement that every member should be a signatory to the NPT was brought up not only by China but several others.

There was similar opposition in the case of the exemption from NSG guidelines at the time of the nuclear deal also, but our bilateral efforts and heavy lifting by the U.S., including a final phone call from the U.S. President to his Chinese counterpart, resulted in the exemption. The strength of the argument was that this would be a one-time exemption with no strings attached.

No Great Gains in The Offing

Interestingly, the NSG is an informal grouping, which is referred to in the International Atomic Energy Agency documents only as "certain states", and there is no precise procedure for seeking admission. But since the group takes all its decisions by consensus, it follows that new members should also be by consensus. For those outside the group, there is an outreach programme which is being pursued vigorously. The outreach programme is meant merely for conveying information and not for consultation. New Delhi hosted an outreach meeting a few years ago, but it was found that the exercise was not of much use in influencing the guidelines.

The pursuit of membership of the NSG by India at the highest level has aroused suspicion that India is aiming to be in the group to deny entry to Pakistan. Such an interpretation is the result of lack of any clarity as to the benefits that will accrue to India by joining the NSG. In fact, membership of the group will not immediately open up nuclear trade as India has already pledged not to transfer nuclear know-how to other countries. If we attempt to dilute the guidelines to liberalise supply, it will be resisted by the others.

Membership of the NSG will only mean greater pressure on us to sign the NPT and the Comprehensive Nuclear-Test-Ban Treaty (CTBT) and commit in advance to a Fissile Material Cut-off Treaty, which would impose restrictions on existing stockpiles of fissile material.

China has given scant attention to the NSG guidelines and has violated them in the case of Pakistan by claiming to act under an agreement reached before China joined the NSG. Unlike India, Pakistan has not even sought an exemption from the NSG. To say, therefore, that India and Pakistan should be equated on nuclear matters is unreasonable, to say the least. But the NSG did not even challenge the supply of two new reactors to Pakistan by China. The NSG's ineffectiveness in countering proliferation makes it even less attractive as a group India should join.

The green signal for India to join the MTCR came when Mr. Modi was in Washington purely by coincidence, as the last date for filing objections happened to be that day. Italy had held up its approval on account of the Italian marines' issue, but did not file a formal objection because of the decision to let the marines go home.

Membership of the MTCR, which restricts the weight and range of missiles, is being projected as clearing the way for NSG. This is not likely because of China except that we can now threaten to veto China if it applies for membership of the MTCR.

When India is not anywhere near the permanent membership of the Security Council and even APEC membership remains elusive, the high-level pursuit of NSG membership may give the impression that India is unrealistic in its expectations from the international community.

Support from Switzerland and Mexico will not make any difference as there will not be a vote on the issue. The U.S. may reiterate its support, but the objection will come from China and even some others. It will be better for India to concentrate on one or two fundamental objectives rather than fritter away our diplomatic resources on matters of marginal interest.

Published: June 7, 2017

Evolving Nuclear Dynamics:
Shifting Global Perspectives

A picture of the globe under the hood of a cobra was a familiar symbol of the precarious state of international security till recently. The accidental or deliberate pressing of the nuclear button has been a long standing nightmare that has haunted humanity. At the same time, using the nuclear genie and harnessing it for prosperity has been the best dream. Today, both the nightmare and the dream have become jaded.

Nuclear weapons have ceased to be viable as instruments of war because of the unpredictability of the consequences of a nuclear war. No one can trust even the use of tactical nuclear weapons without collateral damage for the user. Today, nations can be destroyed with mobile phones and laptops without killing a single human being, making the "humaneness" of cyber-warfare the biggest danger.

The theories of deterrence of nuclear stockpiles have also been discredited after 9/11 brought the most formidable nuclear power to its knees. Non-proliferation today, if any, is not on account of the Non-Proliferation Treaty (NPT), but on account of the futility of building nuclear arsenals. The threat of terrorism looms larger than the threat of nuclear weapons.

After Fukushima, nuclear power too is receding as a sensible component of the energy mix. One clean-up operation after an accident can demolish many years of technological advancement and hopes of having cheap power. The sun shines as a source of energy, not the glittering nuclear reactors which seem to emit mushroom clouds.

Still A Flourishing Industry

Old habits die hard however, and there is constant activity on the weapons and the power fronts. The nuclear and disarmament industry still flourish. Former U.S. President Barack Obama's Prague speech had ignited cautious optimism that nuclear weapons would cease to be the anchor of security, though not during his presidency, not even in his lifetime. Rajiv Gandhi's United Nations Plan of Action for total elimination of nuclear weapons came out of the dusty archives. The 'Global Zero' movement gained momentum, even as nuclear-weapon powers continued investment in developing delivery systems and weapons.

U.S. President Donald Trump had once said that proliferation was good for American allies, but more recently, he said: "It would be wonderful, a dream would be that no country would have nukes, but if countries are going to have nukes, we're going to be at the top of the pack." He even hinted at the use of nuclear weapons in extreme circumstances.

The hope raised by four old cold warriors, George P. Shultz, William J. Perry, Henry A. Kissinger, and Sam Nunn, by setting the goal of a world free of nuclear weapons and working on the actions required to achieve that goal finally receded, and in desperation, the world turned to the good old UN machinery to create illusions of progress.

Emphasising Non-Proliferation

NPT enthusiasts have been disappointed of late that out of the three pillars of the treaty—non-proliferation, disarmament, and nuclear energy for peaceful purposes—the first, non-proliferation, has got watered down and disarmament has become the priority. They also worry that dangerous technologies like enrichment are within the reach of the non-weapon states.

In the context of Japan and South Korea debating acquisition of nuclear weapons, they feel that non-proliferation should be brought back to be the first priority of the NPT. The promotional function of the International Atomic Energy Agency (IAEA) is also a concern for them.

The IAEA has already shifted its focus from nuclear power to nuclear security, as a result. In 1995, the NPT was made a perpetual treaty with no possibility of amendment, but its votaries now advocate that non-proliferation should be emphasised to the exclusion of disarmament and nuclear energy promotion.

The UN General Assembly, with its unlimited agenda, readily jumped into the first UN conference in more than 20 years on a global nuclear-weapon ban, though the nuclear-weapon powers did not join. More than 120 nations in October 2016 voted on a UN General Assembly resolution to convene the conference to negotiate a legally binding treaty to prohibit nuclear weapons, leading to their total elimination. Britain, France, Russia, and the U.S. voted no, while China, India, and Pakistan abstained. Though India had recommended the convening of such a conference, it abstained on the resolution as it was not convinced that the conference could accomplish much at this time.

India said that it supported the commencement of negotiations in the Conference on Disarmament on a comprehensive Nuclear Weapons Convention, which in addition to prohibition and elimination also includes verification. The U.S. and others wanted to accept the reality that such conferences would serve no purpose. The conference has failed even before it commenced.

In the midst of this ferment, a debate has begun in India about a review of its no-first use doctrine. Experts seem to think that India's doctrine is flexible enough to deal with any eventuality, but others feel that we should enter more caveats to safeguard our interests. Perhaps, it is best to let the sleeping dogs lie.

On Nuclear Power Production

On the nuclear power front, the efforts to increase nuclear power production suffered a setback as a result of Fukushima. Many countries that had lined up before the IAEA for nuclear technology for peaceful purposes quietly switched to other sources of energy. The much-expected nuclear renaissance withered away. Except for China, India, and Russia, most nations have shied away from building nuclear reactors or importing them.

India's liability law deterred U.S. companies from exporting reactors to India. The financial problems of Westinghouse, which had agreed to build six reactors in Andhra Pradesh, postponed, if not cancelled, the venture. But India has not fundamentally changed its three-stage nuclear power development, though the thorium stage eludes it.

The need for reduction of greenhouse gases was an incentive to increase nuclear power production, but President Trump's challenge of the whole concept of climate change as a hoax and the consequent reduction of allocation of funds to protect the environment will further reduce the accent on nuclear power. The Kudankulam project is set to move along with Russian collaboration, but its progress has been slow. The nuclear liability law, the Westinghouse bankruptcy and the protests by local people have combined to delay the expansion of nuclear power in India.

Like everything else in international affairs, the nuclear pot is also being stirred on account of the uncertainties of the U.S. government and changing threat perceptions. Nobody thinks any more that peace and amity will break out between the U.S. and Russia, making nuclear weapons redundant. But no one is certain that the nuclear genie will not take new incarnations as a result of the ferment.

Published: April 9, 2017

Space and Nuclear Technologies: Exploring Future Frontiers

Even as billionaire Jeff Bezos was preparing to blast off into space last month, another billionaire Bill Gates took an equally momentous decision to launch his own nuclear reactor with an eye on the possibility of exporting fast breeder reactors to power hungry nations. Both of them characterised their initiatives as essentially aimed at the environment to reverse climate change.

Answering criticism on his expensive and wasteful adventure, Bezos insisted that he had an environmental vision: "We need to take all heavy industry, all polluting industry and move it into space, and keep Earth as this beautiful gem of a planet that it is," he said. Mr. Gates stressed the importance of nuclear power as the clean energy required to meet the requirements of the world, even though the safety of nuclear reactors and the risk of proliferation of nuclear weapons are a growing concern.

The Future of Atomic Energy

Back in 2007-08, the then Director General of the International Atomic Energy Agency (IAEA), Mohamed ElBaradei, had established a Committee of Eminent Persons to look at the future of nuclear power in 2020 and beyond. As an Executive Director of the Commission, I had helped to produce a report, which asserted that "the international community has both auspicious opportunities and significant challenges to tackle as the world moves into its seventh nuclear decade. Expanded use of nuclear technologies offered immense potential to meet important development needs.

"In fact, to satisfy energy demands and to mitigate the threat of climate change—two of the 21st century's greatest challenges—there are major opportunities for expansion of nuclear energy." The report predicted that a "nuclear renaissance" will solve not only the world's energy problems, but also alleviate climate change.

Fukushima And After

But the expectation was short-lived because the completely transformed nuclear power situation was beyond recognition and dealt a blow to plans for swiftly scaling up nuclear power to address not only climate change, but also energy poverty and economic development. An IAEA article, 'Nuclear power 10 years after Fukushima: The long road back', says, as the global community turned its attention to strengthening nuclear safety, several countries opted to phase out nuclear power.

The nuclear industry was at a standstill except in Russia, China, and India. Even in India, the expected installation of imported reactors did not materialise because of our liability law and the anti-nuclear protests in proposed locations. India had to go in for more indigenous reactors to increase the nuclear component of its energy mix. More than 50 nations, which were knocking at the door of the IAEA for nuclear energy for peaceful purposes, quietly withdrew their requests.

After intensive efforts to strengthen nuclear safety, as said in this article, and with global warming becoming evermore apparent, nuclear power is regaining a place in global debates as a climate-friendly energy option once again. Countries such as Japan and Germany re-opened their reactors to produce energy. But even as organisations such as the Intergovernmental Panel on Climate Change (IPCC) and the International Energy Agency (IEA) recognise the ability of nuclear power to address major global challenges, it remains uncertain whether the value of this clean, reliable, and sustainable source of energy will achieve its full potential any time soon.

The Fukushima Daiichi accident, adds the article, continues to cast a shadow over the prospects of nuclear power. Furthermore, in some major markets, nuclear power lacks a favourable policy and financing framework that recognise its contributions to climate change mitigation and sustainable development. Without such a framework, nuclear power will struggle to deliver on its full potential, even as the world remains as dependent on fossil fuels as it was three decades ago.

The Gates Plan

Even when the uncertainty continues and the anti-nuclear lobby is gaining momentum, TerraPower, the nuclear company founded by Bill Gates, has just announced an agreement with private funders, including Warren Buffett, and the U.S State of Wyoming, to site its Natrium fast reactor demonstration project there. Moreover, since it falls within the "advanced" small modular reactor project of the U.S. Department of Energy (DOE), the Department will subsidise the project of one of the richest men in the world to the extent of $80 million this year.

As an article by the non-proliferation sentinels in the U.S, Henry Sokolski and Victor Gilinsky, titled *'Bill Gates' fast nuclear reactor: Will it bomb?'* says, Mr. Gates believes that the fast breeder reactors will replace the current reactors. The DOE and other nuclear enthusiasts also believe that small, factory-built, modular reactors will be cheaper and safer, as well as be an attractive prospect for foreign buyers that will facilitate in reviving America's nuclear industry, enabling the United States to compete in an international market now dominated by China and Russia. Another benefit envisaged is that fast breeder reactors will provide a solid nuclear industrial base for meeting the U.S. military's nuclear requirements. DOE has found bipartisan Congressional support for funding the project.

Mr. Sokolski and Mr. Gilinsky have challenged the move on several grounds such as the failure of earlier efforts to develop such reactors, and the risk of the turning of inert uranium to plutonium, and then using the plutonium as fuel. They have argued in their article that it can even "breed" excess plutonium to fuel new fast reactors. What concerns them most is that plutonium is a nuclear explosive which can be used for developing a bomb. They are afraid that the availability of plutonium through commercial channels would be fraught with dangers.

As their article says, TerraPower announced in March that Natrium would be fuelled with uranium enriched to 20%U-235 rather than explosive plutonium. But the question being asked is if Natrium reactor takes off and is offered for export, will the same restraint apply. Currently, only a handful of nations can make 20% enriched uranium. The critics believe that there will be a rush to make 20% enriched uranium worldwide.

The main objection to nuclear enrichment beyond a point in Iran arises from the fact that it would lead to weapon grade uranium being available for them. The other objection being raised against the Gates project, as cited in the article, is that the principal reason for preferring fast reactors is to gain the ability to breed plutonium. That is surely what foreign customers will want. The way it is configured, the reactor would make and reuse massive quantities of material that could also be used as nuclear explosives in warheads.

Focus on India and China

India's fast breeder reactor, which is not subject to international inspections, is seen as capable of feeding the nuclear-weapon capability of India. And the recent reports that China is building two more fast reactors have immediately provoked international concerns about China's possible weapons plutonium production.

The opponents of TerraPower believe that India and China will be encouraged in their efforts to develop fast breeder reactors and may even want to buy them from Mr. Gates. They also think that the characterisation of TerraPower as small is a gimmick, and they will have to be made big to make them economical. The claim that fast reactors are safer than light water reactors has also been called into question.

It has been pointed out that U.S. Presidents Gerald Ford and Jimmy Carter made it the official U.S. policy to discourage the commercialising of plutonium-fuelled reactors. President Ford had announced that the U.S. would not support reliance on plutonium fuel and associated reprocessing of spent fuel until "the world community can effectively overcome the associated risks of proliferation." The critics do not think that the world has reached such a stage as of yet.

No one can predict whether the space adventure of Mr. Bezos or the nuclear venture of Mr. Gates will benefit the U.S. and the wider world. But billionaires have the sixth sense to know how to multiply their own billions.

Published: March 11, 2011

US-India Nuclear Relations: Challenges and Realities

Lucrative nuclear trade with India, including supplies of reactors, was among the obvious reasons for the Bush administration to think in terms of offering India a special dispensation for full civilian nuclear co-operation.

Varying assessments of the massive increase in jobs in the United States on account of the expected trade in equipment were made. These projections went a long way in vetting the appetite of the industrial sector in the United States and in aggravating the suspicions in the non-proliferation lobbies.

The enthusiasm for the nuclear deal by the US-India Business Council (USIBC), consisting of the big players in India-US trade was attributed to the lure of nuclear trade with India. The USIBC engaged professional lobbyists in Washington to promote the deal on the Hill and elsewhere and there was considerable jubilation in it when the deal was signed.

In India too, the presumption was that significant nuclear trade with the US would follow the deal. Although experts knew that the US had no ready reactors to sell, it was believed that the US industry had already begun to fabricate reactors, using old technology to capture the Indian market.

The US insistence on strict regulations on nuclear trade and its reluctance to give assurances of perpetuity of supplies were seen as mere ploys to get the best business terms for nuclear trade. The argument was that the US would not sacrifice business opportunities for the sake of non-proliferation objectives.

Why should the US work so hard to secure Nuclear Suppliers Group (NSG) waiver for India merely to facilitate supply of reactors by Russia and France to India?

There were whispers in India during the negotiations that we should be Machiavellian in our approach to the United States. Some suggested that India should go along with the US conditions till we obtained the necessary clearances and then not place any orders in the US if the conditions of supply were not favourable to us.

The natural reaction of the US side was to extract a Memorandum of Understanding (MOU) from India that we would seek to secure a significant percentage of our nuclear supplies from the US. It was also insisted on that India should earmark two locations for the installation of US reactors in India.

The Obama administration has maintained this position and one of the trophies that US Secretary of State Hillary Clinton carried back from India was an assurance on locations for American reactors.

But the latest indication from Washington is that the US may not be interested in supplying nuclear material and reactors to India under the new dispensation. This is emerging as a matter of policy as well as a practical measure. President Obama does not want to stand in the way of the implementation of the 123 Agreement, but he is sensitive to the criticism that he is willing to dilute his commitment to non-proliferation for the sake of commercial advantages.

He has, therefore, embarked on a path to do the minimum necessary to let the deal run its course without the US itself contributing to the growth of the nuclear strength of India. He wishes to remain committed to the universalisation of the NPT, while pursuing the vision of a nuclear-weapon-free world in the long term.

The Washington move in G-8 on enrichment and reprocessing should be seen in this context. While the discussions on reprocessing, as provided for in the 123 Agreement, will proceed, supply of equipment and technology in the sensitive areas will be ruled out. The US will also work for a gradual revision of the NSG consensus to put sensitive technology beyond the reach of India and others.

Nor will there be iron glad guarantees of perpetuity of supplies. The US understands that an inevitable consequence of this strategy is that the US will not be able to supply any nuclear material to India at any time. This fact is being accepted as a reality and as a virtue. It will demonstrate to the world that the US is serious about its non-proliferation protestations.

The new men and women in charge of non-proliferation in Washington do believe that the nuclear deal is not in the interest of non-proliferation and they want to curb it to the extent possible without appearing to back off from it.

The US is also reconciled to Russia and France supplying fuel and equipment under the terms of the NSG waiver. It may not be averse to indirect participation in the French deals, if such opportunities arise, but it is gradually preparing the industry to close their options to open nuclear trade with India.

The compensation that the US expects is in terms of defence deals with India, which have as much potential, if not more, for job creation and overall growth in trade. The US has therefore been diligent about pursuing the end user agreement, without which defence deals would not be possible under the US laws.

The US had no doubt that this would be clinched as India had agreed to have similar agreements in the past. Compared to the legal rigmarole that the industry would face in the case of nuclear supplies, the defence formalities are not difficult to complete.

Defence supplies will meet the needs of a vibrant industrial complex, which cannot sustain without exports, while nuclear trade regulations in the US are too complicated to be tackled. The choice, therefore, is clear for the US policy makers.

As for India, no tears will be shed for loss of unreliable supplies from the US as long as the other suppliers keep their commitments.

The new strategy in the US will mean the emergence of tough choices for India in the years ahead. Once the US is out of any obsession with the attractions of nuclear trade with India, it will be more direct in pursuing its non-proliferation objectives with India.

When the Comprehensive Test Ban Treaty (CTBT) and the Fissile Material Cut-off Treaty (FMCT) are mature for ratification by India, the pressure on us will be very great indeed. There will be no industrial lobby to shield India at that time.

If the US is willing to give up its nuclear trade with India and the China factor is diminishing, what other factors will make it possible for the United States to sustain the deal?

Two theories have surfaced in recent days. One is a cynical view that the deal was just a lollipop offered to India to compensate for the massive supply of arms to Pakistan, which was already on the anvil during the Bush era.

India could hardly complain as the beneficiary of a waiver on nuclear matters when the US steps up military cooperation with Pakistan. This theory assumes that President Bush had the foresight to anticipate the Af-Pak crisis.

Another theory is that the real reason for the deal was that the US wanted a massive infusion of Indian nuclear technicians into the country in the next few years, when the US unveils its own plan to reduce dependence on foreign oil.

By offering India the deal, the Bush administration was simply setting up a nursery of nuclear scientists, who could be transplanted to the US at the appropriate time. This may be far-fetched, but the theory exists.

India must brace itself for a new round with the US, not only on the unfinished business of the nuclear deal, but also on the new dimensions emerging in the thinking of the Obama team.

Published: August 21, 2009

I. INDIAN FOREIGN SERVICE

INCREASED RELEVANCE IN A COMPLEX WORLD

Diplomatic Challenges:
A Crown of Political Thorns

Every two years, sometimes more often, national media regales readers with stories on the making and unmaking of Foreign Secretaries. No other post, not even that of the Cabinet Secretary, attracts such national attention and interest. The post brings with it an aura of brilliance, political acceptability, high visibility, and vulnerability. It is a position that legends are made on.

But becoming Foreign Secretary and staying there for a full term is a Herculean task. There are also instances in which unsuspecting officers are plucked out of their comfortable perches in Beijing, Islamabad, and Dublin and installed in the hot seat. Some are born Foreign Secretaries; some achieve the job and some have the job thrust upon them.

The glamour of being Foreign Secretary is not as real as it is made out to be. The pressures and tension emanating from above and below are such that the person can hardly savour either power or glory. As the interface between the bureaucracy and the politicians, he is buffeted by both constantly.

The Foreign Service is highly competitive, if not combative. Its leader needs to have three pairs of hands, like gods and goddesses—one pair to implement orders from above, one to hold on to his/her chair and one to do work. Any slackening will bring instant retribution, and often it would be undeserved and unjust.

Two years of such tension is the reward for brilliance, manipulation or chance—ways to secure the post. Former Foreign Secretaries are a happier lot than the incumbents.

"The making and unmaking of Foreign Secretaries will continue to baffle the public and frustrate aspirants and incumbents, but the method in the madness will surface over the passage of time "

Past Appointments

Any analysis of past appointments will be enough to defy most existing theories about the selection of Foreign Secretaries. Seniority has been the decisive factor in the largest number of appointments. But there have always been ways to get around it by re-arranging the jigsaw puzzle and placing senior people in attractive posts abroad. Merit, subjective at every stage, is a nebulous factor.

The rank allotted by the Union Public Service Commission, by the most objective and diligent process, has been in play only in some cases. Instances of officers at the top swinging from one political ideology to another to earn merit are not rare. Good officers have fallen by the wayside and some have made it with poor credentials.

But the past record of selection of Foreign Secretaries presents a picture of near-perfection in a majority of the cases. The percentage of aberrations is not higher than in the making of Prime Ministers or the selection of Nobel Peace Prize laureates.

Complex Picture

The unmaking of Foreign Secretaries presents a more complex picture. The most celebrated case was the unprecedented sacking of a Foreign Secretary at a press conference by the Prime Minister. The last straw in that case was a factual issue regarding whether the Prime Minister would visit Pakistan or not. The Prime Minister not only contradicted the Foreign Secretary, but also promised the nation a new Foreign Secretary. But it was well known that the chemistry between Rajiv Gandhi and A.P. Venkateswaran was not the best even before the latter was appointed

Foreign Secretary. He was appointed because of his reputation and popularity in the service itself.

"Let us have a bash at it!" Rajiv Gandhi is supposed to have said, while handing him the post. Venkateswaran's removal was a foregone conclusion, and the favourite of the Prime Minister was all set to take over, but the heat of the moment forced the Prime Minister to appoint the senior most officer in the service in his place. That was the only time the Foreign Service openly revolted against a decision of the Prime Minister.

The removal of Jagat Singh Mehta by Charan Singh involved issues of foreign policy rather than personal predilections. Jagat Mehta's rise from High Commissioner in Tanzania to Foreign Secretary was meteoric, primarily because of Indira Gandhi who discovered his potential. But her successors and finally she herself felt that his vision was not in keeping with the dictates of the times.

Jagat Mehta anticipated much of the evolution of Indian foreign policy, like the reduction of rigidity of our nuclear policy and engagement with the United States and China. He had nothing against the Soviet Union, but his stress on other relationships set the Kremlin on fire and the heat was felt all the way in New Delhi when the Soviet lobby took up the cudgels against him.

The fiasco in Lusaka involving his candidature for the post of Secretary General of the Commonwealth speeded up his removal, but it was done in a clandestine manner. He was repeatedly told that his letter of resignation was not accepted, but his successor Ram Sathe was informed of his new post through unconventional communication channels not accessible to the serving Foreign Secretary.

Indira Gandhi herself cancelled a posting the previous government had promised him and he stayed on in the service as an officer on special duty, as a disciplined soldier, till he retired. His vindication came when Atal Bihari Vajpayee honoured him with a Padma Bhushan many years later.

The politically savvy and shrewd S.K. Singh fell victim to his own feeling of invincibility, which prompted him to make an enemy of Prime

Minister Inder Kumar Gujral at a time when the latter's rise to power was not anticipated by anyone. He tried to smooth ruffled feathers to work for the new dispensation, but he was quietly removed with the promise of a political appointment, which did not materialise till the Congress returned to power. Neither the climb to the precarious rock of bureaucratic heights nor the descent is an easy ride for anyone. The satisfaction and pride come only when the person gets back to earth unscathed and looks at the path traversed. The journey to the pinnacle of the Foreign Service has more than its share of storms and avalanches.

The most recent "curtailing" of a Foreign Secretary's term and the appointment of another just two days before his retirement are illustrative of the mix of the many factors which lead to such decisions. Both of them are extremely competent and both, having benefited from political patronage, must accept its shifting sands. Bureaucrats, who get close to the political leadership, rise and fall with their mentors.

The added hazard is that the post of the Foreign Secretary is constantly under scrutiny because of his or her high profile and visibility. The making and unmaking of Foreign Secretaries will continue to baffle the public and frustrate aspirants and incumbents, but the method in the madness will surface over the passage of time.

Published: February 1, 2015

Home Away from Home: Diplomatic Housing Arrangements

Curiosity about life of diplomats abroad pursue me everywhere, even though there are many autobiographies of former diplomats, including mine (*Words, Words, Words,* Pearson 2017) touching every aspect of diplomatic life. Myths persist about the luxury lifestyle on one hand and the miserable existence in expensive metropolitan cities on the other.

What kind of homes do Indian diplomats live in while abroad? How does their life abroad compare with that of the civil servants in India? Are diplomatic wives just glorified housekeepers? How about schools for children and medical care in strange lands? Such is the nature of the barrage of questions that I hear from young people, particularly those who aspire to a diplomatic career or their relatives and friends.

A privilege granted to our diplomats abroad is free furnished accommodation, which befits their status and rank. Quality of housing differs, depending on the countries concerned, but it ranges from adequate to luxurious. As India started acquisition of more and more properties, the housing situation has vastly improved. Ambassadorial homes in most capitals are grand and some of them qualify as classic homes.

We lived in two homes in Tokyo (Japan), a home in Thimphu (Bhutan), an apartment in Moscow (Russia), two apartments in New York (USA), a home in Yangon (Myanmar), and ambassadorial residences in Suva (Fiji), Nairobi, Washington and Vienna. Each one of these places had its own characteristics, advantages, and disadvantages. But one thing in common with all of them was that they were all temporary homes.

So we were able to take the good and the bad in our stride and move on, expecting that in another three years or less, we will make up for the deficiencies. We moved into our home in Kerala also with the same spirit, but found ourselves in the same house for the longest period of time.

In most of the cities that we lived in, there was little choice of houses to make, as we simply inherited them, whether they were owned by the Govt and earmarked for the incumbent of a particular post, or hired by a predecessor. In the case of our house in Tokyo, we had a clear choice, within the rental ceiling and we stayed on in a hotel till we found a place ourselves. One consideration we had was that we should be close to a metro station as driving was hard in Tokyo.

So we ended up in a cottage in a suburb with easy access to a metro station, later finding out that our guests, who came by cars found the distance too forbidding. But our home was ideal for total immersion in the study of Japanese as there were no foreigners in the area and no one spoke any other language. We also had a close look at the domestic life of a middle-class Japanese family.

Our cottage was in the compound of the ancestral home of a senior manager in a reputed firm. He lived in the main house with his wife and son and our cottage was built for his daughter, who had moved to another city with her husband. We witnessed first-hand the plight of the Japanese housewife, who worked tirelessly to run the household. Her husband and son would come home late after entertaining friends in night clubs and would not help her at all and would merely sit in front of the television set, sipping the rice wine, sake.

The Japanese women that time were even less liberated than now and it was common for Japanese girls to aspire to marry foreigners just to avoid the drudgery of home making in Japan. A husband, who shares the burden of the household is a dream for Japanese women even today.

The cottage was very well appointed and equipped, but the furniture provided by the Embassy was not particularly presentable. In our anxiety to make the house look good, we spent money on curtains and also used the carpets we had brought to cover the sofa! It was an agonising moment for us when a child of a friend cut the new lace curtain into pieces just for fun. We learnt two lessons then, not to spend your own money to beautify official homes and not to leave scissors around in the house. Our most distinguished house guests in our first home abroad were Princess Gauri Lakshmi Bayi and her husband, R.R. Varma.

We moved to a more spacious house in the heart of the city after a year and became neighbours of the famous Nairsan, who ran the Nair's restaurant on the Ginza in Tokyo. Nair had come to Tokyo for higher studies, but joined Netaji Subhash Chandra Bose as an interpreter and rose high in the Indian National Army.

Since Nehru did not give him an important position in India, he decided to live on in Tokyo and build an Indira Curry Powder empire. As a part of the Netaji legend, he lives on in the memory of freedom fighters. There was nothing Japanese about the second house we had in Tokyo except one room with the 'tatami' flooring made with a fibre giving a feeling of softness and comfort.

In Thimphu, we had no choice except to move into the house earmarked for the No.2 in the mission on top of a hill around which the entire temporary embassy complex was built. Another huge complex was under construction nearby for the Embassy, but we had left long before it was completed. Apparently, the road leading to the house was not black topped till president V.V. Giri, who was the father-in-law of my predecessor, A.N. Ram, decided to visit the house.

The road was black topped overnight under the orders of the king and we were the beneficiaries of it. But the house, built with mud and bamboo was ill-suited for the Bhutan climate as it had chinks around every window, which brought in cold air from the mountains. Heating the house with firewood was a challenge. Coming as we did from Tokyo, the housing situation appeared to us to be primitive. The compensation for low living was the high importance of the work in a country, which has remained a steadfast friend of India over the years.

Housing in Moscow for diplomats was the responsibility of a government organization called UPDK, comprising mainly of discredited Soviet diplomats. The organisation allotted houses for diplomats in designated buildings, affectionately called "diplomatic ghettos." I inherited my predecessor's flat in Lomonosovsky Prospect near the Moscow State University. It was spacious, well-appointed, and was refurbished for us before we arrived. But the problem in Moscow was that we could not get anything done in the house, except through the UPDK and any problem took very long to fix.

We took it for granted that the house was bugged and that all our activities were constantly watched. India was a great friend of the Soviet Union, but even the best friends were not exempted from spying. The elaborate sentry post outside kept a close watch on our movements and arranged escorts unobtrusively. They would emerge the moment we took the wrong route or went to the wrong housing complex, as they seemed to know better than us where we were supposed to have dinner. The constant surveillance was an irritation initially, but soon we began to enjoy the sense of security.

The test of good housing in Moscow was its capacity to keep it warm as the temperature outside could go down to minus 30 degrees Celsius. Our apartment was so well heated that we could maintain home temperature throughout. The problem arose only when we had to wade through the snow outside. Keeping the roads totally clear of the snow was an art Moscow had mastered out of sheer necessity.

Our Moscow home was frequented by Bollywood legends from Raj Kapoor to Mithun Chakravarty and Hema Malini to Shabana Azmi. No other country had such fondness for Indian stars, movies, and songs. Raj Kapoor's songs were on the lips of every generation of Soviets at that time. Many political leaders, including Prime Ministers came to Moscow during our time. From Kerala, the most popular visitor was K.P.S. Menon (Sr), who came every year during the Onam season. We celebrated Onam in our apartment whenever the Menons visited us. Ramu Kariat and C. Achuta Menon were also among our other distinguished visitors. We were quite nostalgic about our life in Moscow long after we left.

Published: July 25, 2017

Diplomats vs Journalists:
A Comparative Analysis

The professions of diplomats and journalists appear to be very distinct and specialised, particularly because diplomats are government servants and journalists operate individually or work for private enterprises. But when it comes to international affairs, diplomats and journalists are birds of a feather. Diplomats more or less perform the same functions, such as gathering information, reporting, analysing events and making policy recommendations.

The basic difference is that what the journalists write are in the public domain, widely read and debated, but our writings go into the archives, read or unread. How much of it goes into foreign policy formulation and implementation is a matter of conjecture.

When I am complimented today for eight books and a steady stream of op-eds in the last 15 years since I left the Service, I wonder how impressive it would be to publish the dispatches of 37 years on cabbages and kings from a dozen countries.

What distinguishes diplomats from journalists, however, is that we are not only reporters, but also actors at the same time. Diplomats deal with developments as they occur and then they also explain how they have responded to the events even before instructions were received from the Ministry. They will naturally highlight their own role in dealing with the situation, while the Ministry gets a different perspective from the journalists. If reports by journalists are supportive of the reports of diplomats, they gain credibility instantly. But where the perceptions differ, there will be much fact-checking and endless discussions.

Journalistic Diplomacy

Journalistic diplomacy has emerged as an important part of international relations. The knowledge of international relations among the common people is derived from journalists, who provide quick analyses of events around the globe. Very little of diplomatic initiatives reach the people directly. Prominent journalists also connect political leaders, who may not even talk to each other through interviews and columns.

Journalists like Christiane Amanpour and Fareed Zakaria have created more diplomatic tremors than the best of diplomats. Policies are often made more in the open than in closed chambers because of the prodding by prominent journalists. With the communications revolution, journalists steal a march over diplomats by shaping public opinion.

Mutually Beneficial Tie

A continuous dialogue with the journalists is, therefore helpful for diplomats, taking care that they do not misuse the information to create scoops. I have seen several senior journalists providing support to ambassadors, sharing their perceptions of the local scene, which they may know better. KV Narain in Tokyo, P Unnikrishnan in Moscow, Chidanand Rajghatta, KP Nayar, and Aziz Haniffa in Washington were helpful, though they remained vigilant against any failures of diplomats and did not hesitate to report aberrations. They were, in a way, sentinels of our embassies. There have been instances of diplomats, even heads of mission, coming to grief on account of reports in the press.

When It All Goes Wrong

Journalists, by nature, tend to look for sensational news and rush with reports, while diplomats prefer to take their time, analyse and figure out implications of events, particularly for India. The time lag often creates complications and the Ministry becomes impatient initially, but nonetheless appreciate the detailed reports. A celebrated incident in

Moscow was a sensational report by an Indian journalist that President Brezhnev "took leave of his responsibilities" one day in 1975. The story was carried around the globe and there was consternation all around.

Ambassador DP Dhar, who had his own sources of information dismissed the reports, but there were incessant questions from Delhi about the credibility of the report. I recall how Ambassador Dhar had to explain not only why the report was wrong, but also establishing how the story may have been planted on the journalist by interested parties within the Kremlin. Finally, it turned out that Brezhnev had just taken some leave and the report that he took leave of his responsibilities was a verbal inexactitude!

In crisis situations, where diplomats lose contacts with New Delhi, journalists become the only source of information for the Government and things get sensationalised. Our communications were cut by the military Government in Fiji for three days after a military coup (in 1987) directed against the Indian immigrants there and I had to act without instructions. My instinct was to remain neutral and stay in touch with the Governor General, who was still in place to find a solution. But, unknown to me, the press in India deplored the inactivity of the mission and when the communications opened, I was instructed to openly support the Indian community.

The rest is history. I was expelled and we had to close our mission. The Indian community was in distress over the trade sanctions imposed by us. If I had access to policy makers in Delhi at the right time, I would have tried to tone down the Indian reaction to retain our traditional role of reconciling the two communities. But the die was cast by press reports and it took us 10 years to re-establish diplomatic relations.

The interaction of diplomats with journalists in Delhi is much more delicate than in the missions abroad. The normal channel of communications is through the spokesperson of the Ministry, but senior journalists remain in touch with diplomats, with a view not only to get scoops, but also to warn them about the reaction of the public to international events. As the Special Assistant to the Foreign Secretary from 1978 to 1980, I got to know stalwarts like GK Reddy, Inder Malhotra, Subash Chakravarty, and various others around whom I had to be very vigilant about confidentiality of official matters in casual conversations with them.

As responsible journalists, they were themselves conscious of my position and probed the Foreign Secretary rather than me on policy. But I had to face an informal IB investigation about premature reporting of ambassadorial appointments in certain newspapers. Though this was not very sensitive, the PMO was curious as to how these reports appeared and I became a suspect, as I was the junior most person who handled the papers.

As it turned out, it was established that the ship of state generally leaked from the top and I was cleared. When I asked a senior journalist as to why he bothered to report ambassadorial postings prematurely, he said that it gave him credibility in the Ministry and the public eye if his reports happened to prove accurate!

These are mere snippets to show how closely the professions of diplomacy and journalism interact, often to the benefit of the state and sometimes against. But both support each other and work in tandem when important national issues are involved. Leading journalists who operate in Delhi may have plenty of examples to share with us.

Now that I am on the other side of the fence, dabbling in TV and print journalism, I myself have a better sense of the relationship of journalism and diplomacy as interconnected professions supporting each other.

Published: October 7, 2022

Diplomatic Perils: Navigating the Hazards of Service

Diplomatic life has never been a bed of roses. Diplomats are exposed to slander, arrest, expulsion, physical attack, and even assassination for no reason other than being the accredited representative of a country. We are also not unfamiliar with stories of punishment being meted out to the messenger for merely delivering the message.

The recent expulsion and counter-expulsion by the US and India of their diplomats may be linked in some way to their actions, but often the expulsion is a bolt from the blue. A classic case of expulsion was the ordering out of the Australian High Commissioner in tiny Nauru for claiming the expenditure incurred by the Australians in erecting a lamp outside the High Commissioner's residence as aid to Nauru. Nauru prides itself on never receiving any foreign assistance, and the Australian action was seen as a national insult, even though it is dependent on Australia for its very existence.

The pattern of expulsion of diplomats around the globe reveals that it is often the weaker partner in a bilateral relationship that resorts to expulsion of diplomats to make a point. When a country feels powerless to change the opinion of a foreign country, it feels tempted to use its prerogative to expel diplomats. Such actions can only make matters worse in the bilateral relationship. Eventually, the bilateral relationship is repaired, but the sudden dislocation and adverse publicity affect the diplomats concerned and their families.

One consequence of such expulsions is that those declared persona non grata, even for technical reasons, are unable to get back to those countries. In the case of specialists, the expertise lost is regrettable to both countries.

In the case of Devyani Khobragade (2014), the expulsion came as a solution rather than as a provocation. A quiet withdrawal of the officer in September last year would have been a better solution than the series of events that rocked bilateral relations. The reciprocal expulsion of the US diplomat, it turns out, was more than deserved, as he had not only conspired to evacuate Indian nationals to the US on a false pretext, but had made no secret of his hatred of India and Indians.

Gossip about the host country, its manners and its leaders are common in diplomatic cocktail circuits, but to put it on social media is to attract adverse comments, and worse, expulsion.

In our own diplomatic service, we have had several instances of quiet transfers and even expulsions in similar circumstances. Since these are not always publicised, statistics are not available. There have been the highly publicised reciprocal expulsions by India and Pakistan at lower levels. Reciprocal expulsions with friendly countries are done most discreetly and sometimes diplomats under orders of transfer are technically expelled to complete the quota.

The Chinese deliberately publicised the expulsion of two of our diplomats from China during the Cultural Revolution. One of them left the foreign service as a result of the trauma, while the other rose to the highest level in the service. Quiet advice by host governments and financial irregularities have brought back diplomats with little or no publicity.

They will only figure in whispers in South Block corridors. If there is any truth in the reports that the American ire was more against India than against Khobragade, the tragedy of her treatment and expulsion become all the more sad. The bilateral relationship will recover, while she will be deprived of the opportunity to live in the US with her husband and children even after retirement. The present sympathy and support extended to her by the government will diminish and she will have to resolve her problems herself.

Nobody senior from the ministry of external affairs showed up at the airport to receive her. She must have also been advised not to speak to the media to avoid contradictory pieces of information coming out.

The distinction sought to be made between official and private activities with regard to consular immunity is patently unfair. A diplomat lives abroad simply because she is assigned there and her life cannot be divided into private and public. Immunity and compensation should cover all activities, regardless of the venue and nature of the event involved.

Lack of public sympathy for diplomats, who are seen as privileged and spoiled, is universal. Even those who enjoy multiple supporting staff at public expense in India sneer at one domestic assistant that diplomats are permitted. Drivers and cars are provided only to the heads and posts abroad, while civil servants in India take such facilities for granted even at junior levels. Diplomats with no support systems abroad should be treated with the same concern as soldiers in the frontline.

India has had its share of martyr diplomats, some murdered, some brutally attacked, some insulted and expelled, and some quietly whisked away. India has reacted differently to different cases without a formula to nurse the survivors back to normalcy or to ensure that their careers are not affected adversely.

There is no grievance mechanism to deal with the trauma or to compensate the diplomats for their pain and suffering. Each finds their own way to contend with problems arising out of armed attacks or expulsions. No record is available in the public domain of the concessions or compensation given to the affected members of the service. Such information may be of some comfort for those who face danger in the line of duty.

The time has come to ensure that we reduce the number of diplomatic martyrs and have a formula to treat those affected with sympathy and magnanimity.

Published: January 21, 2014

Remembering KSP: India's First Diplomatic Martyr

Long before terrorism and violence became the hazards of diplomatic life worldwide, a young Indian diplomat fell victim to an assassin's bullet in his office in the High Commission of India in Ottawa, Canada, on April 19, 1961. Kokkat Sankara Pillai (KSP) of the first batch of the Indian Foreign Service (IFS) had arrived in Ottawa six months before as the Deputy High Commissioner after having served in Colombo, Port of Spain (Trinidad and Tobago), and New Delhi. Seeing an unexpected visitor at the door, KSP got up from his chair to shake hands with him and the assassin shot him point blank and killed him instantly. KSP did not know who the assassin was and why he shot him. The man walked undetected out of the High Commission and went to a police station and surrendered.

It turned out that the man had come earlier to the High Commission to seek a visa and a work permit for India. The Consular Assistant found out that he was blacklisted in India and stamped "Visa Applied For" (VAF) on his passport and returned it to him. When he discovered later that the VAF stamp amounted to denial of visa, he returned to the High Commission with a rifle to shoot the Assistant, but in his absence, shot KSP. Only a mad man could have committed such a heinous crime.

After expressing deep regret over "the death by shooting of one of our distinguished younger members of the Foreign Service," Prime Minister Jawaharlal Nehru stated in Parliament that "such facts as we have apparently indicate no motive except that some person who is rather demented". He also read out the message from the Indian High Commissioner in Ottawa, which stated: "We are all shocked at the tragic end of a brilliant officer. The shock will be terrible for his wife who is expecting a baby." The assailant, a Canadian of Yugoslav origin, Shani Ferizi, was tried and sent away to a mental asylum for several years.

Tragic News

I remember April 19, 1961, evening very well. We were at the Kakkanad Temple near my village home at Kayamkulam for a festival. The news came like a bolt from the blue that the most famous son of the area fell to an assassin's bullet in Ottawa. A pall of gloom descended on the gathering. For many people assembled at the temple, KSP was more than a diplomat, he was the eminent son of the Kokkat family and even more, the son-in-law of Ambalappattu Damodaran Asan, who was the lord and master of the whole area.

My father was most upset as he had known and admired KSP as a brilliant young lecturer in the University College, preparing for the UPSC examination, which placed him in the elite IFS in 1948. Those were the days when Pandit Nehru personally interviewed every candidate selected for the IFS and handpicked some like K R Narayanan and a few from princely families.

My father was so impressed with him that he wanted me to take him as a role model and aspire to join the IFS and become an ambassador one day. He would tell me how KSP would bring half a dozen books from the University College library every evening and return them the next day. Initially, I took it as an idle dream of a father, who thought that his son could move mountains and set it aside. I was only four years old when KSP joined the IFS!

Role Model

My father sent me to the University College, though he had cheaper options of sending me as a day scholar to one of the neighbouring towns. He insisted that I should literally follow KSP's footsteps. The sudden passing away of KSP, when I had just entered the University

College, shattered my father, but instead of abandoning his dream on that account, he made it his mission to make me fill the void left by KSP in the IFS and in our society. Fortunately, the gamble succeeded and I joined the IFS in 1967.

By then, KSP had become a legendary star on the diplomatic firmament of India and people spoke of him in awe and admiration. All who knew him as a colleague said what a big loss it was for India that he died in his prime.

Taking the story further, my younger brother, Seetharam, 12 years my junior, whose career guide was my academic and IFS journey, joined the IFS in 1980 and that too was because of the indirect influence of KSP. He had unknowingly created two diplomats for India.

My father's fascination for KSP went to the extent of accepting the hazards of the IFS. After a military coup in Fiji when I was High Commissioner there, someone fired a shot at the British High Commissioner's car and when my father heard the news on radio, he was sure that history had repeated itself till I called him.

Every achiever owes his/her success to the dreams of a father as Barack Obama stressed in his autobiography 'A Father's Dream' and the children who are able to fulfil that dream are fortunate. In my case, the story goes back to KSP who ignited the dream in my father. Throughout my career and after, a prayer of gratitude for him remained in my heart, like Ekalavya for Dronacharya. I welcome this opportunity to offer him my "gurudakshina".

The family of KSP invited friends and relatives to record their memories of him on the occasion of the 60th anniversary of his assassination. The rich literature generated on the occasion highlighted his sterling qualities and the gravity of the tragedy. But there was also a tinge of sorrow in one of the tributes that the Ministry of External Affairs (MEA) did not allow his body to be brought back even though his parents were alive. Further, the MEA informed the family that arrangements for their arrival in Mumbai should be made by them.

The Manager of the Central Government Guest House was the only official at the airport. "It is surprising that even after 14 years after Independence, an event of this magnitude catching the attention of the top-most administrators, including the Prime Minister of India, was treated so callously by the powers that be," he wrote.

A young IFS colleague discovered that the Annual Report of MEA for 1991-92 has recorded the tragic incident in a bland manner, without any expression of condolences or the loss sustained by the Ministry. It said, "The First Secretary, Shri. K Sankara Pillai, was shot dead while in office on 19 April, 1961, by one Shani Ferizi, a naturalised Canadian national of Yugoslav origin. The assailant was tried by a Canadian court and has been sent to a mental hospital." This insensitive entry of a tragic event is hurtful even now.

As India's Acting High Commissioner in British West Indies, KSP had presented 24 copies of the Bhagavad Gita to the Chief Justice of Port of Spain on February 8, 1956, for use in the Law Courts of the island. "The Bhagavad Gita that Pillai presented to the Chief Justice had several *slokas* that dwell on the inevitability of death and profound counsel to surviving family members and friends to cope with the grief," wrote K Vijayakrishnan in the *Madras Courier*. Even now, they must be finding solace in the words of Lord Krishna.

Published: April 28, 2020

Elite Diplomacy: Assessing the IFS Entry Criteria

Whether at the time of uncertainty over foreign policy before the Lok Sabha elections, or after Prime Minister Narendra Modi's reinvigoration of foreign policy, foreign service reforms have focussed on expansion, lateral entry of officers, and general dilution of the service's elitist character. But no attention is given to the fact that the Indian Foreign Service (IFS) is already a shadow of its former self, and does not appeal to civil service aspirants.

Most of those who join the IFS are those who did not qualify for the Indian Administrative Service (IAS). If IFS has to perform effectively, its elitism should be preserved, its attractiveness enhanced, and it should be brought to the centre of international relations as it was originally intended to be.

Partners in Foreign Policy

Nobody disputes the academic Amitabh Mattoo's argument that "India's foreign policy must be seen as a shared partnership across departments within the government of India, and academia and think tanks outside the traditional corridors of power." But the answer is not to merge the various partners while destroying the identity of each, but to allow each of them to develop in their own spheres and provide inputs to the Ministry of External Affairs (MEA).

No one seems to suggest that the IAS and Indian Police Service should be expanded through lateral entry to improve their performance.

The logic of this argument for the IFS seems to defy the need to preserve a specialised and professional foreign service. IFS, it should be noted, is no less professional or specialised than the other services.

Foreign policy is framed by various departments of the government, academia, think tanks and the media. They should all have their own defined roles in drafting foreign policy and must remain independent of each other. The MEA should not absorb them into a monolithic institution that has no diversity. Think tanks and the media should shape foreign policy from outside rather than from within the government. Is the right remedy to recruit media experts into the IFS in order to get their inputs on foreign policy? Would they fit into the bureaucratic milieu with its hierarchical and political constraints?

The usual lament is that the IFS is smaller (900 officers) than Chinese (4,000) and American (20,000) diplomatic services. This number is insufficient to meet the requirements of our 120 missions and 49 consulates. It is a fact that India started off with more missions than it could manage. It is not easy or politically correct to close down missions once they have begun; India, therefore, maintains them with a skeletal staff in marginal posts.

Its larger missions are well-endowed and it does not need to be envious of bigger missions maintained by the U.S. or China. The right mix of need and affordability must determine the numbers. The information revolution should lead to a reduction, rather than an increase, in the number of missions abroad. The size of the service should not by itself detract from the efficiency of diplomacy.

Those who argue for expansion and lateral entry seem unaware of the fact that in most of India's important missions, the IFS is in a minority, as it is staffed by officers of other Ministries. Many Ministries have preserved positions in the name of specialisation, but most of them are IAS officers, who may have been recruited specifically for assignments abroad. They may not even have gained experience in the concerned Ministries before being posted abroad. When there is such a practice, there should be no need to induct them into the foreign service itself.

Moreover, Ministries such as Commerce, Finance, Industry, Environment, Science and Technology, Atomic Energy, Space and the

Cabinet Secretariat have officers who specialise in various international negotiations. The missions are merely asked to service these delegations; even the heads of mission receive only a courtesy call and a cursory report. These officers' function, in effect, as diplomats, and they should be added to the strength of the IFS when functional requirements are taken into account. In other words, we have more diplomats in action internationally than the strength of the IFS indicates.

If officers who claim their seniority on the basis of their services in totally unrelated areas enter the IFS laterally, this would only dilute the service's quality. Past experience has shown that such entrants do not leave the service after a term or two, but remain to claim higher positions, spending their whole careers in diplomacy.

If there is a need to induct officers from outside, the procedures available should be used rather than induct those who had once spurned the IFS. The expectations of advancement in the IFS should not be belied. The MEA has already begun to recruit more officers every year, and that is the only way that such a specialised service should be expanded. If necessary, there are retired officers with proven ability, to fill the gaps without claiming high positions and salaries.

Reforms Needed

The suggestion here is not that reform of the diplomatic service is unnecessary. First, it should be made more attractive so that the best candidates are chosen. Like Jawaharlal Nehru did, the aptitude and readiness of the selected candidates should be ascertained before they are chosen. It is patently wrong to take in officers who qualify without English proficiency. No amount of language training after entry into the service would equip them for the rigours of the work abroad.

The recruitment of a large number of doctors and engineers is by no means negative, particularly in the context of the growth of technology. Some of India's best diplomats have come from the medical profession. But we should not lose sight of the recent trend in management to deploy more graduates of social sciences and humanities. Training should be constantly revamped to equip officers to deal with different regions.

The present practice of posting on an *ad hoc* basis should cease. Officers should develop expertise in countries and regions. Multilateral postings should not be meant for rotational blessings, but for those who have the talent and experience. Instead of rotating officers so that they retire comfortably, we should give them other incentives to stay in tough assignments. Those in difficult places must be compensated financially. Postings, an art at present, should be made a science, with a clear criterion. There should be no vagaries of political influence or acceptability.

The real shortage of officers is not in missions abroad, but at the headquarters. Many heads of divisions cover whole continents with very little support. Temporary deputation of officers from various disciplines can strengthen the headquarters till we have a sufficient number of IFS officers to return. The style of the present Prime Minister seems to be to rely on a small number of people to work intensively on issues; this method could be developed into a system.

The role and relevance of the policy planning and historical divisions are often exaggerated. Policy planning cannot be done in a vacuum; it is the territorial divisions which can help formulate policy. The historical division should be a service unit, helping policymakers, as it is functioning right now. Nothing prevents the Ministry from drawing on the experience and wisdom of people from other fields, without absorbing them into the Ministry.

Many youngsters who aspire to the IFS have begun to believe that it really does not call the shots in foreign policy-making, as decision-making has passed on to the technical Ministries. They believe that the MEA has been reduced to a post office. Unless this impression is removed by concrete action, real talent cannot be attracted to the Videsh Bhawan. Foreign services are elitist in most countries, and India should not fritter away its strengths by diluting its specialised and professional character.

Published: June 25, 2015

Rediscovering Purpose:
Celebrating IFS Day

Every service or institution has a foundation day, which becomes an annual event every year. The day is invariably celebrated with varying degrees of enthusiasm, depending on the mood of the leadership or its loyalty to the originator or to the set of events that founded the institution.

But the Indian Foreign Service, which was created by Independent India without a model from the colonial era, rarely celebrated an IFS Day, though old hands recall an odd cocktail party or a tea get-together hosted by the Foreign Secretary in certain years. Till recently, many IFS officers did not even know which day was celebrated as the IFS Day.

The absence of regular IFS Day celebrations had more to it than meets the eye. It was not simply a matter of forgetfulness or apathy to needless ceremonies and unnecessary expenditure.

The Ministry of External Affairs and individual officers entertain even inside the country, accustomed as they are to the representational grant as an instrument of winning friends and influencing people. More fundamentally, the IFS has been the least cohesive of services, because of the very nature of its composition and deployment.

The majority of missions are 'one man and a dog' missions and very few missions have more than a handful of IFS officers working together. In the past, it was not essential for officers to serve at headquarters, where officers have an opportunity to get to know each other.

But even at headquarters, the officers tend to meet only those in their divisions or their bosses, as there is no time for interaction outside their own sphere of work. Constant travel and demands from foreign missions leave them with little time to get to know their colleagues.

These factors turn IFS officers into single palm trees on islands known only to their families and close friends. They may serve in the IFS for nearly 40 years and still never set their eyes on some of their colleagues. They merely become names on the seniority list or bylines on papers and notes that get circulated.

The unique deployment pattern of the IFS makes its members insensitive to the needs and aspirations of their colleagues and gives them a sense that they must fend for themselves by fair or foul means, depending upon their sense of propriety and innate character. They tend to help themselves without concern for others as they rarely see for themselves the frustrations, they may have imposed on their colleagues by advancing their own careers, to the detriment of others.

Many of them have no qualms about utilising a chance opportunity of getting to know their political bosses to get a prize posting even beyond established norms. In the IFS, promotions are a science while postings are an art and, therefore, juniors in lower grades can do better than their seniors by securing plum postings.

The IFS has begun to look like a service without a soul, though it has a strong mind and a heart to serve its national purpose. Things have begun to change in the IFS, but not because of imaginative initiatives of the leadership or even the rather moribund IFS Association, which has to research its annals to find instances of heroic action like when a Foreign Secretary was fired unfairly or when a subsidiary service began to do better than the senior service.

A number of younger recruits have begun to search for the soul of the service, to give it cohesion and to give the members a sense of belonging and pride. The IFS Day celebrations on October 9, 2011 and a decision to mark the day every year are part of an 'IFS spring'.

The information revolution and the advent of social media played a part in the awakening. Unlike many senior people, who got their e-mails printed and dictated replies to their private secretaries even in the initial years of the 21st century, the young men and women who joined the service in recent years realised the potential of the new technology and began to put it to use to bring the service together.

It began with the establishment of a Google group to exchange ideas, to share strategic and literary creations or simply to circulate notable writings outside the circle. It soon developed into a lively, frank, creative, and useful forum as more and more members, young and old, signed up.

From the veterans in their 90's to the youngest recruits, everyone found a level ground to speak out, differ and even agree. From nuclear strategy to table manners, from policy directions to directions to settle back in India after living abroad, there was no topic untouched or unembellished.

It did not take long to move from discussions to formulation of ideas and setting up of data banks. How many in the IFS had written books. No one had a complete list, not to speak of a complete collection. How did the IFS Association originate and why is it stagnant? No one could answer.

Does the IFS have a foundation day, and if so, why is it not celebrated? Do the members get an identity card, and if not, why not? These questions and many others came up and we began to find answers. Nothing frivolous, indecent or undiplomatic came up. A group of young moderators remained vigilant against the least invasion of privacy or breach of secrecy without being accused of censorship.

In future, promotions and posting policies may come up. Right to information will be raised. More transparency may be imposed on the administration. Blue eyed boys and girls may become a rarity. Merit may be recognised and self-confidence may increase. The IFS may find its soul. India may become less of a reluctant superpower. The possibilities are endless.

"You have shown us the way," said Shyam Saran to the young diplomats, "creating a modern networking platform which has brought us all together, from all corners of the world, first as digital identities and now in flesh and blood."

The IFS spring may well have been an offshoot of the advent of public diplomacy. A ministry, which had prohibited the use of official computers for social media and witnessed a minister falling victim to the temptations of Twitter, today not only has multiple websites but also Facebook and Twitter accounts to project its policy.

This liberation led to the extension of social media to the needs of the service and its members. A paperless web of information now envelops the service and encourages greater interaction and action.

Like blogging turned hackers into commentators and literary geniuses, the New Media has turned retired bureaucrats, who were destined to baby sit their grandchildren in high-rise buildings in the United States, United Kingdom, Canada and Australia, into writers, thinkers and even poets. Making a contribution to the collective wisdom of the IFS is a compulsive instinct for the oldest and the youngest.

Technology alone cannot explain the difference that the young officers are making to the service. They are imaginative, ambitious, and motivated. Instead of accepting the status quo, they are seeking a change for the better. They are lighting candles instead of cursing the darkness. A poignant moment came when the dangers to diplomats in these days of international terrorism was dramatically displayed by Malathi Rao. She is the young widow of V Venkateswara Rao, a diplomat who lost his life in Kabul. But she spoke not in sorrow, but with pride of the IFS, which stood by her in her hour of tragedy.

In contrast, in an earlier era, young widows had complained bitterly that the service had left them high and dry. IFS has had its share of casualties in untimely deaths and grievous injuries, which have remained uncompensated and unacknowledged.

Those affected nurse their injuries in body and spirit, taking them in their stride. "We recall those who have paid a price, some with their lives, some with serious injuries. Should not gate number 4 have a list of names on display," asks Leela K Ponappa.

The IFS spring, alas, is still in its dawn and it is yet to infect sections of the old and the young. The attendance at the IFS Day event could have been better, particularly of retired officers who were in town.

Veterans like Pammi Sahay, Shyam Saran and Shivshankar Menon came and spoke in praise of the initiative and the initiators. Foreign Secretary Ranjan Mathai was away in Sri Lanka.

But with better planning and certainty of an event on every October 9, attendance may be better in the future years. The administration and the association may well be less reluctant to lend a helping hand. The IFS spring must infect the seniors even if their stakes in the service diminish over the years.

Published: October 17, 2011

Navigating the Blue Economy: India's Diplomatic Preparation

Diplomats transform themselves into rock stars when the areas they specialise in assume exceptional prominence. Once upon a time, decolonisation was on top of the UN agenda, but today, the stars of that era are hardly remembered. Then came disarmament.

Human rights come alive whenever there's a spectacular violation. The environment has taken the pride of place since the Rio conference of 1992 and those who have played a role in climate change were the stars in Paris. Their future success lies in identifying the next sunrise issue and developing expertise on it.

Addressing a group of mid-level diplomats, on the verge of becoming ambassadors at the Foreign Service Institute in New Delhi, this writer advised them to start specialising in the "Blue Economy", the newest candidate for stardom in coming years. The oceans, which have always been a source of livelihood, trade, colonialism, storms and piracy, present opportunities and challenges.

Professionals connected with the oceans, including the negotiators of the UN Convention on the Law of the Sea (UNCLOS), have been prominent since the 1980s. The traditional blue-water economy has been in operation and diplomats have been playing a role in it.

The new blue economy, introduced by Gunter Pauli in his 2010 book, *The Blue Economy: 10 Years, 100 Innovations, 100 Million Jobs,* has opened new avenues for bilateral and multilateral work, Involving the environment, energy, defence and food production. The blue economy, as distinct from the blue-water economy, encompasses in it the "green economy", with focus on the environment, and the "ocean economy" or "coastal economy", with its emphasis on complementarities among coastal and island states for sustenance and sustainable development.

The newly set up Blue Economy Strategic Thought Forum India, under the auspices of the National Maritime Foundation, has already envisaged the multiple ways in which the blue economy will influence human activities. It defines the blue economy as "marine-based economic development that leads to improved human wellbeing and social equity, while significantly reducing environmental risks and ecological scarcities".

The central principle of the blue economy is the idea of cascading nutrients and energy the way ecosystems do. Cascading energy and nutrients lead to sustainability by reducing or eliminating inputs, such as energy, and eliminating waste and its cost, not just as pollution, but also as an efficient use of materials. The book contains fascinating innovations to open a new world of production and lifestyle.

These game-changing ideas will entice entrepreneurs. Surprisingly, these innovations have the potential to increase rather than shed jobs, as emulating natural systems will mean the deployment of humans rather than machines. Ideas like eliminating air in freezing water, use of food-grade ingredients as fire retardants, growing mushrooms with coffee shop waste, silk as a replacement of titanium, electricity generated by walking and talking, etc, are mind-boggling.

Maritime diplomacy had its heyday back in the 1980s, with the sensational discovery of manganese nodules and cobalt crusts on the ocean floor. The euphoria over marine mining led to the establishment of the International Seabed Authority. The UNCLOS, the "constitution of the seas", which came into force in 1994, became the basis for the legal rights for mining in the open sea.

The interest in seabed mining flagged because of escalating costs, but it's being revived on account of the demand for minerals and metals in industrial development, particularly in China, Japan and India.

The Indian Ocean has been a fulcrum of Indian diplomacy since Independence. During the Cold War, India was extremely active in the

UN Ad hoc Committee on the Indian Ocean in its bid to keep the Indian Ocean a Zone of Peace, which, in essence, meant keeping the Indian Ocean free of great-power rivalry.

But the littoral and hinterland states differed on the meaning of the zone. Many sought the presence of external powers to counter India's growing strength. But even at that time, cooperation for ocean resources was a priority.

Today, India is working with the states in the Indian Ocean region and others to strengthen security and economic cooperation. The re-emergence of piracy has added a new dimension. The new focus on the Asia-Pacific highlights the security and economic dimensions. The US rebalancing of forces and counter-measures by China have created a new cold war. New partnerships are in the making in the Asia-Pacific, seeking Indian participation by competing powers. The blue waters of the Indian Ocean have become a new theatre of tension.

The Chinese initiative—one belt, one road (OBOR)—is a $150 billion grandiose development strategy and framework for China to push for a bigger role in global affairs and to increase its exports. Some see it as an opportunity for India, others as a challenge. The choice has to be made cautiously, balancing our security concerns about an expanding China with economic engagement.

Given the history of Sino-Indian relations, it's difficult to look at OBOR as a benign initiative. But it will be difficult to stay out of a new global highway linking Asia with Europe. The blue-water economy will become central to the development of the entire region. Our competition with China is likely to be exacerbated by the competition for a piece of the blue economy, as evidenced in Bangladesh.

Both the traditional blue-water economy and the new blue economy are important for India's sustainable development. The imperatives of cooperation and the need for adept diplomacy are evident. Prime Minister Narendra Modi endorsed the blue economy during his visit to Seychelles, Mauritius, and Sri Lanka. The joint statement with Mauritius envisages close cooperation in vital areas.

The importance of regional organisations has increased in the context of the blue economy. PM Modi spoke of the blue economy to

SAARC leaders. In September 2015, the Indian Ocean Rim Association (IORA) hosted the first Ministerial Blue Economy Conference and identified priorities. Goal 14 of the UN's Sustainable Development Goals (SDGs)—"Conserve and sustainably use the oceans, seas and marine resources for sustainable development"—makes detailed references to the reduction of marine pollution, conservation of coastal and marine areas and regulated fish harvest. The convergences in the IORA and SDG agendas have to be developed into action.

India's neighbourhood policy assumes primary importance in light of the blue economy. India can profitably integrate its ongoing programmes like 'Make in India', smart cities, skill development. and self-reliance in defence as part of the 'Atmanirbar Bharat' (Self-Reliant India) initiative. Delhi's forthcoming chairmanship of the BRICS will offer a splendid opportunity to highlight the cooperation needed for the blue economy.

Diplomats aspiring to a "blue diplomacy" should begin to grasp the immense possibilities of the blue economy. Although the nodal ministry will be the prime mover, it will be diplomats in coastal and island countries and with the UN, IORA, and SAARC, who will have to operationalise it. The time to start training a diplomatic cadre is now.

Published: February 11, 2016

Lateral Entry Debate: Opening Doors to New Talent

The plan for lateral entry was hatched in a New York think-tank and was embraced by vested interests in India. The thrust of the study was that India did not have enough diplomats to handle the responsibilities of the 21st century.

That the ministry of external affairs (MEA) will soon start recruiting academics and private-sector candidates is no breaking news. The ministry's doors have been so wide open all these years that IFS officers are now a minority in the MEA and our missions abroad.

Out of a total of 4,024 posts, IFS officers occupy only 917. The rest are from the IFS (B), IAS, IPS, and other services, such as the Interpreters' Cadre and the Legal and Treaties Cadre. Our passport operations are handled by a separate cadre altogether. The MEA itself has more than 70 deputationists in the territorial divisions doing the work that was earlier done by the IFS.

The present move is not opening doors but breaking walls, which will endanger the structure itself. A new method of recruitment is being devised outside the UPSC to bring in short-term experts, who are not likely to leave. The move "runs the risk of degenerating into an uncontrollable spoils system", as observed by a serving IAS officer.

The plan for lateral entry into the IFS was hatched in a New York think-tank and was embraced by vested interests in India. The thrust of the study was that India did not have enough diplomats to handle the responsibilities of the 21st century and, therefore, there was a need to recruit people from outside. The point was not about quality but numbers. "Growth in girth is the road to Nirvana," according to these analysts, as pointed out by a former foreign secretary.

The optimum size of our foreign service should not be determined by comparing it to China, Russia, or the US. Indian diplomacy has never suffered because of a dearth of people. It will be uneconomical to match the numbers of richer countries.

India has been wary of expanding the foreign service beyond a point for quality and economy-related reasons. When a Foreign Secretary tried to increase recruitment in 1979, he was accused of extravagance. A second deputy permanent representative sent to our mission to the UN in 1994 was found to be a luxury we could ill afford. If 4,500 IAS officers can manage the whole country, would 900 IFS officers not be enough to man our missions?

Another argument for "opening the doors" is the alleged shortage of research in the MEA. The IT revolution has totally transformed the way diplomats' function. Even while engaged in fire-fighting, it's possible for officers to access information, analyses and insights. Today's diplomats need to multi-task as researchers, analysts, decision-makers and draftsmen.

Political acumen, a general understanding of geopolitical realities and instinct, grown out of years of training and experience in the field, are important factors. If research and access to information were enough, countries like the US would have made no mistakes in foreign policy.

The MEA has also experimented with different structures for long-term and short-term policy planning. The limitations of long-term planning have been in evidence throughout history. What the territorial divisions need is a bridge between themselves and the political masters, a role normally performed by the foreign secretary. A policy-planning division in parallel with the territorial divisions has not been effective. A high-level chairman of a policy-planning body was found eminently beneficial in the past.

The value of the contributions made to foreign policymaking by other ministries, think-tanks, universities, and the media are beyond question. Some of their advice has been decisive in changing the course of policy. But it is best if they operate within their own domains rather than become part of the MEA. The government benefits from multiple entities that study issues and make recommendations. Most democracies rely on multiple agencies and forums for inputs into foreign policy.

The administrative complexities of recruitment into the MEA will also be formidable. The initiative to recruit more IFS officers through the UPSC, taken a few years ago, will be enough to make up for the shortage. By reducing routine training programmes, officers could be deployed more rapidly with quicker promotions. Such a measure would also make the IFS more attractive to young people.

Let the doors of the MEA remain open, but let them not be blown away.

Published: July 11, 2015

Diplomatic Pawns: The Challenge of International Disputes

Among the many hazards that diplomats face today, the most ancient one is expulsion, also known as declaration of a diplomat as persona non grata. It is the most effective bloodless punishment as the person concerned is removed lock, stock, and barrel from the scene, never to return. The diplomat concerned may not be guilty of omission or commission or even aware of the reason why he is being expelled. He becomes a mere pawn in international disputes or he may even be a victim of a symbolic protest or a reciprocal action.

The Russia Example

Russia now, like the erstwhile Soviet Union, may well be the country whose diplomats have perhaps suffered the largest number of expulsions. The recent coordinated expulsion of over 100 Russian diplomats by more than 20 countries is huge even by the standards of the coldest days of the Cold War.

Basically, it was an act of solidarity by the U.S., the European Union, and some others with the U.K. after an alleged attempt by Russia to murder a former Russian spy and his daughter. Russia had denied any hand in the attempted murder, but responded with expulsions symmetrically in accordance with diplomatic practice.

Generally, the countries involved do not go beyond these diplomatic gestures. Slowly and gradually, the vacant posts in the Russian embassies will be filled and diplomats will return to their posts in Moscow.

Austria did not join some of the other EU members to expel Russian diplomats because it felt that communication channels should be kept open, particularly during crisis. The Austrian Foreign Minister recalled the several occasions when Austria had organised historic meetings which paved the way for peace and understanding. Russia welcomed the Austrian position and even expressed willingness to hold talks on the issue of suspected poisoning of the former spy. But for the U.K., the Austrian decision was unfriendly as it revealed the chinks in the European armour.

Russia gloated over the fact that a majority of nations in the world, including China and India, wanted concrete evidence about Russian complicity. It was also a relief for them that U.S. President Donald Trump did not tweet about Russian involvement even though he ordered the expulsion of 60 Russian diplomats.

Russia has a tradition of assigning expelled diplomats to an agency called the UPDK, which takes care of the needs of diplomats posted in Moscow. Diplomats cannot function in Moscow without the UPDK which alone can maintain diplomatic residences. You cannot even drive a nail on the wall without the permission of the UPDK. Domestic staff have to be appointed by it and the same person will come back even if sacked by the diplomat. The Russians at the agency are good diplomats and they seem to have the capacity to relax rules to please Ambassadors.

India's Stand

India takes recourse to expulsion of diplomats only in extreme circumstances when it has clear evidence of wrongdoing. When it expels diplomats, it does expect reciprocal action and accepts it as a necessary evil. India has expelled Soviet diplomats even during the heyday of India-Soviet friendship.

In retaliation, Moscow had technically expelled Indian diplomats, who were already under orders of transfer from Moscow. In a rare case, one of India's diplomats who was expelled in this manner was allowed to visit Moscow as a member of the delegation accompanying the Prime Minister of India. This violation of the code of conduct was later explained as a conscious decision not to hurt India-Soviet relations.

I have the dubious distinction of being the only Indian Head of Mission to be expelled. We invited the expulsion after a military coup in Fiji ousted a Fiji-Indian dominated government in 1987 and changed the Constitution which effectively disenfranchised Fiji Indians.

India refused to recognise the military government, imposed sanctions, and got Fiji thrown out of the Commonwealth. Even in the face of such a position, I was allowed to remain in Fiji for two years before they asked me to leave in 72 hours. I left in 48 hours, saying that I would like to use the remaining 24 hours to go back on a holiday. As it happened, the wheel came full circle and I was invited back to Fiji after 25 years.

Expulsion of diplomats is very often like shooting the messenger for the message. In modern times, expelling diplomats has become the instrument of weak nations to show displeasure to stronger ones even at the risk of facing retribution. Nauru, a little island nation in the Pacific, once expelled the only resident envoy of Australia over a petty quarrel, but restored its vital link in a short time.

The expulsion of Russian diplomats should be seen as part of the emergence of a new Cold War, resulting from the assertive policies of Russian President Vladimir Putin and the aggressive posture of Mr. Trump and his love-hate relationship with Russia. Among the many diplomatic devices which countries possess to express their outrage, expulsion is the least disruptive, though it plays havoc with the lives of diplomats and their families.

Published: April 3, 2018

J. ENVIRONMENT

NET ZERO EMISSIONS —
A MIRAGE

COP28: A Turning Point for Fossil Fuels

Gathering in Dubai, the dazzling city built on oil wealth, it was unrealistic for the 7000 delegates, including 154 world leaders, to expect that COP28 (Conference of Parties) would mark the beginning of the end of fossil fuels as the primary source of energy in the future.

Therefore, like in most conclaves on environment and development, Dubai also created its own "language" to match the expectation with reality. By inventing the idea of transition, rather than phasing out, and stressing the urgent need to develop alternate sources such as renewable and nuclear energy, it is clear that fossil fuels will continue to energise the world as long as they are available in the womb of the earth. As a funny cartoon proclaimed, for oil-producing countries, the best way to phase out fossil fuels is to extract them and put them to use.

Trajectory of Fossil Fuels Debate

The final deal struck by the President of COP28, Sultan Ahmed Al Jaber, after extending the conference for several hours, was the call for a transition away from fossil fuels, after a previous proposal met heated and widespread backlash. "With an unprecedented reference to transitioning away from all fossil fuels, the UAE Consensus is delivering a paradigm shift that has the potential to redefine our economies," the President said.

The proposal announced in the early morning of 13 December and stated in the draft decision entitled "First Global Stocktake" called for "transitioning away from fossil fuels in energy systems, in a just, orderly and equitable manner, accelerating action in this critical decade, so as to achieve net zero by 2050 in keeping with the science."

A global goal to triple renewables and double energy efficiency, declarations on agriculture, food, healthcare, along with more oil and gas companies stepping up for the first time on methane and emissions were the other elements in the package. In effect, the proposal did not mandate an absolute phase out of hydrocarbons. This is the most nuanced and caveated statement he could have produced in the circumstances.

The OPEC (Organisation of the Petroleum Exporting Countries) nations have come a long way from the position they took at COP1 in Berlin in 1995, when they walked out of the Group of 77 as they could not support any alternative to fossil fuels. They implied that the only answer to climate change was adaptation and not mitigation.

COP28 marked a major change, brought about by years of negotiations and the realisation that the world is not divisible into different categories in facing the impending disaster of climate change. The whole world has to swim or sink together. To that extent, the pragmatism and the spirit of cooperation reflected in the decisions of COP28 are laudable.

The debate on fossil fuels reflected the debate at COP26 in Glasgow on a 'phase out' of the use of coal which ended with the acceptance of a 'phase down' at the last moment. It was argued in Dubai that a phase out commitment would likely have required a shift away from fossil fuels until their use is eliminated, while a phase down agreement would have indicated a reduction in their use—but not an absolute end.

Many may have argued that coal and fossil fuels are like chalk and cheese, which cannot be compared. The new formulation satisfied governments, but not young activists, one of whom interrupted a Presidency event while holding a sign that read "End fossil fuels, save our planet and our future." Greta Thornburg, if she was there, would have shouted, "Prove us wrong!"

The final compromise on fossil fuels made it easy for the conference to deflect other controversies. Scores of governments insisted on strong language to signal an eventual end to the fossil fuel era over protests by the members of OPEC and its allies.

"It is the first time that the world unites around such a clear text on the need to transition away from fossil fuels. It has been the elephant in the room. At last, we addressed it head on," said a European delegate. It is a mystery that the US and other western countries championed phasing out of fossil fuels as such a measure would affect them equally. The best explanation is that it was play-acting on their part to concede on such an issue in their effort to safeguard their emission levels.

Why COP28 is being Characterised as Pathbreaking?

John Kerry, the US climate envoy maintained that some fossil fuels may have to be phased out while employing carbon capture technology to reach net zero climate targets by mid-century, but appeared pleased with the transition idea promoted by OPEC countries. Some others like Russia accepted the decision as there was no other alternative. The unstated conclusion was that eventually, only a technological solution like carbon capture will alter climate change. In the interim, humanity should continue to find effective measures to alleviate the adverse effects of climate change.

As for the rest of the agenda of COP28, the global Stocktake completed in September this year concluded that the world was not on track in meeting the Paris Agreement goals. The findings of the United Nations indicated that action set out in countries' National Declared Commitments would increase by 8.8 per cent over 2020 levels by 2030.

The COP expects that the Governments will come up with a road map to accelerate climate action. A number of measures to assist the achievement of the objectives of the Paris Agreement have been outlined in the Joint Statement to maximise synergies among member states, avoid duplication of efforts, and ensure efficient use of collective resources.

The announcement of the operationalisation of the Loss and Damage Fund amounting to USD 700 million to help vulnerable countries recover from climate related damage prompted a standing ovation from the delegates. Hopes were also raised that the fund would be enhanced in future years. The historic agreement was hailed as a welcome breakthrough and one that helped to clear the way for negotiators on other issues.

On the crucial issue of funding, the glad tidings of the Green Climate Fund receiving additional pledges from six countries was a morale booster. The total pledges now stand at a record USD 12.8 billion from 31 countries with further pledges promised.

In addition, 118 governments have committed resources to enhance the capacity for renewable energy. As many as 22 countries have pledged to triple global nuclear energy capacity by 2030, a move to reduce reliance on fossil fuels. These are hopeful signs of tangible progress towards mitigation of climate change.

The young people who attended the conference like my climate activist granddaughter, Durga Sreenivasan, a Robertson Scholar at the Duke University, who conducted policy workshops at the conference, feel optimistic that "the world will make the necessary changes needed for a liveable planet, especially given the long-term benefits of action such as phasing out of fossils and operationalising the Loss and Damage Fund."

COP28 is being characterised as path-breaking as it considered fossil fuels in the context of global warming for the first time and opened the way for a possible transition to alternate forms of energy. But the realisation that fossil fuels will remain the main source of energy for a long time is also embedded in the decisions. The process of bringing the dreams of Rio (1992) into reality will continue its meandering and hazardous course in the years to come.

Published: December 15, 2023

COP26: Phasing Down of Coal
as Part of Environmental Action

If all the trees that went into the millions of pages of documents were saved, if all the aviation fuel spent on jetting off delegates around the world many times over was not burnt out, if the conspicuous consumption in the luxury hotels and conference halls were avoided, and if the millions of tonnes of hot air emitted by official delegates and environmental activists in conferences since 1972 to 2021 had been saved, the global warming today could have been kept below 1.5 degree Celsius.

Or so it seems to me, having been part of the exercise from the Rio Conference of 1992 and the following Conference of Parties and other consultations, roundtables, and seminars till 1997 with the objective of confining global warming to scientifically determined reasonable levels. The irony is that the unique consensus reached at the Rio Conference only became more and more diluted after every meeting of the Conference of Parties.

The story of climate change negotiations goes back to the Stockholm meeting on the environment. Though all the world leaders were invited, the only Prime Minister who attended was Indira Gandhi, who sensed a conspiracy by the developed countries to deny economic development to poorer countries in the name of protection of the environment.

As expected, the rich countries urged the others not to make the mistakes they themselves made at the time of the Industrial Revolution, and give attention to the environment. Gandhi countered this move by asserting the right of the poor countries by stressing that "poverty is the worst polluter" and that "polluters must pay" for measures to balance the environment and development.

Her words at that time have been reverberating in the conference halls since then in an effort to awaken the conscience of the rich nations. The principles of equity adopted in Rio were in response to the mantra Gandhi had given to the developing world.

The Framework Convention on Climate Change (FCCC) was literally a dream come true in terms of the principles of equity in development and the "common, but differentiated responsibilities" to deal with climate change. The Indian delegation was hailed as movers and shakers by the likes of then Senator Al Gore.

The promises and pledges made there raised the hope that a formula had been found to combat climate change by all within their respective capacities and capabilities and the funding for the incremental costs of environment-friendly technology was promised by the rich to the poor, not as charity, but as a historic responsibility.

When the scene shifted to the hard reality of New York politics, the Rio spirit began to wither away and most of the concepts were reopened, leading to an erosion of the consensus of 1992. The industrial interests of the developed nations came into play and the Western delegations began questioning the emissions of India, China, and Brazil, demanding that those countries should also accept mandatory cuts. By the time we reached COP1 in 1995 in Berlin, pressure mounted on us to accept mandatory cuts.

But with a young and inexperienced Environment Minister of Germany, Angela Merkel, who wanted the conference to succeed for her own sake, pushed for a consensus on the basis of Rio and the situation was saved till it was incorporated in the Kyoto Protocol, which eventually failed to take off because the US and others refused to accept it.

Faced with a total deadlock in climate action, China and the US cooked up "voluntary cut for all" as a compromise and despite its rejection by most of the developing countries in Copenhagen, India joined in to break the impasse. The Paris Agreement, an offshoot of

Copenhagen, was hailed as a great achievement, knowing well at that time itself that the objective of limiting global temperature to 1.5 degree Celsius will not be met, and the promised funding will not materialise.

President Donald Trump was forthright in declaring Paris a hoax, and President Joe Biden decided to make a clean break with Paris to move in naming net zero emission years by all countries, and climate action plan 3.0 was born.

The debate throughout the journey from Rio to Glasgow remained unchanged in its essentials. The developing countries battled to retain the Rio principles, while the developed countries tried to get as far from them as possible.

The hot air generated kept contributing to global warming as different formulae were tried out. The Intergovernmental Panel on Climate Change (IPCC), the scientific body responsible to monitor climate change, sounded the alarm bells several times to no avail except to hold more meetings, and even that was not possible because of the pandemic.

The meeting of G20 in Rome and COP26 in Glasgow raised many hopes as several countries had already declared their own net zero emission target years, but the International Energy Agency quickly calculated that even if all the pledges and programmes were to be implemented, the global temperature will still be above 2.4 degree Celsius by 2100.

But that did not stop the speeches and pledges as designation of net zero emission years was an easy way to take credit for setting targets. The new arrangement helped countries to declare their intentions, however conditional they were.

India, which had opposed the idea of designating years, gave in by declaring that it will also achieve net zero emissions by 2070. Moreover, India announced that it would significantly reduce emissions by 2030 and increase its renewable energy sources to gradually replace fossil fuels. The anti-climax came when the whole thing was made conditional to the availability of $1 trillion for the developing countries to replace fossil fuels required for development.

Clearly, the hot air generated for nearly two weeks, taking extra time to fix the final text was not a waste because the focus shifted from collective, coordinated efforts to individual initiatives by countries to battle climate change.

India had always maintained that it will do what it can to reduce the carbon intensity of its economy, but to reach the targets set globally, the developed countries should change their lifestyle, generate savings, and transfer technology and funds to the developing countries. In other words, the luxury emissions of the developed countries should be reduced so that the survival emissions of developing countries should continue without jeopardising the future of mankind.

The way the Glasgow meet ended in extra time by turning the clock back to find a final compromise was typical of the hot air diplomacy, which has become fashionable at the UN. The UN has a growing agenda, but one or two of the agenda items assume prominence. It was decolonisation in the early years, then it became disarmament, then equitable economic development, then human rights, and now, the environment. The pandemic should have been the preoccupation as it is a greater and more urgent existential threat to humanity, except for China blocking Security Council action on it.

India had made it very clear that phasing out of coal and other fossil fuels cannot be envisaged at this time, but the British president of the Conference with an Indian name pressed for it hard till the proverbial Indian wisdom prevailed at the end by replacing "phase out" with an archaic "phase down", which does not make any difference in practice.

It was diplomacy and not science that prevailed at the end as science demands the impossible, while diplomacy deals with the art of the possible. The hope, however, is that science will find away to capture greenhouse gases and dispose them off, and diplomats will find another cause to fight for in global conferences.

Published: November 19, 2021

Beyond Paris: Assessing the Paris Agreement

Nothing that U.S. President Donald Trump touched turned into gold, except perhaps his business empire, but ironically he was the alchemist who turned the Paris Agreement, once considered the product of a conspiracy hatched by the U.S. and China to change the course of negotiations away from the Rio Declaration (1992) and the Kyoto Protocol (1997), into a holy grail worth pursuing.

Many developing countries, including India, which hesitated to sign the Agreement because it had exempted developed countries from their mandatory obligations to reduce greenhouse gas emissions, turned into its devout supporters the moment Mr. Trump denounced it as a hoax and announced his decision to withdraw from it. Today, the Paris Agreement is deemed as the panacea for all environmental ills when the truth is that it is a repudiation of the principles of "common but differentiated responsibilities" and "the polluter must pay".

Mr. Trump was not the only one who called the Paris Agreement a hoax. Many scientists and environmentalists expressed deep disappointment when it was adopted, as the national and international actions envisaged under it were far below the optimum levels. They did not add up to limiting the rise of global temperature to below 2°C, the minimum necessary to save the globe from disastrous consequences. It merely opened a new path to protect the lifestyles of industrialised nations by denying the developing countries their right to development.

Efforts Over the Years

The most hopeful time for global cooperation in protection of the planet was between the time of the Stockholm Conference (1972) and Rio Conference (1992). That was when mounting scientific evidence about the role of anthropogenic emissions in global warming led to political initiatives to harmonise development and environment. Former Prime Minister Indira Gandhi's resounding address at Stockholm declaring poverty as the worst polluter reverberated in many conference halls. The historic consensus in Rio led to the adoption of the UN Framework on Climate Change (UNFCC), which was a model global instrument balancing the right to development of the developing countries and the obligations of the developed countries.

A distinction was made between the "luxury emissions" of the developed countries, which were reduced mandatorily, and the "survival emissions" , which were allowed to increase. Moreover, a huge financial package was approved to develop environment-friendly technologies in developing countries.

But by the time the Conference of Parties held in Berlin in 1955, the developed countries had backed off from their commitments. They made a determined effort to impose mandatory cuts on developing countries. Though the G-77 was split, we managed to maintain the Rio principles with the assistance of the Chairperson, Angela Merkel.

The Kyoto Protocol enshrined the Rio principles. It fixed emission targets for developed countries and a complex set of provisions was included to satisfy their interests. But it was never ratified by the U.S. Congress and the U.S. withdrew its support in 2001.

The end of the Kyoto Protocol and the abandonment of the spirit of the Rio principles were reflected in the Copenhagen Accords (2009), engineered by the U.S. and China and sold to some key countries including India on the argument that a global climate action plan would be possible only if all reductions of the greenhouse gases were made voluntary.

The basic terms of the Copenhagen Accord were brokered directly by a handful of key country leaders including the U.S., China, India, and

Brazil on the final day of the conference. It took another full day of tense negotiations to arrive at a procedural compromise allowing the deal to be formalised over the bitter objections of a few governments. There was a virtual revolt by the developing countries, but the Paris Agreement was virtually born in Copenhagen, and adopted later in 2015.

A Fundamental Change

The Paris Agreement marked a fundamental change in the principles of Rio and for the first time, brought all nations into a common cause to undertake ambitious efforts to combat climate change. It requires all parties to put forward their best efforts through nationally determined contributions (NDCs) and to strengthen these efforts in the years ahead. This includes all parties to report regularly on their emissions and on their implementation efforts.

The Paris Agreement moved away from the principle of common but differentiated responsibilities and all countries were placed on an equal footing by making reduction of greenhouse gas emissions voluntary. The NDCs so far submitted will not result in the desired objective of limiting increase of global warming to below 2°C.

The Paris Agreement requires that all countries—rich, poor, developed, and developing—slash greenhouse gas emissions. But no language is included on the commitments the countries should make. Nations can voluntarily set their emissions targets and incur no penalties for falling short of their targets. It sets forth a requirement for countries to announce their next round of targets every five years, but does not include a specific requirement to achieve them.

The scientific community has already rejected the Paris Agreement as a solution. Further temperature rise, even of 1.5°C, may result in catastrophic and irreversible changes. At 1.5°C, 70-90 percent of coral reefs across the world would die. At 2°C, none would be left. Even a 1°C hotter planet is not a steady state, says a report of the Intergovernmental Panel on Climate Change (IPCC).

The techno-optimism that the wonders of technology will be able to find answers to the dilemma we face without our having to alter our patterns of living is a delusion. The IPCC report acknowledges that "the pathways to avoiding an even hotter world would require a swift and complete transformation not just of the global economy but of society too". This will only be possible if the world rejects nationalism and parochialism and adopts collaborative responses to the crisis. The Paris Agreement falls short of that imperative.

U.S. President-elect Joe Biden has declared that the U.S. will have the most progressive position on climate change in the nation's history. He has already laid out a clean energy and infrastructure plan, a commitment to return to the Paris Agreement, and a goal of net-zero emissions by 2050.

The appointment of former Secretary of State John Kerry as Climate Change Envoy is a clear indication of the importance that Mr. Biden attaches to addressing global warming issues. Having been one of the architects of the Paris Agreement, Mr. Kerry must be aware of its merits and deficiencies.

It is hoped that he will also be aware of the development imperatives of the developing nations. If Mr. Kerry and Mr. Biden insist on matching cuts by the developing countries as a conditionality to return to the Paris Agreement, the whole debate of equity and climate justice will emerge, with India and the U.S. on opposing sides.

Published: November 29, 2020

K. COVID-19

OVERCOMING AN
EXISTENTIAL THREAT

Global Pandemic Pact:
Toward a Unified Response

In an ideal world, the UN Security Council should have met as soon as Covid-19 was declared a pandemic, treat it as the greatest threat to international peace and security, and adopt a resolution to create a structure for urgent international cooperation under Chapter VII of the UN Charter, giving it the responsibility to co-ordinate relief by way of supplies, regulate the use of available resources and to develop vaccines and medicines, which did not exist.

With the traditional proviso for consent of the parties concerned to operate in their own territories, a voluntary "Health Keeping Force" wearing red berets in place of the blue berets of the Peace Keeping Force should have been formed to give assistance, gather data, and educating the population.

The entire machinery of the United Nations, including the specialised agencies, should have sprung into action. But the Security Council was paralysed because of China, which carried the burden of the responsibility for creating the virus, or at least not alerting the world to the lethality of the pandemic they had experienced.

The inaction of the Security Council was particularly deplorable because at the time of epidemics like HIV/AIDS, Ebola and SARS, the entire UN machinery was deployed effectively and the situation was brought under control. This demonstrated the fundamental flaw of the UN, which is that the power of the veto gives the permanent members of the Security Council absolute power even in dire circumstances. This is the first time that the veto prevented the UN from saving the world from an apocalyptic pandemic.

Now, after deaths of millions in every part of the world, suffering and loss of livelihoods and causing irreparable damage to the global economy, the World Health Assembly of the World Health Organization (WHO) has adopted a decision on May 31, 2021 to discuss a new international treaty on pandemics at a special session to be held in November 2021.

Such a treaty would support international efforts to reinforce global health security, in particular, on preparedness and response to health emergencies, in light of lessons learnt from the pandemic. It has been argued that the Covid-19 pandemic is a global challenge and no single government or institution can address the threat of future pandemics alone. A legally binding instrument under international law would enable countries around the globe to strengthen national, regional, and global capacities as well as increase their resilience to future pandemics.

To reinforce the decision taken by 194 nations, 25 enthusiastic heads of state and international agencies have come up with a statement to support the initiative, sensing perhaps that the negotiations will drag on for a long time because of the hesitations of several countries to rush with a treaty. The international community should work together "towards a new international treaty for pandemic preparedness and response" to build a more robust global health architecture that will protect future generations, some world leaders said. "There will be other pandemics and other major health emergencies. No single government or multilateral agency can address this threat alone," the leaders said in their statement.

The question is not if, but when. Together, we must be better prepared to predict, prevent, detect, assess, and effectively respond to pandemics in a highly coordinated fashion. Among the signatories were the heads of government of the UK, Germany, President of the European Council, Spain, Norway and Dr Tedros Adhanom Ghebreyesus, Director-General of the WHO. The Europeans were the main proponents and the others went along with the idea of the treaty without committing themselves to any specific timeframe. The US, China, Russia, and India are not signatories to the statement.

What the WHO is proposing is nothing but a standard practice of multilateral institutions to create a multitude of institutions and a bureaucracy, which will consume available resources on their own upkeep. The treaty would set out the objectives and fundamental principles in order to structure the necessary collective action to fight pandemics.

The expectation is that such a treaty can enhance international cooperation in a number of priority areas, such as surveillance, alerts and response, but also in general trust in the international health system. A globally coordinated approach to discovering, developing and delivering effective and safe medical solutions, such as vaccines, medicines, diagnostics, and protective equipment would benefit collective health security.

The objectives of the proposed treaty are clear enough. But it was not because of absence of regulations that the international community failed to respond to the pandemic effectively. The International Health Regulations (IHR) of the WHO were supposed to create a high-performing system for surveillance of outbreaks of new pathogens that could protect the public health and economic interests of the Global North from the diseases presumed to rage uncontrolled in the Global South.

Such a skewed approach has been proved wrong during the current pandemic. It was the north that was devastated by Covid-19 before it moved to the south. Even a new pandemic treaty is not likely to commit all nations to rise above their national interests to meet a grave emergency. All theories of sovereignty and paramount interests of the countries will be bandied about and the treaty will incorporate the lowest common denominators on the issues discussed. This may elaborate on the existing regulations, but may not make them more effective.

The Security Council has failed humanity many times because of the use of the veto of the permanent members to protect their own interests. Many important issues relating to peace and security are relegated to the General Assembly, whose decisions are not mandatory. In the process, the new treaty will have nothing to compel the member states to ensure international cooperation. There have been calls for a new pandemic treaty that would address gaps in the global governance of threats to global health security. The emerging debate has quickly turned to focus on questions of structure and forms—a UN treaty or a framework convention under the auspices of the WHO.

We have learnt over the years that Conventions and Treaties negotiated in the General Assembly wither away over a period of time. The Framework Convention on Climate Change, for instance, raised high hopes with a bang in 1992, but ended in a whimper, when principle after principle was lost in the subsequent discussions on related protocols and new regulations. A Comprehensive Convention Against Terrorism, which received wide acceptance in the aftermath of 9/11, fell by the wayside due to major differences on the very definition of terrorism itself.

The new pandemic treaty should focus on security of people rather than national borders and highlight the international peace and security dimension of pandemics, requiring the Security Council to act when faced with such existential threats to humanity. Provision should be made for the UN to take multilateral-action across borders, treating health security as part of human security in a "nobody is safe until everyone is safe," policy.

In 2005, the then Senator Barack Obama wrote: "In an age when you can board planes in Bangkok or Hong Kong and arrive in Chicago, Indianapolis or New York in hours, we must face the reality that these exotic killer diseases are not isolated health problems half a world away, but direct and immediate threats to security and prosperity here at home." The Covid-19 has made this assertion prophetic and a new pandemic treaty will be purposeful only if it can meet the challenge of this reality.

Published: June 10, 2021

Zoom Fatigue and Beyond:
The Toll of Virtual Interaction

I was an enthusiastic seminarian ever since I left the foreign service. It was such a delight travelling around, staying in lovely hotels in glamorous cities, big and small, doing intense research to say something meaningful on any subject, relishing the haute cuisine and stimulating discussions. New people, new ideas, new products, and much to unlearn and learn.

Not inhibited by instructions from headquarters and liberated from the conduct rules, one could be innovative, inventive, or simply, funny. It was a mutual admiration society with people whom I had met in different places and worked with, despite having diametrically opposite views. Nobody complained except my wife, who was left behind. Not that she wanted to travel, but she just wanted me to be around.

When I left a star-studded seminar on 'the Strengths of India' at the Central University in Puducherry a day before it ended on March 9th, 2020, the coronavirus was a distant danger, hovering over China. My chauffeur was sneezing and coughing all the way, but I had no fear of infection. I sensed danger only when I had to stand in line for an hour to board the flight from Chennai to Thiruvananthapuram while someone took the temperature of the passengers with a new 'no-touch' contraption.

When I touched down in Kerala, I did not have the faintest idea that I would not board a plane at least for eight months. This is the longest gap in my air travel ever since I joined the foreign service.

The lockdown was a new experience, but the fact that it was going to be imprisonment with the additional risk of getting infected from anyone in the vicinity had not sunk in. The closing down of educational institutions, cancellation of scheduled conferences and travels were a relief initially and it seemed like divine intervention to slow the pace of my retirement activities.

But as the realisation came that success in the Covid-19 era was survival more than anything else, and that the virus was not going to disappear one fine morning, the gloom began to thicken and it dawned on me that, being in the vulnerable age group, it was important not to stir out of home. Television studios, restaurants and hill stations receded into the background and staying home with no physical contact even with dear and near ones became the new norm. It looked as though life had come to a standstill.

Reading and writing were obvious options and I longingly looked at the classics I had collected to read during retirement and the different book plans stacked away in the corner to be pulled out after all the frantic running about for conferences, lectures, TV shows, and seminars was over.

But I realised soon enough that solo exercises like reading and writing did not satisfy the soul. Writing is easy, but writing something that others will read is the challenge. It is a cruel world in which some writers have to run after editors and publishers only to receive rejection slips while some others have publishers running after them with fat cheques.

It gives me great satisfaction when I relate to a live audience or when my TV programmes get a reasonable rating. But all those vanished during the lockdown when interaction became dangerous and the best way of expression of affection was keeping the distance. In a flash, smiles disappeared behind the masks on every face.

The first invitation for a webinar arrived in this grim situation like summer showers. Podcasts and webinars have existed for a long time, but they were rarely used as the alternatives of seminars, and conferences were more productive and interesting. Like online education, which has become the new norm out of the blue, webinars took over the strategic, educational, technological, cultural, and medical discourse rapidly. No travel necessary, no dressing up except for the upper torso, reference material can be at hand, make your own coffee after unmuting the camera. and even go for a walk while others are speaking. No wonder it caught on like wildfire!

It was most enjoyable for a time. It cost the organisers next to nothing, the participants, ranging from school students to Nobel laureates, got over the withdrawal symptoms of the lockdown, the horizons expanded beyond the oceans wherever the internet existed. The world suddenly came within reach. The audience grew from two to several thousands.

Sree Sreenivasan, my journalism professor son, had one or more webinars called 'Sree's Daily Global Covid-19 Show' every day since the first day of the lockdown, completing 218 episodes. We woke up every morning hearing him live. The world of communication changed beyond recognition and people started counting webinars as a blessing of the pandemic.

Today, we live in a webinar-weary world, as everyone started a webinar on their own and the seeming advantages of the phenomenon over personal interactions began to dwindle. The competition for attention, which is scarce in the digital world, became fierce. The UN General Assembly, where nobody could walk without brushing past a celebrity, has a desolate look now. People became more and more nostalgic about the old days. The search for the vaccine, which will be the ultimate redemption from the pandemic, has intensified. But the proliferation of webinars and videos on everything, from itch reduction to cancer cure, befuddle the mind.

Though technology came to the rescue of mankind for communication and learning, its glaring inadequacy was a spoilsport at crucial moments in the webinars. The internet and electricity are still erratic and the art of muting and unmuting of mikes and cameras are still challenges.

The weariness arises also from the pressure from the organisers to join webinars on diverse subjects, which may not be of the required standard. Most of them do not offer any remuneration as it involves only a few minutes of work. There is not much appreciation of the effort required to be put in for every appearance. The incentive of not wanting to be missed out is wearing thin and it is difficult to find excuses. Protocol is rarely respected as the participants never meet personally to complain of breaches. Also, if the time spent on webinars can be productively used by reading and writing, it might be more beneficial. Video recordings accumulate, but there is no time even to check whether they contain any howlers.

With all the weariness, however, I dread the thought that the telephones would stop ringing once and there would be no invitations for webinars. Unless the good old days return and the globetrotting begins, I shall continue to attend webinars with weary eyes as I have agreed to do this a week at midnight to suit the convenience of my journalist hosts in New York.

Published: October 19, 2020

Masks Amidst Cultures:
The Covid-19 Impact

The unique blessing that distinguishes mankind from the rest of the animal kingdom, the ability to smile, disappeared behind masks overnight. It may be an ordinary cloth mask or colour-coded designer masks, but the effect is the same.

Perhaps the only legacy of the Covid-19 pandemic that will stay with us will be the mask and the health checks just like special security checks at the airport were bequeathed to us by 9/11.

This is a pity as smiles are precious gifts that can be given away free with great benefit to the giver and the given alike.

'If you find someone without a smile, give him one!' is the greeting at the entrance of the Yangon airport in Myanmar. An unconscious smile appeared on all lips as they entered, though the people of Myanmar are generally subdued in expressing their feelings.

In fact, every nation has its own style of greeting, but most common is the smile, which has many levels of warmth. The heartiest smiles I have seen are in the South Pacific and it is hard to see a Fijian without a smile.

Even Sitiveni Rabuka, the Fijian Colonel who walked into the country's parliament and marched out Prime Minister Timoci Bavadra and his colleagues at gun point to captivity and proclaimed himself the boss, was seen sporting a broad smile, giving the coup a human face.

Australian women were so enchanted by his smile that some of them asked him to stage a coup in their backyard! The other soldiers, who accompanied him to the bloodless coup may also have been smiling, but they were masked to give themselves a grim look.

The Latin Americans and the Africans come next in keeping a cheerful face in public. The Chinese and the Japanese keep poker faces and they smile only selectively.

Sinologists used to measure movement of the lips of Chinese leaders to gauge the warmth of the friendship. Wearing a mask was common in Japan even when there was no epidemic as they rarely used their smiling talents to establish personal or official relationships.

Even in theatres, where it is necessary to willingly suspend disbelief to enjoy the show, there are people who consider modesty more important than enjoyment.

When a distinguished Japanese diplomat, wanted to criticise his own people, he wrote a book, *Japan Unmasked*, causing a '*shokku*' an English word brought into the Japanese dictionary after 'Nixon Shokku' created by Nixon's visit to China.

In India, it is different from region to region. In Kerala, public display of merriment is the monopoly of drunk merry makers. In Punjab and Goa, newcomers will think that everybody is a bit inebriated.

The pandemic has now become a great equaliser, with the masks having hidden away the variety of smiles that had enthralled the world. Masks have played a role in human history in many areas, including health, entertainment and crime.

Surgical masks are supposed to have been popularised, if not invented by 'The Lady with the Lamp', Florence Nightingale. Most countries and cultures have developed their own masks, which have now become wall decorations. Many of them served as part of stereotyping characters, revealing their nature even before they spoke. They saved the efforts of the actors to contort their facial muscles to create expressions.

Kathakali, an ancient, but sophisticated dance form of Kerala is mistakenly characterised as a masked dance, but the fact is that even with all the embellishments around the face and the massive headgear, the eyes, facial muscles, lips, and even the tongue come into play. A masked Kathakali dancer will be a shadow of his former self.

In the Japanese Kabuki, the faces are so heavily painted to make them look like masks, but the facial expressions remain important in Kabuki.

After a long lull during the complete lockdown, crimes have multiplied in quantity and diversity in different parts of the country, particularly in Kerala.

In the pre-corona days, the accused, often highly respectable people before the crime was committed, used to cover their faces when accosted by cameramen, but today, they all have masks to protect their privacy. This may well be an incentive to crime, particularly burglary.

An ingenious way has been found to save the smile in a studio, where they take a picture of the part of the face covered by the mask and print it on your mask, thus making you look like perpetually smiling.

If it looks really genuine, the wearer may end up in a mental asylum or a court for sexual harassment for smiling meaningfully at women.

As the mask industry prospers and more and more designers go into fashion mask, the fashion industry will suffer.

Who wants to see masked women parading clothes, even if the masks are made of gold and diamonds?

Except for the eyes, there is nothing more beautiful than the nose and the lips. If they are covered, a beauty pageant may be a pain rather than a pleasure. The lipstick industry and even the toothbrush and paste industry will dip in the bargain.

Poets will have to shift their attention from rosy lips and milky teeth to dreamy eyes and shapely eye brows, while describing the heroine.

Politicians will be the winners in the new norm of masked faces. It has been a common practice to create an audience of Trumps and Modis by giving everybody a mask with the face of the popular leaders. People, other than hard core supporters may have been reluctant to don those masks, but now, if you make it part of the mandatory masks, most people except intending defectors will be happy to appear like their leaders.

A blue mask, resembling a UN flag, has been fluttering in social media. On a closer look, it is actually a mask with the strings attached, declaring it the best symbol of globalisation.

Covid-19 has accomplished what the UN failed to do in the last 75 years by making mankind rally around a mask of unity.

Let us hope that it is a temporary phenomenon and we will be unmasked to bring back the smile and the masks will go to the walls as the souvenirs of a nightmare.

Published: June 14, 2020

Aging in the Pandemic Era: Life Beyond 65

The beauty of life is that though mortality is certain, its timing is uncertain. No age has been set for final departure and humans can live in the hope of immortality till the very last moment. Hope is eternal even though existence is transitory. Robert Browning's exhortation, 'Grow old along with me, the best is yet to be', has taught us to await the miracle of a game-changing accomplishment even in the evening of our lives.

Human beings consider themselves indispensable, but the world's graves are filled with indispensable people, who thought that life would come to a complete halt if they ceased to exist. Many believe that age is just a number as long as they have no disability.

Most people realise they are old when others show new respect and reverence to them. The tradition of treating the elderly give them a sense of importance. The Covid experience showed that mortality was high among old people in old-age homes, not in their own homes.

Shakespeare described seven stages in a man's life, but not on the basis of age, but on changing priorities and strength of body. First, the infant, then the schoolboy, the lover, the soldier, the judge, the old man, and 'finally second childishness and mere oblivion, sans teeth, sans eyes, sans taste, sans everything.' No one can escape these stages, but the process of ageing varies from man to man, depending on many factors. We witness everyday aged youngsters and young oldies, making any classification of people on the basis of age meaningless.

Old age does not come overnight. The sky gets dark slowly, writes Zhou Daxin, and asks us to prepare for the inevitable. He says that old people believe that they know everything, but they are as ignorant as children. That is a highly exaggerated notion. But he says wisely that the dictum of old age is not to say "after" or "later" and do everything "now." Old age sets in slowly, almost unnoticed because even with half of the faculties intact, human beings can live near normal lives.

An Egyptian friend taught me early in life that, after 50, if you have no pain in some part of your body when you get up in the morning, that is because you are dead. Pain is thus an assurance that you are alive and that your body is responding to the various afflictions that may be confronting you without your knowledge.

Some say that golf and sexuality go with a man to his grave. Old golfers don't die, they simply lose their drive, it is said. But when you see your drives, which used to cross the water hazard, drop short of it, you know that you are losing it, but you can still win with your wily short game.

I am sure there are some such tricks with sexuality too. A lady whose husband passed away at 85 wondered aloud how long men kept their sex drive.

Recently, more comfort was given to the elderly when the WHO declared that 65 years old is still considered young. Earlier, based on the British Friendly Societies Act, it was considered that old age began at 50 when the average life expectancy was much lower than today.

Now, consider the average health quality and life expectancy-defined new criteria that divided human age as 0–17 underage; 18–65 youth; 66–79 middle-aged; 80–99 old; and beyond, that long-lived elderly. This was a morale booster for people of all ages as people who were middle-aged thirty years ago discovered that those years were youthful for them.

Covid-19 changed all these in one swoop by declaring 65 as old age, thus requiring those above to stay indoors during lockdowns, calling it a reverse quarantine. This was not an advisory, but a legal requirement, which can be enforced by law. Fortunately, since gerontocracy is still the order of the world, implementation of this requirement will be hard.

Prime Minister Narendra Modi himself is past that age and if the Covid Protocol is applied, most in authority will have to stay home. Perhaps the presumption is that the politicians are immune to the morbidity of old age.

When videos appeared in December 2019 of elderly Covid patients being dragged out of hospitals, incredible reports appeared that they were being eliminated to make space for younger patients. Even in the US, the doctors had to choose the patients they wanted to put on ventilators because of the shortage of support systems.

Prohibiting people above 65 from engaging in outdoor activities is as cruel as the suspected Chinese action. There are many people who are very productive in the arts, culture, cuisine and others who have lost their livelihoods. But scribes like me will know that senility has set in only when they get rejection slips from their editors. Indeed, there is life beyond 65 and it must be enjoyed without fetters other than voluntary defence measures against the pandemic.

Published: July 26, 2020

Shifting Priorities: Reflections on the Pandemic

A dictum that we do not remember in normal times is that success is meaningless without survival. But in the last one year, success has become synonymous with survival. Humanity has survived over centuries because of its instinct for self- preservation, but today, the overwhelming urge is to keep alive. This is the big difference that the pandemic has brought about in human behaviour. We have become less daring and adventurous because we know that nothing is more important than holding on tight to the tenuous lifeline.

Even heaven is not tantalising if the prospect of the journey there is near. A recent cartoon showed a priest asking his congregation as to how many of them would like to go to heaven. All raised hands. Then he asked who would like to go first and no hand was raised. With all the challenges and sufferings of living, survival is an unrivalled measure of success.

When Hamlet faced the stark choice between 'to be' and 'not to be', he chose 'to be' as:

But that the dread of something after death,
The undiscover'd country, from whose bourn
No traveller returns, puzzles the will,
And makes us rather bear those ills we have,
Than fly to others that we know not of?
Thus conscience does make cowards of us all.

But Hamlet was sure that he would continue 'to be' and there was no threat of extinction.

Ambition is another trait of human beings, tempered only by the limitations of circumstances. But even the sky is not the limit when it comes to dreams. When the wings of dreams are clipped, people scale down their ambitions to more realistic levels. They still want to climb Mount Everest, swim the English Channel and land on the moon. But as age and diseases rule out certain activities, ambitions are abandoned, but survival is taken for granted and other dreams grow.

However, the pandemic with its threat of unexpected attacks, has made people consider survival bigger than success. The narrowing horizons of longevity have made humans limit ambitions other than survival. Elderly people wash hands more often, wear masks and confine themselves to their homes for sheer survival. They dread loneliness less and infections more.

The pandemic has also changed the priorities of states. Before the second wave struck with pervasive intensity, India's priority was the Chinese presence on our side of the Line of Actual Control (LAC) and the progress of disengagement was closely watched by the world. The Chinese challenge went beyond India and the whole world was preoccupied with the India-China standoff with the possibility of Pakistan opening another front. But the India-China confrontation and the sneaky dialogue with Pakistan with the help of UAE are off the radar, now that the threat is existential from an invisible enemy, with whom negotiations and diplomacy are not possible. Today, survival of citizens has become the priority. Decoupling from the Chinese supply chain and banning Chinese investment have become a faint memory. We are banking on China to supply life-saving drugs and vaccines even when they are occupying our land. The common threat of disease seems to unite the world.

Even while US President Joe Biden claims that he has done well in fighting the pandemic in the first one hundred days, the fear of the future haunts him. When he heard about the extent of the Covid-19 rampage in India, his instinct was not to express sympathy and support to India, but to look for escape routes for himself to preserve his national assets. A State Department spokesperson said that the Biden administration's first obligation was to take care of the requirements of the American people and that 'It is not only in the US interest to see Americans vaccinated; but it is in the interests of the rest of the world to see Americans vaccinated.' The reaction in India was not just one of disappointment, but of outrage that Biden was insensitive to India's interests so soon after the formation of the Quad, which had pledged to work together against the pandemic. In the light of the Quad agenda, the US position was unacceptable. Even though the US made amends subsequently, the self-preservation instinct was stunning.

The pandemic has played havoc with the most vulnerable of us all, the very young and the teenagers. Keeping them away from their friends is traumatic enough, but it is even more difficult for them to be with the parents all the time. The computer games that they had loved till the pandemic arrived cannot replace kicking the real ball with their own feet. The children are the least worried about survival as they do not think of mortality. Moreover, the initial experience of the pandemic seemed to indicate that children were immune to the disease. But the more recent evidence does not rule out the possibility of children being infected. It is the parents who worry about the survival of the children.

India's vaccine diplomacy was an effort to overcome the self-preservation instinct by giving away our limited resources to others without making a careful plan of our future needs and capabilities. Much of Dante's *Inferno* we witness in certain parts of the country is a consequence of not realising that even diplomatic success requires our own survival. Will the many lives were lost without access to oxygen benefit from the sacrifice made? Even a former diplomat became a victim of our policy when he was virtually murdered in the parking lot of the Medanta hospital.

Someone said that nobody will help us if we did not help others. Humanitarian assistance at times of tragedy is not given on the basis of help given in the past. Many countries, who rushed support to India were not countries who received our gifts. In fact, there was criticism in our own country that Covaxin was not fully tested and should not be used. It is quite possible that some of our vaccines are lying unused in warehouses in some corners of the world, when we do not have enough for our own people.

Perhaps one outcome of the devastating pandemic may be a change in our assumptions as to who our friends and adversaries are. Those who help us survive today may turn out to be the builders of our success in the long run. Survival is more important than geopolitics.

Published: May 2, 2021

L. INDIAN DIASPORA

AN EMPIRE ON WHICH
THE SUN NEVER SETS

Diplomacy Beyond Borders:
The Role of Diaspora

If there is one issue on which all political parties agree, it is the imperative to include overseas Indians in India's economic development and to take care of their needs and aspirations. Successive governments have been vying with each other to give more and more concessions to them as acknowledgment of their contribution by way of remittances, investment, lobbying for India, promoting Indian culture abroad and for building a good image of India by their intelligence and industry.

India was initially sensitive to the view that championing the cause of overseas Indians might offend the host countries, who should be fully responsible for their welfare and security. The Indian community and our diplomatic missions interacted on national days or other important occasions, but diaspora diplomacy was low key.

Rediscovering Indians Abroad

Rajiv Gandhi was the first Prime Minister who changed the diaspora policy by inviting Indians abroad, regardless of their nationality, to participate in nation-building, much like the overseas Chinese communities. In return, he promised them opportunities to work with India, like in the celebrated case of Sam Pitroda, who was entrusted with the task of modernising telecommunications in India. The response was not ecstatic, but many volunteered to help out in various ways. But this brought to focus the many inadequacies of the Indian system for the diaspora to collaborate with India or to invest in the country. Grievances like red tape, multiple clearances, distrust of government in fulfilling promises were addressed through hesitant reforms and promotional measures.

The first test of the new diaspora policy came in 1987 when Sitiveni Rabuka ousted an Fiji Indian majority government in Fiji and reduced them to second-class citizens. Rajiv Gandhi, in a major departure from established policy, protested vehemently, imposed trade sanctions against Fiji, got it expelled from the Commonwealth and raised the issue at the United Nations. This bewildered those Fiji Indians who did not want to disturb the race relations in Fiji, but energised the Indian diaspora, generating faith in them that India would not be a silent witness, as it was in the past, to discrimination, racism and disenfranchisement of Indians abroad. The Indian position was instrumental in democracy and racial harmony returning to Fiji after 10 years.

After India and the overseas Indians rediscovered each other under Rajiv Gandhi, there came a host of measures such as a separate Ministry of Overseas Indian Affairs, the Person of Indian Origin (PIO) Card, Pravasi Bharatiya Divas, Pravasi Bharatiya Samman Award, Overseas Citizen of India Card, NRI funds and voting rights for Indian citizens abroad, some from the United Progressive Alliance and some from the National Democratic Alliance governments. The response from the diaspora was diverse, as these affected different categories of Indians in different ways. For the Indian nationals in the Gulf and elsewhere, welfare measures and resettlement facilities were more important, while the prosperous communities in the West, who were clamouring for dual citizenship, felt short-changed. But, on the whole, they were energised into espousing Indian causes in the U.S. Of course, their support to Indian interests was not automatic and they often urged India to modify its policies to suit American sensitivities. Indian-Americans contributed little by way of remittances or investments, but the establishment of the India Caucus in the House of Representatives and turning around doubting legislators into voting for the India-U.S. nuclear deal were major accomplishments.

The Modi Outreach

Prime Minister Narendra Modi made the diaspora a centrepiece of his foreign policy and, during his foreign visits, addressed mammoth meetings of the community to project India's priorities and needs. But he did not address any of their demands or announce any new plans for removing their grievances like travel issues and protection of their properties in India. If anything, the merger of the Ministry of Overseas Indian Affairs with the Ministry of External Affairs, though pragmatic, has been construed as a negative step. The irregularity of diaspora conferences and awards has also caused some concern in the diaspora.

Together with the new hopes and expectations raised by the government, there are new fears and concerns among and about the overseas communities. The volatility in West Asia, together with the fall in oil prices, has caused fears of a massive return of Indian nationals, curtailing remittances and making demands on the job market. In Kerala, for instance, workers from other States have bridged the demand-supply gap in various sectors. The Gulf countries will require foreign workers for some more time, but India's relations with many of them remain in the employer-employee mode. Of course, it was heartening to see Saudi Arabia resolve a serious issue relating to a starvation among Indian workers, but we should be ready for the eventuality of Indian workers returning, though a massive "Indexit" is unlikely.

A recent phenomenon is that of "discovering" Indians wherever there is a crisis. India does not have any precise data on the number of Indians in different parts of the world. The amount of risks that Indians are capable of taking to get medical education, for instance, is phenomenal. Whether it is in Ukraine, Yemen or Syria, Indians are discovered eking out an existence in difficult circumstances. General V.K. Singh (retd.), Minister of State for External Affairs, has become virtually the Chief Repatriation Officer, flying into hotspots with chartered flights to rescue Indians and bring them home. He was often bewildered when many Indians refused to use the facility for return and insisted on staying on in difficult situations either to seek alternative jobs or to settle their claims. Back home, disquiet has been expressed that public money is being spent on bringing people who have gone on their own for their benefit.

Even more serious is the suspicion that some Indians are travelling to the Islamic State areas either to join the jihad or to settle there in what is considered a Promised Land. Adventurism of this kind needs to be stopped. We used to take pride in the fact that Indians never joined terrorist organisations, but the latest trends are very disturbing.

The dilemma for India is whether movements of Indians abroad for education or employment should be curbed. This will be against the spirit of freedom; but there should be at least an accurate count of Indians in different countries and projections should be made of future prospects. States must be prepared with plans for rehabilitation of Indians, with the possibility of offering the same kind of jobs they were doing abroad. Asking them to turn into entrepreneurs overnight would be counterproductive. There should also be a clear division of labour between the Central and the State governments in crisis situations.

The Indian diaspora is more prosperous than before and its involvement in India's development is increasing. Indians overseas are conscious of their opportunities in India. At the same time, new fears about scaled-up return of Indians or their involvement in global terrorism are raising their heads. Firefighting is not enough. We should have a comprehensive plan involving both the Centre and States to invest remittances intelligently and to find alternative ways of livelihood for those who return.

Published: August 22, 2016

Literary Voices Abroad: Exploring Indian Diaspora Literature

The sense of yearning for the motherland is the most overwhelming sentiment of the Indian diaspora, wherever it exists. When travel was hazardous and unusual, the yearning was intense, as they knew well that they would never return home. Though the age of technological advancement has made traveling easier and the distance shorter, their imagination continued to nurse the feeling of inadequacy in being away in a distant land. Their nostalgia, together with a curious attachment to the homeland's traditions, religions and languages gave birth to diaspora literature. The migrant, who leaves his homeland runs from pillar to post, crossing the boundaries of time and money to become one with his new surroundings, but longs to return home at an appropriate time. Consequently, he remains a creature of the edge, the "peripheral man", as V.S. Naipaul calls him. According to Naipaul, the Indians are well aware that their journey to Trinidad was final, but these tensions and throes remain a recurring theme in the diaspora literature.

The literary talents of the diaspora found expression first in adversity and flourished with the advent of prosperity. The writers later began mixing nostalgia with criticism of evils in the Indian society in contrast with their host countries. Some of the most prominent Indian writers in English belong to the diaspora. V.S. Naipaul, Salman Rushdie, Amitav Ghosh, Jhumpa Lahiri and Shashi Tharoor are diaspora writers. Even Vikram Seth and Rohinton Mistry became creative after they began to live abroad. Our own Anita Pratap has said that great creativity comes out of great departures. The greater the pangs of departure, the greater the literature.

V.S. Naipaul is easily the most outspoken critic of India among the diaspora writers. His sarcastic comments on India and the Caribbean and his decisive appraisal of Muslim fundamentalism in non-Arab countries have been topics of ruthless denigration. Undeterred by opposition from his homeland as well as his host country, Naipaul continues at the epicentre of literary development even today. Salman Rushdie spearheaded the renaissance of Indian writing in English with his path-breaking novel, *Midnight's Children*. His work revolves around the Indian subcontinent as a vital theme and his "paranormal pragmatism" has a certain appeal to Indians. Amitav Ghosh has created some of the most lyrical and insightful works on the consequences of colonialism on the natives. Jhumpa Lahiri started a new trend by poignantly portraying the lives of a family of immigrants in her first novel, *The Namesake* through the eyes of a young boy. Shashi Tharoor wrote a biting political satire on Indian politics in his *The Great Indian Novel* by narrating the *Mahabharata* story in modern terms.

Much significant diaspora literature exists in regional languages, including Malayalam. Diaspora newspapers, magazines, television and websites in modern times look critically at India. Their commentaries rejoice over the success of India, but caustically criticize failures. Those in developed countries feel impatient that India is not progressing as fast as it should. They constantly advise India what it should be doing to develop faster, without taking constraints into account.

While the first-generation immigrants from India constantly nurse their grievances against the homeland, the second and third generations look at India without prejudices and take pride in India's accomplishments. For them, India is a brand name, which they can use for their own advancement and they become true assets for the country. This feeling of elation at India's exalted status is present in the writings of young people.

The diaspora literature is fascinating, but it is equally complex and unique. Many writers got recognition initially as the proponents of a new genre belonging exclusively to overseas Indians. But today, many writers have become mainstream contributors to global literature. They have come of age and get counted without their identity as migrants with their feeling of estrangement with both the homeland and the host countries.

Published: April 1, 2017

Fiji Coup and its Impact on
India's Diaspora Policy

When the third ranking officer of the Royal Fiji Military Forces, Lieutenant Colonel Sitiveni Rabuka, marched Prime Minister Timoci Bavadra and his 'Indian dominated' cabinet at gunpoint to waiting military trucks and drove off in the first coup in the South Pacific in May 1987, he was not aware that he would be the cause of a change in India's Diaspora policy.

For the first time in history, India battled an action by a foreign government against the people of Indian origin by imposing sanctions against Fiji, by getting it expelled from the Commonwealth and by raising the issue at the United Nations.

In similar situations in the past elsewhere, India had merely welcomed the Indians who wanted to return to India and made some efforts to repatriate their assets, as in the cases of Yangon and Uganda.

It was evident that Rabuka's coup was meant to disenfranchise Fiji citizens of Indian origin, but in accordance with the established policy of non-interference in internal affairs in such situations, I refrained, as the Indian High Commissioner, from making any statements or visiting the detained cabinet.

During the three days that I had no communication link with New Delhi, I remained totally impartial and held some confidential discussions with the only constitutional authority, the Governor General.

To Rabuka, who was my golf partner earlier, I merely formally conveyed our concern for the lives and properties of the Indian community.

The instructions I received when the communications were restored were a surprise. I was told to support the Indian community against discrimination and the external affairs ministry issued an official statement to this effect. I was also summoned to Delhi for a briefing.

What I heard there from Prime Minister Rajiv Gandhi and Minister of State Natwar Singh reflected a change in the policy laid out by Pandit Jawaharlal Nehru in Parliament to the effect that Indian migrants should be loyal to their countries of adoption and that India would remain alive to their welfare and interests.

I was told that I should return to Fiji and work openly for the restoration of democracy.

Trade sanctions were announced, but the high commission was not withdrawn because it was decided that it was necessary to give moral support to the Fiji Indians.

The new policy, I was told, was that India would stand by their children abroad if there was any affront to their rights and dignity.

Prime Minister Rajiv Gandhi said that he had asked the Indian Diaspora to contribute resources and technology for India's development and the response was heartening.

In that situation, he argued, it should be incumbent on him to support the Indian communities everywhere, if they had any grievances.

It was thus that the new Diaspora policy was born.

The new policy was much appreciated by Fiji Indians, though others raised eyebrows about external intervention.

After two years of uneasy relationship, I was asked to leave Fiji and the mission itself was closed.

But after three more coups and 27 years, democracy has been restored in Fiji and Prime Minister Narendra Modi had a successful visit there.

Much credit is being given to India's tough stand in 1987, and I received a warm welcome when I visited Fiji after 25 years.

Rajiv Gandhi's new Diaspora policy, which paid off in Fiji, had its repercussions worldwide.

The overseas Indian affairs ministry, the Pravasi Divas, the Pravasi Samman, the Person of Indian Origin card, the Overseas Citizen of India card and many other gestures are taken for granted today, but these would not have been possible without the change of the Diaspora policy put in place by Rajiv Gandhi, following the military coup in Fiji and his decision to stand by them, abandoning inhibitions about intervention in the internal affairs of other countries.

It was a new doctrine like the Responsibility to Protect, which developed subsequently at the United Nations. No doubt, the Government of India and the Diaspora have rediscovered each other after the new policy was put in place.

Any number of initiatives of the government and the community can be cited to show how they have helped each other in different countries and situations.

They have learnt to complement each other as it has been realized that the standing of the community is an asset to the government in building relationships and that good relationship between the host country and India is in the interest of the community.

A remarkable fact is that the political parties are unanimous in the view that overseas Indians should be treated with consideration and respect and that no stone should be left unturned to meet their cultural and other aspirations.

In return, the universal expectation is that they will visit India, send remittances for their relatives and invest in small and big enterprises in India.

Even those communities, which are not in a position to do any of these, are also covered by the many measures that successive governments have taken for the welfare of the overseas Indians.

The Indians overseas belong to a broad and diverse spectrum, ranging from the unsung and unacknowledged poor rice farmers in Myanmar to the billionaire businessmen in the US, Europe and the Gulf.

As such, their capacity to contribute to India and their expectations of India are also diverse.

The workers in the Gulf, for example, have existential problems arising out of actions of unscrupulous agents and employers. The government has reached several bilateral agreements with the Gulf States to resolve these issues, bearing in mind that India has a major stake in their continuation in the Gulf.

The biggest remittances come from the workers in the Gulf and not from the professionals in the developed countries, who tend to keep their assets elsewhere.

In the US and Europe, including the UK, the Indian communities look up to India as a cultural and social anchor, more as a nostalgic homeland, rather than a place they like to return to permanently.

They would like India to acknowledge their success and involve them in India's development. They have supported Indian policies and generated interest in India in their host countries.

The India Caucus in the US Congress and the Friends of India in the US Senate are outstanding examples of the contribution they have made to India-US relations.

The community played an exceptionally active role at the time of the US sanctions against India following the nuclear tests in 1998 and the long negotiations on the nuclear deal from 2005 to 2008.

But the support of the community is neither automatic nor continuous. They have been critical on occasions, particularly on consular services and the facilities they get in India with regard to travel, ownership of properties etc.

Their remittances and investments remain low and the contribution from the US was minimal even when the Resurgence of India Bond was issued in 1998. But, on the whole, they take their roles as unofficial ambassadors of India quite seriously and rise to the occasion when India needs them.

The Indian communities in Africa, the Caribbean and Fiji have only emotional and sentimental linkages with India. They make no demands on India, but they preserve their way of life, rituals and religions, as their ancestors knew them. They welcome Indian leaders, artists, film stars etc and bask in the glow of India's clout in the world.

India's policy towards overseas Indians has benefitted India as well as its children abroad, but there is great potential for further growth in the relationship.

The wealth and technology that they wield are immense and they can be of use to India in crucial sectors, provided the community develops faith in the government and considers the growth of India inherently of benefit to them. The facilities and benefits that India extends to them can also be farther expanded.

The recent relaxation of visa restrictions has been welcomed. The demand for dual citizenship and right to vote in Indian elections raise constitutional and legal issues, but ways should be found to meet the aspirations of overseas Indians.

Overseas Indians constitute India's 'soft power', which should be deployed in the country's best interest.

Published: January 7, 2015

Meeting the Coup Leader: Personal Encounter in Fiji

Many people in India may remember Sitiveni Rabuka, a graduate of the Defence Services Staff College, Wellington, Tamil Nadu, and the third ranking officer of the Fiji army, who ousted an Indian-dominated Fiji government in a bloodless coup in 1987.

As the High Commissioner of India to Fiji at that time, I was instructed not to recognise the military regime and to fight for the rights of the Fiji Indians. After two years of a diplomatic battle, Rabuka asked me to leave Fiji in 72 hours. The Indian High Commission and the Indian Cultural Centre were closed down within six months.

Fiji, having lost its innocence, had at least three more coups since then, one even by a civilian. There were as many constitutions and elections, many of them loaded against Fiji Indians whose strength has been reduced to 37 percent of the population on account of migration.

Even today, Fiji has a government headed by a former commander of the navy, Commodore Frank Bainimarama, who has been prime minister since 2007 and has worked with the communities to adopt the first non-racial constitution, under which elections will be held in September 2014.

Commodore Bainimarama has apparently the support of the majority of Fiji Indians, but parties like those of Commodore Bainimarama and Rabuka are yet to take shape. The grand old party of the Fiji Indians, the National Federation Party, may become a multi-racial party.

The Fiji Labour Party, which won the elections in 1987, appears to have lost its prominence. Bainimarama is poised to win the elections, though the scene is not yet clear.

Meeting Sitiveni Rabuka, who had overthrown a democratically elected government, discriminated against the Fiji Indians, brought untold humiliation and suffering to them, tried to disenfranchise them, ordered me out of Fiji and closed down the Indian High Commission, was a difficult decision to take even after 25 years.

Many friends suggested a meeting or a game of golf on which he was keen and we had an hour-long conversation at the Suva Golf Club, where we once played golf together. Rabuka looked the same as I last saw him except for his white hair and bulkier frame.

I thanked him for not declaring me persona non grata (the diplomatic device used to expel me was down-gradation of the mission to a consulate) as such a declaration may have made it impossible for me to visit Fiji again.

I also thanked him for allowing my wife Lekha to stay back for nearly two weeks to pack and ship our belongings. He was totally on the defensive and said he did not order me out and that he was "overruled" in this matter, suggesting that real power was in the hands of former prime minister Ratu Mara, who had lost power after 17 years.

Rabuka also revealed that it was not the pro-Fiji Indian speeches I made that provoked them, but intelligence reports that I was holding meetings in my house to collect money to smuggle arms into Fiji. I said that while India had not recognised his government and managed to get Fiji out of the Commonwealth on account of racist policies, India had not supported any armed struggle.

I had specifically opposed any suggestion of the use of force, as peace was possible only by racial harmony. He said he knew that the reports were wrong, but he could not help it.

I made it a point to tell Rabuka that his coup coincided with the time when Rajiv Gandhi had begun to count on overseas Indians to participate in building a modern India. Gandhi felt his new policy would not be credible unless he stood by Indians in trouble anywhere in the world.

It was for this reason that he instructed me to stay on in Fiji and fight for the rights of the Fiji Indians even at the risk of my being expelled. My struggle for the Fiji Indians was under instructions, I said.

Rabuka found an opening here to draw a parallel between him and me. He said he too was acting under instructions right from the beginning, confirming the general impression that it was Ratu Mara, who had instigated the coup.

"The mistake I made was that I listened to the politicians," he said repeatedly and suggested that he did not have his heart in the coup. But once he was asked to do a job, he did it with conviction, just as I had done. In other words, he absolved both of us of personal animosity.

Another interesting observation that Rabuka made was that the two people, who were actually against me had come to grief—Ratu Mara and his intelligence chief. He said as a believer, he held the view that God would punish those who did harm to those who did their duty. He said he was able to survive because he had no ill-will even to those whom he hurt.

He was aware that he hurt many people, while carrying out his duties, but he could do no more than apologise to them. He admitted that Fiji lost time and resources in the turmoil in the country since May 1987, but he had little choice in the matter.

Rabuka was nostalgic about his days in India, particularly the Staff College. He said he had a great time in India and he had many friends in the Indian armed forces. Soon after the coup, he had called the Indian Army Chief General Sunit Francis Rodrigues, who was his commander in the Staff College, to assure him that he would do no harm to the Indians in Fiji.

When I reminded him about an article written by Kumkum Prakash, wife of a future naval chief, Admiral Arun Prakash, titled 'The Steve I Knew', he was very happy. The article had praised him for his human qualities, sense of fairness, tolerance and humanism and had suggested that the Fiji Indians were somehow responsible for transforming her friend, Steve, into the coup leader Rabuka. He spoke warmly of all his friends and said that his wife too was very happy with them. They called her 'Sai Baba's sister' because of her Melanesian hairstyle!

Rabuka was ecstatic about a Gujarati doctor who operated on both his knees and looked after him in Baroda in 2007. He said his knees were perfect and his quality of life had improved since the operation.

As for his own political future, Rabuka said he had his political party, but since he was not a paid member, he may not be given a ticket. He said he was toying with the idea of a Republican Party, as he was the one who declared Fiji a Republic. He said Ratu Mara was against it, but the instructions came two days too late. He was not against the introduction of the common roll as long as it did not result in the loss of the rights of the indigenous Fijians.

As Rabuka's wife drove into the golf club to pick him up, Rabuka lamented that the prime minister had taken away his official car, his entitlement as a former prime minister and that his pension had been reduced. He had borrowed the car of a friend, who lived in Australia and he had to return it to his friend whenever he visited Fiji. He said the prime minister had benefitted from much that he had done, including the provision in the constitution for amnesty for coup leaders in certain circumstances.

Sitiveni Rabuka, who appointed himself to every high position in the country, including head of the council of chiefs, without being a chief himself, took the wheel and drove off. I felt pity for him for the first time for being powerless and friendless. But his emergence as a nationalist Fijian leader again cannot be ruled out, given the commitment and ruthlessness with which he championed the cause of his people for nearly ten years and then worked with the Fiji Indian leaders like Jairam Reddy and Mahendra Chaudhury. But the general mood in Fiji is to continue on the path thrown open by Commodore Bainimarama.

Published: April 29, 2014

Empowering Young Pravasis:
India's Diaspora Engagement

Pravasi Bharatiya Divas (PBD) conclaves are fast becoming an old boys club. The average age of the delegates should be over 60, with a smattering of curious young people.

The Pravasi Bharatiya Samman, awarded to 15 veterans every year, comes with a perennial fully paid invitation to future PBDs. This will ensure that half the hall will be filled by those with a glorious past, but unable to contribute to the future. Minister Vayalar Ravi, a veteran himself, in an effort to rectify the situation, devoted a session of the Kochi PBD to 'Engaging the Diaspora Youth'.

Speakers lamented that the youth was indifferent to India, that they could not unravel the complexity of Indian culture and that the contradictions of the present Indian scene bewildered them. They were alienated beyond redemption. The second and third generation Indians in the United States was American Born Confused Desis, ABCD, they said.

The speakers failed to see the reality that the younger Pravasis may have no nostalgia for India, but they are able to see India without the prism of past prejudices, frustrations and disillusionment that constitute the psyche of the first migrants from India.

They are able to see that India's growth and development add to their value abroad and that they have the best of both worlds as inheritors of a legacy and beneficiaries of the opportunities and affluence abroad.

The future generations of Indian immigrants are likely to provide the anchor to India in many countries. This is not to detract from the historic contribution of the first generation, but to affirm that the Diaspora youth is not being alienated.

The biggest difference between the first and the subsequent generations of Pravasis is that the first generation went through the traumatic experience of uprooting and resettlement. They left India in a quest for the Promised Land as they felt that they had no opportunities at home. Disillusionment with the homeland was a part of the process.

However much this experience has benefitted them, the reality is that the readjustment was painful. On arrival in a foreign land with nothing but their clothes and a princely sum of seven US dollars, disillusionment awaited them there too. The picture that the tourists see is often different from the world of the migrants.

Many, who migrated, particularly in the early years, felt that they had jumped from the frying pan into the fire. The migrants to Fiji used to say that they were promised *swarg*, but given *narak*. But they persisted and toiled, not only for their own benefit, but also for the country of their adoption.

Indian migrants faced untold hardship, discrimination and prejudices in different stages of their lives abroad. These have been recorded in the rich Diaspora literature. The psyche of the first-generation migrants has a touch of disillusionment even about India, which did not give them enough opportunities.

They are often torn between their nostalgic attachment to India and their duty to their land of adoption. They are also often impatient about the slow growth, corruption and inefficiency in India.

When nostalgia brought the original migrants, now prosperous and patriotic, back to India to do their duty to their families and to feather the nests for the future, they met with exploitation and lack of warmth. Their remittances were welcome, but they were not and their visits became less frequent.

Some lost their investments and homes, which they built for their eventual return. Many of them opted for foreign citizenships, took away their relatives with them what remained in India was only their *man* (mind), with *tan* (self) and *dhan* (wealth) in foreign lands.

The more they followed Indian developments on live television, the more disillusioned they became.

The subsequent generations of Indians abroad are free from such baggage of the past. They may be intolerant of the mosquitoes and the heat when they come to India, but they are proud of their heritage and the achievements of their parents abroad.

India, to them, is a brand, which gives them added advantage in their highly competitive environment.

They use the new opportunities available to them in India for their own benefit. With a few exceptions, the younger Indians abroad are sympathetic and supportive of India's efforts for modernisation. They have greater tolerance of India and greater appreciation of India's strength.

At crucial moments in history, it is the youth that showed greater determination to safeguard their interests by working with India.

When a military coup in Fiji resulted in discrimination against the Indians there, there was a mixed reaction in the Indian community. While all of them were hurt and aggrieved about the developments, many in the older generation were willing to accept the situation stoically and to move out of the country gradually.

But India's efforts to counter the coup and to restore democracy were much appreciated by the young generation. They were willing to stay and fight for their rights in cooperation with India. They demanded military training and arms from India. Some of them even blew themselves up for a cause.

Democracy came full circle in Fiji in ten years because of their heroic struggle and determination, while the older generation took refuge in Australia, New Zealand and the United States.

In the US, the second and third generation Indians stood solidly by India in the crucial days between the nuclear tests of 1998 and the signing of the nuclear agreement in 2008. While some in the older generation were doubtful about the wisdom of the tests, the younger generation saw it as the emergence of India as a world power and extended whole-hearted support.

The young Indian staffers of United States Congressmen and Senators lobbied with their bosses to shed their misgivings and to support India and the nuclear deal. They became prouder of their links with India and prepared themselves to use the new opportunities the warmth in India-US relations had generated.

Many have returned to India permanently to pursue their careers. Others stayed back, basking in the glory of a resurgent India. They joined political action committees, modelled on the work of the Jewish Diaspora and drew up plans for greater India-US cooperation.

The PBD conclaves do not attract the young Indians, as it is the older ones who go for a nostalgic extravaganza. To bring the youth to India, even to a Youth PBD, if held as proposed, there should be ingredients that attract them. The forum should become a true show window of opportunities.

Those below 35 years of age, who are now in key positions in politics and industry must be attracted join the PBD discussions. The younger ones should be brought in large numbers for interaction with young Indians. Investments in the youth will be most valuable.

In the area of culture, the movement of artists should not be only in one direction. Indian art forms have evolved abroad over the years and the innovations made by overseas Indians must be exposed to the Indian audience.

The time has come to cultivate the younger Pravasis, who may not be sentimental, but committed to a modern and vibrant India.

Published: January 24, 2013

M. HIGHER EDUCATION

EXPERIENCES OF AN
ACCIDENTAL EDUCATIONIST

Kerala's Higher Education Odyssey:
Progress and Pitfalls

"Higher Education in Kerala – what is wrong?" was the question asked of me at a leadership programme at the Xavier Institute for Management and Entrepreneurship (XMIE) Kochi. My answer was simple. "We are preparing our students for the 21st century with a 19th-century mindset and a 20th-century syllabus."

Higher education around the world has changed in the last 10 years more than it did in the last one hundred years, but we have remained shackled in our practices, procedures and ideologies. If we go on like this, "God alone can save his country", as stated by one of our best educationists, the late Prof. NR Madhava Menon.

About eight years ago, the then Kerala State Higher Education Council (KSHEC) had identified six areas in higher education which required immediate attention: infrastructure, teachers training, use of technology, autonomy, research, and internationalisation. The Council worked on these and related issues diligently and submitted more than 16 reports to the Government. Most of them still remain buried in the vaults of the Department of Higher Education because of lethargy, turf war, and ideological differences.

Happily, I find that the present Council has picked up a report on the establishment of a Kerala State Assessment and Accreditation Council (KSAAC) and I hope it will be established essentially as an academic audit system. The earlier idea of multiple accreditation agencies being developed for national accreditation is not being encouraged by the NAAC (National Assessment and Accreditation Council).

The unkindest cut of all by the KSHEC is the effort to destroy the one legacy the Council itself had succeeded to establish. Twenty autonomous colleges were approved by the UGC on the basis of a legislation approved by the Kerala legislature on the basis of a KSHEC report prepared by a committee headed by Prof. NR Madhava Menon. These were the best colleges in the state, selected on the basis of the rigorous criteria prescribed by the UGC.

Autonomy was granted only in academic matters to enable the colleges to decide what to teach, how to teach and how to assess the students. This was a game-changing development in Kerala, which was the only state, which did not have a single autonomous college in the state.

While some colleges embraced the new system wholeheartedly, some others, particularly the government colleges, opposed it tooth and nail. The University College, Thiruvananthapuram, did not even permit the UGC inspectors to enter the premises. But those colleges, which faithfully implemented the system vastly improved their performance and created history.

The only negative aspects of the system were the additional burden on teachers and introduction of additional self-financing courses as the Government would not fund the new courses. Opposition to the new system came from various sources, primarily from the Universities, which felt deprived of their authority to oversee these colleges.

Impediments were created to destroy the system. For instance, the legislation had stipulated that if no response was received from the University within 30 days after a proposal was sent to them by an autonomous college, the proposal would be taken as approved. To counter this, one University responded to every proposal asking the college not to take action till further notice!

In spite of these impediments, most of the autonomous colleges did extremely well, increasing efficiency and expeditious announcement of results. For the first time Kerala moved with the times and introduced a reform measure of immense significance.

The change of government in Kerala marked the beginning of the decline of autonomous colleges. The Committee established to oversee the new system was disbanded making it necessary for colleges to go to court to redress their grievances. The Universities stopped approving proposals from the autonomous colleges for courses and the like and made their functioning impossible.

The situation became worse than before in these colleges. The Government took an ambiguous position on autonomy by inviting engineering colleges to apply for it and there were reports of autonomy being given to some more colleges.

The latest news from KSHEC is that a committee established by it has come to the conclusion that autonomy is undesirable and that it should be abandoned. This is two steps back after we had taken one step forward. The Committee has done a hatchet job by giving a recommendation the Government wanted to hear. The Government cannot cancel the autonomy given by the UGC, but it can strangle these colleges by regressive measures.

Those of us who believe that India should have a liberal education system should feel ashamed that we are abandoning a step that was taken after considerable thought and deliberation. All safeguards were provided to maintain the necessary controls even on autonomous colleges.

It will be a sad day if the Government abandons autonomy to tighten its grip over the system, and take higher education two steps backward. I hope that good sense will prevail and we shall continue with the autonomous colleges. Otherwise even God cannot help his own country in educational reform.

Published: May 20, 2019

NEP 2020: Transformative Reforms in Education

The Union Government has recognised that formulation of the Education Policy is so complex that it should be entrusted to a rocket scientist. It had to be done with speed, precision, and pin point accuracy like landing softly on the surface of the moon.

The eminent educationists' officials engaged earlier turned out to be too conservative and rigid. An imaginative outsider was necessary to recommend measures for innovative and game-changing decisions regarding an old established institution.

Dr Kasturirangan, a man for all seasons, rose to the occasion and produced a set of recommendations on the basis of which the Cabinet has formulated a comprehensive framework to guide the development of education in the country.

The first education policy, based on the suggestions of the DS Kothari Commission, was formulated in 1968 and it was revised in 1986 and 1992. In the 28 years since then, the world has changed beyond recognition.

The growth of technology, speedy travel and the knowledge revolution demanded changes in what to teach, how to teach, and how to test. The rest of the world brought about such changes in education that had not taken place in the previous hundred years.

India, on the other hand, sailed along by its old academic vessel, tinkering with it here and there to keep it floating. We had brilliant academicians, entrepreneurs, administrators and politicians, who brought about changes, but without a comprehensive national scheme.

The NEP 2020 is a bold effort to provide the framework for sweeping changes in the whole education system in the nation, keeping in mind the need for access, equity, excellence, and employment.

The NEP proposes sweeping changes in the education system from pre-primary to PhD and skill development. The cumulative effect of the reform will be the creation of a liberal, choice-based education on the lines of the best practices in the world, making use of modern technology, international linkages and projections of employment opportunities and compulsions of the post Covid world.

The idea is to take advantage of the demographic dividend by training our graduates for the jobs of the 21st century. The objective is to make India a hub of Knowledge Economy. Unlike most resources that deplete when used, information and knowledge can be shared, and actually grow through application.

PM Modi observed that the New Education Policy emphasises on inter-disciplinary study and "will ensure focus is on what student wants to learn."

"We are focussing on the quality of education in India. Our attempts have been to make our education system the most advanced and modern for students of our country," he added. "Twenty-first century is the era of knowledge. This is the time for increased focus on learning, research, innovation," he said.

NEP has addressed several issues such as employability, stressful examination, insularity, lack of practical knowledge, language policy, excess of regulatory bodies, new opportunities for drop outs, internal assessment, opportunity for improving grades, banking of credits, role of the private sector and funding. The solutions suggested are expected to be in place in the next 10 years through a process of consultation and consensus building.

In school education, the policy focuses on overhauling the curriculum, "easier" Board exams, a reduction in the syllabus to retain its "core essentials", and thrust on "experiential learning and critical thinking".

In a significant shift from the 1986 policy which created a 10+2 structure of school education, the new NEP pitches for a "5+3+3+4" design corresponding to the age groups 3-8 years (foundational stage), 8-11 (preparatory), 11-14 (middle), and 14-18 (secondary).

This brings early childhood education (also known as pre-school education for children of ages 3 to 5) under the ambit of formal schooling. The mid-day meal programme will be extended to pre-school children.

The NEP says students until Class 5 should be taught in their mother tongue or regional language. This will be flexible in the case of schools like Kendriya Vidyalaya, whose students are likely to move to different states.

NEP 2020 states that universities from among the top 100 in the world will be able to set up campuses in India. While it does not elaborate the parameters to define the top 100, the Government may use the 'QS World University Rankings' as it has relied on these in the past while selecting universities for the 'Institute of Eminence' status.

However, none can start unless the new Ministry of Education brings in a new law that includes details of how foreign universities will operate in India. It is not clear whether the pending law will enthuse world class universities to come to India, particularly since the suggestion is that the universities cannot repatriate profits.

But some top-class universities may come, not for profits in cash, but in terms of knowledge and wisdom. Participation of foreign universities in India is currently limited to them entering into collaborative twinning programmes, sharing faculty with partnering institutions, and offering distance education. Over 650 foreign education providers have such arrangements in India.

In another major reform, the four-year degree programme proposed in the new NEP, students can exit after one year with a certificate, after two years with a diploma, and after three years with a bachelor's degree.

Four-year bachelor's programmes generally include a certain amount of research work and the student will get deeper knowledge in the subject he or she decides to major in. After four years, a BA student should be able to enter a research degree programme directly depending on how well they have performed.

When the four-year degree programme was first introduced in the Delhi University, the criticism was that it was meant to satisfy the requirement of US universities and the proposal was dropped because of the controversy. Henceforth, the Universities will be multi-disciplinary in character.

The IITs are already moving in that direction. IIT-Delhi has a humanities department and set up a public policy department recently. IIT-Kharagpur has a School of Medical Science and Technology. This has been justified on the ground that engineers should know more than just engineering. For instance, a good engineer needs to know the environmental and social impact of the things he builds. Many engineers are also becoming entrepreneurs, requiring knowledge of economics.

The Minister of Education has clarified that NEP only provides a broad direction and it is not mandatory. Since education is a concurrent subject (both the Centre and the state governments can make laws on it), the reforms proposed can only be implemented collaboratively by the Centre and the states. This will not happen immediately.

The Government has set a target of 2040 to implement the entire policy. Sufficient funding is also crucial in implementation of the whole policy. The government plans to set up subject-wise committees with members from relevant ministries at both the central and state levels to develop implementation plans for each aspect of the NEP.

With the addition of considerable private investment in education, NEP expects that India will achieve 50% GER by 2030. The outlay for education will be raised to 6% of the GDP. The present system of affiliation of colleges with universities will be phased out, as has been done in most countries of the world. Higher Education Institutions will have the facility to award their own degrees. It is up to them to decide whether the examinations should be external or internal.

The opposition to NEP has so far been low key. Kerala has complained that none of the submissions made by it has been included in NEP. Kerala is also of the opinion that NEP will benefit only the rich students. The Vice Chairman of the Kerala State Higher Education Council has severely criticised the concept of "Knowledge Economy" as he believes that corporates will manipulate it to their advantage.

Questions have been raised about "traditional knowledge systems" being included in the curriculum and teaching of Sanskrit, looking for elements of "saffronisation." But the Government has pledged that it "will try to take everyone along in the process of making a vibrant India."

It is a matter of satisfaction that a comprehensive road map presented to the Kerala Government in 2011 by the Kerala State Higher Education Council with me as Vice Chairman, covering infrastructure, teachers training, use of technology, autonomy for colleges, setting up of private universities, productive research, and internationalisation have been incorporated in one form or another in the NEP 2020.

But gender justice that KSHEC had stressed is conspicuous by its absence in NEP 2020.

A Global Education Meet, held in January 2016 in Thiruvananthapuram made recommendations to make Kerala an Educational Hub through these measures and the establishment of an Academic City and Higher Education Zones.

But the strong political objection from the opposition towards the end of the term of the previous Government ended the reform process. Very recently, the present Government has picked up for study a few of the old proposals like autonomous colleges and Education Zones.

A thorough reorganisation of the various regulatory bodies has been suggested, but much will depend on the shape and composition of the new bodies, about which there are apprehensions.

Though the National Assessment and Accreditation Council (NAAC) is to be merged with UGC and AICTE, it will function more or less independently.

Presently, NAAC has a reputation of riding roughshod over institutions and teachers by their arbitrary and reportedly corrupt ways. One can only hope that the NAAC will function with more transparency and integrity under the new dispensation.

Published: August 5, 2020

Beyond Blackboards: Modernizing Academic Methods

Minister for Human Resource Development Smriti Irani has spoken of a new education policy. The President indicated the contours of such a policy, stressing the need to use technology such as massive open online courses (MOOCs) and virtual classrooms and to create institutions of excellence in all states. The Rashtriya Uchchatar Shiksha Abhiyan (RUSA) seems to be alive and well. But what is needed is not just a new policy, but a new generation of higher education.

Poor infrastructure and technology, inadequately trained teachers, lack of autonomy for institutions, absence of a research culture and the failure to develop international linkages are the major reasons for the flaws in our higher education system. They are interlinked and need to be addressed through a holistic approach.

The RUSA document, which envisages a paradigm shift in higher education, addresses these and other issues. The thrust of its approach is to free the planning, funding, and monitoring of education from bureaucratic controls. But most states seem to believe that education is too important to be left to the educationists. The changes envisaged run counter to the political and bureaucratic interests entrenched in the present system, but it must be pursued.

Simple living and high thinking are traditional attributes of students, but comfort and convenience are key to creativity, as we see in the best centres of learning. Brick and mortar are as important as brains and dedication for academic achievement. As we train our teachers in modern pedagogy and update their knowledge, online material such as MOOCs and TED talks need to be used liberally.

The system of "flip schools" should be adopted, making it possible for students to listen to lectures at home and do their homework in class with the help of teachers. Resistance to technology, combined with the lack of connectivity and even electricity, pushes us back to the blackboard age. The time is not too far when lectures in class will be outdated. Even the examinations of the future will take the form of "gaming", which tests the ability of students to tackle real situations. Innovation will come from hands-on experience, not from writing essays.

In the separation of universities from research institutions, the fundamental role of learning has been eroded. Patents of products and processes, and even Nobel prizes, should emerge from the laboratories of universities. If Indian universities are not graded high, it is because research is not given priority. Exceptions like the Indian Institute of Science in Bangalore and Panjab University have been noted for their citations. Merging research institutions with universities and linking them to industries will ensure the pursuit of research with a purpose.

The affiliation system and bureaucratic control of funding have sapped the energies that autonomy gives. Things have come to such a pass that many students, teachers, and even managements dread the idea of autonomy. When Kerala introduced autonomous colleges for the first time this year, there was widespread opposition.

Academic freedom should lead to administrative and financial freedom, leaving the government to fashion broader strategies and monitor their implementation. Universities and autonomous colleges should determine what to teach, how to teach and how to evaluate the students.

Globalisation has brought international competition to our doors and we can exploit the demographic dividend only if we integrate our educational system with the revolutionary changes taking place in the rest of the world. Like political power, academic excellence is also moving from the west to the east. Our intellectual strength, the tradition of academic linkages with the world, our innovative skills, and the cost-advantages in India should attract international students, faculty and even great institutions.

But we have isolated our education system by restraining contacts, making it difficult for faculty and students to go abroad. No serious effort is being made to attract foreign students to India. By offering courses that are unique to India and creating comfortable facilities, we should be able to attract foreign students to our shores. The success we have achieved in medical tourism should be duplicated in educational tourism.

Creating a new higher education system is by no means easy. Years of lethargy and the acceptance of mediocrity have created a mindset that is hard to change. Too many vested interests will resist change of any kind, not just stealthily, but also openly in the name of preserving the noble purpose of education against commercialisation and commoditisation.

But unless India catches up with the education revolution around the world, it will not be able to realise its full intellectual potential. We need nothing less than higher education 2.0. We may not get on the list of world-class universities immediately, but we will be on our way there as the system begins to work.

Published: July 17, 2014

Post-Covid Education: Adapting to a New Normal

Having escaped the two World Wars and past pandemics, we thought that 9/11 and the recession of 2008 were cataclysmic. We thought that the world would change on account of those, but life came back to normal fairly soon even though terrorism emerged as a permanent menace. The security hassles at the airports are the only big difference that 9/11 has created, though mankind became more vulnerable despite building up of nuclear stockpiles.

Compared to the Covid-19, striking full force across the world, the disasters of the early 21st century were of limited impact. The year 2020 will be remembered as a turnaround point in human history, not just because many will die, but because the Covid-19 pandemic is forcing us to reinvent ourselves. The only question is whether the course of history will change or whether the pandemic will only hasten the processes which are already in progress.

One area which needs to adjust speedily to the new situation is education, which had already changed in the last few years because of the technological revolution. The use of technology, which was till now an additional support system for effective teaching has become the new norm as normal classes have become hazardous. For parents, teachers, and students, it is possible that some aspects of schooling might not go back to the way they were before.

With Covid-19, educational institutions are rapidly changing the basic way they do their work. Some have become old-fashioned correspondence schools, with the vast majority of interaction happening by written mail. Some have tried to recreate the school setting online using digital tools like Zoom. Others are in-between, directing students to online tutoring and practice programs, and posting videos.

Most people believe that the present arrangements are temporary and they wish to get back to normal as direct interaction between teachers and students as an essential ingredient of education.

In the current crisis, Covid-19 is forcing parents to be teachers and forcing everyone—students, parents, and teachers—to adapt to online learning tools. Some people get comfortable with some of these adaptations. Likewise, while families are now stressed out trying to educate their children, they are also experiencing educational methods and tools that they have never seen before. They are getting more accustomed to them. Mothers and fathers are becoming more responsible to educate their children.

Machine learning is not new to many education systems, though, in India we have absolute faith in the importance of teachers in not only teaching students, but also in shaping their character. Modern methods like Massive Open Online Courses (MOOCs), Flip Schools, etc. were considered dilution of the role of the teachers and were not easily adopted. They were seen as luxuries of the Western world at best and necessary evils to make up for shortage of teachers at worst.

Use of online tools as the main method of teaching will not be easily accepted in India. The lack of adequate internet facilities, lack of equipment, and poor power situation in villages will be pointed out as the problems in adopting online education. But most students will soon have laptops and some type of internet access, narrowing the digital divide.

Teachers are going to like many of the tools and they will have an easier time using them now that students have some experience with them. Online tools can be helpful complements to in-person instruction—instead a replacement for it—allowing teachers to focus more on engaging students and mentoring them. There may also be some shift towards tutoring at home, at least till online tools are installed. Families will get more accustomed to online learning.

However, this approach has the significant disadvantage that families have to play the role of monitor and teacher. Few families want or can afford that, given their work schedules and other responsibilities. Moreover, research consistently suggests that students learn less in fully virtual environments. In-person, teacher-led instruction simply has too many advantages.

A shift to some online tools could shift the role of teachers, making them more like coaches and mentors. They can point students to very good online lectures and then be there to provide guidance and feedback, and to make connections across topics. The roles of students and parents could also shift. Now that they have more places to look, they may be more likely to try and address learning needs on their own. When roles change, everything else can change with it—though in less predictable ways.

There have been many efforts to introduce machine learning in India. The main reason for the campaign for MOOCs was the knowledge gap between college syllabi and the results of modern research. The teachers tend to remain within the confines of their learning acquired several years ago as they neither have the time nor the inclination to acquire new knowledge.

A text book in Kerala had a CD attached to it and it was written in bold letters that the book should not be used for teaching without seeing the CD. Most teachers did not bother because they had no CD player in the school and their personal CD players were not meant for such purposes.

As for MOOCs or its Indian version, Swayam, the teachers found the effort to identify suitable courses and to monitor progress with a view to give credits an unnecessary burden. If MOOCs were used widely, it would have been easier for the system to switch to machine learning when it became necessary because of Covid-19.

Flip schools were also suggested as part of educational reform. Here the students were given lectures on their mobiles to listen to them at home and come to class to do their "homework". They could interact with the teachers and learn the application of lectures for solving problems. Here again, lack of equipment, difficulties in systematic follow up and other inconveniences were cited. Flip schools are likely to become common in the post-Covid-19 system because of its self-learning advantages.

Online examinations will be the biggest challenge in India, where there has been hardly any effort to reform the examination system. Essay writing is a major part of the examinations and collective evaluation is the norm. Online examinations will have to be either objective type or solution-based answering of questions. Some universities have tried, but abandoned the experiment.

Now that this has become a necessity, strenuous efforts will have to be made to redesign the examinations to make them more machine friendly. If the new system works during the crisis period, it can become part of the new norm, which will be economical and hazard free.

An educational system, which was changing rapidly in many countries to suit the current technology and commercial needs, has suddenly and unexpectedly come under extreme pressure to expedite changes overnight so that the learning of students around the globe is not disrupted even for a short period. Those countries, which had a positive mindset about changes in education have been able to accomplish much in a short time.

But India, which has been conservative and reluctant to welcome change, is still far behind. If only the reforms suggested were implemented earlier, we would have been in a stronger position. We have to start on a clean slate and catch up with the transition brought about by Covid-19.

Published: April 29, 2020

Rethinking Higher Education: UGC vs HEC Debate

The Modi government seems determined to change the archaic education system in India. Among its latest proposed measures are replacement of the University Grants Commission (UGC) with a Higher Education Commission of India (HECI), setting up of a separate agency to hold some examinations and giving some institutions in the private sector a higher status to build world-class universities.

All these have been criticised as either unnecessary or motivated by considerations other than educational reform. Unless there is a change in our mindset to accept changes, no reform programmes are likely to succeed. Institutions will come and go, but education will remain anachronistic.

"It does not matter if a cat is black or white, so long as it catches mice." These famous words of Deng Xiaoping should be borne in mind when we look at the new avatar of the UGC being proposed by the Union Government with the HECI. Since the black cat did not catch enough mice, the expectation is that the white one will do it. But happily, the second cat has features other than the colour to give us hope that it may perform better than the first. The declaration at the very outset that the mandate given to the UGC required redefinition based on the changing priorities of higher education is a truism that will not be challenged.

The disappearance of the word, "Grants" from the name of the new body is just a recognition of the fact that funding of state universities and others have already been shifted from the UGC to the Ministry of Human Resource Development (MHRD) through the Rashtriya Uchchatar Shiksha Abhiyan (RUSA), set up by the previous Government. RUSA was meant to be an academic body, but it was soon swallowed up by the bureaucracy.

Equally elementary is the jurisdiction given to the new body for all higher educational institutions, excluding institutions of national importance. (Curiously though, the Chairpersons of All-India Council for Technical Education (AICTE) and National Council for Teacher Education (NCTE) have been included in the Advisory Council. Does it mean that AICTE and NCTE will continue to exist?)

The qualifications and qualities of the high officials of the new Commission have been elaborated, but there is considerable ambiguity about the mandatory provisions, allowing the Government to appoint anyone, including "overseas citizens of India."

Here, doubts have been raised about the possibility of the Government of the day filling up these positions with its own supporters. But this should be taken for granted in any institution under any Government. Even though we do not have the spoils system as in the US, every Government is guilty of nepotism and that will continue regardless of the nature and structure of the institutions.

What India needs is a liberal education, which promotes the autonomy of higher educational institutions for the free pursuit of knowledge, innovation, incubation and entrepreneurship, and for facilitating access, inclusion and opportunities to all and providing for holistic growth of higher education and research in a competitive global environment. This is precisely stated among the functions of the Commission.

Further, it will promote the quality of academic instruction and maintenance of academic standards. Moreover, learning outcomes should be specified for courses of study in higher education and lay down standards of teaching, assessment, and research. Curriculum development, training of teachers, and skill development have also been included as the Commission's functions.

Monitoring the implementation of its decisions has been clearly assigned to the Commission. In other words, the functions are precisely specified and the Commission has no scope for diverging from its mandate. This is the heart of the proposal, which is beyond reproach.

Other important features of the responsibilities of the Commission are the authority to grant authorisation to higher education institutions and to revoke authorisation to them, if the need arises. The procedure for both actions has been laid down in detail. This is an important function, which gives the Commission some teeth.

The thrust of the mandate of the Commission is that it should be an academic body, with minimum interference from the bureaucracy and the politicians. But the Government has no intention to allow it to act totally independently. There will be an Advisory Council chaired by the Union Minister of Human Resource Development, with the Chairperson and members of the Commission as well as Chairpersons and Vice-Chairpersons of the State Councils for higher education as members. The advice rendered by the Advisory Council is binding on the Commission.

In addition, the Commission shall be guided by policy directions of the Central Government and if there is a dispute on policy, the decisions of the Central Government will be final. Curiously, the Commission can give autonomy to other institutions, but the Commission itself will have very little autonomy in practice. The Commission will have no powers for policy making, funding of activities or any authority, which is not subject to the authority of the Advisory Council.

In a sense, the new mandate could have been given to the UGC, without the "G" in it, instead of creating a new body. But the formation of the Commission is a signal that the Government means business to redefine higher education and to reinvent it to use the opportunities and to meet the challenges of the 21st century. Without drastic changes, India will not be able to derive the benefits of the demographic dividend.

One important point that is missing in the new context is the need to empower universities and colleges to re-engineer the education system on the basis of technological advancement. A few computers here and there will not suffice anymore as artificial intelligence and robotics too will energise learning in advanced nations. Many of the plans like revision of curriculum will be overtaken by technological advances unless the new body takes charge of the use of technology in higher education.

The use of Massive Open Online Courses (MOOCs) and "Flip Schools" must be embraced and popularised. "If the poor cannot come to education, education must reach them at the plough, in the factory, everywhere," said Swami Vivekananda. Perhaps, the way to get education everywhere is to embrace technology.

The Union Government has also announced the creation of a National Testing Agency to develop a new examination system. Of course, our examination system is antiquated, with little use of technology. But why this responsibility has not been given to the new Commission is a bit of a mystery. The announcement of creating world-class universities is a welcome development.

The Higher Education Commission should be welcomed as many features in it point to a liberal, students-centric, faculty-oriented education system. To get there, we need a consensus among the political parties about the purpose of education and the best way to achieve it. Narrow political, religious, and sectarian considerations will not lead us to that heaven of freedom in education.

Published: July 14, 2018

N. KERALA

A STATE OF
CONTRADICTIONS

Superstitions and Scams:
Kerala's Vulnerabilities

Kerala is a spoiled state on account of the graciousness and generosity of the rest of the world. Statistics of various kinds are quoted by others to compliment Kerala on its accomplishments. Kerala has the largest number of literate people in India, but this prompts the characterisation of Keralites as intelligent. It is called "God's Own Country" because of the greenery and water bodies even when waste is accumulated here and there.

Since Kerala has the highest Gross Enrolment Ratio, we are rated high in higher education. Kerala is rated as No.1 in reaching the millennium goals, gets an award for Covid care when more than 50 per cent of Covid-19 infections in India occur in Kerala.

Kerala Police are rated No.1 in India even as crimes against women and children are shockingly high. But the "Kerala Model" is fraying at the edges. No wonder YouTube commentator Joe Scaria called Kerala a "Textbook Tiger," perfect on paper, but deficient in practice.

The high prevalence of scandals, scams, gold smuggling, bank bursting, domestic violence and rape is explained away as over-reporting by the media. Femmes fatales operate openly, dominate the news for months together and fade away till political expediency brings them back again. Not a day passes without reports of scams and suicides.

But nothing is as shameful as the antiquities scam, which has exposed the gullibility of Keralites at every level. For a large number of people to invest crores of rupees in such things as the original staff of Moses, Lord Krishna's curd pot, one of the thirty pieces of silver that Judas earned for betraying Jesus, Tipu Sultan's throne and Einstein's skull, the willing suspension of disbelief was beyond imagination.

The list includes a cross made out of the mud that was on Jesus's feet when he was crucified, a thread from the cloth used to wipe Jesus's face during the crucifixion, a nail of Portuguese priest St Anthony of Padua, a piece of St Alphonsa's veil, and a 2,000-year-old jug of Jesus. At this rate, a withered fig leaf could have been sold as Eve's suit in paradise for a crore of rupees!

For several years, a person fooled many people, styling himself as a motivational speaker, doctor, cosmetologist, art promoter and antique dealer, by building influence in high official circles, particularly the police, and parading them as his patrons and protectors. The facts that came out were stranger than any fiction ever created by Hollywood or Bollywood to unravel the tricks of global crimes.

An odd antique may have been overvalued in some places, but manufacturing antiques attributed to pre-historic times and managing to get people to part with their money for them has not featured even in crime thrillers. The police, who officially provided protection to him even after receiving complaints, finally nabbed him after a ceremony attended by many celebrities, very much in Bollywood style.

In Kerala, even as details of the man's deceit and crimes started to unfold, celebrities who took pride in being photographed with him are distancing themselves from him. But like in other scams over the years, the excitement will die down and the criminal may spend some time in prison after an investigation and all others will be let off as lacking evidence about their involvement. The state government is lukewarm about this case because it will hit not only the opposition but also some government appointees.

The disturbing factor of this scam is the evidence to show that the law-and-order authorities themselves and some politicians also fell prey. These are people, who are by training expected to be particularly watchful. The trust that they displayed in a criminal without suspicion is unbelievable and, therefore, the concern is that they have aided and abetted him and protected him in return for various favours. Even more importantly, this case devalues the literacy rate and the degrees awarded by the universities in Kerala.

Kerala students with 100 per cent marks apply for admission in Delhi colleges, but their marks are discounted because of the growing awareness that these marks are often gifts bestowed on students for various considerations. A parent told me that his daughter could not get admission in a top college in Delhi even with 100 per cent marks! Such a reputation will have a cascading effect on Kerala graduates and their chances of getting jobs outside will be in jeopardy.

The scam may also have a devastating effect on business collaboration in Kerala. Scamsters and crooks will come to Kerala, knowing that it is possible to exploit the gullibility of educated Keralites and their greed, manifesting itself in an eagerness to make money in every possible way. The reputation of the Kerala model of development and the ease of doing business will disappear. The criminal will get away, but his imprint will remain on the whole population of Kerala.

A Kerala historian, who is supportive of the present ruling coalition in the state, says that Kerala society is producing decision-makers of the lowest quality. He says that there are capable people in Kerala, but "as a collective, we are behaving like there is no tomorrow." A multinational financial consultant is of the view that the problem of Kerala is not just the brain drain, but also a competence drain.

Such comments have not been made in the case of mounting crimes in Kerala as these are individual cases. The antics over antiquities reveal a deeper malady amounting to a mass hysteria of gullibility. Instead of creating a polarisation on political grounds to save those involved, a deeper introspection is necessary about Kerala society.

Confidence tricksters are not new, but this is the first time that a large number of people were hypnotised into believing that relics of pre-historic times can be traded in this technological age. Technology has the capability to detect the value of art work, but no technology wizard in Kerala has come up with a formula to expose this scam. The damage the scam has done to the image of Kerala should not be underestimated. Never before has the intellectual elite in Kerala been so exposed.

Published: October 9, 2021

Gold Rush: Kerala's Obsession with Gold

Lord Padmanabha, the presiding deity of Thiruvananthapuram, also known as Trivandrum, the capital of Kerala, who is depicted as reclining on a gigantic snake, Anantha, suddenly went up in the estimation of his devotees recently, when it was discovered that he has an inestimable treasure of gold in his custody.

Kerala values nothing more than gold, and it is comforting for the people of the state to know that their erstwhile rulers too had a fascination for the yellow metal, which they stored in the temple as an offering and as an insurance against famine. The innumerable jewellery shops around the temple and elsewhere in Kerala may be handling as much gold as the temple has accumulated. "God's Own Country" is fast becoming "Gold's Own Country."

With only 3 percent of India's population, Kerala gobbles up 20 percent of the country's gold every year, and the World Gold Council estimates that India, the largest consumer of gold in the world, consumes 30 percent of the global supply.

Two hundred thousand people are employed in the gold industry in this tiny state. Such is the love of gold in Kerala that there may be no household without some gold, tucked away as savings, either to be given away as wedding gifts for daughters, or to raise cash by way of gold loans or outright sale.

Buying ornaments and investing in gold is an old tradition, but the proliferation of jewellery stores doing brisk business in gold, diamonds and platinum is a recent phenomenon in Kerala, coinciding with the rise in remittances from the Persian Gulf.

While Indian migrants in the West keep their money in Swiss banks and other destinations, the Indians in the Gulf send their money back home either to purchase land in their villages or to buy gold for their women, or simply as investment.

When the gold prices were favourable in the Gulf, they brought gold there, and many Kerala-based shops sprang up in the Gulf. Now that the international prices are the same, gold shops have come up in every city in Kerala. In small towns in Kerala, the most dazzling buildings are either jewellery stores, silk houses, or combined "wedding palaces." Fashionable eating places or supermarkets are extremely rare even in prosperous towns.

Most film stars of repute are either partners or "goodwill ambassadors" of these enterprises and appear on billboards or television commercials. One of them, Mohanlal, who has interests in different aspects of the gold business, advocates buying gold in various TV commercials throughout the day. He enticingly asks what his fans are doing in the evening and asserts that he cannot celebrate anything without them. He makes it appear as though gold makes the world go round.

If you want to see gold at its most ostentatious, go to a wedding. At these events, when it comes to the precious metal, the rule is the more, the merrier. Many brides are covered in gold ornaments from the neck to the knee, not to speak of the weight placed on their heads. They resemble temple elephants, which are decked from top to bottom with golden decorations during festivals.

Since gold ornaments are highly desirable and they only increase in value, all available money is spent on them with no concern. Beg or borrow, the brides must be decked in gold. They are literally worth their weight in gold. The poorer the people, the greater is the desire to show-off their wealth in gold.

As the lust for gold skyrockets, the demand for imitation gold jewellery has also grown by leaps and bounds. Outside Lord Padmanabha's temple gates, as tall as the Joyalukkas jewellery retailer's building, is Kollam Supreme, a jeweller that freely displays intricate gold ornaments, with no care for security. The secret is that these are just gold-plated ornaments that look like the real thing, with just a gram of real gold used in each of them.

The Kollam brides look as impressive as their richer counterparts at a fraction of the cost. This new brand of ornaments satisfies the intense desire of ordinary people look as affluent as their rich neighbours.

Kerala is littered with small financial institutions that lend money instantly against gold deposits. Muthoot, one of the largest of these lenders, prides itself in completing a transaction within three minutes, and its branches can be seen on every corner in Kerala.

The same family has competing businesses, with each brother advertising in a different colour, red being the most prominent of them. The owner of the red Muthoot was featured on the cover of Forbes magazine for running a big business empire in India based on gold loans. Hundreds of his branches are small establishments, with a simple, but elegant counter in front, and a big fortified room behind.

Those who have feared a crash in gold prices have been proved wrong, as prices are escalating every day, even more than fuel prices. Those who have stocks of gold are overjoyed, and people buy up even at phenomenal prices in the expectation of even higher returns. Soaring prices of any commodity should normally cause concern and raise a hue and cry. But Keralites continue to buy gold in the full confidence that gold prices will never fall.

It's not as if Keralites don't have other avenues for investment. Land is another hot commodity that brings in steady profits. But land transactions are fairly transparent, land registration is cumbersome and expensive, and land holdings are hard to hide. Land transactions also require sound judgment as there is an element of speculation in them. For these reasons, when it comes to their money, Keralites are putting their faith in gold.

Published: December 25, 2012

Political Satire in Kerala:
Embracing Humour in Politics

India may have dented its image as a champion of press freedom after the anti-corruption activist Aseem Trivedi was arrested in September for lampooning the Parliament in a cartoon, but in fact, political satire has a long history in many parts of the country, especially in Kerala.

No-holds-barred portraits of political leaders are daily fare on every local channel, and the targets of such shows even see it as an honour of sorts. Such tolerance for ridicule lies in the fact that mimicry has long been the staple of entertainment in Kerala.

Most of the top movie stars in Malayalam-language cinema, also known as Mollywood, started their careers as mimicry artists at temple festivals and other public functions. In the old days, they imitated sounds around them, like the birds, the animals and the machines. Then they moved on to imitating popular movie stars and eventually to political leaders.

With the explosion of the 24/7 television channels, many of them news channels, the mimicry artists found their way to the small screen. To meet the competition from entertainment channels, the news channels started showing movie clips in the guise of entertainment news and introduced several programs with sharp political satire.

The longest-running of these series is 'Munshi' on Asianet, a daily show poking fun at the prevalent political and social practices. A fixed cast of half a dozen men, who represent not only different political views but also different castes and communities, discuss the day's major event with sharp wit and comical action. They take sides, attack politicians by name, and generally reflect the frustrations of the common man. Finally, the wisest of them all, Munshi, or the Pundit, a wise old man who does not participate in the conversation, sums up the whole situation in a proverb or a pithy quote.

The actors live and work together day in and day out to produce their program, which reminds viewers of the cartoonist R.K. Laxman's Common Man, who appeared every day on the front page of a national daily to offer his commentary on the faults and foibles of politicians.

Asianet has another serial called 'Cinemala', in which actors appear as politicians. Mimicry is used very effectively to bring out the most comical aspects of the political leaders, and the actors bear striking similarities to politicians like the Defence Minister A.K. Antony, the Kerala Chief Minister Oommen Chandy, and the Communist leader V.S. Achuthanandan.

All the channels seem to have found their own versions of Antony, Chandy and Achuthanandan, with varying degrees of similarity with the originals. Just as the real Charlie Chaplin once lost a Chaplin look-alike contest, the real politicians will have a hard time competing with their impersonators, as the latter appear to be more authentic than the former.

Slapstick comedy is not the only medium for political satire. Following the lead of a show called 'Natakame Ulakam' ("All the World is a Stage") on Amrita TV, several others have emerged as one-man talk shows, in which political events are described with various degrees of ridicule. Some, like 'Varanthyam' ("Weekend") on Indiavision and 'Sakshi' ("Witness") on the Leftist Kairali channel, show actual clips of news events to prove the point that facts are often stranger than fiction.

Torn out of context in some instances, the words and deeds of politicians appear ridiculous. One favourite item features political leaders falling asleep on the dais, often when the speaker talks about the need to awake, arise and stop not until the goal is reached. Some shows literally put words in the mouths of politicians by playing the soundtrack of a film.

Asianet's serious news program, 'Cover Story', is the hardest hitting of all the political programs. The anchor, Sindhu Suryakumar, minces no words in her critical analyses of men and matters, and reinforces her arguments with hard facts. She also uses songs and scenes from Mollywood to great effect, but the mood is serious and purposeful. Much to the credit of the authorities, nobody has either tried to intimidate her or to influence her, and she carries on merrily, exposing all politicians.

"In my channel, I am happy to juxtapose a serious program on international matters with a slap-stick on Indian politicians," said T.N. Gopakumar, editor-in-chief of Asianet News. "I professionally believe that this goes to strengthen the aspirations of the people, who exercise their right to vote to elect a better government. Of course, we ensure that satire does not cross the borders, turn into vendetta or malice."

A major dilemma of the politicians is whether to laugh or cry when they become caricatures in popular comedy shows. The appearance of their doubles indicates that they have arrived on the scene, and they may rejoice on that account. Only those who matter politically are imitated and ridiculed. On the other hand, upcoming politicians are not likely to be pleased to see their weaknesses exposed on television.

"As a devotee of free speech, I tell myself that it is flattering to be found worthy of being satirised, so one just grin and bears it and hopes the damage is not lasting," said Shashi Tharoor, a member of Parliament and recently-named minister of state for Human Resources Development. He was recently portrayed in one show's sketch as doing a cinematic dance with his wife, lampooning his image as a romantic Bollywood-style hero.

For more seasoned politicians, it is just an occupational hazard they have learned to live with. Mr. Chandy, the state's Chief Minister, was philosophical about his many appearances on these shows. "Satire is part of the vibrant visual media in Kerala, which enjoys freedom of expression," he said.

Published: November 1, 2012

4

Kerala's Dilemma:
Struggles and Solutions

Mythology, history, tourism, faith, and commerce are jumbled up in the theories about how Kerala came to be known as "God's Own Country". Lord Parasurama, the sixth incarnation of Vishnu, is supposed to have thrown his axe out into the sea to create a strip of land to settle Brahmins there to atone for his sin of having killed many to avenge the death of his father. Naturally, Lord Parasurama's land became God's own.

Travancore, which forms the greater part of Kerala, was handed over by one of the Maharajas, Marthanda Varma Anizham Thirunal, to Lord Padmanabha, the presiding deity of the ancient temple in Thiruvananthapuram, the capital, and ruled it on His behalf till India became independent. Though ruled by a human, the country became God's own.

Tourism promotion demands telling slogans and it is believed that some copywriter literally copied a slogan used by New Zealand tourism and stealthily sold it to Kerala tourism on the ground that New Zealand and Kerala had similar landscapes. Truly, Kerala looks like an unkempt and untidy New Zealand and deserves to be God's own country. For some mysterious reasons, New Zealand does not seem to have protested.

The last theory is about the explosion of faith in Kerala in recent years. The skyline of Kerala changed dramatically in the last 20 years with huge temples, churches, and mosques everywhere the eyes could see. Those who could afford to build new houses of worship, did so, while others built massive gates to miniscule places of worship. In a single trip to Kerala, anyone can see the millions of Hindu gods and many images of the single God worshipped by many. Not surprisingly, the visitors began calling it "God's Own Country"!

I had suspected that the appellation "God's Own Country" is an escape route from human responsibilities. One can always take the line that God alone can resolve Kerala's problems and that there is nothing that we can do about them. We tend to consider human beings of astounding achievements as avatars, as we ordinary mortals, do not need to strive to emulate them!

This has become more evident with the advent of Covid-19 and the consequent lockdown. And much happens which are illegal, unethical, and unacceptable to a democracy, but there is no action, only investigation. The sense of resignation goes with the trust in God that He will settle matters in due time.

In the case of natural calamities, there are certain factors beyond human control and it is only natural to see them as God's fury. Floods are an annual feature in Kerala and they cause death and devastation, which are taken for granted. Many plans are made to prevent floods the subsequent year, but it is cheaper and easier to leave such matters to God Himself.

We celebrate the heroism of the fishermen who courageously save the people in peril, and recommend Nobel Prize for them, but take no action to keep the waterways free or the dams strengthened. A special offering to the gods is a better insurance than anything that Life Insurance Corporation can offer.

Alcohol remains a major challenge in the state; very close to the situation in the former Soviet Union, which collapsed not because of Glasnost or Perestroika, but reduced production of vodka under Mikhail Gorbachev, according to some experts. The belief is that if prohibition is introduced across the board, the state will collapse economically and many will die after taking spurious liquor.

If a daily wageworker does not spend half his earnings at the bars and the beverages corporation outlets, the government will not be able to supply rice at a subsidised price and the families will starve. The authorities can, therefore, leave the issue to the gods. Gold is next only to alcohol as an opiate of the people.

Today, a highly explosive mix of honey-trapping, gold smuggling, bureaucratic bungling, terrorist funding and complicity in all this of a diplomatic mission is rocking the state, but all the action is in the media. Central sleuths of various hues hover around and give bits and pieces of news each day to feed the evening debates on TV channels.

The height of irony is that repatriation flights meant for those in distress are being used for gold smuggling and some say that the chartered flights were financed by smuggling gold. Private holding of gold per capita is the highest in the world in Kerala. God also goes with the gold in Kerala as the most famous temple in the state has the largest collection of gold and gold ornaments and precious stones in the world. What the gods love, the devotees love too.

India used to take pride in the fact that no Indian citizen had joined any of the international terror groups, but now there is evidence of Keralites, disappearing and then surfacing as terrorist warriors. Many take up jobs by terrorist outfits as a livelihood—with the additional perk of the heavenly abode after life. But the shocking thing is that there is no general revulsion to such an approach. The society provides them safe haven and does not ostracise them because they too seem to be doing God's work.

In the initial days of the lockdown, there was a sudden dip in crime and traffic accidents, but they picked up in no time, first domestic violence and then heinous crimes. The most inventive method of murder was committed in Kerala when a husband got a cobra and let it out in his own bedroom to bite his wife. It is a mystery as to how the cobra bit the wife and not the husband.

Serial killings of families with poison is becoming common and parading the unrepentant criminals is a common sight on television screens. The compulsory mask has come in handy to hide the identity of the criminals. Unending investigations and court cases drag on in the belief that justice will be done by the gods.

In this backdrop, the biggest festival of Kerala, Onam, has dawned. Even though there is nothing to celebrate, Keralites must rejoice as they cannot disappoint an old benevolent monarch, Mahabali, who was consigned to the netherworld by an incarnation of Vishnu Himself, and will be visiting his subjects during the Onam season. The festival is the time for Keralites to pretend that they are as happy and prosperous today as they were during his reign.

So huge home-delivered feasts and online festivities are already lined up, regardless of the call to cut expenditure to save for the Covid-19 victims. Malayalis cannot let go a traditional festival even in the midst of disasters. So with festive masks depicting pictures of colourful gods on them and social distancing thrown to the winds, we appease the gods by feasting and drinking. God alone can save His own country and the rest of Kerala can celebrate Onam with gusto.

Published: August 24, 2020

Mullaperiyar Dam Dispute:
A War of Words

Futurologists say that the next world war will be fought over water because fresh supplies will become increasingly scarce. Pakistan has already added water to the long list of disputes with India and people in India have grown concerned about what they say are Chinese efforts to dam the Brahmaputra River.

If the South Indian states of Kerala and Tamil Nadu were independent countries with their own armies, they might have been at war by now over the water held behind a dam in Kerala that supplies Tamil Nadu. Protests and demonstrations have lasted for more than five years and tensions have been so elevated recently that some citizens have resorted to violence as India's federal government, for the most part, has watched helplessly.

The Mullaperiyar dam on the Periyar river sits in and belongs to the state of Kerala. The state wants to repair or rebuild the 116-year-old dam, with its own money if necessary, because it fears that the dam could fail because it has developed leaks and because tremors around it have become more frequent in recent months. An estimated 3 million people live downstream from the dam and could be submerged if it is breached.

More than 100 years ago, Kerala agreed to divert the east-flowing river and leased a piece of its territory to the other state for 999 years. In return, Kerala now receives 1 million rupees, or about $19,000, a year. Historians believe that the king of Travancore signed the deal under pressure in the face of demands of the bigger state that was backed by India's British rulers.

Tamil Nadu, a relatively more arid state that has chronic water problems, has refused to renegotiate the deal or agree to the construction of anew dam. The state's leaders appear to be terrified that they will not be allocated as much water from a new dam as they draw from the river now. That fear persists even though Kerala officials have offered assurances that they will not change the current water sharing formula.

Officials in Kerala have often presented a muddled and inconsistent case for why the dam should be rebuilt. Some have argued that the dam was close to collapse, while others have said that simply reducing the amount of water stored behind the dam and building a tunnel to relieve the pressure of the water would be sufficient to protect the dam.

Independent scientists are divided on Kerala's claims that the dam is in mortal danger, but they are no more convinced by Tamil Nadu's assertions that it is completely safe after 116 years of use. The Indian Institute of Technology Roorkee, one of the country's leading universities, has concluded that the dam will collapse if the area is struck by an earthquake of magnitude 7 or more.

No one is certain whether another dam downstream could contain the water if the Mullaperiyar is breached.

A committee appointed by the Indian Supreme Court to study the issue has signalled that it is more inclined to support Tamil Nadu's position. But as a compromise, it is likely to recommend the construction of another dam downstream. Kerala has not only agreed to bear the cost of such a dam, but also expressed its willingness to jointly manage it with Tamil Nadu. But the feasibility of such a dam is in question and its environmental impact may be significant.

In the case of another infrastructure project, Tamil Nadu officials have protested federal plans to set up a nuclear power plant on its eastern coast at Koodankulam. The state has argued that the plant could expose its residents to radiation. Yet, it does not share Kerala's concern that an old and leaking dam might burst and drown millions of lives. Floods have killed far more people than nuclear meltdowns. About 25 years ago, a dam in Gujarat caved in and killed hundreds of people.

In Kerala, recent protests appear to be stoked by a regional party that is part of the ruling coalition government hoping to gain political points. An appeal by Prime Minister Manmohan Singh has calmed those voices, but a recent visit by Mr. Singh to Tamil Nadu, which is ruled by a different party that is not part of the government's coalition, did not advance the cause of negotiations.

In theory, the dispute could be solved easily if the government repairs or rebuilds the dam while guaranteeing that Tamil Nadu will continue to receive ample supplies of water. Lives would be saved in Kerala and livelihood would be saved in Tamil Nadu.

Instead, the war of words and protests continue, threatening trade and peace between the states.

Published: January 8, 2012

Kakkathuruthu Chronicles: Exploring Kerala's Magical Island

'Sunset in Kerala is greeted by a series of rituals.
Here on Kakkathuruthu, a tiny island in Kerala's tangled backwaters, children leap into shallow pools.
Women in saris head home in skiffs.
Fishermen light lamps and cast nets into the lagoon.
Bats swoop across the horizon snapping up moths.
Shadows lengthen, the sky shifts from pale blue to sapphire and the emerald tinged 'Island of Crows'—the Malayalam name for this sandy spot along the Malabar coast—embraces night.
If dawn is awakening and daytime illumination, then twilight is transcendence, a final burst of vitality before darkness falls.'

This inscription on a magnificent photograph of the island of Kakkathuruthu in the *National Geographic* magazine catapulted the tiny island to international fame.

The suggestion by *National Geographic* was that one should be in Hawaii at 5 am, Paris at 6 am, San Francisco at 7 am, Abu Dhabi at 8 am, Melbourne at 9 am, Tanzania at 10 am, Argentina at 11 am, Namibia at 12 noon, Charleston, South Carolina, at 1 pm, Portland at 2 pm, New Zealand at 3 pm, Croatia at 4 pm, Tokyo at 5 pm, Kakkathuruthu, Kerala, at 6 pm, Cuba at 7 pm, New York at 8 pm, China at 9 pm, Budapest at 10 pm, Monaco at 11 pm, Norway at 12 midnight, 3500 feet on a plane at 1 am, Atacama Desert at 2 am, Tel Aviv at 3 am and end up at Northern Ireland at 4 am.

Such a trip is humanly impossible with existing technology, but a day may come when someone will be able to accomplish it.

I was amazed, however, to find that I had already visited 20 out of the 24 must-see places listed by *National Geographic* in its feature, 'Around the World in 24 Hours' and to add one more to my list, I simply had to drive for six hours from Thiruvananthapuram, have a delicious lunch with former RA&W chief Hormis Tharakan and his wife Molly, ride a country boat for 20 minutes and land on Kakkathuruthu Island in Vembanad Lake, Alappuzha, in time for the celebrated sunset at 6 pm.

As a bonus, Maneesha Panicker, who owns the Kayal resort, and her mother Shantha Panicker served us tea and a delectable *ada* or rice cake cooked in plantain leaf.

The remaining three destinations—Atacama Desert, Northern Ireland and Tel Aviv—will have to wait.

Gone are the days when diplomatic travels took me to exotic places around the world frequently!

When I heard that the once spy chief of India, Hormis Tharakan, was beckoned by the spices and his rich inheritance to settle in Olavipe village near Thykkattussery, 30 km away from Kochi, on a lake and began farming, I had vowed to visit him.

I particularly wanted to see how someone who lived in world capitals and the Indian capital since he joined the Indian Police Service would adjust himself to rural life.

Tharakan appeared to have taken to his rural life like fish to water, when photographs appeared of his rich harvest of paddy that he held aloft in knee deep muddy water.

Hormis Tharakan is an unusual police officer, who is suave, somewhat shy and very well-mannered.

My earliest recollection of him is how, as the serving police chief of Kerala, he got up from his exalted seat at a public function in Thiruvananthapuram and brought a chair for Lekha, my wife, as we walked in.

I was struck that he did not look for a constable to find a chair, as any other police chief would have done in such circumstances. Subsequently, we served together on the National Security Advisory Board, where I learnt about his erudition and intellectual acumen.

The only sign of his last appointment as India's Chief Spy was that he would freeze when any sensitive security related issue was raised.

When news broke about Kakkathuruthu's sudden rise as a desirable international destination, he revealed to us that he lived close to it and that his brother, Michael Tharakan, whom I knew when he was the vice-chancellor of Kannur University, actually lived on Kakkathuruthu itself on the property he had inherited.

I also heard that his ancestral home is now the Olavipe Homestay, created by his brother, the late Jacob Tharakan, who put the village on the world tourism map. This information increased my appetite and I made a plan to visit the area.

As luck would have it, I was invited to receive a 'Lifetime Achievement Honour' from the South Indian Management Association in Cherthala, which included a night on a houseboat at the lovely Vasundhara Savera Premiere resort. The other honourees were 'Agni Putri' Tessy Thomas and Paris Laxmi, the French dancer.

It was a sure recipe for a delightful trip in every way.

We started our journey from Olavipe to Kakkathuruthu, after a sumptuous lunch, on a wooden boat with a tiny engine, trusting the ability of the frail boatman to take us across the Kaithapuzha lake to the Kayal resort, which attracted the *National Geographic* team to pay a visit on their own and felt enchanted enough to include the island in the 24 most attractive tourist destinations on the globe.

There was nothing spectacular about the island or the resort consisting of four cottages. It looked like any other green island, which can be seen in different parts of Kerala. We saw just two Indian guests watching the lake and we were received by Maneesha's mother, the widow of a Youth Congress leader, K Vasudeva Panicker, who was well on his way to political stardom, but passed away at the age of 44.

She told us that Maneesha was on her way to the island. In the meantime, she told us how her daughter had found the island and built the resort, which happily became world famous recently.

We were also introduced to the chef, a village woman, who explained the way she developed the local cuisine to make it palatable to an international audience.

Maneesha arrived soon enough to join us and contrary to my expectation, she tuned out to be an affable and modest young lady, who managed the whole show from her office in Kochi.

She had returned from the US with a master's in engineering and she happened to spot the island, when she was looking for an office space outside the city. She quickly realised the potential of the island and began a resort and fame came to her when she won the award for the best lakeside lodge in the world and was featured in David Rocco's celebrity cookery show.

As a boutique island retreat, Kayal started receiving guests continuously through her international contacts. The international acclaim it received was beyond Maneesha's wildest expectations.

Maneesha said that last December, *National Geographic* Editor George Stone and his team stayed at the resort for four days.

The *National Geographic* team was awestruck by the 'charm of the small island, the lush coconut groves', and the magazine photographers captured the time of dusk on the island in all its beauty and grandeur.

"The best thing that the *Nat Geo* team liked about the island was the sunset, which they watched from a traditional rowboat on the calm waters," Maneesha added.

"When we established Kayal, our idea was to have a small space here with minimal impact on nature and to involve local people in the functioning of our resort," Maneesha said.

Setting an example for responsible and sustainable tourism initiatives in the state, she has ensured a good local participation in all activities, besides organising folk arts performances and entertainment programmes with local flavour.

Maneesha and her mother walked with us after the sunset to the home of Professor Michael Tharakan, the historian, and his wife, a former teacher.

He appeared irked by the sudden publicity that his island had acquired, which meant that scores of journalists landed up to seek interviews from him about the island and its history. He had planned to spend his days quietly to delve deep into medieval history!

By the time we finished our conversation and walked to the boat, the island was in total darkness except for a tiny torch to guide us along the narrow track.

As I left them and sailed away to the mainland, I could see why the trained eyes of the *National Geographic* team picked this pearl as one of the 24 tourist wonders of the globe.

Having now seen 21 of the 24, I felt elated that I was paid to see these beauty spots during my foreign service career, while anyone else would have to spend their lives' earnings to see even a few of them.

Like Kathakali, Kalaripayattu and coconut oil, Kakkathuruthu was also discovered by us only after it was appreciated abroad.

Kerala tourism is understandably basking in the glory of the hard work of a young woman entrepreneur. It will do well to provide some basic amenities to nearly a thousand residents of the island without spoiling its simple splendour and pristine surroundings.

With a little imagination and investment, Kerala could easily develop many more island resorts like Kakkathuruthu.

Published: November 30, 2016

Lessons for Shashi Tharoor from 2014 Diminished Victory

After trailing for several hours behind the Bharatiya Janata Party's O Rajagopal, Shashi Tharoor has emerged victorious in Thiruvananthapuram constituency in Kerala by a margin of 14,501 votes.

This is a remarkable victory when the Congress party was devastated in the rest of India and some Congress leaders lost in Kerala itself. But from a majority of nearly a lakh of votes in 2009 to a margin of below 15,000 votes is a setback.

The Congress will, however welcome his win as the leadership in Delhi has lost many stalwarts and a member of Parliament of his calibre will be a great asset. Tharoor may well become more important in the Congress hierarchy at the national level even though he has suffered a setback in Kerala.

The official explanation that Tharoor was a victim of caste politics in Kerala is only a part of the story. In fact, he was the beneficiary of consolidation of the Muslim and Christian votes in his favour because of their anxiety to save secularism.

There was no evidence that the community of the Leftist candidate rallied around him. It turned out that the votes that went to the BJP candidate were from the Leftist bastions. The performance of Rajagopal was on account of his personal acceptability, his record of service to Kerala as a minister at the Centre, his impeccable political record for half a century and the expectation that he would be a member of the Modi Cabinet.

One reality Tharoor had to contend with from the start was the disillusionment over United Progressive Alliance 2 and the resultant loss of popularity of the Congress party. In 2009, there was a Congress wave as against the Modi wave in 2014, which did not bypass Kerala completely.

But one reason for his poor performance was that the image of Shashi Tharoor today is different from the image he had when he came to Kerala as an international diplomat, a reputed writer and a messiah for change. As A K Antony described him at that time, Tharoor was 'pure gold'.

In the last five years, his personality suffered a battering on account of the various controversies he got involved in.

As the veteran journalist, T J S George wrote about him, 'That is what politics does to people: It dulls human sensibilities and makes the paraphernalia of power look more important than they are.' What sustained him and gave him victory even this time was the conviction of the general public that he is more intelligent and less corrupt than many others.

Another factor was that the campaign team that led him to victory last time was conspicuous by its absence this time. The last team consisted of intellectuals, writers, artists and enthusiastic supporters, who came from such far-off places as New York and Liberia. This time, it was a group of faceless people, many of them sycophants, who kept giving him a false sense of security.

He probably never heard the murmurs about his ego, his disdain for people and the perception about his involvement in his wife's death. Much more experienced politicians have similarly suffered on account of the company they kept.

Though he became fluent in Malayalam in the last five years, Tharoor did not realise how conservative Thiruvananthapuram is. His anxiety to look and behave differently from others was seen as extraordinary pride. Many of his statements betrayed his presumption that his support in Delhi will far outweigh his losses in Kerala. He made no secret of his influence with the Gandhi family. His refrain was that he had used his power and influence in Delhi and abroad for the benefit of Kerala.

A lesson that Tharoor should learn is that in politics, it is important to remove suspicions at the earliest opportunity. No one had any doubt that his Indian Premier League involvement was suspicious, but instead of clearing the charges legally, he found his way back into the Council of Ministers as though nothing had happened.

Similarly, if he had resigned and sought a time-bound investigation to clear him of any guilt the moment the needle of suspicion turned to him in the case of his wife, he would have won much approbation. He did not realise that there were many unanswered questions regarding Sunanda Pushkar and no amount of private grief or lack of complaint by her relatives could place him above suspicion.

Those of us who stood by him and told the world that Pushkar had a serious illness, which could have led to a natural death, could not answer the many questions posed to us by inquisitive people. He offered us no briefing to enable us to defend him. Silence, he thought, was golden in this matter.

The Tharoor campaign ignored the popular sentiment against corruption and some of the programmes of the central government of which he was part and focused on his own achievements in the constituency. The long lists of development activities on flex boards related to spending of the development funds of the MP, which is more an obligation than an accomplishment.

Many hundreds of people who had worked hard for the Vizhinjam Port and the high court bench in Thiruvananthapuram were offended by Tharoor's claim that he had singlehandedly advanced those projects. Many of them had faced the police and even observed fasts, while the MP had only held meetings with authorities.

Having spent several hours of gloom, as Tharoor seemed to appear on the verge of defeat, his friends and well-wishers are relieved that he will continue to represent Thiruvananthapuram in Parliament. He had brought the city into national and international prominence.

With his increased relevance in the Congress party, the voice of Kerala may be heard with greater attention because of him. His victory is creditable when strong Congress leaders like P C Chacko and K Sudhakaran fell by the wayside.

Thiruvananthapuram did not give him a resounding victory, but did not abandon him either. The general tendency of Kerala to stick to the Congress party when it faces total rejection in the North went in his favour.

His many talents, qualities and record of service at the UN are still recognised and admired by a very large number of people. If Tharoor learns his lessons and avoids the pitfalls of the past, he will have a bright political future ahead of him.

Published: May 23, 2014

O. AROUND & ASIDE

A KALEIDOSCOPIC
WORLD

Discovering Slovenia: A Piece of Paradise in Central Europe

My idea of Paradise is a pretty place with mountains all around, a small population, totally peaceful, wonderful monuments not only of history but also of poets, church bells ringing occasionally, charming golf courses, no political rallies and demonstrations, clean roads and wonderful cuisine, easily accessible from my home and some friends from a previous era to relish past associations. My accreditation from Austria to Slovenia was, therefore, a dream come true. Austria itself was a peaceful and orderly place and only my work at the International Atomic Energy Agency (IAEA) added tension and excitement to the post. Ljubljana was just three hours away and after every tense session of the IAEA Board of Governors, I escaped to the peace and tranquillity of Slovenia and stayed not in the city, but in nearby Bled, where President Tito's palace gave us refuge.

India's intimate Nonaligned Movement (NAM) linkage with Former Yugoslavia was still fresh when I was appointed to Slovenia. Two former diplomats of Yugoslavia, with whom I worked at the UN in New York were close comrades and both of them reached dizzy heights in Slovenia after it became independent. Ignac Golob, as the Permanent Representative of Yugoslavia, was an important figure in the diplomatic community in New York. He characterized our relationship as "combative cooperation." Yugoslavia, India, Algeria and Cuba were known as the "Gang of Four" in the NAM, which was fire fighting for unity and integrity of NAM. After he returned to independent Slovenia,

Golob joined a Pensioners' political party and became part of the ruling coalition as the Foreign Minister, a position he adorned with great distinction. Another colleague in New York, Danilo Turk, later became President of Slovenia and made it a point to meet me in New Delhi when he was there on a state visit.

Golob was my guide and guardian throughout my tenure as ambassador to Slovenia and he helped me to establish contacts with the high and mighty in Slovenia, including President Kucan. He helped me with the only two "crises" I faced in my three years in Slovenia. The first related to a vote in the UN on self-determination. This is a hardy annual in the Third Committee of the UN when a resolution, asserting the applicability of self-determination to all peoples, as stated in the UN Charter. But India and some other countries believe that self-determination is applicable only to people under foreign or colonial occupation. As a small country, which became independent from Yugoslavia through a process of self-determination, Slovenia has been supportive of the resolution in the Third Committee. India campaigned actively against the resolution in New York and I was asked to secure the support of Slovenia for our position. I made a special trip to Ljubljana to meet Golob, even though I knew the Slovenian position. He explained the position and said that he would not be able even to abstain from the resolution. But he said that he would do his best to help out a friend. I was delighted to know after the vote that the Slovenian representative was absent at the time of the vote. This was an unusual gesture, which India appreciated.

The other issue was even more delicate. India invited President Kucan to visit India and we had made all the preparations for the visit, including what he would say on India's candidature as a permanent member of the UN Security Council. But just two days before he was to leave for India, India made a request for postponing the visit on account of some inconvenience. I had already reached Ljubljana to meet the President the next day when the message arrived. I immediately contacted Golob and asked for his advice as to whether I should meet the President or simply return to Vienna after leaving a message. Golob sprang into action, conveyed the news to the President and said that the President would receive me at the appointed time. He received me graciously and told me that he understood the situation and looked forward to rescheduling his visit on a mutually convenient date. Sadly, the visit never took place.

A responsibility I had in Ljubljana was a relic of the NAM days, an Institute for Public Enterprises which was set up when Slovenia was a part of Yugoslavia. The Institute continued in Ljubljana under the leadership of an Indian national and India was a major contributor to the Institute. I proposed that Slovenia should take over the Institute and prepared the ground for it before I left. Slovenia may have taken it over later.

Concurrent accreditation of ambassadors to neighbouring countries is largely ceremonial and there is very little possibility of doing sustained work during short visits. It was in recognition of Slovenia's importance that India decided to establish an independent mission there with a full-fledged ambassador, who must be enjoying her stay in Paradise, which my successors in Vienna lost.

Published: 6 July, 2021

The Alleged 'Afrophobia' in India :
Dispelling Misconceptions

An important annual event at the India House in Nairobi is a gathering of Kenyans who have studied in India. It is on those occasions that one realises how many Kenyan ministers and civil servants were educated in India.

They come in vast numbers to these events to acknowledge their debt of gratitude and to reminisce over their days in Delhi, Pune, Chennai and other cities in India. They have good memories of their teachers and classmates and the goodtime they had as scholars.

They also acknowledge how relevant their education in India has been to their present professions. They have no grievances, no bad memories about racial prejudices or unpleasant experiences.

In many African countries, political leaders and the elite have had exposure to Indian education and Indian life. Moreover, India has been in the forefront of the fight against racism and racial discrimination in Africa.

It was ironic, therefore, that African ambassadors were threatening to boycott Africa Day this year and Indians were being attacked on the streets of Congo.

The immediate provocation was the killing of a Congolese student, Masunda Kitada Oliver, in Delhi, presumably in an isolated incident of an altercation with three men over hailing an auto. But the way the incident has been projected as racist and reports that even African diplomats have been facing such racist attacks are a shock to most Indians.

An African envoy went to the extent of saying that 'racism and Afrophobia' were major concerns for African students in India. He alleged that such events had also taken place in other Indian cities.

Indian-African tensions are not uncommon in East and Southern Africa and quite a few from both sides have been killed in squabbles and armed robberies. These tensions are on account of the disparity between the Africans and the Indians and the way the poor Africans are treated by the rich Indians. The Indians live in palatial homes and employ any number of Africans to take care of the household.

I knew of Indian homes where the Africans were employed even to offer *pooja* to Hindu gods. They remain poor in the midst of Indian luxury and pomp. Occasionally when tensions flare up, the Africans, who are accustomed to fighting and kill animals, do not hesitate to kill their masters.

But the issue is not race, it is poverty, envy and greed that drive Africans to take such measures against their Indian masters.

In India, African students are a privileged people, often on scholarships provided by the Indian Council for Cultural Relations, and are mostly at good universities. Many of them have additional sources of income from their families and they live well. Many of them live outside the campuses and drive cars.

Trouble arises when they neglect their studies or engage in illegal activities like smuggling, drug trafficking etc. When action is taken against them by the authorities, they tend to attribute such actions to racial prejudice and hatred.

By and large, foreign students, including African students, are respected and cared for. In Kerala, foreign students are very few, but there have been no complaints from African students about any kind of prejudice.

Some Indians, however, tend to associate African students with violence and scams and they also tend to be prejudiced on account of their colour.

Amar Bose, the founder of the renowned audio equipment firm, himself of mixed blood, Indian and American, has said that he came to

India to study, but he left in anguish because he saw in India the same racial discrimination against Africans as he experienced as a coloured boy in the United States.

In India, fairness of skin is at a premium and consequently, it is possible that the darker hues are considered inferior in some ways.

One evidence of this is the very small number of Indian settlers in Africa who get married to Africans. But it is unthinkable that such prejudices lead to violence and murder. The killing of a Congolese student could well have been for other reasons.

India has had considerable goodwill and influence in Africa, though the Americans and the Europeans have been the biggest investors in Africa. Inevitably, India's relations with African countries have undergone a change in recent decades on account of the competition for influence from the Japanese and Koreans and more recently, the Chinese.

India is not the preferred destination for African students as they do have more lucrative scholarships in other countries. The Indian technical cooperation programmes, with provision for local participation, are not attractive, compared to the more generous offers from China. Indian credit lines are often not fully utilised.

In October 2015, India hosted the biggest gathering of African countries, the India-Africa Forum Summit in Delhi to mark what Prime Minister Narendra Modi called 'a new era of India-Africa relations.' All the 54 African countries participated, as they did at a similar meet in Beijing. Evidently, the African leaders had begun to see the dangers of their overdependence on China and wanted to re-establish links with India.

India made pledges of trade and investment flows and set in motion a number of projects, but there has not been a change on the ground. India has initiated some maritime initiatives in the western Indian Ocean, specifically involving coastal African States and Prime Minister Modi's visit to some of the target countries is on the cards. But the demands of the Africans for fully developing their blue economy go much beyond India's means.

India needs to present an alternative to China in terms of investments, commodities, markets and diplomatic support. There has not been any headway in changing the rigid African position on an expansion of the UN Security Council. Africa's demand for two permanent seats on the Council is still one of the roadblocks.

Against this backdrop, the killing of an African student and the subsequent accusation that Africans in India were victims of racial prejudice have been most unfortunate.

In all likelihood, race may not have been an issue at all in the incident. Fortunately, the African envoys attended the Africa Day event after securing sufficient guarantees from the ministry of external affairs.

However, the African agony over the incident was poignantly expressed in a poem penned by Samuel Panyin Yalley, Ghana's high commissioner, on the occasion, giving a larger dimension to the incident, invoking the old anti-colonial sentiment of being in a cage for no fault of the African. He wrote:

Hear My Cry Oh! Africa

Deep in an unknown chilled cage I lie

Frozen with ice of pain and stained by

My hot African blood suddenly gone cold

Someone must tell me what did I do wrong?

Prime Minister Modi may do well to express our regret over the incident during his forthcoming visit to Africa and reassure the Africans of their security in India.

The vast investments we have made in Africa right from the days of Mahatma Gandhi should not go waste on account of the thoughtless violence perpetrated on the Congolese student.

Our countrymen should also be made aware of the need to be polite and friendly to our African guests, even under provocation. They should know the dictum, *Athithi devo bhava*, whether they are black or white.

The damage done to India's image by this incident can diminish only if such incidents do not recur.

Published: May 31, 2016

Davos Diplomacy: Navigating
Geopolitical Challenges

Thomas Mann immortalised Davos in the Swiss Alps in his intriguing novel, *The Magic Mountain* which reflected his experiences and impressions after visiting a sanatorium there, when his wife, suffering from a lung complaint, was undergoing treatment in 1912.

He enjoyed the beauty and tranquillity of the little village and became acquainted with the team of dedicated doctors, who were looking after his wife.

Davos became a ski resort, sought after by the rich and famous from year to year. After sunset, the skiers sat near fireplaces and began chatting about the problems of the times and returned with new insights.

The fireplace chats became more significant than skiing and became an institution established in 1971 by Professor Klaus Schwab as the World Economic Forum.

Over the years, numerous business, government and civil society leaders have made their way to the high Alps to consider the major global issues of the day and to brainstorm on solutions to address these challenges.

While many global institutions are notable for the breadth of nations or the powerful political leaders attending their gatherings, the World Economic Forum Annual Meeting and all the activities and initiatives of the Forum around the world are distinguished by the active participation of government, business and civil society figures. The Forum engages the most experienced and the most promising, all working together in the collaborative and collegial "Spirit of Davos".

Prime Ministers of India, P V Narasimha Rao, H D Deve Gowda and Narendra Modi visited Davos to participate in the Forum, as India emerged as a significant player on the world scene.

As a member of the delegation of PM Rao and External Affairs Minister Madhav Singh Solanki in 1992, I had a glimpse of the setting and style of Davos.

The most striking thing about Davos was the easy informality of the place. Hotels were nothing but ski cottages strewn all over the mountains and participants had to trudge along the mountain slopes to see each other. More than the formal meetings, any participant could request meetings with any high dignitary over the computer terminals and they were answered positively most of the time.

Heads of state and government, who were distinguished only by the absence of name tags, mingled with the others and the friendships cultivated on the mountains went on to produce political, economic and personal alliances which changed the world in many ways.

Every year, a new issue or a personality dominates the Davos Forum because of their game changing nature. Many Davos milestones included the Davos Declaration signed in 1988 by Greece and Turkey, which saw them turn back from the brink of war, while in 1989, North and South Korea held their first ministerial-level meetings in Davos.

At the same meeting, East German Prime Minister Hans Modrow and German Chancellor Helmut Kohl met to discuss German reunification. In 1992, the theme was inevitably the collapse of the Soviet Union and the newly independent states which emerged out of it.

Bristling with the new openness and hopes, the leaders of these states shared their aspirations with the rest of the world. Another historic event was a meeting of the South African President F.W. de Klerk, Nelson Mandela and Zulu Chief Mangosuthu Buthelezi, their first joint appearance outside South Africa and a milestone in the country's political transition.

India remained on the side lines in 1992, but PM Rao received attention for his new economic agenda presented at Davos.

To be effective in Davos, leaders have to be agile, informal and charismatic. But both our PM and EAM could operate only in formal settings with protocol and note takers, not very common in Davos.

Disaster struck EAM Solanki when it turned out that he had handed over a personal letter from the PM to the Swiss President, seeking a postponement of the Bofors investigations and he had to resign under pressure soon after his return to be the scapegoat to save the PM himself.

Davos 2020, described as "the place where billionaires tell millionaires how the middle classes should live their lives" was preoccupied with the climate emergency. It came to be known as the "global heating Davos", with session after session devoted to the topic.

The adversaries were the most powerful leader of the United States, the formidable Donald Trump who considers that the whole climate change was a hoax and tiny and fragile Greta Thunberg, who has emerged as the conscience of mankind. Trump called her a prophet of doom while she characterised him as a messenger of climate doom.

Donald Trump, who has transformed from a maverick to an unpredictable man with a mission of his own, became the biggest draw in Davos with a kind of love-hate relationship with the chiefs of multinational corporations.

Like it happened at the United Nations General Assembly last year, the audience burst into disapproving murmurs when he boasted that the US was enjoying a "boom the likes of which the world has never seen". But they appeared to favour his continuation in the White House rather than any Democratic candidate. His internal economic policies seemed to make up for his abandonment of globalism. Trump looked like a winner in Davos.

There may have been many deals, big and small, worked out quietly in the corners of Davos, which may be revealed only later. More important were the many contacts made between the government and business leaders.

Global warming was recognised as the biggest existential threat and Davos did its own symbolical bit by asking the participants to travel by train and to plant thousands of trees.

The nuclear threat, the fear of an economic slowdown, the Iran and Korean issues and challenges of technology received scant attention.

The real prophet of doom at Davos this year was Yuval Harari, the bestselling author of *Sapiens*, who dwelt at length on technological disruption, considered more serious than nuclear war and ecological collapse.

"In Davos we hear so much about the enormous promises of technology – and these promises are certainly real. But technology might also disrupt human society and the very meaning of human life in numerous ways, ranging from the creation of a global useless class to the rise of data colonialism and of digital dictatorships." More than anything else, the warning of Yuval Harari will reverberate in the world in the next few years.

The Davos delegates may not have found much time to ski, but skiing on the slippery slopes of the global scene may have been as exciting and hazardous as the ski slopes of the Alps.

Published: January 29, 2020

Middle-East Conflict: A Futile Fight for Common Ground

Jerusalem is the only piece of real estate which is considered the fatherland of three major faiths in the world. For the Jews, it is the sacrificial site of Abraham's son Isaac, who was saved by divine intervention. It is also the site of the first and second Temples. The Western Wall is the remaining relic of one of them, the ideal place for prayers. For the Muslims, it is here that the Prophet ascended to heaven and the al-Aqsa Mosque and the Dome of Rock constitute the Noble Sanctuary. For Christians, the Church of the Holy Sepulchre stands on the site where Jesus was crucified and had resurrected.

No power on earth can claim, monopolize or even seek to elevate its status of this land. We cannot even dedicate, consecrate or hallow this ground, to borrow Abraham Lincoln's words about Gettysburg. The noble souls associated with the land have consecrated it, far above our poor power to add or detract. Turning a centre of pilgrimage into a cause for carnage is pure sacrilege. No new status as a capital of a single country will enhance its prestige or status. Shedding of human blood should be totally avoided there or in its name as it will only desecrate this holy land. Only mutual respect and peaceful coexistence of the three faiths can do justice to its glamour, glory and godliness.

No wonder the United Nations wisely decided to preserve its multi-faith character without assigning it to Israel or Palestine. Only a reckless President Trump had named Jerusalem as the capital city of Israel and set off a chain of events that led to the present bloodshed which has spun out of control in a week.

The latest violence was sparked off by the growing unrest over control of Jerusalem and attempts by Jewish settlers to take over Arab-controlled communities. The tensions have spilled over into the West Bank, where hundreds of residents in Arab communities staged overnight protests against recent actions of Israeli security forces against Palestinians. Casualties have been mounting on both sides, as Hamas continues its bomb attacks on Israeli targets. Clashes between the Arabs and Jews have been taking place in civilian areas.

It is not unusual for fighting to break out between Israel and Hamas, given the way the Palestinians are treated in Gaza, but they do not last long as no war can resolve the issues between them. But Prime Minister Netanyahu, who is struggling to win a majority and to overcome corruption charges, warned in a statement that "This is just the beginning. We'll hit them like they've never dreamed possible."

The United Nations, having failed to deal effectively with the pandemic on account of a Chinese veto, is now paralysed again by the US veto. President Biden had raised much hope of energising the UN after the exit of President Trump, but his honeymoon with the UN came to an abrupt end when he justified the Israeli action by stating that Israel had every right to defend itself. He prevented the Security Council from meeting, not to speak of ordering a ceasefire. It took the Security Council a whole week to hold an open meeting to enable the members to express their views.

The US was isolated, as before, in the Security Council on this issue, but it blocked any statement or resolution. This was in keeping with the US position that extended "ironclad support for Israel's legitimate right to defend itself and its people" and "strongly condemned the launching of rockets by Hamas and other terrorist groups that targeted Israeli civilians" and "reiterated the importance of all involved parties to take steps to restore calm." At the same time, for the record, the US stated that Palestinians must be afforded the right "to live in safety and security" while calling for de-escalation.

Russia and Turkey are likely to lead a move in the General Assembly, which is likely to pass a resolution against Israel with overwhelming majority. To avoid such an eventuality, the US is reportedly applying pressure on Israel to stop the bombing. But Israel has asserted that bombing will continue and that it will take time to end the military operations.

Among the many grievances of the Palestinians against Israel is the discrimination in the supply of vaccines. According to the Times of Israel, Israel had purchased ten million vaccine units of Astra-Zeneca, which are lying unutilised as Israel switched to Pfizer and Moderna versions and completed the vaccination of the whole population of Israel. On the other hand, only 1% of the Palestinians have been fully vaccinated. Israel is trying to divert the vaccine to some other country or just throw them away. It could have been a win-win situation if the vaccines were transferred to the Palestine Authority as a goodwill gesture.

India, as a member of the Security Council, is engaged in counselling restraint since we have good relations with Israel and Palestine. The unfortunate death of Soumya, a young Indian lady in the Hamas bombing impelled India to criticise Hamas for indiscriminate bombing of civilian areas. Israel has made a gesture by the speedy despatch of the body of Soumya to Kerala. The Israeli Consul, who attended the funeral, characterised Soumya as the "angel of Israel" and pledged support to her family.

At the open session of the Security Council, India's Permanent Representative to the UN, Ambassador T S Tirumurti said that the continuing violence, which began in East Jerusalem a week back, is now threatening to spiral out of control. *"The events of the last several days have resulted in a sharp deterioration of the security situation."* Tirumurti reiterated India's strong support to the just Palestinian cause and its unwavering commitment to the two-State solution, while also stressing India's strong condemnation of all acts of violence, provocation, incitement and destruction. "Immediate de-escalation is the need of the hour, so as to arrest any further slide towards the brink. We urge both sides to show extreme restraint, desist from actions that exacerbate tensions, and refrain from attempts to unilaterally change the existing status-quo, including in East Jerusalem and its neighbourhood," he said." "These incidents have once again underscored the need for immediate resumption of dialogue between Israel and Palestinian authorities. The absence of direct and meaningful negotiations between the parties is widening the trust deficit between the parties," Tirumurti said, voicing concern that "this will only increase the chances for similar escalation in future."

Gone are the days when we stood solidly behind Palestine, but the latest Indian statement reiterated its strong support to the Palestinian cause and the two-State solution, which was noted and appreciated widely in India. But by not mentioning Jerusalem as the capital of Palestine and not calling for withdrawal of Israel to the 1967 borders, India has left the contours of a future settlement open to negotiations. Israel had shown understanding of our principled position on Palestine even in the old days and our continuing position on Palestine has not stood in the way of our good relations today. An all-out war is not likely because Hamas will have little support from the Arabs and a final solution is hardly possible when the global situation is in a state of flux. Peaceful co-existence is the only option for Israel and Palestine. The futility of the war is clear and it will not be long before the conflict ends and Gaza returns to an uneasy peace.

Published: May 18, 2021

Fashion and Politics:
The Perils of Apparel

Statesmen and politicians around the world tend to make fashion statements through their attire knowingly or unknowingly. Some win approbation for their originality and appropriateness, while others attract criticism for extravagance or for lack of taste or imagination.

Choosing the appropriate apparel is as important as being well mannered and sophisticated enough to be worthy of the position they hold. It takes considerable effort and attention to make the right impression by the right apparel. Apparel not only proclaims the man, but also makes and unmakes leaders.

Long time ago, when Bhutan joined the United Nations, I was surprised to see that Foreign Minister Dawa Tsering appeared at the General Assembly not in the traditional Bhutanese clothes, which are mandatory back home, but in a well-stitched suit and tie.

When asked, he said that he had observed that those who wore traditional clothes, whether scantily or in panoply, were from the least developed countries. Though Bhutan was one of the least developed countries, he did not want his country to be identified as such wherever he went. Wearing a western suit was the easiest way to attain a level playing field.

Coming to think of it, I realised that no Australian or US diplomat had ever appeared in aboriginal clothes. It was Guatemalan, Malawian and Western Samoan diplomats, who came in colourful skirts and plumes. Now, even they appear in western suits, following the Bhutanese foreign minister's example.

Even the Chinese have abandoned Mao suits in favour of mass produced blue western suits and ties. Today, the General Assembly sessions are no more the riot of colours that it once was. Only a few African chiefs sport their national costumes on the inaugural day.

Indian diplomats wear the *bandhgala* often, but that is hardly noticed as distinct from the suit. I have not seen any Indian in a *kurta* in the sanctum sanctorum of the United Nations. The thermostats in the halls of the United Nations are kept so low that light clothes attract not only stares, but also cold and cough.

Diplomacy is the most conservative profession, when it comes to clothes and fashion. But there are many countries where much variety is offered even for diplomats.

In Tonga, a little island in the Pacific, to which I was concurrently accredited as high commissioner while stationed in Fiji, every occasion had its dress code prescribed. We spent five days on the island to celebrate the birthday of the king and we had to change clothes three times every day—morning coat with tails for breakfast, suit for lunch and the dinner jacket for dinner.

For the audience with the king, we needed to carry a silk hat (never worn), which we had to hire from New Zealand!

On the other hand, in the neighbouring Kiribati, the president appeared in shorts and a colourful *bula* shirt, when I was dressed up in a suit in 35 degrees Celsius to present my credentials.

Seeing my discomfort at being over dressed, he pointed to his shining shoes and said that he was wearing the shoes in my honour. Normally, he would have worn Hawaii chappals!

Generally, in the Pacific, the dress code is fairly relaxed, though members of Parliament wear suits and ties inside the house, regardless of the weather. In many African countries, woollen suits are worn in office, defying the dictates of the weather. The general rule in most countries on the dress code is, 'when in doubt, wear a lounge suit'.

The exceptions to this general rule on dress are made by some to develop fashion statements of their own to make an impact. Mahatma Gandhi made the biggest fashion statement by having no fashion, not even enough clothes to cover himself fully. When he was asked why he went to see the British Emperor half-naked, he said: "His majesty was wearing enough clothes for the two of us."

The hat and cigar of Winston Churchill were a similar fashion statement. Charlie Chaplin's walking stick was in a genre of its own. None of Gandhiji's followers adopted his dress style. Nehru had a rose bud on the lapel of his *achkan*, adding a royal touch. He is reported to have changed clothes three times when he was in Cambridge.

Indira Gandhi wore very fashionable saris and set a fashion trend. Rajiv Gandhi's *bandhgalas* were very elegant. More recently, Hamid Karzai of Afghanistan sported his own fashionable clothes even when he was moving from crisis to crisis. He looked elegant among the suited and booted gentry around him. But the dress sense of an Indian home minister, who changed his clothes three times on a day of crisis led to his downfall.

Shashi Tharoor, who came to politics after many years at the UN, decided to dress like an ordinary Kerala Congressman in white dhoti and shirt and did very well in his first election. But when he adopted his own fashion of colourful kurtas with tricolour shawls, he began to appear different from his colleagues and the fact of his being an outsider came to be accentuated.

There were many factors in his loss of votes in his second election, but his distinctive dress sense was one of them.

APJ Abdul Kalam, when he became President, having been a scientist all his life, developed a new hairstyle and his own distinctive suit. It made up for his short stature and gave him a new personality. Together with his erudition and energy, he has become the most popular former President ever.

Narendra Modi's sartorial journey is the opposite of Mahatma Gandhi's. While Mahatma Gandhi dressed like a peasant after having been a fashionable barrister, Modi adopted aristocratic attire, even while being proud of his humble origins as a tea-seller.

His brand of the kurta became famous for its colours and styles, but his ten-lakh rupee suit with his own name embroidered on it, which he wore at the time of the visit of President Obama, damaged his image considerably.

Arvind Kejriwal, in his humble muffler and Gandhi cap, which he has hijacked from the Congress, swept the polls in Delhi as the *Aam aadmi* not only in name, but also in appearance.

At global summits of groupings like APEC and G-20, the leaders appear in traditional costumes of the host country on one occasion. It must be a major effort to get these clothes stitched to measurements in advance, but it creates an atmosphere of easy informality and even banter, contributing to the success of the summits. There was a chuckle on the lips of the guests at Rashtrapati Bhavan, when Obama said that he was thinking of wearing a 'Modi kurta' at the banquet.

Striking a balance between elegance and image is a challenging task. Mahatma Gandhi succeeded by stressing his humble image, while others suffered setbacks on account of their flashy and extravagant attire. Kejriwal stumbled upon his own fashion statement, which caught the imagination of the people of Delhi. Apparel can be used to great advantage by statesmen and politicians, but its perils are also real.

Published: February 18, 2015

P. PERSONAL MEMOIRS

VIGNETTES OF A
SPECKLED LIFE

From Dream to Reality:
A Diplomat's Journey

When I finished my schooling in my home town Kayamkulam with a first class, my father, K. Parameswaran Pillai, decided that I would go to a university and that too in Thiruvananthapuram. Many had advised my parents to put me into the one-year teaching course. But my father, a school teacher, has always set the goals for me and my siblings and my mother, N. Chellamma, ensured that we could pursue them.

Thus, I joined the Intermediate College in 1960—new place, new surroundings, and a new medium of instruction. It was a total culture shock for me as I had studied in Malayalam medium school till then. I didn't understand most of the things the teachers taught because except my second language, Malayalam, everything else was taught in English. Later I realised that it was good that they didn't use Malayalam in class because that's how I picked up English.

There was this outsider tag always associated with me and that continued even after I joined University College for BA English. I was tempted to take up science, but my father was adamant that I should take up English since he believed that I was destined to join the foreign service. The reason behind this dream of his was Shankar Pillai, a teacher of University College, whom my father had met. Shankar had cleared the Indian Foreign Service (IFS) exams, but was killed by a madman at his office in Canada. My father thought I would replace him one day in the foreign service.

Things changed for the better within two years at University College especially after I got high marks in the second-year examination of my BA course. Though I was still an outsider for those from the capital city, it did not take long for the situation to improve. In fact, I should thank one of our teachers, Sudhakaran Nair, who took all of us around and brought us together.

I can go on and on about my teachers, which includes people like G. Kumara Pillai, Ayyappa Paniker, Hridayakumari, Santhakumari, Chellamma Philip, K. K. Neelakantan, K. Srinivasan, John and Vaidyanathan, among others. Ayyappa Paniker sir has been the one who left behind a lasting impression on me. Though I couldn't understand his brilliance and sense of humour while in college, in my later years I was fortunate to get to know him more. His intelligence kept me in awe. He introduced me to the world of global literature and encouraged me to read more. As for Hridayakumari teacher, it was my dream to speak like her!

We did give nicknames to a few teachers. Sankara Narayana Iyer sir was called 'Vada' sir, probably because he used to bring vada for lunch. It is learnt that once some of the students tied a vada on the fan when he walked into the class. Then there was 'Punchiri' Mathai, who always had a strange smile on his face. Vaidyanathan sir was called 'Vadi' because he was very tall and straight like a stick, and looked more like a soldier.

Another major influence has been my principal N. S. Warrier sir who instilled in me a liking for foreign affairs. He was very much interested in what was happening around the world and used to call me to his office to discuss that with me. He believed that I have a future in foreign service. In fact, as I was active in Students Congress then and decided to stand for the post of Chairman, he immediately wrote to my father about that. I had to withdraw from the move.

I used to move around with a group of four, some of them my seniors. We used to watch English movies at Sreekumar Theatre, where a new movie was released once in every three days. Then the charge was 24 paisa!

The five years on the University College campus, pursuing BA and MA in English, have been the most formative and memorable years of my life. I am deeply hurt by the fact its days of glory is now a thing of the past. After passing out, I taught at Mar Ivanios College for over a year. By then I had cleared IFS and it was time to explore new pastures.

Published: June 12, 2014

College Chronicles: Nostalgia
from the University Days

Every time I passed the historic buildings of my alma mater, the University College in Thiruvananthapuram, festooned with red flags and graffiti of revolutionary slogans, the word that came to my lips was "Ichabod" (Hebrew for no glory, inglorious or where is the glory?).

The story of Ichabod is narrated in the first Book of Samuel as a boy born on the day the Israelites' Ark of God was taken into Philistine captivity. The mother of the boy was so distraught that she thought that the arrival of her son had deprived Israelites of their glory. It is by this name that Max Beerbohm called his melancholy essay on the loss of his travel labels affixed on his hatbox.

Indeed, the glory of the University College had long gone by the time I returned to Thiruvananthapuram in 2004. The campus was already colonised by some students and the whole place had a deserted look. A sense of fear seemed to hang in the air. The classrooms were shabby and broken chairs and tables were lying around in the classrooms. The toilets were dirty and unusable. I could not believe that the University College, once a pride of Kerala, had come to such a pass.

I stepped into the University College for the first time in 1961 to join the English BA course and the atmosphere was exhilarating. A sense of history descended on us the moment we stepped into the classrooms. Most of the teachers were legendary and their presence in the class inspired us. Classes were small and the friendships we made remained intact even long after we left the College. A sense of responsibility and scholarship dawned on us because of the atmosphere of learning and excellence. The five years that I spent in the college were most fruitful and rewarding.

We were overawed by the scholarship, dedication and fluency of the teachers. Hridayakumari in white khadi was the very symbol of low living and high thinking. Sitting in her class, I wished I could speak English like her one day. G. Kumara Pillai was awe-inspiring in his demeanour and his gravitas, but maintained a cheerful face. Sudhakaran Nair was friendly and eloquent. Ayyappa Paniker, as a newcomer, appeared shy and unsure of himself. He had not become famous poet yet and we were unable to comprehend his erudition and witticisms. Induchudan, more an ornithologist than an English teacher, kept the team going. K. Srinivasan, Vaidyanathan and Sankaranarayana Iyer were sincere and scholarly. Chellamma Philip and Santhakumari among them live to tell the story of those glorious days. The college and faculty were a perfect fit.

Not that it was all study and no play in the golden days. We had our fun, our frolic, our groups, our party politics and even conflicts. We have angered teachers like Hridayakumari and G. Kumara Pillai enough to force them to turn us out of the class. The provocation in the case of Hridayakumari was that all the boys in the class decided one day to boycott her class for no reason.

We just went to the Coffee House. When she came to the class the next day, she asked all of us to leave the class without any questions or explanations and we marched out without a protest. It took us three days and several apologies to be admitted back into her class. The loss was entirely ours. In the case of G. Kumara Pillai, it was an innocent instance of a boy exchanging some notes across the aisle with a girl. Pillai found the distraction too serious to ignore and out went both, perhaps to have coffee together.

College elections were bitterly fought even those days and they were on political lines. But the difference was that the campaigns and contests were very friendly and the results were accepted with grace. The main parties were the Students Federation (SF) and the Students Association (SA) and the latter had the upper hand. I was myself very active in the SA leadership, but I nominated a friend of mine as the speaker as I wanted to focus on studies in the final MA. During the recent debate as to whether student politics should be permitted on campuses, I had favoured student politics as I felt that the students gained much by the experience on the campuses. I pointed out that many of the political leaders of today had come from campus politics.

By all accounts, the situation in the University College today is a far cry from the happy situation of our times. This is definitely a reflection of the deterioration of politics in general. Violence and murders have become common in Kerala politics and no party is innocent in this matter. But the situation in the University College is unprecedented in the sense that one group of students is really ruling the campus. This has been happening for years when the state Government was in the hands of another party, which had decided to let the sleeping dogs lie. Occasionally, tales of violence came out, but the teachers and the students have been accepting the situation without much protest. They claimed that the situation was under control and that there was no interruption of studies. Now we know that illegal means were used to pass the examinations by stealing answer papers and forging documents. The last straw was an attempted murder of a student who is a member of the same outfit, which had occupied the college.

The outcry over a stabbing incident led to some action against the criminals, who were masquerading as students and some remedial action has been taken. Many deep-rooted conspiracies have been unearthed and the gravity of the situation has come to the fore now. But the glory of the University College cannot be restored in a hurry. The malady is deep and it may aggravate again unless the political parties, which are exploiting the situation change their ways.

As many have suggested, the location of the University College at the centre of the city is a part of the problem. Relocation of the college has been tried in the past. A change of location may be helpful, but if the college can be cleansed of the criminal elements and studies resume, it can become a centre of excellence once again. The various alumni associations, which merely reminisce over the past glory, must get involved in the rebuilding of the college. The history of achievements of the last 150 years must inspire the students and the authorities to rebuild the college and restore its academic value and lost glory. I dream of the day when it becomes a temple of learning once again.

Published: July 19, 2019

Settling Down: A Diplomat's Quiet Retreat

For a village boy like me, Thiruvananthapuram was the maximum city, the promised land. My father who had spent two years in a college here late in his life was impressed with the opportunities in the city and decided to send me here for college education. The newly found freedom and the dazzle of college life appealed to me. The rigours of learning English and my outsider status were impediments, but my good performance in college gave me confidence.

The only role models I had were the brilliant teachers in the English Department of the University College such as K. Ayyappa Paniker, G. Kumara Pillai, Hridayakumari, K. Srinivasan Santhakumari and I aspired to be one of them. There was no world beyond Thiruvananthapuram.

My father, however, had bigger ambitions for me and he told me about a young professor, Shankara Pillai, who was preparing for a career in the Indian Foreign Service. When Pillai joined the IFS and got posted to exotic places, I learnt more about diplomacy as a profession, set my heart on it, and got selected. Sadly, Pillai fell victim to the gun of a madman in Ottawa, when he was India's Deputy High Commissioner there.

My heart was in Thiruvananthapuram, but, like the Biblical prodigal son, I set sail for my 40-year Odyssey which took me to many countries and gave me the experience of a lifetime. I had with me a piece of Thiruvananthapuram in my wife Lekha, who was born and brought up here. We decided that we would return to live in Thiruvananthapuram one day.

During my frequent trips to the city in the 40 years I spent away, I noticed the slow but steady development of Thiruvananthapuram, which strengthened my resolve to return to it. It had developed a modern skyline and a good health-care system without destroying its traditional features like the Golf Links, Museum and the palaces. On the one hand, a quaint golf club was there for fitness and on the other, a multi-speciality KIMS Hospital if fitness failed.

As we were packing to return to the city, we sounded out others about our plans to settle here, but most of them discouraged us. They felt that we would find the city dull and lacking in social life, entertainment, and intellectual stimulus.

Ideal Weather

But 15 years later, we have no regrets. There were moments of disappointment but not discontent. The best part was the weather which did not dictate change of clothes to survive. Having lived in temperatures ranging from minus 40 degrees to 40 degrees Celsius, a mean temperature of 25 degrees seemed ideal. Initially, we decided to live in a suburb, without realising that 18 kilometres was a long way off because of the poor roads. We also tasted the deception of a builder who built a house at half the price we paid him. Later we learnt that what he did was the rule rather than an exception.

The Technopark is the institution that brought Thiruvananthapuram to the modern age. I had met G. Vijayaraghavan in New York when the project was only a twinkle in his eye. I knew then that his vision would become a reality soon. The glistening steel and glass structures and restaurants with international cuisine are the offshoots of Technopark. No other institution has changed the city as much.

Religious Places 'Grow'

A new phenomenon in the city is an explosion of religious faith. What were small temples, churches, and mosques have grown into gigantic structures and new ones have sprung up. There has also been a proliferation of rituals. Perhaps the feeling that humans cannot be trusted has led people to hold tightly to gods and goddesses.

Cultural events also have multiplied. Apart from the Soorya programmes, which are held virtually round the year, there are government-sponsored events to mark every national and state festivals. The International Film Festival of Kerala and the Mathrubhumi Festival of Letters have become regular features. The city's residents have developed more interest in national and international genres of music and dance as evidenced by the fact that artists from other states and countries are performing more frequently here.

Noise Stays Intact

The proliferation of public meetings has made the city noisier. The city must formulate a code of conduct about the number of people on the dais and the length of their speeches. The massive use of electricity for illumination and expenses on flowers in plastic and glass monstrosities which are given as souvenirs are wasteful. Noise pollution is as acute today as it was when I learnt driving in the city many years ago. My trainer insisted that I should keep my hand on the car horn so that it sounded continuously like a fire engine. Sounding the horn is still a ritual here, while in other countries, it is used most sparingly.

Mercifully, the trees in most of the city have been saved, mainly because of activists like the poet Sugathakumari. In the climate change debates at the UN, I used to plead for development as against environment, but I found that the Western argument for environmental protection seemed to appeal to the intelligentsia in the city. We must strike a balance between environment and development and should not become environmental fundamentalists.

The Invisible Waste

Thiruvananthapuram is still a conservative, largely bureaucratic city, as distinct from a more cosmopolitan city like Kochi. Public services are fairly satisfactory, but it does not have a waste disposal system. In some mysterious way, the city remains free of accumulated waste as it happens in other cities when the system fails even for a day.

The one thing that does not change about the city is the acceptance of Sree Padmanabha as its presiding deity. The revelation that the Sree Padmanabhaswamy temple holds immense wealth has vastly enhanced its value. But there is no consensus as to how to put the wealth to productive use. Proposals range from exhibiting it to turning it into bonds and using the money generated for the development of the State.

I believe there were plans for leaving the ancient city as it is and to build a new city as was done in the case of many world capitals. But the decision to merge the new with the old has given the city a charm of its own. Glitzy jewellery stores surround the ancient temple, the spires of the Kowdiar Palace add a royal touch to the skyscrapers, and modern wax models coexist with metallic statues of the Maharajas.

Published: August 29, 2020

Ayurveda Experience: Insights into Traditional Healing

An Indian Ambassador has to be a walking encyclopaedia on everything from the Indus Valley Civilisation to Infosys.

This was difficult, particularly before the advent of Wikipedia. In countries like Fiji, the Indian envoy is the arbiter on their religious rituals and social habits, which are no more in vogue in modern India.

In my case, a non-Hindi-speaking Indian envoy was a curiosity and I had to take a crash course in spoken Hindi, though it is slightly different from the Fiji Hindi spoken on the islands.

I am sure the Fiji Indians must have been bewildered by the diversity among the Indian representatives sent there, but we managed with some bold innovative interpretations of Indian culture and rituals.

In different countries, different aspects of Indian life and culture get projected depending on the state from where the majority of the Indian community comes.

With a large number of Keralites there, Austria has several Ayurveda centres, some run by Indian doctors, who practiced allopathic medicines also.

Ayurveda is not just an alternative medical system, but a part of the wellness culture in Germany and Austria.

I had the privilege of inaugurating some of these centres in Vienna as the Indian envoy to Austria. I made it a point to do that, knowing well that Ayurveda is a part of the soft power assets of India in the region.

On one occasion, after I had waxed eloquent on the medical and philosophical aspects of Ayurveda as though from my personal experience, an Austrian journalist asked me whether I had personal experience of Ayurveda treatment.

I was startled for a moment because I never had such treatment and I did not want to tell a lie.

On the other hand, I knew the credibility of what I said would be lost.

In a moment, I found an answer: "For an Indian, Ayurveda is a way of life and an elixir which helps him from the cradle to the grave. From the honey that is given to a newborn baby to the water of the Ganges given to a dying person, we are linked to Ayurveda," I said.

The journalist and the audience appeared satisfied.

Very recently, I narrated this incident at an event in Kottakkal, one of the most prominent Ayurveda centres in the world, which drew wild applause.

Incidentally, I was invited to Kottakkal, not to speak on Ayurveda, but on the 'World of 2017 and Beyond'!

The main takeaways from that visit were the generous hospitality and courtesies of the doyen of Ayurveda, Dr P K Warrier and an Ayurveda secret revealed by Metroman Dr E Sreedharan.

He said that he learnt from a recent experience that the best cure for gout is water in which papaya peels are boiled.

Against this backdrop, my wife and I decided to go for an Ayurveda wellness treatment, when the opportunity arose recently.

My hesitation to go for such an experience was on two counts. Ever since I was a child, I had hated the idea of oil baths and had refrained from using oil when I began to take baths on my own.

The other reason was the extreme intrusiveness of massages without clothes. Of course, it is true that though we spend much on clothes and ornaments, all of them have to come off to enjoy some real pleasures.

The choice of place was made because of our friends from the US, Gopal and Nalini Pillai who have been coming to Krishnendu, an Ayurveda hospital not far from my hometown, Kayamkulam near

Haripad. The hospital is headed by Dr Mohan Babu, a fourth generation traditional Ayurveda practitioner. The place is modern, but the ambience and treatment are strictly on traditional lines. The doctor himself is a living model, as he looks much younger than his age, obviously because of the Ayurveda way of life.

I was still sceptical as we checked in after an examination by the doctor using modern clinical methods. Of course, mine was *sukha chikitsa* or comfort treatment, not for any particular ailment.

The experience was much better than I had expected, though I was still irritable with the near nudity and the oil all over me.

Two able bodied young men started to work on me with extraordinary efficiency and scientific precision.

Though I was told that I could choose the level of pressure, I let them do as they thought appropriate and they followed a pattern of individual and synchronised massage.

They kept checking with me whether I was comfortable, but otherwise, I was just a human body to be massaged into shape.

My CV or personality was of no consequence to them. It was oil first from head to foot and then massage. Then a thorough rubbing with a herbal package in a piece of cloth. It was so well orchestrated that there was no moment to waste. Only the minimum conversation, all about postures and pressure.

After a couple of days, things moved on to massage with a pack of medicinal hot rice paste, but again with business-like movements. Clearly, the treatment is scientific, but artistically delivered.

My wife had the same experience from the sprightly and helpful young women who worked on her. It is the Ayurveda culture, happily preserved at its best at the Krishnendu hospital.

Speaking to those who have experience of other resorts and hospitals, the general situation in the reputed ones is similar, but the system varies from place to place on the regimen to be kept during treatment.

Some are very strict about diet and permission to go out during the course of the treatment. Much to our relief, the regimen at Krishnendu was fairly liberal within limits.

The friendliness and care of the doctors and the staff were striking. The food was modest and healthy, but tasty and fresh.

The benefits of such treatment may not be visible immediately, but the general feeling of wellness, rejuvenation and relaxation is palpable.

A former President of India had the habit of undergoing Ayurveda treatment every year in Kerala and he remarked once that he felt ten years younger every time, he took the treatment. The joke was that after seven visits, he became so young that he had to crawl back home! We had no such feeling, but felt that the time and money spent at Krishnendu were very much worth it.

No wonder our friends and many others come all the way from the other end of the world for Ayurveda treatment at one of its most authentic sources.

Published: March 9, 2017

My Nobel Moments: Recollections on the Stockholm Ceremony

A conspiracy by my children to give me a break from my solitude in Thiruvananthapuram landed me in Stockholm for the Nobel ceremony and the king's banquet on December 10, 2023.

They must have discussed and decided that I was not likely to get a Nobel in this birth and, therefore, I should get the second-best experience of witnessing the Nobel ceremony and enjoying the banquet.

My son, Sree Sreenivasan, is on the board of the Nobel Outreach Committee, which develops activities to inspire generations and to disseminate information about the Nobel prize.

I was surprised that even the Nobel Prize needed social media to make its presence felt in the world.

Every entity strives to transmit as much data as possible on the Internet so that Chat GPT has enough material to answer questions.

Sree was invited this year to the Nobel ceremony and the king's banquet with a guest.

Normally, his wife Roopa Unnikrishnan should have been the guest to go with him, but she and the rest of the family voted for me for the privilege and I gladly agreed to accept the honour.

My travel became even more pleasant because I discovered that our ambassador in Stockholm was young Tanmaya Lal, who had worked with me 20 years ago.

Also, I did not need a visa for Sweden.

Ambassador Lal and Sumita Lal gave us a warm welcome dinner at their elegant home and other courtesies throughout our stay.

I was curious when the ambassador's multi-purpose assistant, who introduced himself as Rana, turned out to be Rana Pratap Varughese, from my neighbouring town, Thiruvalla in Kerala.

His father, who lived for long in Rajasthan had given him the name of a Rajput hero. Since all the guests were expected to wear the most formal 'white tie and tails', I drove from the airport to the tailor.

Sree, who had reached Stockholm two days earlier, had prepared the ground for my 'trial' of my strange outfit.

The tailor took an hour each for both of us to be fitted with an enormous number of white and black pieces of cloth and both of us looked like penguins!

But since the event was only the next day, we had to take off each piece and pack them to take home. We were left wondering how we would put those clothes on again.

I remembered what Gandhiji said when he was asked why he did not cover himself adequately when he called on King George V.

"His Majesty was wearing enough clothes to cover both of us!" the Mahatma said.

Though images of the Laureates were on the wall, it was hard to distinguish them from the guests.

We took pictures with some people and some of them turned out to be Laureates.

Since it was an informal reception, we were able to slip away to the ambassador's private dinner with Indian delicacies.

Memories of events of twenty years ago enlivened the conversations as we updated each other about our careers and children.

Traditionally, the Nobel Prizes for Physics, Chemistry, Medicine, Literature and Economics are given by the king of Sweden in Stockholm and the Nobel Prize for Peace is given in Oslo by the king of Norway on the same day.

The timing is fixed in such a way that those in Oslo could fly to Stockholm to attend the ceremonies there.

As it happened, the Peace Prize event was poignant because the prize was received by the two children of the winner as she herself continued in an Iranian prison.

The children told a stunned audience that they did not expect to see their mother ever again.

In Stockholm, three were awarded the prize for Physics, three for Chemistry, two for Medicine, one for Literature and one for Economics.

Awards in each category was introduced in detail, then the king presented the prize to each of them. A standing ovation was given to each winner, but no opportunity to speak.

They were able to reply only at the end of the king's banquet by midnight.

As the audience, we simply had to rise and applaud each winner.

Walking on the ice without dropping our unfamiliar and ill-fitting suits was the only hazard.

Those who did not enjoy first class Western music had the additional ordeal of having to keep awake for hours.

The ceremony ended early the next day and all of us were taken to our respective hotels by buses.

The monarchy is very much alive and well in Sweden and the royalty was present for the ceremony and banquet. The king said nothing except for a one-line toast to Alfred Nobel.

The respect given to the royalty was beyond belief in democratic Sweden. Sadly, the backdrop for the Nobel Prizes were two wars in Europe and its vicinity.

But that did not affect the pomp and glory of the Nobel ceremony. It was lovely to be there to enjoy the magical atmosphere of celebrating the spectacular accomplishments of extraordinary men and women who had enriched the world of sciences, literature and peace.

Published: December 19, 2023

6

Sree's Journey: Reflections on Family

Things happen in life in strange ways. I was not scheduled to return to Thiruvananthapuram till late last night after participating in the 50th anniversary celebrations of the Chinchwad Malayalee Association near Pune, together with former chief minister Oommen Chandy.

But I felt I should return sooner as my son Sree Sreenivasan and his twin children, Durga and Krishna, were at home. My hosts helpfully suggested that I could drive to Mumbai and catch a flight, that would bring me to Thiruvananthapuram in the afternoon.

The celebrated expressway from Pune turned out to be much more hazardous than I had expected with heavy rain above and pot holes below.

Once we reached Dharavi of the *Slumdog Millionaire* fame, I thought that there was no way I could catch the flight. But my skilful driver, who makes this trip twice a day, assured me that he would get me there on time for the flight.

He expressed surprise, however, that I was not nervous or anxious about missing the flight! I did not believe his promise, but there I was on the flight as the doors were about to close. The flight, of course, did not take off for another hour!

Back in Thiruvananthapuram, my wife Lekha had lined up several options, the most important being a visit to the famed Ganesha temple, the most auspicious place to start anything new.

We delayed the visit to the temple as I had promised to take the children for a round of golf and then it was time to try out the new restaurant, 'Upper Crust', which, we thought, might suit the palates of the three American citizens.

But Lekha had her priorities right and she had a kind of premonition that something good would come out of the visit. And there it was that the news came that Mayor Bill de Blasio of New York City had just announced that my son Sree was appointed the Chief Digital Officer of New York City.

We knew this was coming, but to receive the news at the Ganesha temple was sheer delight. It was the culmination of a totally unexpected experience of seeing a well-settled 45-year-old son with a wife and two children suddenly without a job.

When Sree accepted the post of Chief Digital Officer at the Metropolitan Museum of Art three years ago, leaving a comfortable position as the first Chief Digital Officer at Columbia University, we saw it as a splendid opportunity for him to spread his wings and to find greener pastures.

To those who wondered whether it was wise to leave Columbia, I said the American system of 'hire and fire' was much more congenial to career development than the escalator system in many countries, including India.

Success comes only to those who dare and act, I said to Sree after he took me around the Met just before he took the plunge. Having changed 10 schools in 12 years, he was fully prepared to accept change. His brother Sreekanth too has shown great resilience in facing the challenges of change.

The Met, with which Sree had a 30-year-old love affair ever since we lived on Madison Avenue in the 1980s, took to his new career like fish to water and enjoyed the experience. Hardly had he mastered his new art and taken the Met to greater heights came the news that the Met could not afford him and, even more, his ambitious plans to make the Met the most digitalised museum in the world.

I characterised it as an effort to turn the Museum into a virtual university with every art object as a lesson. When Sree broke the bad news to us, it was a shock, but I stuck to my position that the 'hire and fire' system had its blessings and challenges and both should be accepted with equanimity.

I said as much to PBS, which interviewed me on 'Sreexit' from the Met. As it happened, I was in New York for a few days during this period. Our family had great faith in the abilities of Sree and his wife Roopa (Roopa Unnikrishnan, champion shooter, Commonwealth gold medallist, Arjuna Award winner, Rhodes Scholar) to rise to the occasion and they did.

The news of his exit came on my birthday and somehow, I felt that it was auspicious and that he would soon be back in a position commensurate with his vast abilities and experience in the digital world, which he had mastered without any technology training.

History graduates from St Stephen's rarely become tech gurus. But what astonished us was the way he handled the new situation. He turned adversity into an opportunity. A *Quartz* article noted: 'But while many high-profile executives might have responded by withdrawing to lick their wounds and work their networks behind the scenes, Sreenivasan went in entirely the opposite direction. The same day the news broke about his dismissal, he posted a note on Facebook. Sreenivasan shared the Met's company-wide memo and his gratitude to his bosses and team, and he outlined some loose plans (a book, consulting, a speaking tour, and a family vacation in India). Perhaps most importantly, he said he was open to any and all meetings and included a link to a form inviting friends to offer advice about what he should do next.'

The responses he received were overwhelming, but he and we realised that it was a cruel world out there and it would take time. Tantalising offers came from different parts of the world, but he made it clear that he would not move out of New York till his children finished Hunter College in the next five years.

Nothing would have suited him better than the offer he received from New York City. From a single institution in New York City, he is moving to the City Administration itself. As an observer of the fortunes of the Indian community in New York, Dr Thomas Abraham noted, Indians are not rare even in the White House, but New York City does not have many Indians in high positions.

He saw some poetic justice in Sree's appointment. Indians had made a great contribution to the growth of New York as a maximum city.

As we bask in the glory of Sree's new appointment, we are counting the blessings of the 'hire and fire system,' which recognises merit and offers exceptional opportunities.

Lord Ganesha appeared to have a particularly benign smile on us that evening when we folded our hands in gratitude.

Published: August 2, 2016

In Tribute: Remembering Lekha Sreenivasan

Confronting death is a painful experience, particularly when it happens to someone who has been part of your life for 55 years, growing together, sharing joys and sorrows. In the case of my wife, Lekha Sreenivasan, it came unexpectedly, when it appeared that she was on the verge of recovery.

She had a lively conversation with our son a few moments before she passed away. In one second, her "breath became air" as in the case of Dr. Paul Kalanidhi, a neurosurgical resident who died at the age of 36, having chronicled his lifelong quest to learn what gives meaning to life in the face of death.

I do not know whether Lekha had a premonition of death as she never discussed it, but in the last two years, when the world itself was in the grip of fear of death, all her actions, particularly her turning to writing her story indicated that she was aware that her time was coming.

It seemed that, even in the midst of her busy schedule of helping the needy through Karuna Charities, which she founded many years ago in New York, she felt that she reached a moment in life where she must give an account of herself, provide a ledger of what she has been and done and meant to the world.

She found a joy unknown to her in her prior years that does not hunger for more and more, but to record her past for posterity. She saw in it a way out of her aches and pains, her breathlessness and oxygen dependence and the many pills she swallowed. As she feared, she could not see her work completed and left us with peace on her face, as though in sleep without medicines and oxygen mask, which sustained her.

Like in the case of Dr. Paul Kalainidhi, it was the urge for narrating her life that brought her back to life. As Dr. Kalainidhi wrote, "The monolithic uncertainty of my future was deadening; everywhere I turned, the shadow of death obscured the meaning of any action. I remember the moment my overwhelming unease yielded, when that seemingly impassable sea of uncertainty parted." She faced each day like Samuel Beckett did, saying to herself, "I can't go on. I'll go on."

Interacting with family and friends was the source of her solace, but her inner struggle was entirely her own. The only sign of her state of mind was that she was insecure when I travelled out of town. She even felt that the pandemic was a blessing in disguise as my travels were severely restricted on account of it. Her elephantine memory helped her recall events with clarity and precision.

Her book, *Better Half of Diplomacy*, being published posthumously is a sincere, truthful and transparent narration of her experiences in different parts of the globe. I discovered on the day of her demise (January 9, 2023) and later that there were many people who cared for her and loved her for what she had done, not just as a diplomat's wife, but as a compassionate human being, who dreamt of wiping every tear from every eye.

Of course, many eminent people, including the Honourable Governor of Kerala Arif Mohammed Khan, Chief Minister Pinarayi Vijayan, former Defence Minister A.K. Antony, former Chief Minister Oommen Chandy, the Leader of the Opposition V.D. Satheesan, BJP State President K. Surendran, four Ministers of the LDF Government, Shashi Tharoor MP, Baselios Cardinal Cleemis, K. Muraleedharan MP, Binoy Viswam MP, M.K.Raghavan MP, former Ministers, Ramesh Chennithala and Pandalam Sudhakaran and many others from different walks of life came to pay tribute to her.

But, to my surprise, many poor and sick people, the beneficiaries of Karuna Charities International she founded in New York, came with tears flowing down their cheeks, wondering how they would pay the medical bills and school fees of their children next month.

It was clear that unknown to me, she cared for them and kept her charity work going with the help of her friends even when she herself was sick. Obviously, she had held them close to her heart as she did her family and friends. Even as we grieve for her, we celebrate her life with the conviction that she made a difference in the lives of many poor and hungry people.

Published: January 22, 2023

Epilogue

Reading the Tea Leaves

Whenever I am asked to speak on the world of 2047, I say that the only one thing certain about that year is that I shall not be around to see it. But that truth enables me to make predictions without the possibility of being called upon to explain why I went wrong. But there is no doubt that the global order, which was built brick by brick by the winners of the Second World War, has collapsed as evidenced by the fact that all the crises of the 21st century are still smouldering, if not raging. The elaborate scheme of preventive diplomacy, ceasefire, peacemaking and peacebuilding in the UN Charter has collapsed and ad hoc arrangements outside the Security Council have not worked. The Permanent Members, by their lack of unity, have fatally undermined the Security Council. The present intolerable situation is seen optimistically as things getting worse before it gets better. But a global nuclear war is not unlikely on account of Ukraine or Taiwan. Moreover, there is a possibility of the world ending in a whimper and not a bang, with cataclysmic climate change, devastating pandemic or invasion by a threatened animal species or mishandling of Artificial Intelligence. In other words, all the leaves at the bottom of the Chinese tea cup give no reason for optimism. All indications are that the world is inexorably moving towards the dance of Kalki rather than Krishna's dance of joy. Any other future will be a bonus for mankind.

As for the immediate future, the trends are disturbing, as events in the 2020 have dealt a body blow to the efforts being made to build alternative structures like G20, the Global South and the alphabet soup of bilateral and multilateral engagements, which have proliferated. The ravages of Covid-19 still haunt the world. The way China prevented the Security Council from meeting to discuss the most existential threat to humanity was the unkindest cut of all. China got away with murder when the World Health Organization failed to establish the origin of the pandemic even though there was evidence of Chinese culpability. The credibility of the Security Council hit rock bottom when individuals and countries had to fend for themselves in a sea of uncertainty. The Russian invasion of Ukraine created a new situation where a permanent member attacks a member country of the UN and uses its veto to protect itself. The war in Gaza is still being defended by the US, although it shows some signs of pangs of conscience over the enormity of the loss of lives in the war. The Israeli tail is still wagging the mighty US dog. The fact that the last global order was established only after a devastating war casts a shadow of war over a crumbling global order.

India's future is on the upswing, though it cannot be insulated against global trends. Threat from China looms large even though Pakistan has ceased to be a challenge. The other neighbours of India are not as friendly as they should have been, even though India's "Neighbourhood First" policy has been in evidence. The recent moves of the Maldives President (Mohamed Muizzu) to seek security and prosperity from China rather than India is ominous. The fact remains that in the long run, the neighbourhood will remain volatile. The experiment of SAARC has failed and BIMSTEC does not have the political or economic glue to make it viable as a regional organisation. China will remain the greatest threat to India even in the next century. An economic or environmental collapse of China cannot be ruled out because of the dictatorial actions of the Chinese rulers, but they have proved capable of brave decisions to avert a political collapse.

In the evolving conflict between democracies and autocracies, India has to stand with democracies, and the recent history of India indicates that we are preparing for a tight embrace of the United States and the West. The Quad is a baby step towards a full-scale alliance in the context of the unprecedented treaty between China and Russia. The China-Russia "no limits" partnership of 4 February 2022 was conceived to highlight the possibility of Ukraine and Taiwan becoming the hotspots of a global conflagration. A major war is likely to reshuffle the world to create a new world order. This will also result in the creation of a new world organisation dominated by the West and a new cold war will begin. Most of the treaties including instruments for disarmament, human rights and environmental protection will be renegotiated without the proverbial burning of the midnight oil, but through Artificial Intelligence or its other manifestations. By then, robots will occupy the White House, the Kremlin and South Block, but human failures and foibles will still play a role in governance. The battle of the robots, if any, will be put down by built-in mechanisms. Human migration to distant planets will ease the pressure of population on Earth and power generated on other planets will illumine the Earth. It may be the height of irony that our succeeding generations will look up to our time with nostalgia.

Human creativity will diminish and poems, plays and novels will be written, not by humans, but by machines. A single language, understandable to everyone will replace our Tower of Babel. Happiness may become a tradable commodity of high value because it will be manufactured. All indications are that human existence in the future will be more hazardous and uncertain. Like the young people of today, they will blame the earlier generations for not doing enough to preserve the environment for the succeeding generations. For those of us in the evening of our lives can only pray for our successors.

About the Author & the Editor

Ambassador **T.P. Sreenivasan** has the distinction of having served at the Ambassadorial level at the UN in New York, Nairobi and Vienna, where he was the Governor for India of the International Atomic Energy Agency. He was the first to be posted to the US three times, including as Ambassador and Deputy Chief of Mission in Washington. He has also been High Commissioner to Fiji and Kenya and posted in Tokyo, Thimphu, Moscow, New York and Yangon, besides serving in New Delhi.

After his return to Kerala in 2004, he has been the Director General of the Kerala International Centre, Vice Chairman of the Kerala State Higher Education Council, Director of the NSS Civil Service Academy, Mentor and Professor of Eminence at the Somaiya Vidya Vihar University, Mumbai, and Visiting Professor at the Central University of Kerala, Kasaragod.

He has authored 10 books, contributed columns in several Indian and foreign journals and lectured in India and abroad. He has received several awards, including the Sree Chithira Thirunal National Award and K.P.S Menon Memorial Award.

As the editor of *Diplomacy Liberated*, Wing Commander **Ragashree D. Nair** brings a wealth of expertise in international relations, honed through a distinguished 15-year career in the Indian Air Force. Throughout her service, she held key positions at major airbases, providing invaluable insights into security dynamics, a crucial aspect of modern diplomacy.

An alumnus of Management Development Institute (MDI), Gurgaon, she holds multiple postgraduate degrees and certifications, including in human resource management, brand management, and linguistics. She currently serves as the Co-Chair & CEO of Medicaid Ethos Private Limited and as a Director at Nuttmeg Products Private Limited.

Recognised for her leadership, she has received accolades such as the ET Ascent Women Leader Award 2022 (Karnataka) and the 100 Prime Women Icon Award 2022.

Based in Trivandrum, she contributes significantly to local management associations and civil services education.